THE GODDESS OF LOVE

Aphrodite rising from the sea, the 'Benghazi Aphrodite' from Cyrenaica, based on the picture by Apelles. Hellenistic marble statuette. University Museum, Philadelphia.

Geoffrey Grigson

THE GODDESS
OF LOVE

*The birth, triumph, death
and return of Aphrodite*

Constable London

First published in Great Britain 1976
by Constable and Company Limited
10 Orange Street London WC2H 7EG
Copyright © 1976 by Geoffrey Grigson

ISBN 0 09 460170 4

Set in Monophoto Garamond 11 pt
Filmset and printed in Great Britain by
BAS Printers Limited, Wallop, Hampshire

Tais Philtatais

And so, O Goddess, ever honour'd be,
In thy so odorous Cyprian empery.

George Chapman

Zürne der Schönheit nicht, das sie schön ist . . .
Jede irdische Venus ersteht, wie die erste des Himmels,
    Eine dunkle Geburt aus dem unendlichen Meer.

(Do not be angry with beauty, because it is beautiful . . .
Every earthly Venus, like the first Venus of Heaven,
    Is a dark birth which emerges out of the endless sea.)

Friedrich von Schiller

Preface

This book—not, as I am all too aware, by a classical scholar—was written because in poems and pictures and in statuary, in museums across the world, we are always encountering Venus, or Aphrodite as we should now call her, by her proper name. Did I know why Ronsard invoked her splendidly as

> Idalienne, Amathonte, Erycine,

or why she was to be observed (according to Drummond of Hawthornden)

> At the first glace of morn
> In Cyprus gardens gathering those fair flowers
> Which of her blood were born,

or why

> The Graces naked danc'd about the place,
> The wind and trees amaz'd
> With silence on her gaz'd,
> The flow'rs did smile, like those upon her face?

Roughly; but not sufficiently. So I began, with visits above all to Cyprus and the Aegean, an exploration of which this is the result, in words and images; a partial portrait of a goddess who captivated the people of the West, and left them an inheritance, in which a natural awe remains active.

Somewhere I have read of an antiquary (I think it was) coming to Aphrodite's Idalion—Dali in Cyprus—and finding a young Englishman there, near the site of Aphrodite's temple, alone on the naked hill, reading to himself Bion's *Lament for Adonis*; Adonis, Aphrodite's semi-divine lover, having died at Idalion from the tusks of the wild boar. I should be pleased, if some readers and perusers of this book, who are not too captious in their greater knowledge of Mediterranean, Aegean and Near Eastern antiquity and art and literature, are led by it to visit either dry Idalion or the magnificent Adonis Source in the Lebanon, or dusty Paphos, or the foamy Cypriot beach where Aphrodite came ashore, or Knidos on the Turkish coast, where Praxiteles' statue of Aphrodite was enshrined, or Mount Eryx in Sicily, where Venus Erycina lived among her temple doves, including the wild turtle doves which migrate between Africa and Europe. I would be pleased if some readers looked with a new concern at slender Hellenistic Aphrodites which have found refuge in this and that museum, or at Aphrodite's pictured descendants—since she is present even in modern times in nudes, say by Renoir or Matisse.

I am grateful to many people who have helped me over this or that detail; to my old friend and agent David Higham, who pressed me to go on with rather an intimidating project; to Jane Grigson; to A. L. Lloyd, another old friend, who allowed me to include his translation of a tenth-century Andalusian-Arabic poem about quinces; and to my friends Professor Edward Schafer and Phyllis Schafer, and Wayland Young and Elizabeth Young, who have lately been investigating some of the Near Eastern lands of Aphrodite; and I am grateful too—'What fair pomp have I spied of glittering ladies'— for my recollections of several exquisite if some of them bitter-sweet exemplars of the nature and meaning of Aphrodite.

The translations, unless otherwise ascribed, are my own.

Geoffrey Grigson

Contents

Illustrations

Illustrations 12 and 13 are by courtesy of the Lebanon Tourist and Information Office,
London; 27 by courtesy of the Italian State Tourist Office; 4, 7, 11, 18, 19, 21, 25, 26, 31,
34, 38, 41, 47 & 48, 49 & 50, 52, 53, 54 and 66 by courtesy of the Mansell Collection.

The Birth of Aphrodite

A Mouth Lovelier than the Virgin's

Answering our needs, offspring of our wants, our desires, our hopes, our dread, our insecurity, our insufficiencies and uncertainties, our fancies, gods in the West came slowly to a mature personification. Then they died slowly. But even then their death was often incomplete. Something of the old god survived in a new god, in a new personification, persuasively introduced, and answering, under a new name, to mutations and alterations in the human condition.

Aphrodite of the Greeks, Venus of the Romans, may be dead, but she has died away less completely from our emotion than the other high gods of the Mediterranean, in their white temples. She began as a conical stone, as if the symbol and the weight of a blind urge, she became, always young, but always experienced and experiencing, the divine woman, conceived in shapes and attitudes of grace, necessary in the lives of the young, appealed to by girls who shared her own femininity and asked her for help in the business of attraction, and by young men who asked her to make the girl, or girls, they wanted, give as she had given, Aphrodite in her time having condescended thrillingly to mortals or semi-mortals as well as to other gods.

In her statues, in the mind-images men and women had of her, she became both tender and exquisite, but not a simpleton. She was the goddess of I want a man, I want a woman, as well as I want a particular man or woman, the one I happened to see yesterday walking under the olive trees. She was the goddess also of love between women, between Sappho, for instance, and her girls, and of love between men or between men and boys. Prostitutes, too, can be as beautiful as virtuous daughters. This goddess of love extended her patronage to whores. Look up Greek words derived from her name and you find that *aphrodiastikos* meant lecherous, that *aphrodiazein* meant to copulate, that *aphrodisia* were brothels, and that a lessee of a public brothel was an *aphrodiastes*; and in her myth it was remembered, from the first grand celebration in Greek poetry of her nature and her origins, that she was Aphrodite Philommedes, Aphrodite the Lover of Genitals—a fact we may forget in our deference to the Venus of Botticelli or a naked girl by Modigliani.

One of the great Christian fathers, Clement of Alexandria, remembered this in the second century after Christ, when he exhorted the Greeks away from the old gods to the new tripartite god. He remembered that Aphrodite was Philommedes, born of the foam which spread around the *medea*—the 'lecherous members' Clement called them in disgust—of Ouranos, when they fell into the sea, after Kronos, the son of Ouranos, cut them away with his sickle. For the Greeks there was a pun in this name. If their goddess of loving, their goddess of all sexual desire between gods, men, birds, and beasts and all creatures, was Philommedes, Lover of Genitals, she was also Philommeides, Lover of Laughter, lover of the gaieties of that love which comes at last, after all difficulties and anxieties, to its climax, in that mutual co-instantaneous pleasure which remains beyond description, though not beyond verbal or pictorial indication; that transitory sensation in which we are taken for a moment out of life or more exactly into life's absolute intensity.

It was hard for such a goddess to die altogether. All the time her circumstances remain in the relations of men and women. She comes back. We see the Evening Star in the green or yellow or deep blue sky to the left of the sunset, and we remember that the Evening Star is her planet, if not herself. Doves cross her Mediterranean to Europe every spring and pair off and start their peculiarly gentle murmuring out of sight inside the new leaves, and we remember that doves belong to Aphrodite or Venus.

Again and again she has been reborn in poems, and in paintings.

In Bury St Edmunds of the fourteenth century, a monk, John Lydgate, invokes her, in her star-shape:

> Fairest of stars, that with your persant light
> And with the cherishing of your streames clear,
> Causen in love heartes to be light
> Only through shining of your glad sphere,
> Now laud and praise, O Venus, lady dear,
> Be to your name, that have withoute sin
> This man fortuned his lady for to win.

In Florence of the fifteenth century—the Renaissance reanimating the past and establishing her again, newly vital, in poems, in pictures, in statues—Sandro Botticelli, a painter exceptionally handsome and still young, and unregenerate, sets Venus on her shell, with whatever neo-

platonic allegorical excuse, naked and among roses. And he gives her face
the peculiar expression which comes on the face of women in that climax of
making love.

In France of the nineteenth century, after Venus had lost her substance
once more, she returns warm to life behind the back of bourgeois prudery,
and a Provençal poet Théodore Aubanel earns a reproof from his archbishop
for writing with passion of the statue of the Venus of Arles:

> O blanche Vénus d'Arles! ô reine provençale!
> Aucun manteau ne cache tes épaules superbes;
> On voit que tu es déesse et fille du ciel bleu . . . .
>
> Montre-nous tes bras nus, ton sein nu, tes flancs nus;
> Montre-toi toute nue, ô divine Vénus!
> La beauté te revêt mieux que ta robe blanche;
> Laisse à tes pieds tomber la robe qui à tes hanches
> S'enroule, voilant tout ce que tu as de plus beau;
> Abandonne ton ventre aux baisers du soleil! . . .

In England of the nineteenth century, the young Swinburne comes into
the open and startles the respectable by telling Christ, in the name of
Venus, that the girl of his pseudo-medieval poem has a mouth lovelier
than his mother's:

> She is right fair; what hath she done to thee?
> Nay, fair Lord Christ, lift up thine eyes and see;
>   Had now thy mother such a lip—like this?
> Thou knowest how sweet a thing it is to me . . . .
>
> Behold, my Venus, my soul's body, lies
> With my love laid upon her garment-wise,
>   Feeling my love in all her limbs and hair
> And shed between her eyelids through her eyes.

And in another poem more famous than that *Laus Veneris*, that 'praise of
the goddess of love', Swinburne of 1866 assures the Christian Victorian
god, the pale Galilean, whose breath has turned the world grey, that he
will die no less than Cytherean Venus, that his mother 'came pale and a
maiden, and sister to sorrow', whereas Venus

Her deep hair heavily laden with odour and colour of flowers,
White rose of the rose-white water, a silver splendour, a flame,
Bent down unto us that besought her, and earth grew sweet with
    her name.
For thine came weeping, a slave among slaves, and rejected; but she
Came fleshed from the full-flushed wave, and imperial, her foot on
    the sea.
And the wonderful waters knew her, the winds and the viewless
    ways,
And the roses grew rosier, and bluer the sea-blue stream of the bays.

(Hymn to Proserpine)

Swinburne is a hundred years behind us. No doubt in our close of the twentieth century gods are not to be invoked, only recollected, contemplated, and analyzed. Aphrodite or Venus is excavated, she is hauled out of the sea, she is in museums, she is in editions, she is translated. The last great poet to have written a sensuous if deeply meaningful poem about Aphrodite seems to be Rainer Maria Rilke; a poem of storm, birth, spring, love, then storm again producing death:

So the goddess came to land.

Behind her
As she went off fast along the youthful shores,
All morning the flowers and the haulms
Came up, confused, and hot,
As if from an embrace. And she ran on and on.

But at midday, in the roughest hour,
The sea heaved once more and threw out,
On to that same spot, a dolphin,
Dead, and ripped and red.

An *ex post facto* poem.

But Aphrodite direct? Literal Aphrodite, as she was to ordinary Greeks, in their emotions, less with her dolphins than with her doves?

Contemplating everything she embodied, we no longer have to apologize, or pretend, or evade, or wear masks. In his *Laus Veneris* Swinburne a century ago had to mask himself as a medieval Frenchman, in his *Hymn to Proserpine* he masked himself as a superseded pagan priest, and still nearer our own time classical scholars and classical archaeologists remained under compulsion to tut-tut about Aphrodite, and to emphasize that she wasn't, of course, altogether Greek, and to underplay her in Greek life, while also exaggerating the pure spirituality of her various cults.

That is long over. We can recognize and admit the frankness of the Greeks about desire, or about the facts—or their fancies—of the sexual case. It is true that to look back at Aphrodite or Venus—

> The blood of Venus enters her blood, Love's kiss
> Has made the drowsy virgin modestly bold;
> To-morrow the bride is not ashamed to take
> The burning taper from its hidden fold*

—is in a way to look back with regret to love as a circumscribed lyric, love unsoured, uncomplicated, untwisted, in a halcyon era that never was, entirely. We look back to a dream, the core of which is a warm reality. In the French folksong the girl tells the king's son who has killed her white duck that he must pay her four hundred francs:

> Que ferons-nous de cet argent?
> Nous ferons bâtir un couvent
> Pour mettre les filles de dix-huit ans.
>
> Et les garçons de vingt-cinq ans.

Of that impossible convent Venus or Aphrodite would be the abbess.

The Descent of Aphrodite

Where did Aphrodite come from? Where was she born, since we talk so much of her birth? These are not quite the same questions. According to the primal Greek myth of Aphrodite, as set out by Hesiod in the hexameters of his *Theogonia*, or 'Genealogy of the Gods', she grew in the divine foam which the severed member and testicles of Ouranos stirred up in the sea; which must have been the Aegean. The pregnant foam floated to Kythera, the island off the eastern prong of the Peloponnese, and from Kythera across the Mediterranean on to Cyprus; there, having come to full growth

---

*From Allen Tate's translation of the Latin *Pervigilium Veneris*, the best English version, though Coventry Patmore more happily turned the famous refrain *Cras amet qui nunquam amavit, quique amavit cras amet*:

> Let those love now who never loved;
>   Let those who have loved love again.

1 *Petra tou Romiou. The foam beach at Achni on the south coast of Cyprus where Aphrodite is supposed to have come ashore. Photo: Doros Partasides*

and perfection in her sea matrix, she was born, the moment of birth being when she stepped ashore, a new goddess.

Cypriot tradition says that she stepped ashore at a point on the south-west coast of the island, not far from her temple city of Old Paphos, where a peculiarly thick and creamy foam boils up and surges on to a shelving beach, under pink rocks and cliffs.

History, or historical inference, shows that she came to Cyprus (if by way of Kythera) from the Phoenician mainland. And her true genealogy must go back from Phoenician goddesses, Phoenician queens of heaven, of love and fertility, to mother-goddesses of Assyria, and Babylon, and Sumeria.

First of all, let us follow Aphrodite back in that ancestral direction; or let us begin with what have been called the 'Venuses of Prehistory', the 'Venuses of the Old Stone Age'.

Right across the Old World from the Atlantic to Russia statuettes have been found of a shape which suggests a divine fertility, a concern for pregnancy and increase. These naked female statuettes—some of ivory from the tusks of the extinct mammoth, some made of stone or clay or lignite— usually emphasize the breasts, the swollen belly, the buttocks, and some- times the privates. Breasts, belly and backside, for instance, round into the balloon shapes of the squat limestone 'Venus of Willendorf', a tiny figure, in fact, less than four inches long, which was discovered in a cave in Lower Austria in 1908, under deposits of glacial dust, or into the mammoth ivory curves and volumes of the Venus of Lespugue, in the Musée de l'Homme in Paris, which was found in Haute-Garonne.

It is as if, 25,000 and more years ago, pregnant goddesses, of whatever name and whatever cult, helped to ensure children for the strength of the community and young for the population of wild animals on which the hunting communities lived, in the Ice Age. The line of descent and inheri- tance and adaptation may be gapped, but it is only reasonable to suppose that the idea of such divine, fertile and maternal power would never be lost; that it would be adjusted to new conditions of life, in particular to the gradual elaboration of farming in the Middle Eastern lands, the rearing of food animals, including fish in tanks and pools, the planting of crops, the deliberate raising of fruit. It can be supposed, with reason, that goddesses of birth and upbringing, goddesses of fertility, would throw their bene- ficence over the vegetal as well as the animal and the human; that their divinity and its extra functions would spread; that they would acquire new names in new countries, dividing, subdividing, yet continuing to overlap, and combine again, in their new personifications.

As consciousness of life increased, as life split into separate activities,

2 The 'Venus of Lespugue'. Mammoth ivory figurine c. 25000 B.C. Musée de l'Homme, Paris.

each separated and individualized process, each phenomenon, each abstract energy and activity, would acquire its own divine being—the being or personification of its vital force; and the likelihood, as cultures became less crude, would be that goddesses, for instance, in their woman shapes, would lose their Willendorf lumpiness, and more and more come to match conceptions of grace and perfection. It is that long journey, with a quickening

later in the new civilizations of the Middle East and the Eastern Mediterranean, and a final quickening among the Greeks, which joins those
conveniently and after all not quite so misleadingly named 'Venuses' of
the Old Stone Age to the historic Aphrodites and Venuses.

Where Aphrodite originated is Sumeria, via the Babylonians, the
Assyrians, and then the Phoenicians. She is nearly, but not quite, the last
shape, the last personification, of the needs which five thousand or more
years ago were expressed for the Sumerians in their goddess Inanna,
consort of the shepherd god Dumuzi, queen of heaven, goddess who was
also the Evening and the Morning Star; sometimes a fierce goddess,
but above everything the goddess of the bed and fertile abundance, beautiful
in her lapis lazuli necklaces, and with her antimony shadowed eyes. In
the Sumerian city-states and temples, she co-exists with a no doubt older
mother-goddess, Ninhursag, but as if Ninhursag was the creator of life,
and Inanna the goddess by whom life continued. So according to a hymn

> all the living creatures of the steppe,
> all four-footed beasts under the wide heaven,
> fruit-planting and garden, flower-beds and verdant reeds,
> the fish of the pond, the birds of heaven,
> all wait upon my lady, when it is quiet (at night),
> all living creatures, men in their numbers bow the
> knee before her . . .
> My lady looks down kindly from heaven,
> they all come forward to the holy Inanna.*

From Inanna, centuries ahead, Greek Aphrodite would inherit perhaps
her doves, and certainly in Cyprus and Corinth and on Mount Eryx, her
temple prostitutes with whom worshippers carried out a rite of union and
fertility; and Inanna's divine husband Dumuzi was to become Aphrodite's
Adonis, dying from the sharp tusks of the boar.

Inanna of the Sumerians gave way early in the second millennium B.C. to
Ishtar of the Babylonians and the Assyrians. Ishtar of these Semitic peoples
appears as the Evening Star, bringing man and woman to bed: she appears
as the Morning Star, waking men to go fighting in wars, a decidedly violent
goddess, a wielder of weapons, as well as the goddess of love. Inanna's
Dumuzi becomes Ishtar's Tammuz; and Ishtar, too, has sacred prostitutes;
and is served by priests who have been castrated.

Next among the Western Semites, among the Phoenicians, who spread

*Quoted by Helmer Ringgren, in *Religions of the Ancient Near East*. S.P.C.K., 1973.

themselves up and down the Palestinian coast about 2000 B.C., Ishtar is
Astarte; and at their nearest point Astarte's Phoenicia and Aphrodite's
Cyprus (which was first of all Astarte's Cyprus) are no more than about sixty
miles apart. At the eastern tip of Cyprus, the windy Mediterranean on either
side of you, you can scramble on to a rock (once crowned by a temple of
Aphrodite—see page 129), and make out on the horizon, if indistinctly, the
range of bare limestone heights, which was the Olympos of the Phoenician
gods.

The Phoenicians—dwellers in what the Greek called Phoinike, the 'land
of purple', the land where they made the Tyrian dye, and prepared the
purple and violet fabrics which kings and queens and courtiers and their
ladies required in all the countries and city-states of the Near East—traded
and founded their settlements around the coasts of Cyprus and across the
Mediterranean. In one guise or another, under one name or another, it
seems that Astarte went with them, and that in Cyprus, in this rich island of
flowers, corn and copper, they set her up along with her temple girls; and
it was there, we may suppose, that the Greeks encountered her and adopted
her and began to transform her to their own ideas. And the Phoenicians
seem to have taken Astarte into Greece itself. Kythera, off the Peloponnese,
where Aphrodite had the most ancient of her Greek temples, may have
served them as one of the fishing stations where they collected the small
molluscs which gave the dye, the preparation of which was no less complex
than the preparation of the famous blue dye from the woad plant.

Along with their bales of purple and violet cloth no doubt the Phoenicians
brought Astarte or Aphrodite to Corinth, which became so celebrated for
its Aphrodite worship; and to Athens as well. What the Greeks called both
the mollusc and the dye was *porphura** (from which our word 'purple'
descends), and it was a legend that a King Porphurion, 'King Purple',
established Aphrodite's cult in Athens.

So Astarte or Aphrodite would have entered Greek life, not inapprop-
riately, together with the most rich and royal of the fabrics of antiquity.

Astarte's cities were strung down the Phoenician coast. Nearest to
Cyprus was the Bronze Age city-state of Ugarit, or Ras Shamra, Headland
of the Fennel. There Astarte still went under the Babylonian name Ishtar.
Southward she was worshipped at Byblos, Sidon and Tyre; and then, further
south, near Israel and Egypt, she was the great goddess at Askalon, the
city-state of the Philistines or Peleset, as the Egyptians called them, those
mysterious people who were not Phoenicians, though they came under
Phoenician influence, and took over Western Semitic gods and goddesses.

*The 'purple' adjectives in Greek were *porphureos*, from *porphura*, the 'purple-fish', and
phoinikios, from *phoinix*, 'purple', as in Phoenician; and also the Phoenix.

3 *Astarte. Found near Seville. Bronze from the Nile Delta, 8th century B.C. The Phoenician inscription on the base names the two men who gave the statuette to Astarte. Museo Arqueológico, Seville.*

At Askalon the Philistines called her Atargatis.

The Cypriots claimed, or so Herodotus wrote in the fifth century B.C., that their original Aphrodite had been this Atargatis of Askalon. She was worshipped there and elsewhere as a goddess whose body ended in a fish tail, as if a mermaid. Fishes were sacred to her, and were kept in temple tanks and ponds. Water and fish alike symbolized her fertile power. She too had her fertility prostitutes, and her eunuch priests, and her temple doves. Doves strutted and flew round all the houses and streets of Askalon, holy birds which mightn't be killed or eaten, or even touched. Dolphins, too, were associated with Atargatis, symbolizing her power over the sea, her ability to give good sailing to ships of Askalon, the ships of these Sea People, who caused such upset to the Egyptians, in the reign of Ramases III (1198–1166 B.C.).

The Sea Peoples had or acquired their towns in Cyprus; and seem to have maintained a friendly intercourse with the Mycenean Greeks. And in Cyprus the Sea Peoples and the Mycenaeans come together. Legend declared that Cyprus became Greek, or began to do so, after the fall of Troy. Teucer, the grand archer of the Greeks, was held to be one of the first settlers. When he came home from Troy to Salamis, he was rejected by his father Telamon, so taking his people with him he sailed back to the east, and founded for himself a new Salamis, on the south coast of Cyprus, on the edge of the sea. At the other end of Cyprus, Agapenor, son of the king of the Arkadians, who lived among blue mountains and the meadows of the Peloponnese, made a city for himself at Nea Paphos, which he founded near the rocks on which his boat came to grief, on its roundabout return from Troy.

Egyptian records complain not only of the Peleset or Philistines, among the troublesome intruding Sea Peoples, but of the Tjekker. These indeed may have been the people of Teucer, who established themselves on the eastern confines of Cyprus. Their city—their Salamis—was not the 'modern' Salamis, the Graeco-Roman complex of theatre and gymnasium and re-erected columns bowered in the yellow bloom of Australian eucalyptus, a hundred yards from the sea, but Enkomi, a mile or two inland, where archaeologists have uncovered, among poppies and Crown Marigolds and wild scarlet-flowered gladioli, the brown, humble-seeming ruins of what was once a rich city of traders and copper smelters.

Enkomi and the Tjekker—we are getting nearer the real birth of Aphrodite, for the archaeological facts seem to be that the Greeks—Achaians from around Mycenae—began entering Cyprus in the 13th century B.C., and mingling there first with the Cypriot inhabitants, then with the intruding Tjekker and Peleset; and that Cyprus became thoroughly hellenized between 1230 B.C. and 1190 B.C.

It was a reversal. Here were Greeks from the west in a Cyprus which for a thousand years had been in rapport with the lands of Astarte and Atargatis to the east; which were only a day's sailing away—so long as Astarte-Atargatis gave a fair wind.

These Achaians, these Mycenaeans, revered a fertility goddess of their own, and baked little clay figures of her, plumped with breasts and marked with a pubic triangle. Now, in Cyprus, they encountered a superior divinity of fecundity and love and the sea. Astarte or Atargatis filled out an insufficiency. And when the newcomers adopted her it seems that they knew her, or were introduced to her, not by the name Astarte or Atargatis, but as Ashtoreth.

This does point to Askalon, and the connections there between the Philistines and the Israelites, since Ashtoreth was the Hebrew name for Atargatis (as in the Bible—'And the children of Israel did evil again in the sight of the Lord, and served Baalim, and Ashtoroth, and the gods of Syria, and the gods of Zidon, and the gods of Moab, and the gods of the children of Ammon, and the gods of the Philistines, and forsook the Lord, and served him not.' *The Book of Judges*, 10,6.).

'Ashtoreth' was a name, a word, the Greeks could not pronounce. They tried, they turned 'Ashtoreth' or 'Astoreth' into 'Attorethe', and then 'Aphthorethe', in the end settling for 'Aphrodite'. ('Atargatis' they changed, in a similar way, to 'Derketo'.)

Reverencing her as goddess of the sea, and goddess of the fertilizing waters, whether of sea or rain or river or fountain, and goddess of love, the Greeks supposed that the first syllable of their mispronounced name for her was their own *aphros*, 'foam'.

Out of the sea-foam was she born—a happy piece of that folk-etymology we incline to when our fancies do not have to obey a science of language.

So we come back to those questions of how and where Aphrodite was born, in the imagination of the Greeks—back to that myth of the great severed member of Ouranos wriggling off Cyprus in the spermatic foam; by which the Greeks began the wonderful and admirable transformation of the Semitic goddess into the love goddess of western men, western poetry, and western art; including the art of sculpture which was little developed by Phoenicians or the Sea Peoples who were absorbed by Phoenician culture.

Towns in Cyprus identified as Idalion, Soli, Marion, Kition, and Salamis were listed by Ramases III as among his enemies—meaning, it has been presumed, that they were towns which had become strongholds of the Peoples of the Sea. All of them were known later as centres of the cult of Aphrodite. Marion is the modern Polis, in a special country of love (page 49),

Kition is the modern town of Larnaca, where in the middle of the streets and houses archaeologists have been revealing a large, important temple of Aphrodite or Astarte, a Phoenician temple, built in the ninth century B.C., in which, as elsewhere in the island, Astarte and Aphrodite became more or less fused—for the Phoenicians of Kition Astarte, for their Greek neighbours Aphrodite.

In Larnaca museum there is a votive statue from this temple, in limestone, a young man with a dove in his left hand, the likeness of a postulant of the goddess, at some time in the fifth century B.C. His clothes and his feet still have traces on them of red colouring, which recalls a description, from one of the epic texts discovered in the excavations at Ugarit, of a sacrifice made by a mythological Phoenician king. He first 'washed himself and made himself red', before taking hold of the animals he was to offer to El and Baal.

The Egg and the Foam

That Aphrodite grew in the foam was the principal, but not the only, explanation of her birth. Early on the Greeks had another way of suiting her to the authentic company of the Greek gods, and one that had nothing to do with the sea. They conceived that she was the daughter of Zeus by the shadowy goddess Dione. Homer, for instance, writing before Hesiod set down his genealogy of heaven, always says that she was the child of Zeus and Dione (though he already associates Aphrodite with Cyprus, in the *Iliad*, and with Kythera as well, in the *Odyssey*).

If, as scholars of mythology have suggested, Dione was an earth-goddess, this would make Aphrodite the child of earth and sky, of earth which receives, and sky which, with thunder and lightning, sends down the rain of fruitfulness.

A very different story, one which must have originated in Syria, was recorded by the mythographer Hyginus, writing in Latin in the second century A.D., many hundreds of years after the time of Homer and Hesiod.

It is said that an egg of wonderful size dropped from the sky into the river Euphrates. Fishes rolled it on to the bank, doves sat on it and warmed it, and hatched out Venus, who was known later as the Syrian Goddess. Venus was of surpassing worth and holiness, and Jove granted the fish the privilege of being translated to the stars. On this account fish and doves were reckoned to be divine by the Syrians, who do not eat them.

4 An Astarte from Kition (Larnaca), Cyprus. Terracotta figurine c. 500 B.C. British Museum, London.

Evidently this was first told about Atargatis, not the Atargatis of Askalon, but the Atargatis of the great temple at Hierapolis, in Northern Syria, not many miles from the Euphrates: it is Atargatis taken from the waters of life by her sacred fish, and brought to birth by the warmth and attention of her sacred doves.

Aphrodite of the Greeks needed a better story than that; and one in which the narrow waters of a foreign river would be replaced by the wide waters of Ocean around Cyprus and around the shores and islands of Greece. The myth as told by Hesiod will be better understood if we begin with a genealogical tree, not of the whole complex variable family of the great gods and the younger gods and the lesser gods, but simply of the descent of Aphrodite and of her divine relationships as Hesiod supposed them to have been.

Hesiod first of all describes how Gaia (Earth) fell out with her son and husband Ouranos or Heaven, the enmity between broad-breasted maternal earth and paternal heaven. To Ouranos Gaia had borne, not only the Titans, and the three one-eyed Cyclops, but the three monsters with a hundred arms, the most terrible of their children. Ouranos loathed them. One by one he pushed these hundred-armed monsters back into Earth, who groaned with their presence, and planned revenge for what she considered a vile act.

Earth thought out a plan. First she made a great sickle with flint teeth, and then asked her sons to help. They were all afraid except Kronos.

Gaia gave Kronos the sickle, and made him hide. Then when it was dark, the randy Ouranos as usual came and stretched himself on top of her. Kronos at the right moment caught hold of his father's genitals with his left hand, and hooked them off. Drops of the blood of Ouranos fell on Gaia and made her pregnant with the Erinyes, the Giants and the ash-tree nymphs. Kronos threw his father's genitals behind him into the waves of the sea, where they were tossed around for a long while—

> And their immortal
> Flesh stirred a white foam around them; in which
> There grew a girl, who floated first to the most holy
> Kythera; and from there passed on to Cyprus in
> The sea, where she stepped out a goddess beautiful
> And feared, and grass sprang up under her slender
> Feet. Aphrodite she is named by gods and men,
> Because she grew in *aphros*, foam, and Kytheraia
> Because she came to Kythera, and Kyprogenes
> Philommedes, lover of genitals, since genitals

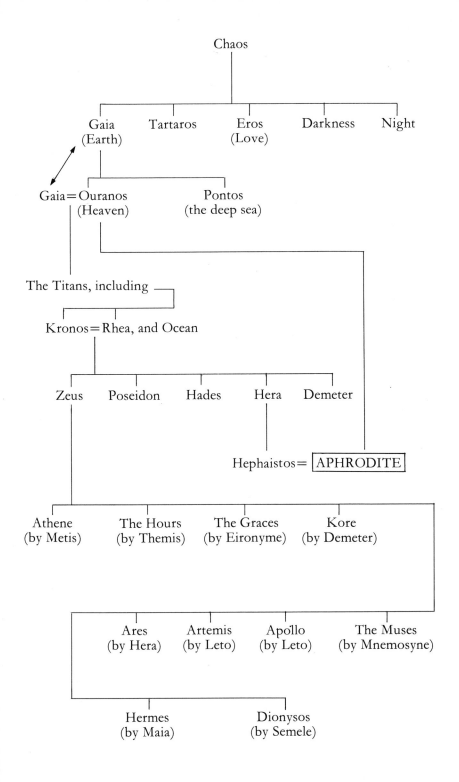

Occasioned her. Eros was her companion, and fair
Desire followed her from the moment she was
Born and when she joined the company of the gods.
And from the beginning she has been honoured
And apportioned among the immortal gods and men
With conversation between girls, and deceiving smiles
And sweet delight and love and gentleness.

According to Hesiod, the new-born Aphrodite was straightaway accompanied by Eros. Before long this winged Eros was taken to be the child of Aphrodite; he was to dwindle to the badly brought up child directing his fatal arrows at this breast and that. But for Hesiod he precedes Aphrodite, as one of the ancient primal gods.

Also in Hesiod's account something we all know about is missing. There is no shell, nothing is said of Aphrodite floating on half of a scallop shell across the light waves of the Aegean, and Mediterranean, in springtime. We think of the shell as the means by which Aphrodite was transported to her Cypriot landing, we have been accustomed to it by Botticelli's *Birth of Venus*, which is perhaps the most famous and familiar master-painting of the world (a narrowing world: Edgar Snow has written in one of his books of seeing a colour-print of Botticelli's Venus pinned up in the flat of a Chinese steel-worker, in a town near the Great Wall).

Botticelli of course did not invent that scallop shell. Some four centuries after Hesiod's time Aphrodite and the shell began to appear together, in the arts of the fourth century B.C. Then in the second century B.C. little coloured figures were commonly made—to put in tombs or to offer at the shrines of Aphrodite—which show Aphrodite not so much travelling on a shell as appearing from a shell.

From a scallop she is actually emerging, new-made and naked, as if she had grown inside the scallop rather than in the sea itself.

I do not think this new, or later, image entirely contradicts Hesiod's story. Instead the Shell-Venus seems to correct and amplify the myth—while suggesting another mode of birth—in a way which agreed more with Phoenician, Philistine or Syrian accounts of the Astarte goddess. Perhaps a little more common sense had been required, a sea-womb, a sea-receptacle. Why shouldn't the foam, the sperm of the genitals, have ripened in the soft bed enclosed and protected by the two valves of the scallop?

Two valves, not one, are shown in many of the little terracottas (Plate 6).

5 The Shell-birth of Aphrodite, with roses and winged Erotes. Pottery oil-flask. Attica, late 5th century B.C. Museum of Fine Arts, Boston, U.S.A.

The valves are opening and revealing this new pink Aphrodite, who is kneeling, not standing, inside. *Kteis*, the Greek word for a scallop (literally a comb, from the ridges and channels which fan outwards across the shell) also meant the private parts of a woman. So there, in this sea-womb, this sea-matrix, is the new goddess perfected. And we may suppose that the scallop had just propelled itself upwards—Aphrodite Anadyomene, Aphrodite rising up—and spread its valves to reveal her. Also in her terracotta shell Aphrodite sometimes holds a man's member in her hand, completing her image as the goddess both of the *kteis* of women and its counter-organ in men; that goddess who was, as well, in Hesiod's description, Philommedes, Lover of Genitals, queen of what roundabout writers sometimes call 'the satisfying crisis of the sexual act'.

Aphrodite's origin in a *kteis* does come nearer that other watery origin from the egg which the fish rolled out of the Euphrates. And certainly

6 The Shell-birth of Aphrodite. Terracotta figurine from Southern Italy. Hellenistic, 2nd century B.C. British Museum, London.

the shell as womb does fit the goddess of the waters, of the sacred fish and the sacred dolphins, and of fair voyaging in space and in love.

One Greek writer, Diphilos, of the fourth and third centuries B.C., the time when the scallop-Aphrodites were first being made, seems to have mentioned, as a piece of everyday knowledge, that Aphrodite was shell-born. Plautus latinized his comedies (which are all lost in the originals), and in one of them, the *Rudens*, Plautus makes a character say to Venus that since she was born from a shell, as people affirm, of course she will be kind to the two girls, the two shell-fish, the pair of cunts, as might be said today, thrown up by a storm below her temple (*concha*, the word used by Plautus, has the same two meanings in Latin as *kteis* in Greek, shell and private parts of a woman).

Both Phoenicians and Greeks might have noticed one delightful peculiarity of the scallop, which could have fitted it all the more to be Aphrodite's matrix. If you open a fresh scallop (our own *Pecten maximus* of northern waters will do: Aphrodite's scallop, Mediterranean or Aegean, is actually a different species of about the same size, *Pecten jacobaeus*) you will find around the inside edge or fringe, among the short white tentacles, a number of glittering eyes, upwards of thirty of them. They form a kind of necklace of Aphrodite. Perhaps these minute pearly eyes round the scallop explain why Aphrodite's Phoenician forerunner was known in some of her cults as Margarito, or as the Lady of the Pearls. (It is no good looking for this necklace of eyes in a scallop bought from the fishmonger. He will have cleaned away everything except the white and orange flesh.)

2

A Goddess Transformed

Paphos

'Paphian', after all the poems of all the centuries, is still the most resonant of the Greek epithets for Aphrodite; and in Cyprus there remain three places named Paphos, a port, a town, and a village tacked to the earthquake-scattered scraps of Aphrodite's most celebrated and longest-lived shrine.

'O Paphian Aphrodite'—but there is not a sign of her at Nea Paphos, or Kata Paphos, the port, where Agapenor founded his city, and where the pilgrims of the Ancient World landed for the yearly flower-garlanded procession to Old Paphos. This Kata Paphos does have its youthful antiquities, its pretty mosaics of the House of Dionysos of the third century A.D., under a corrugated iron roof, its underground Hellenistic tombs or tomb-houses, with their often colonnaded courts, by the hard and noisy edge of the Mediterranean, brown against blue.

Otherwise Kata Paphos is a low, arid, nearly empty junk-yard of our own century, a few warehouses, a quay, plenty of rust, plenty of collapsed fences, a prospect of the dismal and the unsuggestive rottenness of time, the site of a Roman capital also thrown down by earthquakes, and deserted—it was malarial into the bargain—for modern Paphos, or Ktima, two miles away on higher ground. Here you find still less of the Paphian Aphrodite, in a modern town, a modern suburb without a centre, which has only the benefit of unrelenting sunshine, and which is being transformed as fast as scaffolding and concrete can manage into something still less pleasurable and still more undivinely pretentious.

So to the third Paphos—Palea Paphos, Old Paphos, or Kouklia, ten miles away along shadeless roads, on a low shadeless hilltop where the limestone comes up to the surface, set back from a coast not at all impressive or attractive in this stretch. A white village, which motor-coaches penetrate between walls to an adjoining muddle of dust, weeds, orange peel, chocolate papers, and blocks and drums of limestone.

The first temple here was built not long before 1200 B.C. With the

Phoenicians it became in the ninth century Astarte's temple, and so, with the Greeks dominant, it was claimed for Aphrodite (even then the Paphian goddess was sometimes referred to as Astarte Paphia—Astarte of Paphos).

As late as the third century of our era Palea Paphos, or Palaipaphos, under the Romans, was still a city of wealth, spreading around the temple. As late as the third century Clement of Alexandria still had reason to jeer at the Greeks because they weren't ashamed to go on worshipping Aphrodite, whose initiates here at Old Paphos gave coins to her as if she were a whore, and were given in turn little phallus-images (of a kind which can be bought from Turkish Cypriots who deal illegally in antiquities) and cakes of salt symbolizing Aphrodite's emergence from the sea.

When the temple site was being excavated in a rough way in 1888, one item found by the English archaeologists was a bronze-gilt pin (now in the British Museum) which speaks more illuminatingly and persuasively of the goddess than the whole litter of stones and the footings of walls, which cannot much inspire the coach-loads of tourists and Cypriot school-children. An inscription pricked up the length of this pin says that it had been vowed to Paphian Aphrodite by Eubola, wife of Aratos, a courtier of one of the Ptolemies who ruled in Cyprus, with Old Paphos as their capital, from late in the 2nd century before Christ. At the head of the pin is fixed an egg-shaped bead of Egyptian porcelain, capped with a pearl. Below this egg four doves spread their wings, and drink from four lotos flowers, set between four goat heads.

Lady of the Pearls, Lady of that egg which fell into the Euphrates, Aphrodite of the Goats, of the kids whose entrails were inspected here at Old Paphos by Aphrodite's priests (see page 207), Aphrodite of the Doves, Aphrodite who borrowed the sweet scented lotos flower from Egyptian Isis (page 197)—so much of the Paphian goddess can seldom have been symbolized in one small object.

The Beach of Achni

After all, legend may prove more evocative than myth or archaeology. A visit to Aphrodite's rocky landing-place may put us more in touch with her than continued poking about in the dust, rubbish and glitter of Old Paphos, ruined by earthquake and ages and stone merchants.

It was natural for the Cypriots to claim that Aphrodite came ashore somewhere close to her greatest shrine. In the first century A.D. the geographer Pomponius Mela compiled a survey of most of the known world, of which the heart was the Mediterranean. He wrote that Cyprus was left, in his day, with only a few cities, of which the most excellent were 'Salamis,

Paphos, and Palaepaphos, where the natives claim that Venus'—he wrote in Latin—'first emerged from the sea'.

Perhaps even then the Cypriots were claiming, as they still do, in their tourist literature, that where she came ashore was the beach named Achni, below the Petra tou Romiou, five and a half miles from Old Paphos, under the main road from Paphos, or Ktima, eastward to Kourion, where Apollo had his great Cyprian temple, and to Limassol.

> A savage place! as holy and enchanted
> As e'er beneath a waning moon was haunted
> By woman wailing for her demon-lover—

does that apply, as in Coleridge's *Kubla Khan*? Yes, and no. When I first saw the place I had been thinking of Hesiod—not *Kubla Khan*—and of the description of Aphrodite's landing, in a fragment of one of the Homeric Hymns. But the sun was covered, and if holy and enchanted (in spite of the new motorway crossing the chasm and pressing against the beach) this place of the rocks was savage distinctly. The Petra tou Romiou spoke more of its own legend: it had been hurled against the Saracen fleet by Dighenis, the legendary hero of medieval Cyprus, when the Saracens jeered at him and called out *Romios! Romios!* (Greek!). Rocks large and enormous; and behind them, the striated limestone cliffs which concealed hills further back rising to a thousand feet, were bare, grey and lifeless, and unrelated to love.

The landscape demanded a transformation or an epiphany; which came the moment the clouds passed off the sun, the sudden light bringing out the colours. The company of these grey rocks rooted in the shelving beach and in the sea, and these grey cliffs above them, changed to Aphrodite's colour; which is pink. Also the dark dull blue of the sea changed to the blue of Persian tiles.

The foam here is extraordinary. It gleams, it drives ashore. The black-based pink rocks lift heavily out of the blue; a selvedge of white divides them from that blue of Persia, and in great swags the divine foam runs up a shoulder or shelving of sand, the swags intersect, and then the foam slides back over the dark slope of the sand to meet more foam advancing. A rose landscape, a rose and blue landscape, without roses, noisy with the agitations of the sea (which means that you cannot hear any of the invisible lorries which pass on that new motor-way behind and above). The only birds about are jackdaws, as if a reminder that Aphrodite had her chthonic connections. No white gulls, no white doves, no rock pigeons fly down to greet Aphrodite.

7 The Birth of Aphrodite, helped from the sea to the beach by two of the Horai, the Seasons. Centre panel of the Ludovisi Throne. Greek, c. 470–460 B.C. Museo Nazionale Romano, Rome.

It would be pleasant to suppose that the processions to Old Paphos and the temple began from this Achni beach, and not from Agapenor's Kata Paphos a few miles to the west. But here no harbour or city ever existed. It would be pleasant, too, to think that the writer of a love poem of the second century B.C. (either Poseidippos or his friend Asklepiades) had this beach in mind:

> By your beach, goddess of Paphos and Kythera,
>   Kleander saw Niko swimming in the blue-waved
> Sea, and O he was on fire with love, O what parched
>   Coals that sea-wet girl set glowing
> In his heart. There he stood shipwrecked on that
>   Shore which welcomed her so gently from
> The sea. But they are in love now. They weren't useless
>   Prayers he prayed then on that shore.

Today, if Aphrodite walked naked out of the everlasting foam on to her beach, she would have to spend her first minutes on this earth scraping ship's oil off her feet and legs. And the same goes for every modern Niko who comes to Achni and Petra tou Romiou, and risks a swim.

Forgetting that benison of our grubbier time, there is another detail to consider in the folklore, in the pink and the white, of Aphrodite's beach. The small, white and rather endearing flowers of a Star-of-Bethlehem (*Ornithogalum tenuifolium*, one of the commonest spring flowers of Cyprus) grow here on the hard soil above the sand and shingle. Cypriots say that these white flowers were first imprinted here—like the white clover which Bronwen imprinted on the grass of Wales—by the naked feet of the new-born Aphrodite.

Aphrodite came ashore, and flowers were born. Roses came into being (page 190). The young flower-goddesses, the Horai, the Hours, the goddesses of the Seasons, were there waiting for her in the west wind, they fitted her out (one of them, the Season-goddess of the spring, the proper time for this event, is to be seen welcoming Aphrodite in Botticelli's painting). Then she was taken off to join the rest of the high gods, becoming one of the Twelve Olympians.

There are lines from the early, lost *Cyprian Lays*, written perhaps by Stasinos, in the eighth century B.C., which describe the clothes she put on, embroidered and scented with spring flowers:

> She clothed her body in garments the Graces
> And Hours had made and steeped in the flowers of spring,

Of kinds which come with the seasons, larkspur,
Crocus, rich violets, exquisite, delicious,
Nectareous flowers of the rose, ambrosial cups
Of narcissi . . . and of the lily . . . .
. . . Every season
Had perfumed the garments divine Aphrodite put on.

Stasinos came from Cyprus and those flowers are ones a Cypriot would have known—larkspur in the fields, purple, lilac or yellow crocuses, mountain violets, roses, the very fragrant spring-flowering *Narcissus tazetta* with a yellow cup, and for lily perhaps the pink gladiolus or Sword Lily (*Gladiolus triphyllus*), which does blossom, in fact, on the very steep ground above Aphrodite's beach, in the Cyprian spring.

In the Homeric fragment I mentioned (a fragment of one of the songs a Greek bard would have sung to introduce his lays) less is said about Aphrodite's flowers—only violets are mentioned—and more about the golden jewellery which the Hours hung around her, as if to signify that she had joined as well the territory of sentience, the territory of gods and men and creatures:

My song shall concern Aphrodite, revered,
In her crown of gold, the beauty, protecting each
High town of Cyprus which is in the sea:
There the moist breath of the west wind conveyed her
Over the sounding swell of the sea
In the softness of foam, there the gold-circleted
Hours welcomed her gladly, dressed her in clothes
Of the gods, and placed on her undying
Head that crown of the finely-worked gold,
And hung her pierced ears with earrings
Of splendour made of the gold-coloured
Copper out of the mountains, there they placed
Laces of gold round her tender neck and her
Silvery breasts, such as the gold-circleted Hours
Wear themselves in the gay divine dance
In their father's house. So they tricked out
Her body and led her away from the sea
To the gods, who then welcomed her
Gladly and gave her their hands, and stared
At her beauty, Kytherea bound with violets,
And each burned to make her his wife.

Those few lines, as it happens, were discovered in a manuscript, in Florence, in the fifteenth century, just in time to help the poet Poliziano to describe Venus in his *Stanze* and to help the artist Botticelli with details of his painting; to which it may be added that the Greek bard's talk of the moist west wind conveying Aphrodite over the sea in the softness of the foam does leave room for thoughts of a shell. The lines—for Botticelli and for ourselves—do not contradict the possibility, even the plausibility, of Aphrodite riding on the shell, in the foam, and across the sea, though probably the bard had in mind, not a shell but a chariot, in which Aphrodite had crossed the waves and had then been drawn up from the sea, and in which she continued to snowy Olympos (Plate 8). Or was it shell to shore and then chariot or car or carriage to Olympos?

8 Aphrodite rides off from the sea to Olympos, drawn by Zephyros and Iris, Hermes stepping up behind. Greek terracotta plaque from Lokroi, Southern Italy, c. 460 B.C. Museo Nazionale, Taranto.

Gods do not walk: they ride, like the grandees of earth, and there is evidence of Aphrodite's chariot or car or carriage (I prefer to say carriage, because chariot suggests war and wounds and death, and Athene) on this occasion, not in poetry, but in reliefs and vase-paintings. Sometimes the carriage she stands in is harnessed to a swan (occasionally a swan itself is her vehicle, Aphrodite riding between its wings and clasping its neck; but the swan is Apollo's bird, properly). In other representations she stands in her two-wheeled carriage and drives a team which consists of Zephyros, the West Wind—here is the real meaning of the West Wind's moist breath conveying her over the sounding swell of the sea in that early fragment of song I have just quoted—and Iris, the goddess of the rainbow.

Iris is a heavenly messenger, but also she was the wife of the West Wind.*
According to some the two were the mother and father of Eros, who was there at Aphrodite's Cyprian epiphany, though before long it was accepted that Eros was Aphrodite's child, by Ares the brutish god of war. In one terracotta relief (Plate 8) Aphrodite holds the reins, and Zephyros and Iris pull the carriage, Zephyros holding Aphrodite's dove in his right hand and Iris holding Aphrodite's alabaster vase of perfume. Behind Aphrodite, behind the carriage, wings on his hat and his feet, bearded Hermes, the messenger god (who was to be one of Aphrodite's lovers) is stepping on to the carriage as if to point out the way.

2 Kythera and the Akamas

Already, as in Homer's *Odyssey,* and in the long Homeric hymn or lay which recounts her love for the mortal Anchises, and in Hesiod's account of the gods, Aphrodite is called Kythereia, the goddess of the island of Kythera. But we do not gain much from searching for her on that not very large, remarkable or beautiful island between Crete and the Peloponnese. She had her temple there, Herodotus says it was built by the Phoenicians, Pausanias adds that it was the most sacred and most ancient of her sites in Greece. Kythera, Kythereia, Cythera, Cytherea, Cytherean—like Paphos and Paphian, the words sound their flute music through Greek, Latin and European poetry, but Aphrodite has not been revealed on Kythera, and the probable site of her temple on its mountainside has not been tested yet by excavation. The visible evidence there, rough columns inserted during the Middle Ages into a chapel of St Kosmas, suggest that on Kythera Aphrodite was endowed with no more than a 'small Doric

---

*Other accounts say that Zephyros was married to Chloris, whom the Aemaus identified with their Flora, goddess of flowers.

building of the late sixth century B.C.'.

Kypris, Cypris, Cypria, the Cyprian, Kyprogene, the Cyprus-born—the other, greater island remains Aphrodite's home of homes, though she came to have her temples in every city of Greece, and of the Greek settlements overseas.

Beyond the cliffs of Achni, of her landing place, it is no great distance to country of anemones and cyclamen and to the flowers of the Troodos Mountains, or eastward to square miles of the Mesaoria lucidly and fluently yellow in spring with Crown Marigolds (the wide yellow of them shows from the air), and red with poppies. Among flowers, Aphrodite enjoyed shrine upon shrine, at Old Paphos, Idalion, Amathos, Tamassos, Soli, Kythrea, Kourion, Golgoi, on the rock at the eastern tip of Cyprus (page

9 Aphrodite's Phoenician temple at Paphos, showing the sacred cone. Cypriot coin of Roman imperial date. Cyprus Museum, Nicosia.

129), and on the blue peak of Olympos, the breast-shaped mountain as it was called by Strabo, which is now Stavrovouni, the Mountain of the Cross, capped, in place of the temple, with a monastery to which St Helena gave the cross of the Good Thief, who was crucified alongside Christ, as well as a portion of the True Cross, which she was taking home from the Holy Land to Byzantium, by way of Cyprus. (An Italian on the way to the Holy Land in 1335 visited Stavrovouni monastery. He saw and put his finger on the cross, and mentioned that it was invoked by seamen in bad weather, no doubt when they came in sight of blue Stavrovouni. Greek sailors, too, would have looked up in the same way to this mountain, this Olympos, and invoked the Aphrodite who protected sailors and gave good voyages.)

At Tamassos—according to Greek or Cypriot-Greek legend—Atalanta lost her marriage race, owing to Aphrodite and the three golden apples, or quinces. At Idalion, in the vanished forests of lowland Cyprus, Aphrodite was deprived of her Adonis (who must have his own chapter) by the wild boar. At vanished Aphrodision Cypriots of the sixteenth century claimed that Aphrodite was born (as if, in those parts, they knew nothing of Aphrodite stepping to land on south-western Cyprus). At Kythrea, where a great fertilizing spring pours out of the hillside above the village and runs under the dapple-shading plane trees of a café and turns the grist-mills, they claim that Aphrodite was brought up.

Another local legend says that Aphrodite used to bathe herself (after bouts of love) in a spring in the Akamas, at the western end of Cyprus, overlooking Khrysokhou Bay. This is the spring variously called by Cypriots the Brusis ton Eroton, the spring of the Loves, the Cupids, and the Loutra tis Aphroditis, the Bath of Aphrodite. The Cypriots declared that Aphrodite slept with the Greek hero Akamas beside this spring— Akamas the Athenian, who was one of the warriors inside the Trojan Horse, having come to Cyprus after the Trojan War.

Years ago it was best for anyone who wanted to visit this Bath of Aphrodite to go by boat from the fishing village of Lachi along what was then only a track from the grubby, remote, but ancient little town of Polis. Now there is a road—through a February-green parkland of olive trees set against the peacock colours of the sea—to the farm and the tourist pavilion three or four hundred yards from the spring; which means cars and feet and a sullying of the hidden cleft in the rocks, screened by fig-tree branches, where the water descends.

Even so, the place is delicious, reached by a luxuriant path through pink and white flowered cistus, long stemmed cyclamens (often growing out of holes in the limestone boulders), small blue squills, and arisarum, and tall Naples Garlic, and reed. Maidenhair Fern hangs from the dripping rocks, that fern which came to be called in Latin *capillus veneris*, the hair of Venus, meaning either her pubic hair or the hair she wrings out, new-born from the waters, in so many of her statues.

After that, a six-mile walk on from this grotto, round a mountain—again flowering with cyclamen and with narcissi and cistus and much else—and then between wheatfields and the sea, will take an energetic investigator to a little well, dug between a grove of small pines, and the edge of a blue crescent of a bay, which is also associated with Aphrodite and her ablution. Goats, sheep and birds and humans came there for water, and this bay, without foam, is yet so perfect in shape and colour that one can fancy Aphrodite also landing there, on her island, in the spring sunshine.

Aphrodite's particular fame in this neighbourhood of the Akamas perhaps goes back to Hellenistic times, or earlier still. Grubby Polis, where old Turks creep in black baggy pantaloons, leaning on their sticks, was preceded by the town of Arsinöe, built by the great Ptolemy Philadelpos (308–246 B.C.) and named after his sister-and-wife Arsinöe, who was deified as an Aphrodite blended of the Greek or Cyprian goddess and the Egyptian Isis. Here, as in Egypt, this Arsinöe-Aphrodite would have had her temple. Arsinöe succeeded a more ancient town, Marion, and Marion may have been a town of the Philistines, or another of the Sea Peoples (page 31), who seem to have brought Aphrodite or rather Atargatis to her transformation, to her birth or rebirth on the island. No doubt stories about Aphrodite were localized in the district, if only in rivalry with Paphos, Tamassos, Amathos and Idalion.

At Ferrara, in the early years of the sixteenth century, the young poet Ariosto knew of the Spring of the Loves, the Bath of Aphrodite. He inserted two stanzas about the spring in his *Orlando Furioso*, luscious, yet I would say not altogether imaginary, as if (though there is no record of it) Ariosto himself had journeyed to 'L'isola sacra a l'amorosa Dea', and then, as in his poem, had gone on from a disappointing Paphos to this 'land full of love and pleasure', himself making the last few miles by boat. He gives the feel of the approach to the spring, and has the topography right, more or less:

> Up from the sea six miles or seven gradually
> The pleasant hill ascends. With myrtles,
> Cedars, orange trees and bays and with
> A thousand more sweet trees the place
> Is full. Thyme, marjoram, roses, lilies
> Spread from this odoriferous ground
> A sweetness every wind that breathes
> From land takes out to sea.

From a limpid spring a second brook runs
    Down and waters all that slope. It may be
    Said this place of pleasantness and joy
    Is lovely Venus's, and every woman and girl
    Who comes to it is rendered prettier far
    Than others elsewhere in the world. For she
    Inspires all those who burn with love,
    The young, and old to their last hour.

Now, as then, the journey to the grotto (and on to the well) is worth making, in an Aphroditean sense. The grotto, something like the Castalian Spring in miniature, still suggests, when you penetrate to it, love, freshness and refreshment and fertility—lyricism in a dry land, a dry life.

10 Aphrodite with a dove. Greek terracotta figurine from Kameiros, Rhodes, c. 540 B.C. British Museum, London.

3

Adonis and Others

Divine Acquisitions

Greeks of the first millennium and the second millennium B.C. were on the move. Greek invaders in the second millennium pressed down from the north and broke up the civilization of the Mycenaean Greeks. Their pressure drove previous inhabitants overseas into the Aegean islands and into the coastal lands of Asia Minor and into Cyprus. Bringing their own gods, these incoming Greeks acquired new ones, and were glad to, since the divine circles of paganism were far from being jealous, exclusive and impenetrable. So new-born Aphrodite was not alone. She was only one among such divinities gained from new contacts and conquests.

The newcomers from the north, for instance, acquired Athene from the Mycenaeans. She had been the Mycenaean citadel goddess, their goddess of war, and was to be, as well, the Greek goddess of both war and wisdom, born, as the later Greeks were to explain, with her spear in her hand out of the head of Zeus, the Father of the Gods. Even Apollo, hard as it is to believe, may not have been Greek originally. His name is not Greek, and like Aphrodite, this well-spring of culture may have been a god from the east, from the mountain country of Lycia, not so far away from Cyprus. Artemis, Apollo's twin sister, the Lady of the Wild Creatures, may have come from Phrygia, to the north of Lycia—from the land of the great mother-goddess Kybele, the land of the Phrygian mode and the traditional invention of the flute, and King Midas whose touch turned everything to gold; the centre land of modern Turkey around and south of Ankara.

If Aphrodite's naturalization or domestication seems less complete than that of such other high gods who were brought into the company of snowy Olympos, one reason is that she arrived or was accepted rather late. The Greeks were always to remain conscious of her relationship to the east, and to goddesses still worshipped by the Phoenicians and Syrians; and, an

11 Colossal head of Aphrodite. Greek, c. 500–475 B.C. Museo Nazionale Romano, Rome.

island of wonder on her account, divine Cyprus lay, like the often insane impact and effects of love, just beyond the horizons of normality, an island of desire.

Improved she certainly was; and by a people who without saying 'foreign devil' to their neighbours, were conscious of their ability to improve everything they borrowed. But in such borrowing characteristics had to be adjusted, an incoming divinity was required to supply what was missing, and no more, and had to be relieved of contradicting or discordant relationships, more or less. So the joins between the new and the old, the Greek and the eastern, remained visible.

This is clearest in the usual story of Aphrodite's birth. Only at remote Dodona, in the north-west of Greece beyond the Pindos Mountains, at the primitive cult centre of Zeus and the oak-tree and Dione, served by ascetic priests with unwashed feet and pigeon-priestesses or dove-priestesses, was Aphrodite rather crudely accommodated in the genealogy of the gods as the actual daughter of Zeus and Dione, the vaguely indicated consort of the Father of the Gods, whom Hera replaced. The story of the divine semen of Ouranos ripening in the foam of the Aegean into the young goddess of roses and love obviated too much awkwardness of upset and adjustment; according, at the same time, with the full poetry of Aphrodite's nature and function. Even then the new or not so ancient goddess retained traces of her old eastern self, for instance in the husband she acquired, in her liaison with Ares, the sharp and nasty god of war, and in her love affairs with the hero Anchises and the young and handsome Adonis.

2 *Astarte and Baal*

Let us look first of all into the association of Aphrodite and Adonis, since it belongs most vividly to the island of Aphrodite's birth. Other high gods of the Syrian and Phoenician city-states, other inhabitants of those clouded divine heights of Mount Sapan which can just be seen from the eastern point of Cyprus, must have crossed to Cyprus with the goddess about to be born as Aphrodite. Across the water the ruling triad of the eastern gods was made up of El, Hadad or Baal, and herself, Astarte-Aphrodite, Ashtoreth-Aphrodite, Atargatis-Aphrodite, as we may call her for indicative convenience. El was the creator; the ever young and vigorous Hadad or Baal took care of his creation, and Astarte-Aphrodite caused his creation to reproduce; and just as Astarte derived from Ishtar of Babylon and Assyria, so Hadad or Baal derived from the Babylonian and Assyrian Adad, god of thunder, lightning, rain and abundance. He was the 'Rider on the Clouds', which capped the heavenly Mount Sapan (which was the Kasios of the

Greeks, and is today's Jebel-el-Aqra). The storm-clouds collected, the lightning flashed and forked to the dry earth, and Baal, the 'Lord', was at his work, at once frightening and beneficent. Falling on the parched soil of the Syrian and Phoenician coast-lands, Baal's rain brought the plants up again, and life was renewed.

Mist and Dew were the daughters of this god, who had the strength of bulls, and wore a horned helmet, and carried his lightning in one hand and his club in the other. His myth says that he was overcome by the death-god Mot, the god of the yearly dry season which shrivels the vegetation in these hot lands of the Eastern Mediterranean. The dryness would have prolonged itself into everlasting drought if Baal's wife and sister Anat had not found him in Mot's subterranean realm, taken him up, and buried him on Mount Sapan, where she resurrected him after a while.

It is the story of the death and return of the Sumerian Dumuzi, and of the Babylonian and Assyrian Tammuz.

Figures of Baal in terracotta and in bronze have been found in Cyprus. But then (taking a backward look at the table of divine genealogy on page 35) think of the situation on Mount Olympos or in Greek consciousness. The great gods, with Zeus at their head, are in firm possession. It is desirable to have this new goddess in the pantheon where she will exercise a function of divinity—a love function—not exercised by the other queens of heaven. But she cannot rule with Zeus on Olympos, as with Baal on Mount Sapan. The great Hera does that already; and she can only take her place below Hera, who is the sister and wife of Zeus, and below Athene and Artemis, two of the three goddesses—since she inflamed gods as well as men—who were always untouched by her power.

For Baal or Hadad, the thunder god of Mount Sapan, there is no room at all on Olympos. But he does not quite disappear. It is Baal or Hadad who survives, in Greek mythology, as Aphrodite's Adonis, diminished, transformed, semi-divine, but not eternal. Adonis, for the Greeks, is all that is left of the Phoenician god, whose epithet was '*Adon*, 'lord'.

The Birth and the Death of Adonis

Whatever happened to '*Adon*, the lord, in Cyprus, he was taken care of variously in Greek myth. Paphos being the grand centre of the island worship of Aphrodite, the Greeks supposed him to have been the son— incestuously conceived—of Kinyras, king of Paphos. The incest was the fault of Myrra or Smyrna, daughter of Kinyras. She was in love with her father. Her nurse helped her to come to his bed twelve nights running, Kinyras in the dark not recognizing her. When he discovered that he had been coupling with his own child, Kinyras ran after her with his sword. Myrra appealed to the gods to make her invisible, and before Kinyras caught her, she was changed by the gods to that tree the gum of which is *murra, smurna,* or *myrrh*; whereupon her pregnancy by Kinyras became the pregnancy of the tree. It broke open ten months later—one month extra for a tree—and gave birth to the holy Adonis. (Myrrh can be counted part of the migration of the gods from east to west. It was burnt on the altars of the Phoenician and earlier gods for its sweet scent. The Greek *murra* was borrowed from the Semitic name. *Commiphora myrrh*, the myrrh-tree, does not grow in Cyprus, but in Arabia, the source of the temple supplies, and in Africa.)

To continue the story of Adonis, the baby born of the tree was so beautiful that Aphrodite determined to save him from destruction. She hid Adonis in a coffer, then handed the coffer to Persephone, the goddess of the Underworld, who opened the coffer and looked at the baby and refused to give him back.

Aphrodite appealed to the gods. Zeus decided that Adonis should spend part of the year with Persephone in the Underworld, and part of it with Aphrodite in the sunlight. So much or so little did the Greeks retain from the Phoenician myth of Baal or Hadad's descent into the land of the god of death, and his return, which had enabled the waters of abundance to fall once more.

Adonis now grew up at Paphos no less beautiful as a young man than as a baby. Aphrodite loved him to madness, and was afraid that he would be killed or injured if he insisted on hunting big game in the Cyprian forests. He went after wild boar against her advice. A boar broke cover and drove its tusks into his white flesh (according to some the boar was Ares, made jealous by Aphrodite's love for Adonis). Aphrodite in her bird-drawn carriage heard the groans of Adonis, and came down to find him laid 'all along for dead upon the yellow dust' in a pool of blood.

The First Anemones

To cheat the Fates, as far as that was possible, Aphrodite at once decided to create an everlasting memorial of Adonis by turning his blood into a flower:

> Of my greefe remembrance shall remayne,
> Adonis, whyle the world doth last, from yeere to yeere shall growe
> A thing that of my heavinesse and of thy death shall showe
> The lively likenesse. In a flowre thy blood I will bestowe . . .

This sed, she sprinckled Nectar on the blood, which through the powre
Thereof did swell like bubbles sheere that ryse in weather cleere
On water. And before that full an howre expyred weere,
Of all one colour with the blood a flowre she there did fynd.*

So anemones were born—the Crown Anemones or Poppy Anemones
(*Anemone coronaria*) which are the prettiest of early spring flowers on the
hills of Cyprus and Greece and the Lebanon, ancestors of the modern
St Brigid Anemones, which are the blood of Adonis in the gardens and
the bright seedsmen's catalogues of Europe and America.

In Cyprus nothing more brilliantly, in a more startling way, suggests
Aphrodite and Adonis as coupled powers of spring and renewal than a
flash in February or March of the first anemones among the scrub of a neglected field or a neglected olive orchard, say on the lower slopes of the
Kyrenia mountains, when there is a wind in the pines, above that Persian-
tile blue of the Mediterranean between Cyprus and the snow peaks of
Anatolia. Also anemones have the mythological good sense, or the mythological good manners, to grow at Idalion, more or less in the middle of
Cyprus, anciently reputed to be the exact place where Adonis fell to the
boar. Raided by tomb-robbers and old-fashioned archaeologists, Idalion
is now a muddle of half-excavated grey mounds and slopes and old fields,
surrounded more or less by an horizon of blue mountains. A platform
on top of one terraced hill is where Aphrodite had her temple, when
Idalion was a Graeco-Phoenician city. Up and down these slopes the
anemones—the primal anemones, one could say—come out just about
the time when blossom, pink against the blue of the horizon, is dying
away on a few scattered almond trees below the temple platform. The
Greek Cypriots of the neighbourhood call this hill the Peak of Gabriel.
My thought on reading this was that Aphrodite's birds had brought her
to earth, to the body of Adonis, on this temple site, and that the Cypriot
Christians had substituted one epiphany for another at this point, the
Virgin Mary for Aphrodite, imagining that Gabriel flew down here from
heaven to tell the Virgin that she was to become the mother of Christ,
making Idalion into a local Nazareth.

As for the name by which the Greeks knew these mythical and actual
flowers, it looks as if *anemone*, the flower moved easily by the wind, *anemos*,
must join Aphrodite as a borrowed word which was then explained by
folk-etymology. Just as Aphrodite derives not from *aphros*, 'foam', but from
Ashtoreth, so *anemone* derives, not from *anemos*, but from the Semitic

*From Golding's translation of Ovid's *Metamorphoses*.

na'aman, which meant the one 'who was pleasant', the one 'who was lovely'.
Sir James Frazer, in *The Golden Bough*, mentions the 'wounds of Naaman'
as an Arabic name for this Crown Anemone.

I have been writing as if this anemone of Baal and Adonis, of the 'lord' and
the lover of Adonis, always had flowers the colour of blood. The colours
vary. In a single field, a single clump, whether in Cyprus or the Lebanon,
you find anemones not only red, but white, pink, blue, purple, and lavender;
which is perhaps why the stories of Adonis, Aphrodite and anemones also
vary. For instance, the poet Bion, who lived about 100 B.C., and came
from the anemone countryside of the ancient Greek city of Smyrna (Izmir
in the modern Turkey), says in his *Lament for Adonis* that it was the tears of
Aphrodite which caused the anemones to grow—as if he had been thinking
only of the white anemones—while the blood of Adonis produced the
first roses:

> Tears fall from the Paphian goddess, blood from Adonis,
> And they change on the earth into flowers.
> Her tears are anemones now, his blood is roses.
>   Adonis, Adonis, O. sweet Adonis is dead.

Ann Matthews in her *Lilies of the Field* (1968), a handbook to the best of the
wild flowers of Cyprus, maintains that the first anemones to open are the
white-flowered ones, down on the plains, where they show as early as
December. In the hills they open later, along with the red, pink, lavender,
and purple-blue forms. Perhaps this explains the supposition that the
first anemones grew from the tears of Aphrodite and were white.

The Gardens of Adonis

These accounts of the birth, then the death of Adonis duplicate, in a changed
diminished form, the same vegetative myth of Baal or Hadad being slain
and coming back with the waters of life. But Adonis, keeping the god's title
or epithet as if it had been his distinctive name, wasn't worshipped by the
Greeks. For them he was a demigod, commemorated by the blood-red
anemones, who belongs to the company of the great Aphrodite. Without
a wide or proper cult of his own, for the Greeks he retained no more than
traces of his old foreign condition of divinity, in their myths and at last in
the yearly rite of the Adonia, the mourning for Adonis, which the Greeks
observed for centuries in Athens and elsewhere.

This was a Phoenician custom they borrowed, perhaps from the neighbourhood of Byblos, in the modern Lebanon, where *'Adon*, the Lord, was

revered, in association with Astarte. Lucian visited Byblos in the second century A.D. He saw the Adonis ceremonies there, in the temple of Aphrodite, and recorded the local belief that Adonis had been killed in the gorges of the 'river Adonis', which turned red, as if with his blood, every year when the rains came and washed down the coloured earth into the river. (Byblos is the modern Jbail, north of Beirut, and the river is the Nahr Ibrahim, which pours out of a cave opposite the site of an Astarte, or as it became an Aphrodite, temple near the village of Afqa.)

In Athens, as in Byblos, there was weeping and wailing when the Adonia came round, and the Athenians placed little 'Gardens of Adonis' outside their houses. These were old bowls or broken crocks filled with rootless slips of lettuce, dill, fennel and other plants. Watering kept them as fresh and green on the first day of the Adonia as the rest of the world's revived vegetation (in Athens the Adonis ceremonies were held in April). Then on the second day they stopped watering the 'gardens' and the slips at once drooped and shrivelled in the hot sunshine, and the 'gardens' were thrown into springs or streams.

Such ritual gardens symbolizing the return and death of the *'Adon* are mentioned by the Hebrew prophet Isaiah, of the eighth century B.C., when he talks of the Israelites deserting Yahweh for the Phoenician religion of nature:

> In that day shall his strong cities be as a forsaken bough, and an uppermost branch, which they left because of the children of Israel: and there shall be desolation. Because thou hast forgotten the god of thy salvation, and hast not been mindful of the rock of thy strength, therefore shalt thou plant pleasant plants, and shalt set it with strange slips. In the day shalt thou make thy plant to grow, and in the morning shalt thou make thy seed to flourish; but the harvest shall be a heap in the day of grief and of desperate sorrow.

Perhaps it was about Isaiah's time that the Adonia ceremonies became established in Greece. Nearly five centuries later Theokritos describes the rather grand celebration of the Adonia in the royal palace at Alexandria. His poem is anything but mournful. Two young married ladies of Alexandria, Praxinoa and Gorgo, chatter their way to the palace, and the grand moment comes when the singer of the year addresses a song to Aphrodite (in fact to Ptolemy II's queen Arsinoë, who was identified and deified in her lifetime with Aphrodite and Isis), telling her that Adonis has

12 and 13 (Overleaf) The source of the Adonis River in the Lebanon.

come back from the dead. The song begins

> Aphrodite of the golden eyes, Lady
>   Whose loved homes are Golgoi
> And Idalion and Eryx up on high,
>   Adonis has come back.
>
> Look, in the twelfth month Adonis
>   Has come back to you, led
> From incessant Acheron by those soft-
>   Treading, kindly Seasons who
>
> Are slowest of the Blessed Ones, yet
>   Longed for, since each time
> They bring some gift with them to all of
>   Mortal kind . . . .

And the song goes on that next day Adonis—or the life-sized figure of him bedded there beside Aphrodite, with flowers and fruit and Adonis Gardens in silver baskets—will be taken down to the shore and dispatched on his return journey across Acheron, that river which borders the deathly kingdom of Hades and his queen Persephone or Kore.

Aphrodite, the Smith-God, and the God of War

With the reduction of Baal or Hadad to Adonis, Aphrodite-Astarte lost either divine companion or divine consort. In her new sodality she needed a new husband, and here again the join between old and new shows, because a husband was appointed for her in the peculiar person of Hephaistos, himself an intruded deity in need of a wife. He found his place as the god of the new working of iron (which the Hittites in Asia Minor invented in the thirteenth century B.C.), the god of metals, the smith-god, and the Greeks had taken him as well from the Asian world, though they made him the son of Zeus, by Hera, a suitable parentage for the god of weaponry and the fabricator of his father's thunderbolts.

His name, like Aphrodite's, is not Greek; and, as Apollo may have done, so Hephaistos entered Greece from Lycia. Northwest instead of east of Aphrodite's island, his native mountains rise, less than 150 miles away, over the modern Gulf of Antalya. There he began his godly existence as a fire deity, in a district where natural gas comes out of the rocks, the mountain land of the Khimaira or Chimaera, the monster who breathed fire (the fires of the ignited gas) and combined in his body lion, goat and dragon.

His cult went from volcanic area to area, from Lycia to Lemnos, near the Dardanelles, from Lemnos to the Lipari islands, the Hephaistiades (where he is more familiar to us, under his Roman name, as Vulcan, hammering in his underground smithy with the help of his shaggy one-eyed Cyclops). Homer says in the *Iliad* that Zeus threw him out of heaven for interfering between Zeus and Hera, his father and his mother. He fell steadily for a day, and then came to earth on Lemnos, an island of a civilization older than the arrival of the Greeks, where hot springs still flow in evidence of earlier volcanic activity.

In his smithy Hephaistos forges not only iron thunderbolts for Zeus, but spears, arrows, and armour, and necklaces and pieces of diverting mechanism for his divine customers. He lives in a bronze palace, served by artificial girls he has fashioned out of gold. One of his master works was the bronze giant Talos, who guarded Crete, stalking around that long island of King Minos three times a day, catching strangers as they came ashore, clasping them tight, and then heating himself until they were dead by roasting or grilling.

A talented and useful god; but an awkward one and a black husband for golden Aphrodite. The fall from heaven to Lemnos had made him lame; he was thick-necked, hairy, sooty, and comic. When he limped from god to god on Olympos with the two-handled nectar cup, the gods, according to Homer, found his gait and person irresistibly funny.

Hephaistos and Aphrodite have no children, and she cuckolds him again and again, above all with Ares, the thoughtless god of destruction and slaughter and the savagery of war. Hephaistos made a metal net of the finest invisible mesh and threw it over Ares and Aphrodite as they lay together. They could not escape and he exhibited them to the hilarity of the rest of the gods.

It was told of Hephaistos that at a time when Aphrodite had been short with him he was visited by that other one of the queens of heaven, Athene, in search of arms. He tried to make love to her, chased her and spilt his seed on her leg. The virgin goddess, who was always proof against love, disgustedly wiped the seed off with a piece of wool, which fell to the ground, where from the sperm was born Erichthonios, who became king of Athens. The story recalls the way Aphrodite came into existence, but also it suggests that this foreign husband of the foreign goddess of love and beauty did not quite 'belong', any more than she did.

Aphrodite and Hephaistos, Aphrodite and Ares, are contrasting and complementary pairs; and Ares, again, was not certainly of Greek origin. Aphrodite's association with this divine savage speaks once more of her extra-Hellenic origins, and of the adjustments required to accommodate her on Olympos. Beautiful like herself, her predecessors Astarte, Ishtar and Inanna had all combined in themselves love and war, fertility and fierceness, had all been terrible with weapons. The gentle dove might be Astarte's bird, fluttering and cooing around her temples, but Astarte handled the axe, and threw the spear, and drove the chariot on behalf of her Phoenicians. The Greeks already had established Athene as their war-goddess: armoured Athene with her spear, armoured Athene who invented the chariot, as the Greeks maintained, the goddess of the citadel who defended and beat off aggression. They did not require a goddess who would compete with Athene or be her double in that role, so Aphrodite lost that contrasting aspect of herself in most places where she was honoured in Greece (though not everywhere: she was armed Aphrodite, a wooden image in armour, in her temple on Kythera, where her Greek worship was first established; she continued to be the warrior Aphrodite for the severe Spartans, also for some of the cities on the Asian coast). For the most part her old warrior's nature was reduced simply to her habit of misconducting herself with Ares.

He was a god whom the Greeks did not much respect; they found him less worshipful, soldier's braggadocio not being a good thing in itself, than mythologically useful as a foil to their adopted and adapted love-goddess. One of the children of Aphrodite and Ares was Harmonia, as if the concord of opposites (Lucretius was to write of Venus enfolding Mars with her sacred body and giving him rest). Another mythological item is that Ares enraged Aphrodite by making love to the beautiful Eos, the dawn-goddess. Aphrodite condemned Eos always to be in love with someone; a proper association of dawn and love, and the parting of lovers as the sky begins to lighten and turn red.

4

Eros and Hermes and Priapos

Eros

The story of Aphrodite's affair with Adonis has its double or parallel in the story of the goddess falling in love with the handsome shepherd Anchises, on Mount Ida, as a result of which she became the mother of Aeneas. But I shall leave Aphrodite and Anchises, and Aeneas and Aphrodite's share in the foundation of Rome, till I come to the Roman transformation of Aphrodite into Venus, only recalling at the moment that Ida, the Anatolian mountain or mountain range of myths and legends which towers south-east of Troy (from Ida the gods watched the Trojan War), was a chief district of the worship of Kybele, the great bisexual Mother Goddess of the Phrygians, and that the name Anchises is held to be a form of Agdistis, which was Kybele's other name. It was from Kybele's divine life-history, so intricately netted are Aphrodite's relationships and ancestry, that the association of Aphrodite and Anchises arose.

Like Adonis, Anchises was all that remained for the Greeks of another god out of the foreign past of their Aphrodite. Established, elevated into one of the twelve great Olympians, Aphrodite in her chief duty as goddess of love had to be adjusted, in the course of time, to a couple of ancient gods already in her line. The first of these simpler expressions of love and its inborn drives to generation was Eros, Love himself, no little cupid creature, as he was to become centuries ahead, but a long recognized divinity, fundamental to life, young, handsome, winged, since he was always on the sudden business of the heart, and pictured sometimes (but through his later connection with Aphrodite) as carrying a rose in his hand.

Refer to the table of gods on page 35, and there you find him as a primal god who existed before almighty Zeus and the brothers and sisters of Zeus and the children of Zeus, and before Kronos and Rhea who were the parents of Zeus, and before Heaven; a god, in short, as ancient as Gaia, the Earth, and like her the offspring of Chaos; a god without whom there could have been no life, and no succession of life. Hesiod wrote

First of the first Chaos occurred, but next
Wide-breasted Earth, the always firm base
Of everything, and dismal Tartaros in wide-wayed
Earth deep down, and Eros, handsomest among
The undying gods, dissolver of limbs, subduer
Utterly of the wits and sense of every
God and all mankind.

Early on, Eros and Aphrodite transmitted to men on approximately the
same wavelength, or at least in the same programme of love, although
Aphrodite's power and influence were greater. Hesiod says that Eros went

*14 Winged Eros, with a rose in his hand. Bronze mirror case. Etruscan, 5th century B.C.
British Museum, London.*

with her when Aphrodite came out of the sea and was conducted to the assembly of the gods. But they were separate, and only gradually did Eros, though half-independent still, come to act as Aphrodite's agent, in the preliminaries of love, driving victims, as Ibykos wrote in the sixth century B.C., like game into the unbreakable nets of the Cyprian. Sometimes Eros is the god, sometimes he is the noun meaning love, less than a personification. The sixth-century poets talk of him rather more as a god. Sappho (interested most in the love of women for women) repeats Hesiod in saying that Eros loosens the limbs—turns us to water, in our phrase; Eros shakes us. If he is a god, he is also the irresistible beast, the force of nature who is at once sweet and bitter:

> Eros shivers my heart,
> Like a wind down the mountain
> Which falls on the oaks.

In the high classical time of the fifth century Sophokles writes a lyric (in the *Antigone*) about the power of Eros over gods and men, the journeys of Eros—he will find you out anywhere, away in the country or overseas. He will turn you mad, subdue you, impoverish you, he will drive just men to injustice and dishonour, Aphrodite looking on and enjoying the sport. But this is the Eros of thought and appraisal, even though abroad on his golden-feathered wings.

Here and there Eros had his centres of worship; in particular, not far west of Athens, at Thespiai in Boeotia, below Mount Helikon. There in his temple he was honoured in the shape of a tall phallic pillar. Later on his temple acquired one of the celebrated statues of antiquity, a properly youthful, winged Eros carved by Praxiteles. He gave it to the very rich hetaira Phryne; Phryne came from Thespiai, and presented the statue to the temple, a right gift from a courtesan who made a fortune out of love (Praxiteles was one of her lovers). In the end this statue of Eros was taken off to Rome for Nero, and was lost in the great fire of Rome in A.D. 80, which came soon after the lava of Vesuvius had buried Pompeii and Herculaneum. In the National Museum in Naples they have—from under the lava—a marble Eros copied either from the statue Phryne gave to Thespiai or from another statue of the god which Praxiteles carved for the Eros temple at Parion, one of the Greek towns of the Troad, on what we call the Sea of Marmora. The features and the look and the inclination of the head of this young Eros at Naples are enigmatic and magnetic with a sense of desiring, vaguely, and being desired. He looks—I would suppose him to be sixteen or seventeen—like the dream lover of all masculine homosexuals, ancient or modern, though no doubt that wasn't the way Phryne looked at the original. Still, Eros was both the homosexual and the hetero-sexual instigator of love. Thespians, after their marriage, would go to his temple, face the Praxiteles statue, and ask Eros for his favour.

Since he was male, the Greeks did take to seeing in him more the god of homosexual love, and of the good looks of young men—witness a poem by Meleager, of the late second century B.C.:

> The Cyprian's a woman: she pelts
> Us with insane fire for girls.
> But Eros drives our appetite to
> Males. Then which must I
>
> Lean to, his mother or her child?
> I tell you this, the Cyprian
> Will confess it's her pert child
> Who comes off always best.

By Meleager's time Eros had become very much that pert, spoilt, dangerous manikin of love, who wasn't any more the primeval issue of Chaos, and the primal urge to love and procreation, but the child of Aphrodite, fathered on her by Hermes (whom I come to next), or by Ares, the most notable of her divine lovers, or by Zeus; always fluttering around, always uncontrol-lable, disobedient, unpredictable, armed not only with the torch that spreads the insane fire of love, but with his bow (not acquired till the fifth century) with which he shot the arrows of infatuation into his victims, like some Anglo-Saxon elf or Irish fairy shooting the flint arrow-heads of disease into men and cattle.

The poet Apollonios, of the third century B.C., in his long telling of the story of Jason and Medea and the Argonauts, and one of the more cele-brated Greek wall-paintings from Pompeii show us Love diminished to that fractious child of Hellenistic and Roman convention, who was to return to frailer, flimsier existence on the Rococo ceilings of eighteenth-century Europe or in the mildly erotic paintings which François Boucher designed for the Pompadour and her friends. In the wall painting Aphrodite has penalized her child for some outrage or other by taking away his quiver, and on her shoulder sits one of the Loves into whom diminished Eros has been still further diminished and subdivided. In the *Argonautika* the goddesses Hera and Athene call on Aphrodite—she is rather surprised and pleased that they should visit her—and ask her if she would be so good as to persuade Eros to shoot one of his arrows at Medea, so that she will

15 Eros in flight. Hellenistic terracotta figurine from a tomb in the Greek town of Myrina (Anatolia). 2nd century B.C. Museum of Fine Arts, Boston, U.S.A.

fall in love with Jason. Well, says Aphrodite, I don't know—I don't know
if he will take any notice of me, etc., etc., but I will try. She finds Eros
cheating Ganymedes (the beautiful boy who handed their divine drink
around to the gods) in a game of knuckle-bones, and to persuade him to
interrupt his game and take a shot at Medea, she promises Eros a golden
ball, a trick ball, which Zeus had played with as a child. Eros goes off with
his bow and arrows, but not before he has tried to winkle that magic ball
out of his mother for nothing, before the job was done.

Serious it was—and is—to be hit by one of his arrows. To quote Meleager
once more:

> Love is a terror, a terror,
>   But how does it help if
> I sigh and repeat over and over again,
>   Love is a terror?

> The Boy listens in. Then
>   He laughs. To him insult is
> A pleasure. If I curse,
>   He grows stronger.

> O how did you manage,
>   Cyprian, born of the blue-
> Green sea, all the same to bring
>   Out of the water flame?

Grandeur at first, frippery at last, is the story of Eros, tagged in the end to
Aphrodite's power, and bequeathing—but that is not fair—his name or his
name-adjective to the dirty books and pictures of our century: 'erotic',
'erotica'.

2. Hermes and Aphrodite

Little terracottas and other likenesses exist of naked Aphrodite standing
cosily by a 'herm', a square-sectioned pillar of stone which ended in a bust
of Hermes, bearded and benign. The right place for such a herm was by the
edge of a track, or a road, or at a crossroads, since Hermes (though he was
not the only god to be set on a herm) showed the way to mortals; he was the
divine guide, named, so it is generally concluded, after a *herma*, a cairn, a heap
of stones. In many countries, from Greece to Wales or the Highlands, cairns
have served as a primitive indication that you are on the right road. But

then on the flat front of the Greek herm protrudes its masculine member, erect; which in a terracotta partly explains Aphrodite's presence alongside, since these two, Aphrodite and Hermes, share in the concerns of fertility.

In brief this is the story of Hermes: he was born—the sauciest and one of the most attractive of the Greek gods—in a cave on the side of Mount Kyllene, in Arkadia, the highest mountain but one of the whole Peloponnese, the mountain which is now called Ziria, a rocky, remote, snow-crested lump standing over the Gulf of Corinth. His father was Zeus, his mother was the nymph Maia. He was new-born, in his cradle, in his mother's cave, when he began his tricky, always engaging role in Olympian life by toddling off to steal cattle which belonged to his brother, or half-brother, the great Apollo. He gave Apollo the lyre which he had brought with him, and had just invented and made, in his cradle precocity. Between the gift and his cheerful impudence, Hermes won Apollo round, and was made his herdsman, after all. And here it is that Aphrodite and Hermes meet, the goddess from elsewhere, and the country god of Hellenic credentials (though he could have been an aboriginal Arkadian god adopted by the Greek immigrants): they meet in the life and increase of animals. 'Muse,' begins the Homeric hymn to Aphrodite,

> relate me the works of Aphrodite the golden,
> The Cyprian, who excited sweet desire in the gods,
> Who overcomes in their tribes mortal men,
> And birds on the wing, and all of the beasts,
> The many that dry land breeds, or the sea.
> All these depend on the works of the sweet-
> Wreathed Kytherean . . . .

Just as the animals were a part of Aphrodite's concern, so Hermes, this old Arkadian god of shepherds, herdsmen and farmers, was thought of in the sheep-pen, in the stockyard, in the byre; he made the ram couple with the ewe, the bull with the cow, the stallion with the mare, the shepherd's dog with the bitch. There are likenesses of him as Hermes Koriophoros, Hermes who carries the ram, the shepherd with the ram—not the lamb, not the ewe —across his shoulders.

According to the Homeric hymn which tells of the infant Hermes and his theft of Apollo's cattle, and Apollo's liking for him, although he grew up to be the genial confidence man of heaven and the patron of thieves, Zeus made him not only the master of sheep and cattle and dogs, but also the master of the enemy creatures, the birds of prey who might pick off the lambs, and the lions, and the wild boars. Aphrodite's power over the animals comes face to face with his own, the power of this country god whose phallus, modest and not a grand knockabout rubicund job like that of Priapos, but still a phallus, mildly ornaments the roadside herm, also helping the traveller on his journey by averting the evil eye.

Hermes may become a very nobly proportioned young anthropomorph in the statues made of him by the fourth-century sculptors (such as the famous copy in the museum at Olympia of the lost Hermes with the child Dionysos, by Praxiteles), statues suited to him as the rapid Messenger of the Gods, the guide who brought Persephone up from the underworld, who led the way for Eurydike, when she almost managed her return to life and light, and who conducted Aphrodite to her love Anchises on Mount Ida; but he begins crudely, more crudely even than the herm by the side of the road, or the herm inserted in a pile of stones. Indeed in some of his shrines, for instance at Kyllene (the harbour town on the west coast of the Peloponnese, not the mountain), he was worshipped with great reverence in the unabashed shape of a standing penis, on a pedestal, according to Pausanias's *Guide to Greece.* And he was taken to be the father of that other, on the whole less amiable, always erect and randy godling of the wild and the mountain (and of the Peloponnese in particular), the hairy, goat-legged, goat-footed Pan, who invented masturbation.

In some places Aphrodite and Hermes were worshipped together—in the Peloponnese, for instance, at Argos and at Megalopolis as well as Kyllene. And to match likenesses of Aphrodite standing by a bearded and modestly ithyphallic herm, there is a dedicatory poem of some charm, suggesting the tone of these matters in Greek life, by the poet Phanias, of the late second or first century B.C.:

> Hermes of the Wayside, this portion of
>   A fine bunch of grapes,
> This lump of lardy cake baked
>   In the oven, a black fig,
> An olive soft on the gums, these
>   Parings of a round cheese,
> A little corn from Crete, a heap
>   Of fine ground meal, then
> To finish with, this cup of wine,
>   I give to you. Permit the
> Cyprian, my goddess, to enjoy them too,
>   And I will offer on the pebbly
> Beach, I promise, a white-footed kid
>   To the pair of you.

16 Aphrodite crowning a 'herm' of bearded Hermes. Hellenistic terracotta figurine from a tomb in the Greek town of Myrina (Anatolia). 2nd century B.C. British Museum, London.

How well that matches the terracotta (Plate 16) from Myrina, on the Ionian coast. Aphrodite puts a wreath on Hermes' head; and at the foot of the herm there it is, an offering of grapes and fruit. The terracotta would have been made and the poem written at about the same time, around 100 B.C.

In the myths not very much is explained or recounted about the association of Hermes and Aphrodite. They had children together. One was the beautiful young Hermaphroditos, who found himself united to his chagrin with the nymph Salamakis, the two of them sharing one bisexual body (Hermaphroditos may have come to Greece from Cyprus, from Amathos, where Aphrodite and Adonis were worshipped).

According to some ancient accounts another child of Hermes and Aphrodite was that posthumously maligned, but in his long day homely and popular god of vineyards and gardens, Priapos.

The Misshapen Godling

To be just to Priapos, let's begin with some poems about him. There are many of them, earthy, gentle, comic, bawdy, and sometimes brutal—though the brutal poems came rather from Latin than Greek writers.

First, a poem from the Latin in which Priapos speaks to a girl, who looks at his rough, excessive figure in some garden or orchard or vineyard:

> Silly girl, what are you laughing at?
> Neither Praxiteles nor Scopas made me,
> I wasn't polished by the hand of Pheidias.
> The foreman adzed the block of wood
> And told me I was Priapus.
> And yet you stare at me and giggle.
> You think it's funny I should have
> A gate-post sticking from my thighs.

There he was on guard, a figure hacked out with an adze, and whittled into exacter shape, from a piece of old fig wood—not necessarily because fig-trees had their bawdy connotation, but because they were everywhere, and old bits of fig wood would have been around in gardens, easy to carve. Figs, though, being figs, this wood Priapos was usually made of, established a joke. Don't come here and steal the fruit or the lettuces: if I catch you stealing the figs it's my weapon which will be stuck into your fig, etcetera. And small Priapos was, or became, mostly his large weapon, which jutted upwards and outwards, instead of lying flat or flattish, like that unexaggerated member on a herm. A post it was; and a post which was painted the

17 Priapos anointing himself with oil. Hellenistic bronze statuette. Museum of Fine Arts, Boston, U.S.A.

brightest possible red, at any rate in Roman gardens. Furtiveness, secretiveness—none of that. Priapos exhibited himself for everyone to see, sticking out from the leaves. Some of his bronze figurines even lift up their clothes, for better visibility, and the fold of the clothes serves as a bag for fruit and garden stuff, a juxtaposition of the products of life and the principle of life, or the agent of life.

In one hand, too, Priapos often carried a small hook for cutting and pruning—and for attacking scrumpers, as with his other weapon.

Try Theokritos on this god, less than half a century perhaps after his entry into the mental realm of the Greeks:

> Goatherd, turn from the path under the ilexes and find
> That new-cut fig wood image erected in a holy garden
> Where water springs from the rock always and flows
> Hedged in with bay-trees, myrtles, scented cypresses,
> Where vines now set with grapes sprawl round and climb
> And blackbirds eagerly and clearly utter songs
> To spring, and brown nightingales reply from
> Honeyed throats—that fig wood image with the bark
> Still on, which has no ears or legs, yet all the same

Displays such splendid tackle for the Cyprian act.
Sit there. Pray that kind Priapos to free me
From the pain of loving Daphnis. If he does I offer him
A kid. If he says no, to bring him round I offer him
Three animals, a rough he-goat, a calf, a lamb I've reared
By hand. O may that Priapos listen to your prayer.

In the Greek poems about him he is less threatening than protective.
Theokritos, pastorally combining the fresh and the artificial, gives him in
his lines more of a role in love than a role in gardening. Other poems,
simpler and more direct, speak of Priapos with gratitude: he has loaded the
vines, he has given fruit to the tree, he has kept off the birds, he has brought
fish to the hook or into the net. Odd little creature as he may be—or may
have become—ugly and old or middle-aged, he has given a livelihood to
gardeners, fishermen, shepherds, and beekeepers.

In poems in *The Greek Anthology* fishermen as wrinkled as sea-rocks and too
old to work any more, dedicate to Priapos their nets and rods, their floats;
old gardeners dedicate to him all their garden tools, their gardening cloak,
now ragged and worn-out, and their hide boots. Like Hermes, he is given
sacrifices, figs, pomegranates, quinces, walnuts, olives, cucumbers, wine.
And he has—or should have—his share of newly landed fish.

From the Greek of Quintus Maccius (of the first century B.C., or early
first century A.D.):

> For you, Priapos, lover of the sea-worn rocks of this
>   Offshore isle and its rough headland,
> The fisherman Paris has hung up the brittle shell
>   Of a crawfish which he caught luckily
> In his pots. Having baked the meat, he kept that
>   For himself, mumbling it happily between
> His half-decayed teeth, and to you he has given
>   This stinking left-over. So allow him,
> God, in the luck of his catch no more than enough
>   To quieten his rumbling belly.

The moral of that is one which was familiar in Greek life, Don't cheat the
gods: they like their proper attention.

Affection marks poem after poem about Priapos. Archias, a Syrian-
Greek from Antioch who lived in Rome in the first century B.C., makes
Priapos give this seashore account of himself:

I am small Priapos, I live on this breakwater
By the beach, with friendly gulls. Pointed I am,
I have no feet. Children of busy spearers of fish
Could well have carved me, along an empty strand. Yet
If a fisher with his net or rod calls out to me, I go
To him quicker than the wind. And I detect
As well all things that swim below the sea. Gods
By what they do are known, not by their form.

Tibullus, a generation or two later in Rome, talks to Priapos, who

. . . lives naked through the chill of winter,
Naked through the rainless heat of summer,

and gets good advice from him in his love affair with a boy, Priapos talking
less like everyman's little daimon of the garden than like a wise and tender
spirit of love. He tells him not to waste time or youth:

How soon
Youth goes! Time does not hang around,
Time does not come again. How soon Earth
Loses her bright colouring! How soon
The high poplar drops its beautiful leaves!

. . . The snake shines new, its
Years sloughed off. But fate will not let
Beauty stay. Bacchus and Phoebus only have
Everlasting youth.

Aphrodite's rapprochement with little Priapos was necessarily a late
one, less of worship than of myth, once more; a matter of tidying up the gods
and their relationships. The powerful Greek cities of the Asiatic shore had
founded new colonies northward to the Black Sea; several of them along
the south of the Dardanelles and the Sea of Marmora. Here the Greeks had
first discovered Priapos, a fertility god in these coastlands of grapes and fish
and oysters. They adopted him, as a god of this northern country of the
Troad, just as their forefathers had adopted other gods whom they found in
possession here and there, tickled evidently by his robust combination of
vitality, utility and comedy. On the Dardanelles and the Sea of Marmora his
chief cities were Lampsakos and Priapos, and Lampsakene coins pictured
him attached, so to speak, to his member. He was known in Athens by the

fourth century B.C., but it was Alexander the Great's invasion of Asia Minor, in 334 B.C., which spread the knowledge and the range of Priapos and established him in the gardens of the Greeks, wherever they settled, and of the Graecized peoples, and the Romans.

Such a god, comic or no, humble or no in particular ways, had to be related somehow to the great gods of fertility. To Aphrodite he could be no more than child, in a franker and rough relationship to Eros. Some stories made out that if Aphrodite was his mother, his father was Hermes, others that his father was Adonis; but neither fitted the Lampsakene shore—so why shouldn't Priapos have been fathered by the great god of ecstasy, orgy and the vine, Dionysos, whom the Greeks believed to be a god from Phrygia, and who in his Phrygian context was a god of vegetation?

But then how could the most beautiful of the goddesses and one of the handsomest of the gods have had between them an offspring so grotesque?

An explanation was devised; and I shall give the story as it was neatly summed by the English poet and mythologist William King, one of the friends of Jonathan Swift, substituting Greek names or forms for his Latin ones:

'The more common opinion is that (Aphrodite) conceived by (Dionysos) before he undertook his expedition into India; but during that time she married to Adonis. Upon the return of (Dionysos) she met him in a triumphant manner, and crowned him with a garland of roses, but would not accompany him any longer, being ashamed of her inconstancy. In this condition she retired to (Lampsakos); where, being about to be delivered, (Hera) pretended to come to her assistance; but hating any thing that might be of the offspring of Semele (the mother of Dionysos, by Zeus, Hera's husband), she made the infant so deformed, that his mother could not endure the sight of him. Having given him the name of (Priapos), she left him at (Lampsakos), where he was educated; but after some time, for his vicious practices, he was banished the country.'

That did the people of Lampsakos no good: 'The inhabitants thereupon being infected with a grievous disease'—Priapos hitting back at them in the part he knew best, evidently—'consulted the oracle of (Dodane) which advised them to recall (Priapos) into their country: which they did, and built temples, and offered sacrifices to him, and worshipped him as the protector of their vineyards and gardens, who could defend their fruit from mischievous birds and thieves, and punish such as endeavoured to hurt or blast them with their inchantments.'

According to one Greek account, Zeus as well as Dionysos had been making love to Aphrodite, so the disgusted Hera touched Aphrodite's belly with her finger, causing the child's unshapeliness, which so upset

Aphrodite, lover of the beautiful, when he was born, that she exposed him on the mountainside. A shepherd found him there and brought him up, in that way causing Priapos to become, as well, the god of shepherds and sheep-pens.

Aphrodite and Priapos, mother and misshapen son, also shared in the protection of seafarers, gods, both of them, of the calm sea and the fair wind. As a harbour god Priapos helped both the seagoing merchant and the offshore fisherman caught by some squall off the mountains:

> Time again for a boat to run and to rip.
>   Seas are not any longer furrowed and
> Roughened and dark. Swallows are shaping their round
>   Nests already under the eaves,
> Grasses laugh on the meadows. Sailors,
>   Listen, it's me, it's *Bromios' son,
> The Harbour Priapos, speaking. Time to pull on
>   Your sodden ropes, time to haul
> Your lurking anchors out of the harbour
>   And hoist your strong sails.
>   (Antipater of Sidon, in *The Greek Anthology*)

Following all the ancient poets who spoke kindly and affectionately of Priapos, I can think of only two or three English poets who have been civil to him. One was Swinburne (himself, tiny and with a mop of red hair, not unlike an ineffectual little Lampsakene) who wrote with such surprising acuteness of Aphrodite, another was the more robust Walter Savage Landor. Landor wrote a *Greek Anthology* piece on the girl who comes to deck a Priapos, but is careful to approach him from behind, though blessing him for being so just and kind as to have awarded her the prize for grace. In another poem he wrote of a spring below which

> red Priapus rears
> His club amid the junipers.

And it is pleasant to think that Goethe, also mad on Greece, owned and appreciated a little bronze of Priapos, flower-crowned, bearded, holding up fruits in his dress so as to reveal that notorious member. It is still in the Goethe-Nationalmuseum at Weimar.

Our way has been to overlook the reasonable frankness of the Greeks

*The god who was *bromios*, noisy; i.e., Dionysos, who gave rise to noise and excitement.

and hide this little god in the secret penetralia of museums, in the secret cabinet of the Naples Museum, along with other risqué objects from Aphrodite's Pompeii, or in forbidden books such as the one, in the time of Goethe and Landor, by which the connoisseur Richard Payne Knight (1750–1824) earned himself opprobrium and the title of 'Priapus Knight' (oddly it was Priapus Knight's money which enabled his younger brother Thomas Knight to become one of the greatest gardeners of all time, raising new varieties of fruit and vegetables which would have been a delight to the garden god).

Our language has elongated Priapos into words for obscenity, sexual turpitude, and pathological misfortune (*'Priapean*, grossly lustful and obscene.' *'Priapism*, persistent erection of the penis'). The standard modern book about the little god, his looks, his functions, his character and his worship, by a German scholar, hides its not very shocking information away in Latin, under the Latin title of *De Priapo* (1932). At school how ingeniously masters of the classical sixth form evaded Priapos, just as they evaded so much else that might have clouded the perfect polish of the miracle of the Greeks.

He has his twentieth century problems elsewhere. In Turkey, for instance, in what was once his own particular territory. If you go into the Archaeological Museum at Ephesus, or at Seljuk rather, the attendant asks if you wouldn't like to see the god Bes, to begin with. If you agree, in slight bewilderment, that you would like to see him, the attendant goes over to the wall and pulls up a shutter, and there, behind glass, illuminated, is revealed, in a niche, not Bes, not that fat jovial divine dwarf from Egypt, but short little Hellespontine Priapos, in terracotta, carrying his enormous all in front of him. After which, Dirty Foreigner, you can buy a postcard of this tawny godling, photographed against a background of blue. If you should be a Turk, no Priapos, no postcard. The postcard says in English 'Only to be sold to *foregain* tourists'; and then, in Turkish this time, 'Must not be exhibited openly'. The English on the card goes on to affirm that this terracotta Priapos was found in one of the rooms of the brothel of Priapos's own city of Lampsakos.

In our world perhaps only the Japanese would understand why the Greeks and then the Romans liked Priapos so much, and were so amused by him at the same time. The English poet James Kirkup, in one of his books about Japan,* describes how he went with Japanese friends to the festival of an ithyphallic deity—or rather a deity who was all a large gleaming phallus, somewhat more of a Hermes than a Priapos, since he looks after

* *Heaven, Hell and Hari-kiri* (1974).

roads and travellers. The festival was affectionate, a matter of much 'grave hilarity' and many cups of the best saké. It was with that kind of gaiety, I suspect, that they treated the 'Hellespontine god', the 'country child of Dionysos', this peculiar offspring of Aphrodite; and I shall round off these comments on him with a Priapic afterthought.

In the second century of our era, when paganism was fading, and new religions were competing in the Mediterranean and the Near East, one of the Gnostics, Justin of Monoimos, declared that Priapos and God the Father had been one and the same. Not quite so mad a notion as you might think, because Justin argued that Priapos—this is like Hesiod's Eros—had 'created before anything existed'. Priapos had once been a powerful god in Asia Minor; and a seriousness remained—it is there if we look for it—below the comedy and knockabout and domesticity of his transformation.

ƒ

Aphrodite in Essence

Homer's Aphrodite

On the edge of modern Athens a great tract of half broken-down indust-
rialism surrounds the fenced site of the Eleusinian Mysteries, the Mysteries
of Demeter, the goddess of life and death, of the birth and reaping and
rebirth of the corn, which initiated the Greeks into their profoundest
intimations of the divine. And then over the centre of modern Athens
may hang, any day, until the wind carries it off, a yellow smog from the
factories, the foundries, and the chemical works. It can be smelt and it
contradicts the past. Then it lifts or vanishes, and there, as it should be, is the
white Parthenon in the sunshine, immaculate (though the chemical
acids now bite at the marble) above the tawny and the grey, and the cease-
less chase and hum of lorries, buses, cars, and taxis.

Aphrodite had her Athenian temple below the Akropolis and the
Parthenon, a powerful universal goddess, whose personality survives,
but junior in the hierarchy of the gods to Athene who owned the great whale-
back of Athenian limestone and the great temple on it, and the great city,
the protectress, the citadel goddess of war and wisdom, one of those three
immortals, with frosty Artemis and respectable and inviolable Hestia, the
hearth goddess, who could not be subdued and taken prisoner by love. The
ironic thing is that the junior goddess endures—though we call her Venus—
whereas for other deities (except perhaps for Apollo, and the Muses)
we have to grub in the books and in the museums.

> Belle Déesse, amoureuse Cyprine,
> Mère du Jeu, des Graces et d'Amour,
> Qui fait sortir tout ce qui vit, au jour,
> Comme du tout le germe et la racine;
> Idalienne, Amathonte, Erycine . . . .*

*From Ronsard's *Voeu à Venus, pour garder Cypre contre l'armée du Turc*, in *Amours Diverses*.

It is not to the others that many such poems have been written, since the death of Greece and paganism.

What isn't known—though we may guess—is when Aphrodite exactly made her entry into Greece, or into human consciousness, and how soon she was established in her firm, yet slightly ambiguous position, rather towards the edge of the divine family. In those oldest structural master-pieces, those oldest poetry temples of Greek civilization, the *Iliad* and the *Odyssey*, she is already the accepted Greek goddess, rather than the naturalized alien. That is to say, she was already in her full or main development by the end of the eighth century B.C. Perhaps by that time the Greeks of the main-land and the islands had been under the spell of Aphrodite for a century or two.

She was to change in detail, her statues were to develop from the conical dark, well oiled stone of Paphos or from rough wooden images or archaic marbles into which men had to read the charms of the most exquisite of the gods, she was to lose her clothes, and stand up on the plinth eventually as the naked, pink-tinted goddess of Aegean, Mediterranean, Adriatic, and Black Sea youth. Her wooden temples were to be built and rebuilt in stone; in one shrine and another she would be distinguished by special epithets, emphasizing particular elements in her divine character or particular directions of her power. But the goddess the Greeks recognized, however thinly or conventionally or automatically in the end, continued to be the Aphrodite they read about in Homer. To be sure then of what she was in essence, it is to the *Iliad* and the *Odyssey* that we have to go first of all; and next to those two *Hymns to Aphrodite*, which were thought to be Homeric, though they were written perhaps a century later than the grand epics.

Since the Greeks—or most of them—did not think of Aphrodite as a warrior-god, and since the *Iliad* is about war and violent death, Homer does not have so much to say about Aphrodite, who likes to laugh and whose face dissolves into dimples, as about Zeus and Hera, Athene, Ares, Poseidon, and Apollo. But since she favours the Trojans (a relic of her Asiatic origin), just as Athene of the Brilliant Eyes is in favour of the Greeks, she intervenes—and rather unfortunately for herself or for her reputation among the gods, if not altogether among the readers of Homer. She is feminine, but a mug at violence, unlike Athene, Guardian of Cities, who is formidable, if moral, with her huge bronze-headed spear. Aphrodite's favourites on the favoured side are Paris and Helen, who are the cause of war between Greek and Trojan, a war which has become one of the most famous ever indulged in by mankind.

Homer knows all about that, though he does not know, or does not mention, as if perhaps it still had to be invented, or was current only in some other part of Greece, the story of Paris and the golden ball and the three goddesses, Hera, Athene and Aphrodite, a story which was so much to appeal to artists and poets in antiquity; and later, when classical learning was revived at the end of our Middle Ages.

Like the wicked aunt in our fairy-tales, Eris, or Strife, was not invited to the wedding of Peleus and the sea-nymph Thetis, so she had thrown a golden ball among the heavenly guests, on which she had written—to live up to her name—that it was for the most beautiful of those who were present. Hera, Athene, Aphrodite, each claimed the distinction. Since the young Trojan was reputed the handsomest of mankind, Zeus decided that he should judge between these three Queens of Heaven; which he did, on Mount Ida, in the Troad, where he was shepherding his flocks. Facing him in their nakedness, each of them promised Paris a different reward. Aphrodite promised that this best looking of men should marry whoever was the best looking of women; and it was to Aphrodite—but her beauty made the choice unavoidable, whatever might follow—that Paris awarded the golden ball, in the first of beauty contests.

Helen, wife of Menelaos, king of Lakedaimon, or Sparta, was the best looking of all women, Paris eloped with her, and the Greek kings combined to bring her back; and so the Trojan War began.

In the *Iliad*, Paris's own brother Hector taunts him for being a woman's man, without courage, gifted by Aphrodite with no more than charm and good looks. When he fights Menelaos outside Troy and is likely to be killed, Aphrodite snatches him up in a mist, and returns him to his scented bedchamber. Then she appears to Helen, who is awed by her divinity and her beauty,

> By her so radiant eyes,
> White neck, and most enticing breasts,*

but is already having second thoughts, and she insists that Helen and Paris go to bed once more.

Aphrodite's other interventions do not succeed so well. When the gods fall out over Troy and the Greeks, and take to fighting, and Athene knocks down the detestable Ares with a boundary stone, Aphrodite, as lover of the

---

*This and the following quotations from the *Iliad* are given in George Chapman's translation of 1611.

---

18 The 'Aphrodite of Capua'—looking at her reflection on the shield of her lover Ares. Marble copy, c. 320–200 B.C., of a Greek original. Museo Nazionale, Naples.

god of war, manages to take him out of the fight, only to be laid out, together with Ares, by another blow from powerful Athene.

Earlier, when she was spiriting her mortal son Aineias (Aeneas) from his fight with Diomedes, King of Argos, Diomedes had chased the two of them and had been rash enough and forgetful enough of the respect owed by mortals to immortals, to scoff at her, and pierce her wrist with his spear, drawing ichor

> Such as flows in blessed Gods, that eat no human food
> Nor drink of our inflaming wine, and therefore bloodless are,
> And call'd Immortals.

In a chariot borrowed from Ares the wounded—or scratched—Aphrodite managed to get away—Apollo has taken care of her son—to Olympos, where she was comforted and healed by her mother Dione (Homer, you will remember, making her the child of Zeus, by Dione—not a word of Hesiod's sea-tale of Ouranos, Kronos and the sickle and foam); and Zeus after some superior sarcasm from his consort Hera and Athene, rather puts her in her place, in a kindly way:

> The Thunderer smiled, and call'd to him love's golden Arbitress,
> And told her those rough works of war were not for her access;
> She should be making marriages, embracings, kisses, charms,

since 'affairs in arms' were the business of Athene and Ares.

Patronising or no, there we have the first basic formulation of Aphrodite, or rather the first which has descended to us, and the one which continued to be valid among the Greeks.

Aphrodite was—and was to remain—the most single-minded of the gods. Everything else that imagination devised or improved about her, was subsidiary to that statement by Zeus, or was accommodated to it: her role was to be love's golden arbitress.

Again and again in the *Iliad* her beauty is emphasized (a beauty in those earlier times which came easier in words than in wood or stone); and not contradicting what may be called Aphrodite's erective power, her beauty leads to April, to the Seasons and the Graces and the Muses, and to love in the centre of the arts. (Here perhaps there is room for Schiller on beauty and Aphrodite—Schiller's demand that we should accept beauty without resenting the unfairness of its distribution:

> Zürne der Schönheit richt, das die schön ist . . .
> Jede irdische Venus ersteht, wie die erste des Himmels,
>   Eine dunkle Geburt aus dem unendlichen Meer.

19 Bronze head of Aphrodite, from Satula, Armenia Minor (North-east Turkey). Hellenistic 2nd century B.C. British Museum, London.

(Do not be angry with beauty, because it is beautiful . . .
Every earthly Venus, like the first Venus of Heaven,
    Is a dark birth which emerges out of the endless sea.*)

In the *Iliad* she is already 'golden', which is not, as we might think, an epithet indicating vaguely that she was bright and precious. 'Golden Aphrodite' is the Aphrodite hung with the gold necklaces of a queen who is also divine, and awesome; and in the lay about herself and Anchises, the rather later 'Homeric' hymn, the earliest poem we know which is altogether about Aphrodite, she allows Anchises, when they are together on the bed, on Mount Ida, to take off

                              her glittering adornment,
      Her pins, her twisted armlets, her flower-shaped
      Earrings, and her necklaces

—golden jewellery such as that which shines so surprisingly out of the past as you enter the Mycenaean room at the National Museum in Athens. Gold is the metal of queenship and divinity; and necklaces—if not so splendid as the ones out of the tombs at Mycenae—were to be standard on the marble statues of Aphrodite in each *naos*, each inner chamber of her temples.

The story too (in the *Iliad*) of Aphrodite's *kestos*, the beautifully embroidered band which encircled her neck and then coiled between her odorous breasts, already indicates and emphasizes the universality of her power in life. In this *kestos*

Were all enticements to delight, all loves, all longings were,
Kind conference, fair speech, whose power the wisest doth enflame.

Its magic made the wearer irresistible. So, according to Homer, when the Greek party among the gods wanted Zeus out of the way for a time, while they hatched mischief against the Trojans, Hera sidled up to Aphrodite and gave her a lying excuse for borrowing the *kestos*, which Aphrodite was kind enough, and foolish enough, to untie and hand over to her. Hera knew that if she wore it Zeus couldn't help coming back to her bed again: they would make love, and Zeus would doze off, and not realize what was afoot.

Statues of Aphrodite were often hung with her *kestos*, as well as with her

*From Schiller's poem *Das Glück*.

golden necklaces. One such statue, preserved in Byzantium as late as the sixth century A.D., was described then as 'an Aphrodite born of a noble sire. And on the breast of the goddess from her neck the *kestos* flowed and fell in coils'.

When Lucian, in the second century A.D., wrote about the character of the worship of the Syrian Atargatis, the 'Syrian goddess' from whom Aphrodite seems to derive, he said that her temple statue in Hieropolis wore the *kestos*, which was only put around statues distinguished as the Eastern Aphrodite, the Aphrodite of Heaven—the love goddess. (Not long ago a no doubt well educated manufacturer of women's underwear marketed a brassière called the Kestos.)

It is true that in the *Iliad* Aphrodite does seem to be patronized as well as elevated. Hera, and blue-eyed Athene—they are grander, their powers are more diverse, they indulge themselves in sneers about the more or less single-minded goddess of love.

Some writers on Greek religion see in this treatment of her by Homer a sign or consequence of that fact that she came late into the close community of the gods, where she had to find her ecological niche. Perhaps. And perhaps there is some extra confirmation of this in the *Odyssey*, where Aphrodite is not one of the *dramatis personae*, appearing only off the stage. Demodokos the bard entertains Odysseus and his host King Alkinoos and the evening's company, in Book VIII, with the lay of how Hephaistos netted Ares and Aphrodite on his bed, and exhibited them to the lecherously admiring and envious gods, Hephaistos remarking that she is enslaved by her own passions. When the net is removed, Aphrodite behaves rather like an outraged hen in the farmyard, fluffing out her feathers after the cock has dismounted, and pretending that nothing has happened. She goes off to her own Cyprian headquarters, at Paphos, to be bathed and oiled and clothed by the Graces. Her *amour propre* is restored.

Not the behaviour of a truly Greek divinity? Or the way to treat such a divinity?

Men and gods may want to push love and herself to one side when grave or prosy concerns engage them. They may patronize her. But then see what she can do to them. Helen, in the *Odyssey*, home again with Menelaos after the sack of Troy, talks rather smugly and in rather a middle-aged way of how Aphrodite had enticed her to Troy from her country, her child, her husband's bedroom and her husband, and how she had come to think the worse of her behaviour. And then we reflect—we are meant to reflect—that if it hadn't been for Aphrodite and the power of love there would have been no Trojan War. Zeus may have put Aphrodite in her place, but all that biting of weapons, that spilling of black blood, that glinting of fierce eyes, that intolerable quantity of death and unhappiness, had been caused by love.

Love is sweet, love is serious and must be reckoned with. For good and for bad Aphrodite is a great goddess who springs, not from Zeus and Dione, not from the sperm in the Aegean or the Mediterranean, but from the nature of living things; and essentially from the nature we know best—our own; where she remains.

The Graces

'The more a man cultivates the arts,' Baudelaire commented to himself in *Mon coeur mis à nu*, 'the less he erects.' He added that 'fucking is the lyricism of the people,' which is true enough. It may not be the lyricism of the *curé* or the painter or the poet. But then the 'people' is a capacious term; and Baudelaire—he was younger then, in his twenties—also said that love was the great thing in life for all of us; to which he added a general rule that we should eschew sentimentality and evasion: 'The long and short of the matter: in love, beware of the *moon* and the *stars*, beware of the Venus of Milo'—i.e., beware of whatever has become a correct, permissible, ideal image of love or beauty—'beware of lakes, guitars, rope-ladders, and all novels, even the most beautiful novel in the world, even if the author were Apollo himself! But love the woman you love properly, vigorously, boldly, orientally, ferociously.' And in that command there returns something of a Greek acceptance, a Greek common sense and honesty. Sappho would have concurred.

Love is the lyricism of the people: being in love, acting out love—however briefly, one minute from start to finish according to American statistical enquiries—is about as near as most people get in their lives to experiencing lyric pleasures or ecstasies: poems or songs about love are the songs most people most enjoy. And Baudelaire added that only love 'merits the turning of a sonnet and the putting on of clean underclothes'. Love approaches and identifies itself with poetry: Aphrodite was attended by the Charities, the Graces; and the Graces lived on Olympos beside the homes and the shining dance-floors of the Muses.

If as a verbalism only, we go on paying more respect to the Muses than to the Graces. We could still, if we were a little old-fashioned, talk of the Muse of T. S. Eliot or the Muse of Pasternak. The Muses were the goddesses of poetry, music, and dancing, they were daughters of Zeus, the master of heaven. The Graces were also among the daughters of Zeus, three of them in most accounts, givers of delight, which began as sexual delight. If they were not present when Aphrodite came ashore, the fine transparent embroidered clothing she put on was made for her both by the Horai, the Seasons, who dressed her and went with her on that primal occasion, and by the Graces.

As a rule this young triad of delightful goddesses would dance together, arms around each other's shoulders, or with the Muses or with Aphrodite. Homer in the *Odyssey* not only talks of the Graces bathing and scenting and dressing Aphrodite at Paphos, after her smith-husband released her from the net: he has a mention as well of Aphrodite putting on her crown, and associating with the Graces in the joys of their dance. Hesiod wrote of their beautiful complexion and their sparkling eyes, and their glances of love:

> And from their glancing eyes poured out that love
> Which takes from the limbs their strength.

Their names—the names by which they were usually known to the Greeks— he gives as Aglaïa, the Bright One, Euphrosyne, the Glad One, and Thaleia, the One of Abundance; and he mentioned, not only that they are neigh- boured on Olympos by the Muses, but that they were worshipped first of all at Orchomenos. This was the very ancient city in Boeotia, west of Thebes, and nowadays, with its Mycenaean remains, only a two hour's drive from Athens along the motorway past the drained Lake Kopais. Stones from the temple of the Graces are built into the Byzantine church at Orchomenos. In their first temple on the site the Graces were honoured in the shape of three stones which had fallen from the sky; and anciently the Graces were celebrated there by their own festival of music and poetry called the Charitesia.

Another revered temple of the Graces stood in the once sacred city of Elis beyond the mountains on the west shore of the Peloponnese, in the countryside of Olympia and the Olympic Games. Love was forward in Elis. Here as well was a grand temple of Aphrodite Ourania—Heavenly, Eastern Aphrodite, Aphrodite, Queen of Heaven, from Cyprus—and inside the temple stood an image of Aphrodite, in ivory and gold, by the great Pheidias. In their temple of the Graces the Eleans worshipped the triad in the form of three wooden statues, clothed and gilded, whose faces, hands and feet were of white stone. Pausanias, in his traveller's handbook of Greece, recorded that one of the Graces held a rose—which was proper for a goddess who expressed the aesthetics of love, one a knuckle-bone, which Pausanias explained as a symbol of the still unspoilt, uncontaminated graces of the young who played with knuckle-bones, and one a sprig of myrtle, which was sacred to Aphrodite (page 194). Pausanias affirmed, too, that among the gods the Graces belonged most of all to the train of Aphrodite.

Pindar, of the fifth century B.C., is the poet who is always calling on the Graces and doing them honour. They have fair hair, Pindar writes, they give delight, they give life its vigour, and make it bud, they sing by the Kastalian Fountain, which still pours down through the rocks at Delphi of Apollo and the Muses. It is by the power of the Graces that the tongue draws its words from deep in the mind, it is by the clear light of the Graces that Pindar (and every other good poet) writes his songs. And it was to praise a boy from Orchomenos of the Graces who won an event in the Olympic Games in 488 B.C., that Pindar wrote them a brief ode:

> You whose portion
> Is beside the waters of Kephisos,
> Who live where fine horses abound,
> O song-celebrated,
> Queenly Graces of Orchomenos the fertile,
> O watchers over the ancient Minyans,
> Listen. Listen to my prayers. For it is you
> Who help men to all
> That is sweet and delightful,
> Whether it is the skill of a man, or
> His looks or his fame.
> For not even the gods
> Can command their dances and banquets if the holy
> Graces are absent, who are the housewives
> Of all things in heaven, enthroned alongside
> The god with the bow
> Of gold, Pythian Apollo, revering the eternal
> Lordship of the Olympian Father.
>
> O Lady Aglaïa,
> And Euphrosyne, lover of song, children of the
> Powerfulest god, now listen, and Thaleia,
> Delighter in song . . .

The Graces, like love itself, and like Aphrodite, tended to be taken from religion into philosophy, or into metaphorical states between the two: goddesses, as time went on, less of the glances of love than of the felicities of culture. Theokritos was to end a poem on the meanness of rich patrons by asking 'What can men, who do not turn to the Graces, find worth desiring?' Plato gave his austere follower Xenocrates the famous and sensible advice 'Sacrifice to the Graces'; yet, like Aphrodite, the Graces were to lose their clothing in later Greek (and Roman) art, and so retain something of the divine lyricism of bodily desire.

When they were allegorized by painters of the Renaissance in Italy, for instance by Botticelli in his *Primavera*, by Raphael in his picture of the trio holding the sacred apples (properly these should have been the quinces) of Aphrodite, by Correggio—who gave them a most endearing femininity— in his fresco in the Camera di San Paolo, in Parma, they were still of the company of Aphrodite as Venus; still, whether clothed or naked, or next to naked, delicious creatures of the spring.

They remained of the company of Venus, however subtilized in other respects, when Pierre de Ronsard, in sixteenth-century France, imagined them dancing with the Muses on the river meadows below the manor-house in the Vendômois, on the façade of which his father Loys de Ronsard had set in 1515 the dedicatory words *Voluptati et Gratiis*, to Pleasure and the Graces. They were made to dance later in Edmund Spenser's *Faerie Queene*, allegorized, intellectualized, spiritualized, but continuing to be 'daughters of delight, Handmaides of Venus', who

> to men all giftes of grace do graunt,
> And all, that Venus in her selfe doth vaunt,
> Is borrowed of them.

There was something of apology, during the Christian centuries, about this refining of the Graces; and about beauty, let alone beauty resplendent in women (witches, for instance, came to be thought of, not in our pantomime image of crones with greasy hair and decayed teeth, in black Welsh hats, but as firm-breasted young women of naked beauty). We are luckier, we live with Renoir's pictures—the pictures of 'the last superb master of the body of woman'—and we all know what brush he painted them with (according to elderly crusty Cézanne; who also, the prejudice against the nude dying hard, called Renoir a pimp). We can again be more honest in our own delight; and in our retrospective examination of the Graces and Aphrodite. Love being what it is, we can understand why it could be thought of, before the Christian moralists, as beautiful or divine—whatever its kind, its accompaniment, and its consequences.

Below Aphrodite and the Graces, the foundation under the foundation is simple: the coupling in the creature world of the male and the female was an antique concept of religion. The urge to the act was powerful, its pleasure was intense, and all life depended on it—even by analogy the vegetal life.

About Aphrodite and love there is little which is unexpressed, without complication, in the epithets which were applied to her and in the special titles by which she was reverenced in one temple and another throughout the Grecian world.

Love persuades us irresistibly: she is Aphrodite Peitho, Aphrodite of Persuasion (that was her name on Sappho's island of Lesbos), and Aphrodite Epistrophia, the Aphrodite who Turns our Hearts, Aphrodite the Twister, as well as Aphrodite Psithyros, Aphrodite who Whispers, and Aphrodite of the Mandrake, that is to say of the love-drink, the aphrodisiac made from the roots of the mandrake (which is one of the common spring-flowering plants of Cyprus and Greece).

Aphrodite is beautiful, to accord with the beauty of love: she is Aphrodite Parakyptousa, Aphrodite the Side-Glancer, who looks at us—and we are lost—sideways, from the corners of her eyes, and Aphrodite Baiotis, Aphrodite of the Little Ears, and Aphrodite Kallipygos, Aphrodite with the Lovely Backside (which she turns to look at in one of her statue types).

She brings lovers together, somehow—'Love will find out a way': she is Aphrodite Machinitis, Aphrodite who Contrives.

She gets men and girls married, she gets them into each other's arms, she gets them to bed, and is Aphrodite Nympha, Aphrodite of the Bridal, Aphrodite Harma, the Aphrodite who Joins (whence the Greek goddess Harmonia, her extension and her associate; and our word harmony), which was her title at Delphi; Aphrodite Thalamon, Aphrodite of the Bride-Chambers, the bedrooms; and Aphrodite Praxis, Aphrodite of Success, of the good result, the happy issue, the ultimate moment of love, the orgasm, in our ungraceful word. She is Aphrodite Charidotes, Giver of Joy. She is Aphrodite the Whore: Aphrodite Hetaira, Aphrodite Porne, the goddess whom whores and hetairai looked to as their patroness.

She is fatal, Aphrodite Androphonos, Slayer of Men; as well as Aphrodite who gives Comfort, by whom we are soothed, Aphrodite Paregoros; and (as she might have been for Renoir painting his naked housemaids in middle age and old age, or for Picasso) she is Aphrodite Ambologera, Aphrodite Postponer of Old Age.

And Aphrodite Antheia, Aphrodite of the Flowers.

20 Aphrodite. The 'Bartlett Head'. Marble, by an Attic master of the 4th century B.C. Museum of Fine Arts, Boston, U.S.A.

Aphrodite for Poets

A god is always difficult to define: he is a personalisation of desires, emotions, needs, which change; take him to bits, and he is almost infinitely extensible, he extends through time, and alters with time. The effects of every viable or once viable deity range between a maximum of the ordinary and a maximum of the extraordinary, between commonplace and exceptional, the conventional and the imaginative, the cliché and the 'real'. The Christian god, for instance, is not quite the same for Clement of Alexandria, who denounced Aphrodite's dying worship, and, let us say, for the solemn monk from St.-Calais who found himself designing the grim architecture of Durham Cathedral; or for the monk and George Herbert; or for Herbert and a modern Anglican vicar and the retired businessman, or brigadier, who is the vicar's warden and reads the lessons on Sunday.

Much the same has been true of Aphrodite. She existed with differing intensity for different periods as well as persons; for petitioners who wanted her assistance and carried a dove to her temple, for the priestess who took charge of her worship, and the sacrifices; for coroplasts, or image-makers, who turned out by hundreds and thousands little coloured Aphrodites in terracotta which would be offered to her by pilgrims, or would be set in ships, or put into bedroom shrines, and for the great sculptors who carved and polished her great temple statues. She was different in intensity of significance for light and graceful erotic poets or poets as passionate as Sappho or as profound as the dramatists of the fifth century in Athens.

Still, there was always a core. As the goddess of physical coupling, body to body, she expressed feelings which, if strong even in unlikely victims and weak in others, were at least common to every man or woman, in the normal or abnormal ranges of appetite. She was necessary, or so the Greeks felt; therefore her temples, large or small, stood everywhere, in the sunlight of the Aegean, the Mediterranean, the Adriatic and the Black Sea; her name was spoken by everyone, as a common fact of life for more than fifteen hundred years. And wasn't she to be found, in her Roman guise, frisking wildly on a mosaic floor (Plate 65) in a villa as far north, as far away from Paphos, as the Yorkshire Wolds, in a parish where a huge phallic stone almost touches the parish church—and still further north, on the line of Hadrian's Wall, in a rough relief (now in the Museum of Antiquities at Newcastle upon Tyne) which shows her either at the bath or rising from the sea and wringing the Mediterranean out of her hair (Plate 60)?

It is a special rather than the common Aphrodite who figures in the

21 Aphrodite with the Beautiful Backside. Marble. Graeco-Roman copy from Nero's Golden House at Rome of a Hellenistic statue. Museo Nazionale, Naples.

22 Head of Aphrodite, from Salamis in Cyprus. Marble, 4th century B.C. Cyprus Museum, Nicosia.

grander poems or fragments of poems and plays which have come down to us, of a date after Homer, Hesiod and the Homeric Hymns. They insist on life more than love, and may quieten any timid apprehensions we may have that in all of her ancient career Aphrodite was up to no good. Aischylos, for instance, in a few lines from his lost play *The Danaides* makes Aphrodite speak marvellously of the yearly, seasonal marriage of Heaven and Earth:

> Sacred Heaven longs to wound the Earth,
> And longing moves the Earth to marriage.
> From this Heaven in love the rain falls down
> And impregnated Earth then bears for men
> Demeter's sheaves and that which feeds their herds.
> Also this moist marriage gives their perfect
> Season to the trees. I help these things to be.

Whatever Aischylos thought, that was all the same the oldest Aphrodite newly expressed—ancient Inanna, Ishtar, Astarte, goddess of the life of plants, no less than the life of creatures, as the consequence of love. It was the grave poet balancing the indulgent sweetness, the bitterness, the cruelty, in a way the universal crudity of the acts and states of love, by insisting that it was also the cosmic condition of life. 'She haunts the whole of nature,' as Louis Séchan and Pierre Lévêque say, in their handbook to the greater gods of Greece.

Euripides, after Aischylos, had it both ways. Expert in the forces of our human existence, Euripides celebrated that Aphrodite, that abandonment to orgiastic love, which the women longed for in his play *The Bacchae*. They were off with the wine-god of our irrational, emotional, ecstatic urges (wine was called 'Aphrodite's milk', by Aristophanes, because it increased lasciviousness); and in one of the choruses of the play they long for Dionysos to take them to love and Cyprus:

> O to visit Cyprus,
> Aphrodite's island,
> Where her Erotes
> Dwell, who stroke
> Their spell on
> Mortal men . . . .

—wild love, wild intense desire, wild lust, though lust is a word of sin, and sin belongs to Israel and Christianity. For the Greeks love was as inescapably love as the wind blew or the rain fell or the sunlight was warm.

There is more of this to be read in *Hippolytos*, which Euripides filled with the force of love and the vengefulness and cruelty of its goddess, when she was improperly used. Young confident Hippolytos is fool enough to say that she is the worst of gods, he prefers Artemis and chastity and the chase, and she won't have it. Men—there must be nothing too much in their behaviour vis-à-vis the gods—must know their place and give the gods the honour they require. So Aphrodite makes married Phaidra fall in love with Hippolytos, who does not want her and tells her so. Hippolytos has to die, and Phaidra as well—she hangs herself, and at least avoids dishonour.

Even then, to blame Aphrodite would be to contradict the clear nature of things, and Phaidra's nurse is allowed to say

> If the Cyprian falls on us, it's no good
> Resisting. If we yield, she will come on us
> Gently. If she finds us disdainful, she will
> Abuse us O you can't think how severely.
> She ranges the sky, she is there in the waves
> Of the sea. Of the Cyprian all things were
> Born. It is she who sows and gives love by
> Which all of us on the earth have our being.

Love is balanced again between excess and the inevitable.

So it went on in that line until centuries later, in Rome, Lucretius began his philosophical, more or less scientific or scientifically intended poem about the universe with an invocation to Aphrodite, as Venus, which is both poetry of noble order, and surprising.

Aphrodite for Philosophers

Yet before Lucretius, and long before him, there is another philosopher to be considered in particular relation to Aphrodite; Empedokles, that most extraordinary of Greeks who came from the great yellow-rocked city of Akragas (Girgenti) in Sicily, a poet-philosopher like Lucretius, but much else; that human being, reduced or elevated to a 'naked, eternally restless mind' (Matthew Arnold's description) who plunged out of this life, or so tradition says, into the fires and gases of Etna.

Writing philosophy in verse at the same time that Euripides and Sophokles were writing their plays, and a hundred years before Praxiteles was carving his statues of a naked Aphrodite, Empedokles considered Aphrodite, or at any rate Love, less as a divinity than as a force of nature. He conceived that in nature the prime forces were Love and Strife. Love united opposites,

Strife divided their unification, and brought into being new opposites which could in turn be united. Yet if for Love this philosopher of the Greek world beyond Greece used the word *philia*, his synonym could be *Aphrodite*, and when he writes of Love, Joy and Aphrodite in the few fragments we have of his long poems *On Nature* and *Purifications*, then the creative sensuality of the goddess still affects him, in the elevation of his ideas.

23 *Aphrodite, the 'Kaufmann Head', from the Karian city of Tralleis (Aydin, Anatolia), copy of the Aphrodite of Knidos. Marble, 4th century B.C. Musée du Louvre, Paris.*

On her let your spirit gaze, not sitting
With eyes bedazzled. For it is she whom
We know to be planted deep in our fabric.
She it is by whom men are impelled to
Have thoughts of love and perform works
Of peace. Aphrodite and Joy are the names
Which men give her . . . .

Empedokles wrote that in the Golden Age, when they worshipped no
gods of battle, and no Zeus, no Kronos, no Poseidon, but only Kypris
the Queen, only Aphrodite, they did so with bloodless sacrifices:

With sacred presents, with painted images,
And with subtle perfumes, with offerings
Of unadulterate myrrh and of odorous
Frankincense they appeased her, and on
The ground they poured out libations of yellow
Honey. Her altar was not wet with the pure
Blood of bulls, since men found it most hateful
To tear out the life and eat the fine limbs.

When he describes Love as the great force he is still affected, his words are
still affected, by Aphrodite the goddess, by her religious individuality
and power, and by all that his co-evals felt of her in the common life of the
Greek cities, the common life of men and women:

At one time in life's season of flowers does
Love bring together the limbs that belong
To the body. At another, cruel strife
Divides them and they wander alone by
The breaking waves of life's sea. It is so
With the plants and the fishes that have
Their homes in the sea. It is so with the beasts
Who couch on the hills, and so with
The tumbling birds who wander around on the wing.

In each Aphrodite fragment it seems to me that the grace of the goddess
(which the sculptors of the next century after his will reveal in full in their
tinted statues), the scent of her body, and her quinces and her myrtle bushes
and her roses, and the tenderness of her doves, are present in the philosophic
sense imparted to her.

This man, who exclaims that heretofore (in his or his soul's transmigration) he has been a boy and a girl, a bush and a bird, and a voiceless fish leaping out of the sea, finds phrases about Aphrodite in which his abstract thought retains her sensuality. Declaring that flesh and blood arose from the mixture of the four elements, Earth, Fire, Water and Air, Empedokles says this happened after Earth had anchored 'in the perfect harbours of the Cyprian'. Wonderful. And it is clear what he meant when he spoke, in a bare fragment, which amounts only to those few words, of 'the cleft meadows of Aphrodite'—meadows in which there are flowers, and from which children are born.

Bits and pieces by him are so charged as to be unforgettable. If only the whole of these poems by Empedokles, or more of them, had come down to us, after fifteen hundred years!

Lucretius

This is how Lucretius, centuries later, begins his poem of the universe, mentioning, as a Roman, first of all, that Aphrodite or Venus was the mother of Aeneas, taken to be the official founder of Rome, but then, in his surprising way, plunging into her creativity:

> Mother of Aeneas, darling of gods and men,
> Venus our nurse, below the wheeling
> Stars of heaven you fill ship-bearing
> Sea and fruitful lands with life. Through you
> All manner of things alive first are
> Conceived and then emerge and see the light
> Of day. Goddess, ahead of you storms clear,
> When you arrive clouds empty from the sky.
> And sweet Daedalian earth brings out its
> Flowers for you. The flats of ocean smile
> For you, and through the calm of heaven light
> Spreads and shines. The day Spring shows herself
> The west wind's generative breath regains
> Its life, the birds of the air make you
> And your arrival known, their hearts pierced
> By your power. Then rich provender
> Makes wild beasts leap and swim quick streams.
> Captives of your charm follow, wherever
> You may lead. And so through seas and heights
> And grasping streams, through leafy homes of birds,

> And the green fields, into the hearts of all you
> Strike persuasive love, by which eagerly,
> Race by race, they multiply their kind.

Lucretius goes on that the goddess alone governs the nature of things: nothing comes out into our resplendent realm of light without her, she is the condition of all that is delightful and lovely—so he hopes for her aid in the writing of his poem of the universe.

An odd beginning, yes, to an epic of the mind which proceeds to put love into its place, and the gods out of theirs, dispensing with them in the Lucretian world of reason and scientific laws, in which all men lived, or should have been living, by the free exercise of their wills. The gods, Lucretius said in his poem, might exist, but they were distant, shadowy, insubstantial beings too concerned with their own affairs to bother about ours. To suppose they had been generous enough to create this splendid natural world for us, as our everlasting home, was rubbish. And scornful he was, before he reached the end, about the messy state of being in love and about kowtowing to Venus-Aphrodite on that account.

Scholars have been worried by those opening lines to that same deity. How could a philosophical poet who did not care a straw for gods, write to one of them lines which seem so happy and so much from his heart? Lines it is hard to explain as a surrender to cliché, a rather feeble surrender to the conventions of how an epic poem should begin—'Sing, goddess, of Achilles' wrath', and so on.

I feel that it was perhaps the greatest of possible compliments to Aphrodite, as if that goddess of everyone's heart was the one deity Lucretius could not quite bring himself to shrug off. One authority, the French writer Robert Schilling, has suggested that the famous opening of the *De Rerum Natura* spoke for the Epicurean realm of serenity, less for a goddess than a condition. Before he finished with her at the beginning of the poem, Lucretius recalled how Venus-Aphrodite had slept with the God of War: 'You alone,' he said to her, 'can give men the serene benefits of peace.' And he would have known the tradition that on Aphrodite's temple at Paphos no rain ever fell, the sky above her temple complex remaining always blue and tranquil.

That does not seem satisfying to me. I like to remember that the greatest poets are not superhuman—or altogether above inconsistency. In his earlier years—we do not know a thing about them—years before philosophy took hold of him, mightn't Lucretius have had reason to feel some special tenderness for Aphrodite or Venus which he could not forget? Even if there was truth in the legend of the death of Lucretius—that, another suicide like Empedokles, he killed himself in madness induced by drinking a love philtre?

Once, so a story goes, a wise young boatman on the Nile delighted the wandering teacher Appollonios of Tyana by assuring him that he sacrificed to Aphrodite seven days a week. She had caused him a deal of trouble, but she might do him good, he was sure Aphrodite was very influential in the affairs of the heart.

Perhaps young Lucretius once had reason to think the same.

Perhaps he reflected that in her supposed dealings with men and women Aphrodite's inflictions of cruelty were outweighted by her bestowal of pleasure. Hadn't she been a giver of joy, sometimes, if not always of the serenity Epicurean Lucretius would have liked?

Yet this Roman philosopher and poet paid her one of the happiest, though not one of the most passionate, compliments she ever received.

Sappho's Aphrodite

Between Lucretius and Sappho, born about 612 B.C., there were five hundred years, and I am sure the Aphrodite we can understand, or even accept, remains the one Sappho invoked: Sappho, on Lesbos, asking in verses both stately and passionate, in which the feeling is locked but not frozen, for Aphrodite's help in the agony of a desired girl's indifference to herself. It is the one complete poem by Sappho that we have:

> Deathless Aphrodite on your throne
> Of colours, daughter of Zeus, weaver of
> Guile, do not break my spirit, Lady, with
> Grief and distress.
>
> But come to me as before when you have
> Heard my far away spoken words and
> Attended, and have left your father's
> House and arrived
>
> In your harnessed carriage of gold drawn by
> Your quick fine sparrows beating their rapid
> Wings round black earth through the mid
> Space of heaven.
>
> Quickly they came. And, happy one, your
> Deathless face smiling, you demanded what

> It was now, and why I called now, and what
>   My mad heart most
>
> Wanted to happen. Who is Persuasion
> Now required once again to restore
> To your friendship? Who's upsetting you
>   Now, my Sappho?
>
> She may run away, but soon she shall
> Follow, she may refuse gifts but soon
> She will give, and she will love soon, even
>   Though she's unwilling.
>
> Come to me like that again and release
> Me from my grievous distress. Do for me
> What my heart yearns to have done, and yourself
>   Fight on my side.

That is where Aphrodite in essence is to be seen and felt, that poem from the deep heart—and not from the ice-box—which all Greeks would have understood. No doubt essential Aphrodite is to be seen in the best of her temple statues, some of the less damaged ones. But the statues (which I shall come to in a later chapter) could not be so personal. They established, or they followed, types of Aphrodite, whereas Sappho's poem is spoken by an individual, by a great poet and by a woman in love.

Perhaps for today's reader, certainly for today's translator, Persuasion with that capital P sticks out of the poem a little awkwardly. But then Persuasion—*Peitho* in Greek—was not quite the personified abstraction it cannot help being for ourselves, with our different habits of thought and usage. Like Eros as he developed, Peitho was rather more than a projection of Aphrodite's own power. If she was enticement, she was also a sub-divinity, also something of a person. Hesiod, before Sappho, made her present at the moment when Aphrodite came to shore; and in a fragment of one of her poems Sappho describes this Peitho as 'Aphrodite's maid shining with gold'. She had special cause, as well, to write of Peitho, since she and her fellow islanders on Lesbos worshipped the two together or the two in one, Aphrodite-Peitho. Pindar in his song for the athlete Xenophon who vowed extra temple prostitutes to Aphrodite at Corinth (page 124), addresses the girls as servants of Peitho, servants of Persuasion, and then goes on to praise Aphrodite. The two are both separable, in the one context, and inseparable.

On the whole Aphrodite, as we find her, is revered for sweetness rather than hated or feared for cruelty; which corresponds to the psychology of love. We may be cruelly used, but we don't expect to be, we don't think about that till it happens, and we are ready to forget it the moment the pain is over. Sappho wrote another poem—extraordinary that it was discovered on a potsherd in Egypt as late as this century, and sad that parts of it were missing—about the special sweetness of Aphrodite of the Flowers, Aphrodite Antheia, or rather about this sweetness of flowers pervading and surrounding a temple of Aphrodite:

> . . . [come]
> Here to me out of Crete, to this
> Holy temple, by which your pleasant
> Orchard of quinces grows and on your altars
> Incense burns,
>
> Where cool water murmurs through the quince
> Boughs, and all the place is in the shade
> Of roses, and sleep from the trembling
> Leaves flows down,
>
> Where the horses' meadow is thick with
> Flowers of the spring, and winds breathe
> Gentleness around . . . .
>
> Here, Cyprian, take . . . and with your
> Grace pour out festivity's nectar
> Into cups of gold . . . .

Translators of this poem usually say apple orchard, apple boughs, but I suspect Sappho was speaking of a sacred orchard of quince trees (compare the poem by Ibykos about spring and quinces and vines and Aphrodite and love, on page 98). Quinces, both downily surfaced and hard, and sharp in taste, and ripening to a lovely yellow and to the most intriguing scent, were her special fruit, and the Greeks used their word *mélon* for different kinds of tree fruit, often without a distinguishing epithet. A *mélon* might be an apple, a sour crab, a peach, an apricot or a quince; or from the firmness and softness of young quinces the word might be used for a girl's breast.

At any rate, there, in those few lines about a temple of hers somewhere out in the country, in April, I think we can feel the special mellifluence of

Aphrodite of the Flowers, who was also—but I come to that in the next chapter—Aphrodite of the Prostitutes.

Until quite recently, twenty, thirty years ago, bizarre evasions have been played with Sappho and love and Lesbianism, Lesbian passion, in the few scraps of her love poetry which have luckily descended to us. By classical idealists who had forgotten

> The isles of Greece! The isles of Greece!
> Where burning Sappho loved and sung

and had perhaps never read Swinburne's 'Sapphics', and who certainly didn't care to think of his

> Lesbians kissing across their smitten
> Lutes with lips more sweet than the sound of lute-strings,
> Mouth to mouth and hand upon hand, her chosen
> Fairer than all men,

Sappho was exalted (or degraded, according to one's stand in such concerns) into a Princess Ida or a Miss Beale and Miss Buss running a finishing academy for the young ladies of Lesbos 2,500 years ago. And since the refusal to face the obvious about Sappho accords with a determination to evade the obvious about Aphrodite herself, about Sappho's goddess, I allow myself a scrap of Sapphic dialogue between such a Slippery Insider and a Sceptical Outsider:

Sceptical Outsider.   You say she wasn't a Lesbian?
Slippery Insider.   Not exactly. I don't like that word.
S.O. Didn't she write love poems to girls?
S.I. Yes and no.
S.O. Just as other Greek and Latin poets wrote love poems to boys?
S.I. You have a dirty mind. You don't understand the Greeks. You don't understand that Sappho was a lady. She came of a very good family on Lesbos. She was a moral—
   (S.O. gives a grunt)
   I repeat highly moral head of a religious cultural guild in Mytilene. She taught young girls about the service of the Muses and how to write Sapphics. She was nothing if not pure, serving a pure Aphrodite—
S.O. *(laughing indulgently and interrupting an aerial giggle which may have come either from Aphrodite or the ghost of Sappho):*

I see you have never heard of the late Vita Sackville-West, a minor English poet, modern—more or less.

S.I. Sappho wasn't that kind of lady.

S.O. I'll agree she wrote better poems.

S.I. What you don't want to understand is that our Sappho provided her girl graduates with entirely proper poems to be recited at their weddings when they were married in the proper way.

S.O. *(producing a current encyclopaedia).* Hang on and I'll read you something. Here's one of your lot saying something different. The tone in which Sappho addresses young women 'leaves little doubt that she was temperamentally a sexual invert'.

S.I. Yes, but go on, go on.

S.O. 'However the uniform respect with which all early writers . . . speak of and to her excludes the possibility of any uncleanness in her conduct.'

S.I. You see?

S.O. I see.

In fact there is no evidence, none at all, for Sappho's religious guild, or Sappho as a teacher of poetics or the rest of the tales of the Slippery Insiders. Even as late as 1955 a Cambridge professor of Greek, Denys Page,* had still to demolish this blarney of the scholarly moralists who refused to recognize that Sappho, and the Greeks, and Aphrodite as well, knew more than they did about the kinds and inclusiveness of sex, and were honest about it.

Descending from Sappho to pedestrian verses written in the last centuries of paganism and the first centuries of Christianity, when the Greek world was under the generals of Rome, there has come down to us a hymn to Aphrodite which, for the Orphic religionist, the Orphic believer in the pure life and the divine soul of man, and in rewards for the soul after death, and its migration into other bodies, catalogues all or most of the accepted powers, functions, special pleasures and special interests of Aphrodite, the Cyprian-born goddess of Greece and all the Hellenized lands, including perfumed Syria and Egypt (where she drives over the flat plains of the delta in her golden carriage).

These are the first lines:

---

*In his *Sappho and Alcaeus*. One of the Slippery Insiders he demolished on Sappho's account, was that peculiar Oxford bachelor, the late Sir Maurice Bowra, whose wit wasn't matched by as sharp an insight into poetry or the heart of women, or the heart of love.

Heavenly Aphrodite, much hymned, lover
Of laughing, sea-born, birth-giving goddess,
Lover of feasts which last through the night,
Majestic, strength in the night, connector,
Weaver of wiles, mother of need, since the
World lies under your yoke and you rule
The Three Fates, and are parent of all
Things in the heavens and in the fruit-filled
Earth and the depth of the sea, majestic
Comrade of Bakchos, whose joy is abundance,
Maker of marriage, mother of desire,
Source of persuasion, granter of favour,
Worker in secret, seen and not seen . . . .

The hymn is a collective of the past, of all or most of the concepts of Aphrodite, from Homer downwards. But *au fond* she is still, throughout, the mother of desire, the goddess of the appetite of body for body, she who entices and persuades (as she persuaded Helen to go to Troy), she who induces coupling, however exalted this divine nature of hers may be in one or other direction.

To the end she is the goddess of the poet, and above them all of Sappho, that 'lewd, love-sick female', as the Christian apologist Tatian called her in the second century, complaining to pagan Greeks that this damsel of theirs sang her own wantonness, while his Christian girls were chaste and sang more nobly of divine things as they spun from their distaffs.

6

Prostitutes of Aphrodite

Hetairai and the Sacred Whores

Latin grammars used to quote from Horace—and perhaps still do—*non cuivis homini contingit adire Corinthum*, 'It isn't everyone who gets to Corinth.' But they did not explain to schoolboys why everyone or anyone should have wanted to go to Corinth in particular—which was for its prostitutes, all the common prostitutes in their brothels by the two harbours, all the higher class or well-to-do, but no less shark-like *hetairai*, and all the prostitutes actually vowed to Aphrodite, who were to be found in her Corinthian temples, especially the temple, one of the richest in Greece, on the grand rocky bluff of the Corinthian acropolis. Corinth was the luxury city of the Greek world, until the rise of Alexandria; and prostitutes there as elsewhere naturally looked up to Aphrodite as their special goddess. She roused desire: if there was no desire there would be no customers.

The *hetairai* of the Greek cities, as everyone knows, were a cut above the girls of the brothel or the street corner. *Hetaira*, a little euphemistically because they were all in the same trade, meant a companion. 'Courtesan' has been the usual translation, as if that was not quite so rough a word as whore or tart, and not quite so inclusive as our semi-legal, semi-official word prostitute.

Hetairai worked on their own, and often added some education, some cultural sophistication to their liveliness and their good looks. Many of them, like the grander whores of every age and country, became rich. Since Aphrodite was the goddess of all bodily love, it was not shocking for Greeks that superior whores, or hetairai became models for the greatest pictures and statues of Aphrodite.

Phryne, who came to Athens from Thespiai, sixty miles or so to the north-west, was the model for the entirely naked statue which her lover Praxiteles created for the Aphrodite temple high above the harbours of Knidos on the Asiatic shore of Greece; and she sat to Apelles for his much imitated picture of Aphrodite just risen from the sea and wringing out her hair, so that

the drops of water made a veil around her body. She was rich, and for her body's sake Praxiteles gave her his statue of Eros, which she presented in turn to her native city—not a gift which the Thespians saw any reason to refuse. At Lokroi Epizephyrioi in Grecian Italy, across the sea from Corinth, an *hetaira* named Polyarchis gave the temple of Aphrodite an image of the goddess carved in wood and decorated with gold—a 'golden Aphrodite'—as we know from an epigram by the Lokrian poet Nossis (end of the fourth century B.C.), who looked on herself as a Lokrian Sappho:

> Let's go to the temple, and see Aphrodite's
> Statue. How the gold shines!
> Polyarchis set it there, whose splendid
> Body brought her wealth.

Another poem, ascribed in *The Greek Anthology* to Nikarchos of the second century B.C., tells how a girl disenchanted with spinning and weaving and all the chores which withered and wasted the flower of a girl's life, made a bonfire of her gear, outside the door of her house, and chose garlands and music and the sweet life instead: she became an *hetaira* and in her new career she naturally called on Aphrodite

> Cyprian, she said, you shall have ten per cent
> Of all I earn,
> Just find me work, and you shall have your cut,

a request which would certainly have been backed with regular sacrifices.

There was a convention, too, of writing poems in which retired prostitutes would take the paraphernalia of their old body trade round to Aphrodite's temple and dedicate them to her, much as a retiring fisherman would dedicate his nets and creels to Priapos or Hermes. Nikias, in such a poem, gives up work when she is past fifty, and presents Aphrodite with her sandals and her hair pieces, her mirror, her girdle, and various unmentionables, as she calls them. Plato is supposed to have written the epigram in which Lais, the most beautiful and most celebrated of all the *hetairai* of Corinth (whose grave was suitably ornamented with a carving of a lioness devouring a ram), resigns her profession when her looks have gone:

24 *Aphrodite rising from the sea, the 'Benghazi Aphrodite' from Cyrenaica, based on the picture by Apelles. Hellenistic marble statuette. (See also Frontispiece.) University Museum, Philadelphia.*

25 The young wife offers incense to Aphrodite. Side panel of the Ludovisi Throne. Greek, c. 470–460 B.C. Museo Nazionale Romano, Rome.

26 The hetaira *plays her flute to Aphrodite. Side panel of the Ludovisi Throne. Greek,*
c. *470–460 B.C. Museo Nazionale Romano, Rome.*

> I, Lais, who made a fool of Greece
> With the insolence of my beauty,
> Which brought young lovers
> In swarms around my door,
>
> Give this mirror to the Paphian,
> Since I do not wish to see
> What I am now, and what I was
> I can't see any more.

Between the whore and the wife, or the *hetaira* and the wife, Aphrodite's role is neatly indicated in the carved reliefs (Plates 25 and 26) of the Ludovisi Throne, of the first half of the fifth century B.C., which the Romans seem to have taken from Greece and set up in the temple of the Venus of Eryx which they built in 181 B.C., near the Colline Gate in Rome. I would not call them the most beautiful of Aphroditean sculptures, but there on the front panel Aphrodite rises from the Cyprian waters, two of the Horai, the Seasons, welcoming her and clothing her, as in one of the Homeric Hymns, themselves standing bare-footed on the shingle of the beach. There is the goddess, the operator of desire and life. On the left-hand panel an *hetaira*, as if the fun and games and music of desire, sits naked, playing her flute, as if at some jollification in Athens (*hetairai* were often skilful musicians, like the *Yoshiwara* girls of Japan). On the right-hand panel, a young married woman, discreetly clothed, pays her respects and her debt to Aphrodite, who has gained her a husband, by making an offering to her of the sweet savour of incense.

Old-fashioned classical scholars had to accept that the Greeks they admired so much and with such reason, were given to frequenting whores somewhat excused as *hetairai*, but they didn't like it (and anyway they never showed themselves much in favour of the existence or the worship of Aphrodite, or of her intrusion into the Greek family of gods). What they liked even less was the thought of sacral whores crowded into Aphrodite's temple on the Corinthian Acropolis. That is something, too, which Greek guides, with a university education, don't mention as they take you round Old Corinth, or round the small museum, where there is an Aphrodite or two, saying not a word about their ancestors and the temple ladies. And the Greeks who worshipped Aphrodite, and who knew that desire is desire and that a whore can have her wild and exciting beauty or elegance, and that hypocrisy and Aphrodite were not bedfellows, weren't quite happy themselves about prostitutes in a Greek temple. The Greeks, shocking as it may seem, might come to worshipping an Aphrodite Hetaira (as in

Athens), an Aphrodite Porne, Aphrodite the Whore (as at Abydos on the Hellespont), an Aphrodite of the Hole, an Aphrodite (as in Syracuse) of the Beautiful Backside, or an Aphrodite of Copulation, simply, or an Aphrodite who Rode Astride, or an Aphrodite who Opened Herself Up, like a carving of a Sheila-na-gig on a Romanesque church; but if they visited Corinth and climbed up to Akrokorinthos and paid their money and enjoyed the girls, they were still aware that temple prostitution came from the East, from foreigners.

They knew it went on in Cyprus, that splendid yet not so Greek, if Greek-speaking island, more than halfway between Greece and the Levant. They knew it remained part of the cult of the Phoenician Astarte in this place and that around the Mediterranean, but it did not fit into the Greek measure of things. Various Greek writers mention temple prostitution, and then pass it by rather quickly, without much detail.

Sumer to Corinth, via Cyprus

In fact, sacral prostitution went far back into Semitic religion, to the temples of the Assyrians and the Babylonians; and earlier still to the Sumerians and their religion.

The gods required the service of men. Men and all living things required to be fertile. Men relied on rain which fell, water which flowed, crops which grew, fruit which ripened, cattle, goats, sheep, and wild animals which reproduced their kind. Enlil and Inanna of the Sumerians, Tammuz and Ishtar of the Babylonians and Assyrians, Baal and Astarte of the Phoenicians coupled and gave life; their coupling was imitated by god-kings and high priestesses in the Sacred Marriage, in the temples of Inanna, then Ishtar, and then Astarte.

The gods were pleased. Everything which made for abundance and fertility in this analogical way, was activated. But sacred coupling went further. Worshippers at large were enjoined to couple with girls who were vowed to Inanna, Ishtar, or Astarte. The act with these lesser ritual performers was also good in the sight of the goddess and her consort. It was also holy, encouraging or triggering the corresponding powers and processes in nature.

Piecing clues together, it seems there were holy professionals and holy amateurs. In the temples, served by castrated priests, the holy professionals occupied upper chambers with windows. Jezebel of the Old Testament was a Phoenician prostitute of the kind: 'And when Jehu was come to Jezreel, Jezebel heard of it; and she painted her face, and tired her head, and looked out at a window . . . And there looked out to him two or three eunuchs'

—two or three of the castrated priests. In the Metropolitan Museum in New York there is a Phoenician ivory of a girl looking out of a temple window, above pillars which end in lotos flowers (see page 197). In the Louvre girls look out of the window of a terracotta model of Aphrodite's temple at Idalion.

From what Herodotus reports of Ishtar's temple in Babylon in the fifth century B.C. perhaps holy professionals had come to succeed an earlier, more embracing rite of holy amateurs, which survived here and there. Once in her life—presumably on some special, crowded feast day—every woman, whether she was rich or poor, had to go up to this temple of the goddess of love and abundance, and sit there, wearing a plaited bandeau around her head, until sooner or later—later if she wasn't good-looking—she was chosen by a man. He would throw a silver coin in her lap and claim her 'in the name of the goddess'. Ishtar took the silver coin, the man took the girl, then and there.

By coupling with this stranger, the woman did her duty to the goddess. Then she went home, nubile.

It looks as if this festival of the visit to the goddess came round once a year, in the spring, and then continued to exist in various places, alongside the temple provision of the holy professionals, the holy women at the window. Herodotus isn't clear on this, but certainly the occasion he describes in Babylon resembled a crowded fiesta. He added that much the same practice occurred in Cyprus. Where? At Palaia Paphos, at the great shrine of Astarte Paphia,* who became Aphrodite Paphia? Probably; as a main feature of the yearly festival which brought the pilgrims in such lyrical procession from the port at Nea Paphos.

The account of Herodotus moved the modern Greek poet George Seferis to one of his poems about Cyprus. Seferis does not share the pained disapproval which Herodotus expressed. Instead he imagines an occasion of very possessive, sacred, mysterious emotion. On a visit to Paphos, Seferis found himself in the churchyard which surrounds the very small white church of Katholiki tucked into the ground alongside the scattered drums and debris of the great temple (The church was once called the Church of the Blessed Aphroditissa). There was an olive press in the churchyard, and he caught a whiff of olive oil. That was his cue. It made him think of a girl who had oiled her limbs and hair, and sat waiting in the temple precinct, two thousand years ago, and a few yards away, for the strange man:

---

*Inscriptions to Astarte Paphia have been found at Old Paphos, as well as the more usual ones to Aphrodite Paphia. She would have remained Astarte to Phoenician donors.

Oil on her limbs,
smelling maybe a trifle sour
like this small church's
oil mill
like its rough porous
unturning stone.

Oil on her hair
encircled with cords,
other scents too maybe
we do not know
poor ones or rich ones
statuettes with fingers
applied to small breasts.

Oil in the sun;
leaves tremble
the stranger has stopped
heavy the silence
dividing her knees.
The coins have fallen;
'You I call to the goddess . . .'

Oil on her shoulders
and on her writhing middle
dappled legs in the grass,
and that wound in the sun
as it tinkled for vespers
as I spoke in this churchyard
to a crippled man.

On one of the temple stones here at Old Paphos candles are still offered
by nursing mothers to the Virgin Mary, the 'Virgin who gives Milk'.

What kind of men were the strangers who made their choice and threw
the silver coins, and then lay with the girls, and 'bruised the breasts of their
virginity', as Ezekiel wrote with Hebrew disdain?

Were the men only theoretical strangers? Young, handsome, the
'desirable young men, horsemen riding upon horses', of the First Book of
Kings? Considerate, brutal? Could the girl refuse when she saw the wrong
man eyeing her or coming up to her?

Hard though it is for us to conceive how such a custom worked and continued, would this sacramental initiation into the act of love so much have horrified girls brought up to expect it as inevitable and normal? Must we think it worse or more damaging than the legitimized private rape which the beginning of a marriage has so often amounted to, through history?

Certainly in her own island of Cyprus her great Paphian temple was not the only place where Aphrodite was served by girls at a festival or by temple women who slept with worshippers, or both. The little earthenware shrine in the Louvre seems to show they were present at Idalion, and from what Strabo wrote they must have been the attraction of that temple of Aphrodite which once stood on the extreme eastern end of Cyprus, on a rock topped in spring with wild flowers from which one can just see the Syrian mountains trodden by Baal and Astarte. This is a windy, shadeless, unfrequented temple site which guidebooks say little about, though it is beautiful, or at least very moving in itself, approached by a southern coast road through the most paradisiacal scenery of the island, through a medley of fields, hills, flowers, forest, sand and blue inlets, in spring all the possible divinity, richness, and freshness of growth. Strabo says briefly that the temple could not be entered or seen by women, meaning, apparently, by married women, as if none but virgins climbed to it, on the errand which brought such girls as well to Palaia Paphos.

The Greeks contemplated Cyprus much as North Europeans were to contemplate Venice or Florence. In Venice or Florence the world's most accomplished and elegant whores were available, and in Venice beyond the waters there was Titian painting them—if you could afford such a memento —as goddesses of love naked on a couch. In Cyprus, in that rich far away island, there were roses, Aphrodite and girls. Desires were satisfied there in practices pleasant to think about, which wouldn't quite do at home, or fit into that Greek sense of measure in life and religion.

Corinth was the grand exception. Corinthian temples of Aphrodite, especially the temple on the highest point of Akrokorinthos, the citadel, were at any rate the only ones in Greece itself where Aphrodite kept her girls; and if we could go back far enough we might find that the foundation of the cult was due to Phoenician traders or to Mycenaeans from Cyprus, already worshippers of the Paphian goddess—Mycenaean Greeks who had settled in Cyprus and traded with the homeland. Prostitutes and doves also lived together in the famous temple of Aphrodite or Venus which stood on Mount Eryx, now Monte San Giuliano, in north-west Sicily, a

27 Mount Eryx (Monte San Giuliano), Sicily. Site of the Phoenician temple of Astarte, which the Romans transformed into the temple of Venus Erycina.

maritime site which is every bit as dominating and magnificent as the citadel at Corinth. The Elymians, the ancient inhabitants of this corner of Sicily, may have come from the eastern Mediterranean which could explain their worship of a goddess who was identical, prostitutes, doves, open-air altars and all, with the Aphrodite of Paphos, or very like her. Or again Mycenaean Cypriots may have introduced Aphrodite to Mount Eryx, since they had their contacts with Sicily. The Phoenicians possessed themselves of Eryx, worshipping Aphrodite as Astarte, then the Romans ousted the Phoenicians—the Carthaginians—and captured Eryx in 241 B.C., and Astarte changed her name again to Aphrodite, or rather to Venus. The Romans made much of their new prize, which fitted in with the story of Aeneas, child of Aphrodite by Anchises, as the semi-divine founder of Rome. The temple became rich, and important visitors from Rome would enjoy the view and the sacred harlots. But Eryx, if Graecized eventually, was not Greek by origin, and though Greek legend held that the temple was founded by Eryx, King of the Elymians, and that Eryx was a son of Aphrodite and the sea-god Poseidon (or of Aphrodite and Boutes, the Argonaut whom Aphrodite rescued when the magical song of the Sirens made him leap into the sea), we cannot blame the Greeks for its copulatory worship or copulatory indulgence.

The Lokrians

The minor exception was in a Greek colonial, if not in a Greek mainland, city. Lokroi Epizephyrioi, the city of that love poet Nossis (page 113), in Magna Graecia, Megale Hellas, the southern Italy of the Greek coastal colonies, seems to have had its prostitution temple. We do not know much about the Aphrodite worship in this temple. But one of the Roman historians, Pompeius Trogus, left a story of something which happened there in the fourth century B.C., when the Lokrians had forgotten or neglected their devoir, in this line, to Aphrodite. He says that when the Lokrians were in danger of being defeated by their particular enemy and rival, the nearby city of Rhegion (today's Reggio di Calabria), they promised that if they won, they would prostitute their daughters thereafter on the feast of Aphrodite (presumably their Aphrodite was eastern also in retaining her concern for war as well as love, a 'bringer of victory', as she was also at Argos and elsewhere). All went well, but later on they backslid, and then found another war going badly for them. They were under the thumb at the time of Dionysos the Second, the expelled tyrant of Syracuse. Dionysos told them they had better remember Aphrodite. His plan was that their wives and daughters should dress up in their best and go along to the temple. There a hundred of them would be chosen by lot, and stay on call in the temple for a month, all the men of Lokroi having previously taken an oath not to touch them. When the month was over no other Lokrian girls would be allowed to marry till each of the allotted girls had been found a husband. The Lokrians agreed; the ladies were assembled, whereupon the soldiers of Dionysos arrived and stripped them of their finery. Whether they had the girls as well isn't recorded. Their ornaments—their jewellery—Dionysos kept for himself.

Beneath the lines of this story, it does look as if Aphrodite's Lokrian temple had once been staffed with sacral prostitutes, like her temple at Corinth, and her temples on Cyprus. Perhaps the Lokrians had imitated the Corinthians. Lokroi stands about opposite the Gulf of Corinth, right in the line of trade from Corinth and the East to Italy and the West. But since Lokroi was not founded until about 700 B.C., sacral prostitution there could not have been very old, unless the Lokrians took over a cult which already existed on the spot, as at Eryx.

No doubt the practice had been abandoned, though not forgotten, when Dionysos the tyrant came up with his plan.

In the fifth century the Lokrians made terracotta plaques of high quality and metal-like precision. Most of these have to do with the Lokrian worship of Persephone. Aphrodite is figured on some of them, as on the plaque I have mentioned (Plate 8) of Aphrodite riding away from the Cyprian foam to Olympos.

Corinth's famous prostitution temples flourished certainly because of the position of Corinth along the sheltered seaway between east and west (and the narrow land way between north and south). Cargoes from Asia Minor, the Syrian coasts and Egypt were transported from one gulf to the other, one harbour to the other, across the isthmus, and later the ships themselves were drawn across on rollers. So Corinth became exceptional in its wealth and its ways, used to rich merchants and travellers from the Levantine shores of Astarte, or from the Cyprus of Aphrodite.

The girls who plied in the high perched holy brothel of Akrokorinthos were numerous, and celebrated for their good looks. Rich Corinthians liked to buy girls on the slave market and dedicate them to Aphrodite. There happens to be a poem, gapped but complete enough to make sense, occasioned by a dedication of such girls to this Corinthian Aphrodite. It was written by the great Pindar in 464 B.C. for a Corinthian athlete named Xenophon, who had promised Aphrodite no fewer than a hundred girls if he won the crown at the Olympic games that year; which he did. After his victory the girls were acquired and brought up to the temple, and, as they danced, Pindar's high flying strophes were sung in front of Aphrodite's statue:

You girls who take men with pleasure; who in
Corinth the rich serve Persuasion; who burn yellow
Tears from the green incense tree, and again
And again send your thoughts flying
          Up to the Erotes' mother,
Aphrodite of Heaven,

Children, she has granted you this, that
Without blame you collect the fruit of your
Tender season on the beds of desire. Beautiful
Wholly is that requirement . . . .

Yet I must wonder what the Lords of the Isthmus
Will now say of me for devising and linking
          With prostitute women my
Opening sweetness of song?

Purity's touchstone has tested our gold
. . . .

O Lady of Cyprus, Xenophon is on fire with thanks
That his prayer was regarded; for that he has driven
          These hundred girls to graze
Here in your precinct.

What did the girls think? Perhaps that this mixture of piety and poetry
was a load of rubbish, though becoming a temple prostitute up on the rock
might have been preferable to slaving in a private house down below.

Corinthians and visitors to Corinth no doubt became more concerned
with the looks and the skill of these girls of Aphrodite than with any sacramental rites of universal fertility which may have been in Pindar's head.
But the girls of the temple did more than entertain their customers. They
are known to have taken part in ritual processions and in ceremonial prayers
to Aphrodite; and after all Aphrodite remained a goddess to keep in with
in personal life. Didn't she satisfy or assist desire, whether in ordinary
heterosexual lovers and lechers, pederastical lovers, or lesbian lovers (not
that the Greeks were quite easy about lesbianism), or her own greedy
hen-sparrows and cock-sparrows; and having emerged from the sea,
couldn't she also quieten the sea?

At least it may be imagined that visitors, as they came out of the temple
on Akrokorinthos, regarded the two more than sky-blue gulfs below, and
reflected that they had spent their money sensibly as well as enjoyably.
They had gratified the goddess. Now she would get them home safely.

7

Aphrodite and the Sea

Temples by the Shore

Aphrodite's temples were frequently set on high places and dangerous places, above the sea, and her temple statues—Hellenistic ones—frequently show her naked with a dolphin.

This favourite Aphrodite displayed her concern for seafarers. In April, Aphrodite's month, the season of voyages began, and Greek ships started to creep again around the Aegean, the Adriatic, the Ionian Sea, the Mediterranean and up north through the dangerous narrows of the Hellespontos and the Bosporos into the Black Sea, their masters, crews and passengers hoping that Aphrodite would keep the sea calm and twinkling. So she was Aphrodite Euploia, 'Aphrodite of Good Sailing', Aphrodite Galenaia, 'Aphrodite of the Calm', Aphrodite Pelagaia, 'Aphrodite of the Ocean'. It was one more role which she inherited from her more immediate oriental predecessors, and for the Greeks a role more acceptable than remaining an Aphrodite of the dedicated temple prostitutes—both more acceptable at large and more useful, given an extra force certainly by the story of her maritime birth. In her temples on the citadels of Corinth and Eryx she was the love goddess, and the city goddess, and the sea goddess, as in her oriental past; and her high porticoes were visible, comfortingly, to sailors as they came up the Saronic Gulf or the gulf of Corinth and as they rounded the toe of Sicily.

Another of her splendidly positioned temples—lately investigated by archaeologists—presided over 'steep Knidos', in Asia Minor, set on a high terrace above the two harbours of the city. This was the temple of that undraped Knidian Aphrodite by Praxiteles, the one for which Phryne was the model. The oldest and the holiest of all her temples in Greece itself, the temple on rocky, rather unwelcoming Kythera, off the eastern prong of the

28 The 'Marine Aphrodite'. Marble statue found at Rhodes. Hellenistic, 1st century B.C. Archaeological Museum, Rhodes.

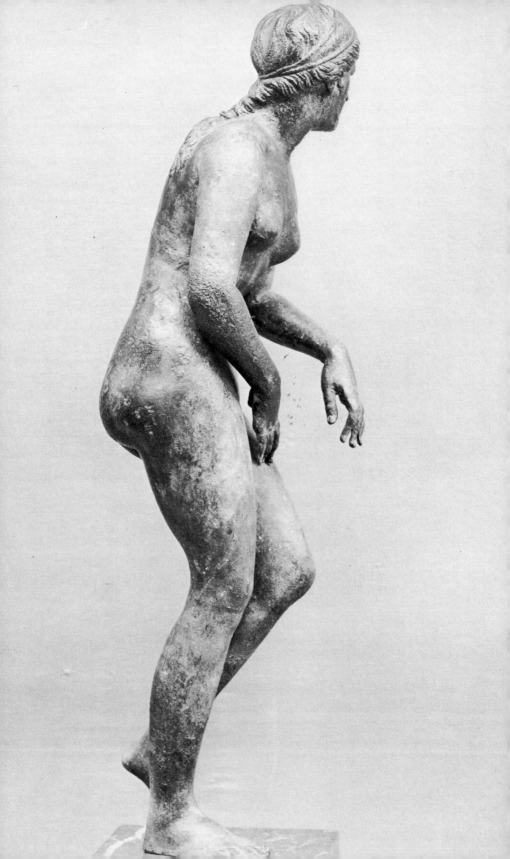

Peloponnese, stood high enough on a mountainside or hillside terrace to be visible to every merchant ship from Libya or Egypt or the Phoenician coast, which put into the harbour of Skandeia down below.

In Cyprus several temples of Aphrodite looked from high places out to sea. Paphos, her aboriginal and her greatest shrine, is not, it is true, so impressive on that account. The high ground its ruins stand on is reached by a gradual slope, and it is then only moderately high, though it affords a view of the restless wind-driven sea a mile and a half away.

Out on the edge of the plains near Larnaca, eight miles in from the sea, the Aphroditean temple site which does strike a colour image into the imagination and then the memory, is the blue mountain of Stavrovouni, now capped —but that is quickly forgotten—with its monastery of the Cross. Insisting on itself from every direction, and from the Mediterranean, Stavrovouni is the blue symbol and blue reminder of Aphrodite's former domination of Cyprus. The obscured temple site I spoke of in the last chapter, the site on the eastern tip of Cyprus, is less grand, but imparts rather more information about Aphrodite and the sea. This temple can never have been very rich or very large on its constricted level of rock, which gives an eastward view to Astarte's Syria, but it recalls another epithet, a slightly ambiguous one for the Aphrodite revered by sailors. As well as Euploia, Galenaia and Pelagaia, Aphrodite was called Akraia, which meant both Aphrodite of the High Place, such as an acropolis, and Aphrodite of the Extreme Point, Aphrodite of the Headland. This headland, this extreme point of Cyprus, running out in rocks and small islands, and open to gales from the north or south, was particularly dangerous. From her platform the Cypriot Aphrodite gazed down on ships making a fair voyage or ships in trouble, very much, as one Greek poem calls her, the Watcher or Guardian of the Surf.

Cyprus here levels to a low neck of stony and scrubby wilderness, 200 yards across from sea to sea. Out of this rises a last hill, a last cube of steep-sided, grass carpeted rock, on which the temple was built. The scholar D. G. Hogarth in his *Devia Cypria*, his notebook of an archaeological journey through Cyprus in 1888, says that the stones from this now vanished temple of Aphrodite were shipped off for the building of Port Said, a work which began in 1859, along with the excavation of the Suez Canal.

You must climb up to the platform for your Cypriot view—given a clear day at Cape Andreas—of Astarte's Asia and the Bald Mountain, Jebel-el-Aqra, above and between Antioch and Ras Shamra, the holy Mount

29 Bronze statuette of Aphrodite, a variant of the Aphrodite of Knidos. Late Hellenistic. Metropolitan Museum, New York.

Kasios of the Greeks, the holy Mount Sapan of the Syrians, on which Astarte and Baal and the rest of the Canaanitish deities assembled. It is faintly there like a ship which doesn't move after all, a tiny black smudge on the horizon. Travellers rounding this perilous cape on their way to Seleukeia Pieria, the port of Antioch or to Tarsos, would have looked up at the white columns of Aphrodite's temple, and perhaps caught a gleam of a naked Aphrodite—a dolphin Aphrodite—standing in her temple, which functioned here as a spiritual lighthouse, sending out the light of her divinity to smooth the waters. She could be there still, waiting under the sea for a skin-diver, some zealous and indignant early Christians having perhaps carried her to the edge of the cliffs and tumbled her over. Or perhaps it was an archaic Aphrodite which D. G. Hogarth noticed when he was exploring Cape Andreas in the eighteen-eighties. Squared stones still lay in heaps on the landward side of the temple rock, and among them Hogarth found 'a headless stone statue, female, and with the arms close to the sides', a stiff piece of 'rude workmanship'. Near it was 'a draped leg of a later period'. Nothing so exciting remains there today. All I could find was two fluted drums of marble, which must have been rolled down to the neck of land, and abandoned there because they were too weather-worn to be worth loading into the barges for Port Said. They lie hidden in the scrub, birds on migration flitting out to rest a second or two on their roughened surface.

This Aphroditean headland does bring two poems to mind, all the same. One of them, by Theodoridas, a Sicilian who lived in the second half of the third century B.C., underlines the ancient need of a temple on this point. It was written actually about the headland, about an occasion when Aphrodite's divinity failed, or declined, to work. A merchant named Timarchos had been wrecked here on the rocks which extend the headland immediately below the temple, and were called the Keys of Cyprus, the *Kleides Kuprou* (these outliers are still known as the Klidhes Islands):

> The Keys of Cyprus, and extreme Salamis, and the fierce
> South-wester destroyed you, Timarchos, with your
> Ship and your cargo, and your sad mourners, poor man,
> Have received your black, black ashes.

Were his ashes sent home—perhaps to Sicily, after his body had been washed ashore and burnt on the low peninsula?

The other poem was written by Anyte of Tegea, who lived about a

30 Aphrodite, with dolphin and lotos leaf, the 'Aphrodite of Itálica'. Marble. Hellenistic, 3rd century B.C. Museo Arqueológico, Seville.

hundred years earlier than Theodoridas. It describes, or at least indicates just such a temple and *temenos* of Aphrodite of the Headland:

> This is the Cyprian's ground: always she has been pleased
>   To gaze from land across the glitter of the sea.
> Her bright statue makes the waters tremble all around,
>   And so brings the voyage of sailors to its happy end.

Anyte may have found herself especially close to the Cyprian goddess because of the links between Cyprus and Arkadia where she lived. Tradition held that Nea Paphos had been founded by the Tegean hero Agapenor, when he and his Arkadians were wrecked on Cyprus on their way back from the Trojan War (probably for Nea Paphos we should understand Old Paphos, thinking of Agapenor as the founder of the great temple). Anyte no doubt had frequently burnt incense to Aphrodite in her temple in the market place at Tegea.

There must have been hundreds of little shrines of Aphrodite round the Greek or Hellenized coasts such as the one in Plautus's play *Rudens* (adapted, remember, from the Greek), outside Kyrene on the North African coast, above the rocks where the two girls Palaestra and Ampelisca are wrecked and come to land: a poor little temple looked after by an elderly priestess, in expectation of offerings, an altar outside, a statue of Aphrodite inside.

Naturally, too, the Greeks combined the Aphroditean notions about love and travelling by sea: they thought of Aphrodite giving—if rightly approached—as fair a voyage across the not always placid seas of love as in the dangerous seas of the Mediterranean.

In *The Greek Anthology*:

> Revere the Cyprian. And I will breathe a fair wind
> On you in love and over the bright-eyed sea.

> (Anon)

> Watcher over the Surf, I send you these cakes
>   And gifts of simple offering, for tomorrow
> I traverse the wide Ionian Sea, hurrying to our
>   Eidothea's arms. Shine with fair

31 Aphrodite with a dolphin, found in Cyrenaica, the ancient 'Garden of Aphrodite'. Marble. Hellenistic, 3rd century B.C. Museo Nazionale Romano, Rome.

Favour on my sailing and my love, Cyprian,
Queen of the bedroom and the shore.

(Gaitoulikos, ? 1st century A.D.)

Queen of this beach, housed by
The strong swell of the sea,
My home here is simple but
It pleases me,

Because I delight in the wide
Frightening sea
And in seafarers who look
For assistance from me.

Give me my due, and fair wind will
Flow out from me
Behind you in love, or
Across the grey sea.

(Antipatros of Sidon, late 2nd century B.C.)

2. The Blessed Dolphin

The dolphin was a respected, indeed a sacred denizen of the Hellenic seas. It was the King of the Fishes, it was the favourite of Poseidon, the god of the sea, dolphins having discovered where Amphitryte was hiding from him in the depths when he wanted her for his wife. In Crete Apollo had been a dolphin god. The second of the Homeric Hymns to Apollo tells the wonder tale of how Apollo, in the shape of a huge quivering dolphin, leapt aboard a Cretan merchant ship on its way to Pylos on the south-western tip of the Peloponnese. The great dolphin could not be dislodged, it lay there, its quivering made the ship tremble from stem to stern. The ship would not answer the helm, but drove on with a following wind, past sandy Pylos, and up the Peloponnesian coast. The wind changed from south to west, and the ship swung to starboard into the Gulf of Corinth, continuing until it beached on the sand at Krisa, below Parnassos and the new temple Apollo had established for himself on its slopes.

32 Aphrodite riding a dolphin. Greek terracotta figurine c. 460 B.C. Musée du Louvre, Paris.

Apollo resumed his godly shape, telling the Cretans that they were to take charge of this temple, at Delphi, *Hoi Delphoi*, the temple of the god who was also a dolphin (*delphis*), a mythic piece of folk etymology.

Powerful Dionysos had transformed evil men into good dolphins, in a maritime adventure recounted in another of the Homeric Hymns. Pirates saw him standing on a headland, came ashore and seized him, thinking such a well-favoured young man must be royal and good for a ransom. Back in the ship, the ropes fell off Dionysos, wine started to flow everywhere, a vine curled along the yard-arm, clusters of grapes hung down. Dionysos turned into a lion, there was suddenly a bear stalking in the ship. The lion leapt on to the captain, and the pirates jumped into the sea, where they were transformed straightaway into unpiratical dolphins, the first of their kind.

Up and down the eastern shores of the Mediterranean the dolphin had been associated with the Phoenician Astartes; and it went well with Aphrodite of the Fair Voyage, in thought and in statuary, a beaked, pug-faced, marble creature coiling at Aphrodite's feet, sometimes ridden by her executory child Eros, or carved with the flowers and leaves of the sacred lotos, the sacred water-lily (growing in the waters of the Nile, the lotos— see page 197—belonged in particular to Isis, who became identified or merged with Aphrodite).

The dolphin was a creature of fine weather. Every sailor, every merchant, every traveller in Mediterranean and Aegean waters was used to the sight of dolphins. They saw 'families' of dolphins swimming round and under their ships, or running races, curving in and out of the sea, leaping clear and coming down slap on the surface.

> The calmest stillest seas, when left by them,
> Would rueful frown, and all unjoyous seem.
> But when the darlings frisk in wanton play
> The waters smile, and ev'ry wave looks gay.

—wrote a young English poet of the eighteenth century, William Diaper, about dolphins, in his translation or version of Oppian's long poem about the inhabitants of the sea.

A sea-creature of high spirits, then—and high virtue. The Greeks knew that dolphins were exemplary parents, and that mother dolphins suckled their young with rich milk (there is an etymological link between *delphis*, the Greek for dolphin, and *delphus*, Greek for the womb, which may have to do with the dolphin as Aphrodite's animal. Here is a 'fish' which has a womb, a 'fish' which couples and bears young, a love creature in the fruitful cold realm of the sea). Every Greek knew that dolphins were fond of music and kind to human beings in distress. Everyone knew the story, which Herodotus tells, of Arion on the dolphin's back—how the sailors of a ship bringing this poet back from Corinth, where he had been giving successful and well rewarded performances on the kithara, made it clear to him that they were going to throw him overboard and steal his earnings. Arion asked if he could sing one more song—his dirge, his threnody, according to Lucian's dialogue of *Poseidon and the Dolphins*. Then he put on his special singer's robes, took his stand on the poop, performed, and jumped into the sea, out of which he was fished by one of the dolphins attracted to the ship by his singing and playing. Arion rode safely on the dolphin, who put him ashore at Tainaron, the southernmost point of Greece; and there, in a temple to Poseidon, the journey was commemorated by a bronze group of the dolphin and the poet.

Pausanias mentions this bronze, which recalled to him another of the many tales of a dolphin which befriended a human being. He said he had seen the famous tame dolphin which lived in the harbour of an island near Lesbos, and was devoted to a boy who had been brought up with it, at whose summons it would come to give him rides.

Poets may like to remember that dolphins showed respect—posthumous respect this time—to another poet, and a greater one than Arion. It was said that Hesiod, to avoid a Delphic foretelling of his death, went to Oenoë, above the Corinthian Gulf, but there he unwisely seduced the sister of his two hosts. They murdered him, and took his body down to the sea and threw it in the Gulf. Dolphins found the dead Hesiod and brought him back to land for burial, either at Oenoë or at Askra, not far away, where Hesiod had his cold unprofitable farm. Writing in the second or third century A.D., Aelian declared that all good men with a feeling for music give a decent burial, in their turn, to washed-up dolphins when they come across them. To be neglectful of dolphins, he adds, is a sign of being indifferent to the Muses and the Graces. Oppian, too, pronounced an anathema on dolphin-killers:

> Hunting of dolphins is abomination. A man
> Who wilfully brings about their death,
> Can approach the gods no more. They will
> Not love him for his offerings. His touch
> Pollutes their altars, and he defiles all
> Those who live below his roof. As much
> As they loathe the murdering of men
> Do the gods loathe to have death's doom
> Brought on these chieftains of the deep.

Aphrodite's dolphin is an extension and a symbol of her own preference for quiet seas, as calm as her doves. This kindly, noble, musical animal, this servant of the high gods, intimated rescue or safety. If your ship went down on the way to the Nile or the Pillars of Hercules, dolphins might pick you up, in a manner of speaking; or if dolphins appeared, the sea might renew its tranquillity.

8

Aphrodite's Temples

Destruction and Transfer

Not much is left above ground of the major or the minor temples of Aphrodite in Greece or the cities of Greek foundation. Time's slow ruination, earthquakes, removal of stonework for other purposes and other buildings—her temples suffered in the usual ways.

The noble fifth-century temple at Segesta in Sicily may have been hers, may have been another shrine for the Paphian Aphrodite or Astarte, like the one (page 120) which stood on Mount Eryx not far away. It is an enclosure of columns which never held up a roof and never contained an inner chamber for housing a statue of its god or goddess, suggesting, even if it was unfinished, a temple designed in classical form for the open air cult of Eryx and Paphos. But there is no proof of its dedication to Aphrodite.

Otherwise there remains no grand, serene building, in which Aphrodite once dwelt, as complete as Athene's Parthenon, or Apollo's temple at Bassai, or Aphaia's among the pine trees on the roof of Aegina, or Hera's at Paestum in Italy, or the great temple of Olympian Zeus at Empedokles' city of Akragas (Girgenti), on the south coast of Sicily. And for that disappearance of Aphrodite temples Christian zeal and repugnance may be to blame as well as the ordinary forces of destruction.

Clement of Alexandria (c. 150–c. 215), who gloated over temples that had been accidentally burnt or abandoned, and jeered at statues of gods and goddesses which deserved destruction, showed special disdain for Aphrodite, and for her 'lustful orgies': she resembled (in the way she had encouraged Helen to go off with Paris) a 'dirty-minded little waitress', and Clement was scornful that great painters and sculptors should have modelled their Aphrodites on whores, on *hetairai*. 'I must leave you to judge,' Clement exhorted his Greeks of the last decades of the second century A.D., 'whether it is a respectable proceeding to prostrate yourselves to whores.' Two more pagan centuries had to go by before Clement's Christianity began to triumph and look secure, in A.D. 424, under Constantine the Great.

Constantine, too, was severe on Aphrodite, so perhaps then or later more Aphrodite temples than we know about were destroyed with a special glee. Constantine, now Emperor of East and West, did not forbid the old religion, he discouraged it, and he sequestered the gold and silver of the great temples to build Christian churches in his new Constantinopolis, his new Byzantium. But two Aphrodite temples he did throw down, two Atargatis-Aphrodite shrines where sacral prostitution continued, though with some excuse, since, however Hellenized or Graeco-Romanized it had become, they were in the ancient realm of Baal and Astarte and the rest of the Syro-Phoenician gods. One was in Heliopolis, Baalbek, in the modern state of Lebanon, between the Lebanon and the Anti-Lebanon ranges, of which the three greatly revered gods were then Zeus, Aphrodite and Hermes. The other, on the Mediterranean side of the Lebanon, up on the snowline, and some 30 miles in from Byblos (Jbail) on the coast, was no less than the temple near Aphaka (Afqa), which looks across to the Adonis river at the point where it tumbles out of a huge limestone cavern—the river which turns red with the blood of Adonis, or with the iron-stained earth carried down in February in its flood-waters (Plates 12 and 13).

Of all the neighbourhoods concerned with Aphrodite this most inter-mingles richness and wildness, rock and water and vegetation, radiant light, and the special colours of height and depth, down, down, and down, an enormity of the womb of landscape, cherishing, concentrating, the myth of Aphrodite and Adonis, and his death from the savage boar. It is like a *poème barbare* by Leconte de Lisle.

The road from Jbail to the limestone declivities above the river gorge and below the summits of the Lebanon wriggles upwards some four to five thousand feet through a fertility of terraced vineyards and terraces of mul-berry trees, and sprawling olives with ancient trunks. The snow has melted, springs are full, and flowers are out, cyclamen among them, and the brilliant anemones of Adonis. The road tilts up, and tilts down again without mercy into the gorge, to a bridge and the platformed remnants of the temple which Constantine's soldiery destroyed or at least desecrated. The cave opens in the banded limestone, the banded cliff face, above bridge and temple. There is a refreshing fertile noise of waters falling out of the cave and from limestone clefts to the one side and the other.

The way the remnants of this temple to Aphrodite or Astarte-Aphrodite or Atargatis-Aphrodite lie fallen in one direction suggests that Constantine's work was completed later by an earthquake. Eusebios says in his *Life of Constantine** that his master's destructive method was to have pagan

*Tr. E. C. Richardson, 1885.

temples decanted of their wealth and their mystery. Doors were pulled down, tiles were taken off the roof, and the temples were left open to the weather, their statues having been dragged out with ropes.

This temple near Aphaka, in its out-of-the-way situation, Eusebios called 'a hidden and fatal snare of souls', dedicated to 'the foul demon known by the name of Aphrodite'.

'Here men undeserving of the name forgot the dignity of their sex, and propitiated the demon by their effeminate conduct; here too unlawful commerce of women and adulterous intercourse, with other horrific and infamous practices, were perpetrated.'

This Christian bishop and historian understood Aphrodite better than some of the early Fathers of the church who had inveighed against her. He wrote (in his *Oration in Praise of Constantine**) that Aphrodite was the generation of bodies elevated into a deity, just as Pluto embodied the opposite principle of death and the dissolution of bodies. The pagans described 'their very lust and passion and impure disease of the soul, the members of the body which tempt to obscenity, and even their very uncontrol in shameful pleasure, under the titles of Eros, Priapos, Aphrodite and kindred terms'.

In Baalbek, 20 miles away across the Lebanon, more than a dozen columns of Aphrodite's great temple stand upright. Dionysiac carvings, which caused it to be mistaken in modern times for a temple of Dionysos, or Bakchos, the wine god so associated with Aphrodite as the sire of her bizarre child Priapos, remain sharp and clear.

In this temple, according to Eusebios, 'those who dignify licentious pleasure with a distinguishing title of honour, had permitted their wives and daughters to commit shameless fornication'.

But then all turns on the religion—on the point of view.

No doubt other Aphrodite temples were among the first to be destroyed or turned inside out with an extra-special Christian gladness or zeal or fanaticism like that of the Tudor commissioners who despoiled abbeys and cathedrals and brought the bright glass of saints tinkling to the floor. Even then sacred places, sacred buildings, are apt to retain their sanctity, by transference, the god of the new religion taking over from the god of the old. Some of Aphrodite's temples, like those of other gods, were transformed into Christian churches; or Christian churches were built out of the materials on top of the old footings or alongside the ruins. In Heliopolis, for instance, a second smaller temple of Aphrodite became a church dedicated to Saint Barbara. In Karia, in Asia Minor, north of the island of

*Tr. E. C. Richardson, 1885.

Rhodes, Aphrodite's temple in her prosperous city of Aphrodisias was turned—with some juggling around of the columns, of which more than a dozen are still erect—into a basilican church. In mainland Greece, too, several Aphrodite temples were succeeded by Christian churches. For instance, under Hymettos, just outside and above Athens, Aphrodite was worshipped by the source of the Ilissos, and her temple there, near the Kaisariana Monastery, was replaced in the fifth century by a basilica.

Many sites where there once stood an Aphrodite temple seem marked by a special sweetness of surface and contour. But I would not make too much of this. Such a site, now exercising the charm of loneliness, will probably have been urban and busy; and Greek landscape has, in any case, its special sweetness and the Greeks knew how to relate building and landscape, surely without recourse to a conscious and elaborate symbolism of landscape. One writer on Greek temples, Vincent Scully, in *The Earth, the Temple and the Gods*, has tried to work out such a relationship between the character of the sites selected for temples and the character, in each case, of the gods they were provided for. Aphrodite's temples 'had to do with the appearance of unexpected and irresistible forces, expressing a nature at once aggressive and transparent'— with a view of a sexual cleft of rocky horizon, or the sexual shape of some conical hill or the drama of an upsurge of rock.

Perhaps; though the choice of such divine landscape criteria must remain too subjective, I would suppose. The circumstance which determined that one of Aphrodite's temples should be set on this hill or that headland must often have been simple obedience to Aphrodite's familiar maritime or city interests. And even then it was natural enough, or logical enough, to set temples on prominent, isolated hills. Where else should a high god live except on high? Hills are a customary focus of religious awe, which increases if they are capped with a temple or a church. When Aphrodite, in the Homeric Hymn about herself, appears to Anchises among the shielings on Mount Ida, and strikes love into his heart, Anchises does not at once realize her identity: he simply concludes that she must be divine, and immediately says

> I will make you an altar on a high
> Point that can be seen far around, and there
> Will I offer you, at every season, rich
> Sacrifices . . . .

The Goddess in her Dwelling

It was the gods who differed, one from another, rather than their temples. Large or small, urban or rural, the temple was the house in which the god lived for the moment and was manifest on earth in his statue. Its prime and its simplest element was the hall, the inmost part, the *naos* (a word related to the Greek verb *naiein*, to dwell, to inhabit), in which the worshipful statue was placed. This *naos* was entered from the east end, through a pillared porch, and then through doors—great bronze doors or grilles in an important temple.

When the doors were open, light enough, softened by the porch and the overhang of the roof and the ceiling, flooded in and illuminated the statue at the far end of the *naos*, or 'dwelling'. Round this 'dwelling' and its porch—if the temple was more than a simple shrine—marched the rectangle of white, unpainted columns upholding the ceiling and the roof and providing a shady colonnade, a cool surrounding veranda.

The most important thing of all, the stone altar, rectangular or oval, stood as a rule in the open, in front of the porch and the steps which led up to it; and all around altar and temple and statue extended the special sacred domain of the god, his *temenos*, that which is cut off or separated from ordinary existence, outside. Before he could come out of the profane world into the *temenos* and approach the altar or the 'dwelling' and the god, the visitor or worshipper needed to be clean in spirit; he was purified, water was poured over his hands by a temple guardian.

It is fair to argue from a late dialogue,* about whether it is better to love young women or boys, that Aphrodite's temples were often distinguished by one charming feature. A speaker in the dialogue describes a visit he and some friends had made to Aphrodite's temple at Knidos, where they wanted to see the statue of the goddess by Praxiteles, much as we go to Florence to see the *Birth of Venus*. He says that as they approached, sweet breezes, 'Aphroditean breezes', blew on them from the *temenos*, because instead of being paved with flagstones in the usual barren way of temples, the open space by this temple was a delicious garden of trees and shrubs, the usual thing in a *temenos* of Aphrodite. There were myrtles especially, because the myrtle (page 194) was sacred to Aphrodite, there were planes, cypresses, bay trees, and plenty of the ivy and the grape-clustered vines of Dionysos (his wine being coadjutor to the business of Aphrodite).

That wasn't all. The speaker in Pseudo-Lucian's dialogue mentions casually that in the deepest shade of this garden there were pleasure-benches or pleasure-booths for those who wished to enjoy making love. People of fashion made use of them now and then, but on feast days they were very popular with the common people of Knidos who went to it

---

*_The Erotes_, ascribed to Lucian, but by an imitator, writing early in the fourth century A.D., some two centuries after Lucian's time.

33 and 34 *Aphrodite of Knidos. Marble, Graeco-Roman copy of the lost original which Praxiteles carved* c. *350–330 B.C. Museo Vaticano, Rome.*

earnestly—*aphrodisiazein* is the word Pseudo-Lucian employs; they were *aphrodisiazontes*, 'aphrodisi-*azing*' in earnest within a few yards of one of the masterpieces of Greek art.

It is a fascinating scene to imagine. The young fresshe folkes of Knidos, on holiday, climb up on a bright Ionian morning to the *temenos*, they are purified, they enter, and approach the altar. Two by two at the altar they make their offerings, the temple has its share, the goddess has her share and the holiday-makers have their share. The sweet smell of burning frankincense masks the other smells of burning. The sacrificing holiday-makers also have their share of the wine which they have brought for Aphrodite: they enter the 'dwelling' and have an inspirational look at naked Aphrodite, by Praxiteles, holding her hand in front of her privates, and then they walk out of the heat into the deep shade, underneath the tall cypresses, which also exude a perfume, and the very tall old plane trees, and perform as the goddess enjoins, in a garden of fertility.

It is as if the Pseudo-Lucian had let a cat out of the bag. If this happened in the early fourth century A.D., why not before? If at Knidos, why not elsewhere in the islands and on the Greek mainland, in the *temenos* of other temples of Aphrodite? Why not among the quince trees and roses and flowers and cool waters of that temple which Sappho had described (page 107)? In the most entranced of the Latin celebrations of love and its goddess, the *Pervigilium Veneris*, the 'Night Watch of Love', written, perhaps as late as the early fourth century A.D., about a spring festival in a Sicilian temple of Venus, these love booths in the precinct appear again, woven of green shoots of Aphrodite's or Venus's myrtle:

> Tomorrow in the shade of the trees will
> The Joiner of loves entwine the green huts
> Of switches of myrtle.

No wonder Clement and other Fathers of the church set themselves so much against Aphrodite: it wasn't all myth or mythical love-making, or a matter only of sacral prostitutes at Corinth or Eryx or in the Cypriot and Phoenician temples. Aphrodite said to the populace *Go to it*—and they went to it. And the cynic might recall *la fouterie est le lyrisme du peuple*—though I wouldn't be the one to insist that such holiday goings on at Knidos or that Sicilian temple were Aphrodite altogether without the Graces.

9

Sacrifice

To What Green Altar?

Ruins are disinfected by time, or put another way, ruins promote a kind of disinfection of the past. Our imaginations and our dream of antiquity gild the originals, of which ruins are romantic indicators. Some of us smell the incense in the ruins of Tintern or Fountains. If we could go into the past, if we were taken out of the present into a stuffy afternoon we should smell other smells indicating as much or more of the real thing as it used to be. Try an experiment. Try going on a warm day into the monastery of the Armenians, in the Venetian lagoon. You encounter smells which may dilute for you the romance of abbey ruins—the cheesy smell of bodies in their thick robes, the smell of the stalest air which has been going in and out of the monkish lungs, the stale stench of food hanging around in the refectory.

It is a lesson which may be applied to bright temple ruins, or to the neat drawings which reconstruct the temple of Zeus at Olympia or Apollo's temple under the cliffs of Delphi. Here is a *temenos* imagined with a tree or two. Here are Greeks strolling in grave meditation. What the reconstructions cannot show is the smell of blood, the smell of sacrifice.

Sacrifice seems to me the practice in civilised antiquity which is hardest to accept or to understand—always allowing that civilisations are for ever imperfect. Writing in an earlier chapter about Priapos, I quoted (page 75) a short pastoral poem by Theokritos, which the Greeks of his day would have found tender and charming in its evocation. There are the bay trees, the myrtles, the scented cypresses, the loaded vines, as in that temple Garden of Love at Knidos. It is spring, blackbirds and nightingales are about, and Theokritos thinks it in tune with the season and the pastoralism to talk in his poem of sacrificing a kid, a calf, a lamb which he has reared himself, creatures as young as the time of year; and for a moment a modern reader forgets that sacrifice is a nasty word which translates backward, from now more or less empty metaphor, into blood, into death, into slicing the throats of those young white creatures.

About the *temenos* of each great temple there must have been something of the noise and stench of the abattoir. Cattle were drawn in, knives were sharpened. It was all very well for an exquisitely besotted Keats to ask

> To what green altar, O mysterious priest
> Lead'st thou that heifer lowing at the skies
> And all her silken flanks with garlands drest,

when off his Grecian urn the poor beast was about to have its throat cut and its warm sloppy stinking entrails inspected and its flesh divided into tasty portions for god, priest and people.

In the Homeric Hymn about Apollo and his dolphin voyage and his new oracular temple at Delphi, the simple-minded Cretan sailors who find themselves so suddenly changed into temple attendants, do what Apollo tells them, and march off singing up to Delphi and Parnassos—and then have cold feet. How are they going to keep alive up there? The land is poor, it is not good enough for vines, there is not grass enough for grazing. Apollo tells them they are blockheads: don't they realize he has put them in charge of a rich temple where the supply of animals will never fail? If every one of them, knife in hand, were to be slaughtering sheep all the time, there would still be more to come, still be plenty of eats for them, with all the tribes of man attracted to his shrine. There you have the economics of sacrifice; and Delphi, too, must have been something of an abattoir—even though smells dry up in hot air and gobbets of ropy blood look somehow less terrible in brilliant sunshine.

What about sacrifices and the temples of Aphrodite?

Blood and Purity

No less than any other god, Aphrodite expected the scents which rose from the altar, the smoke of flesh and incense which hung in the bright air and vanished on its way to heaven. It was food turned by the purity of fire into an ethereal substance suited to the less palpable corporeality of the gods.

Had you asked a Greek why animal—and vegetable—offerings were made to the gods, he would not have replied like some anthropologist who has studied the world literature and the world-wide performance of the rituals of sacrifice. He would have said that of course the gods—and Aphrodite among them—expected sacrificial offerings: they had always been given them: why imagine they will show favour to you, if you do not show respect for them? He might have quoted Peisistratos in the *Odyssey*, who remarks when he is interrupted in a sacrificial feast or a festival sacrifice to Poseidon, god of the sea, that man cannot neglect the immortal gods.

Gods are nothing if not powerful, and to those with power, if you want their protection or intervention, you bring tribute. Each sacrifice is a gift.

But why a gift especially of the flesh, and fat, and blood of animals?

That further question might have puzzled your Greek informer into saying, 'But why not?' Perhaps he would have continued that he might, and that on proper occasions he did, present the gods with cakes prepared on the family hearth, and with honey and wine and olive oil and milk and curds and fruit, and of course incense. But those were offerings which wouldn't entirely satisfy the gods, and wouldn't satisfy the temple people, or his own clan, or his family or himself. He would explain that they all liked roast meat on special occasions, that they all went shares at the sacrifice.

He would not have had much more to say on the difference between bloody sacrifice and bloodless sacrifice, and he would have offered no theories on sacrifice as communion between god and man or about the offering of blood as the essential fluid of life. Early or late, a devout or conventional Greek before, and a less devout but still pagan and conventional Greek after, the rise of Christianity, would have defended sacrifice as something which had always been practised, and which it was common-sense or natural to continue. And the gods being gods, it must of course be done properly, with the customary procedures.

Those sacrificial procedures were much the same for all the Olympian gods. Greeks went to their temples for public festal sacrifices and for private or family sacrifices, to which guests might be invited. They loved these outings. The annual feast day began with a procession and was capped with singing and dancing, after the sacrificial eatings and drinkings. On public occasions and private occasions they honoured the god by coming in their best white clothing; and the time for a sacrifice—to most gods— was in the cheerful freshness of the day, in the morning sunshine.

The pure gods expected purity in those who arrived to sacrifice and pray and offer thanks and make requests. Hence the ritual purification with water at the entrance into the *temenos*. In the first book of the *Iliad* Agamemnon offers bulls and goats to Apollo, but this sacrifice down on the beach cannot go ahead until Agamemnon and his men have all dipped themselves in the purifying waters of the sea. Telemachos, again, in Book Two of the *Odyssey*, when he wants to pray to Athene, goes down to the sea, the nearest water, and washes his hands in the grey surf before raising them to the goddess in the special attitude of prayer. It was the same when the worshippers arrived at the *temenos*. The holy water sprinkled on them at the gateway by temple guardians or attendants freed them of stain and fitted

36 Aphrodite with a goat. Greek terracotta relief from Gela on the Sicilian coast, c. 500 B.C. Ashmolean Museum, Oxford.

them to enter an enclosure within which everything was sacred—not only
the altar, the temple, the shining statue of the god or goddess in its 'dwelling'
inside the temple, but the trees which grew around, the statues which stood
here and there, as votive offerings from the well-to-do, each set on its
marble base with the donor's inscription (hundreds of such bases were
recovered from the excavations around Aphrodite's temple at Paphos,
and may be seen there in the dusty museum), and the separate treasuries
which housed other precious things which had been presented to the deity.

Sacrifice depended on your means. If you were well off, you could afford
an ox or two oxen (Pythagoras, in the sixth century B.C., was supposed to
have sacrificed an ox to the Muses every time he worked out a new theorem
in geometry). Pigs, sheep, goats, piglets, lambs, kids cost less; and so on
down the scale, a poor man's offering of a cockerel or a dove not being less
acceptable to the gods, or a rich man's offering of many four-footed beasts
necessarily more acceptable—though the rich might not think so.

An important, much frequented temple would have its own supply of
sacrificial animals, its own herdsmen. When the animal was selected, under
the eye and guidance of the priest or his subordinates, and paid for, it was
decorated with ribbons and garlands, for the god's pleasure, like a cart-
horse at an agricultural show. Barley meal was sprinkled on its back, and it
was led to the altar. All the more propitious if the creature seemed to go
willingly, seemed to be offering itself to the god.

Singing and music were part of the ceremony. A ritual cry of rejoicing
was sent up to the god, asking that he should be there to receive the
sacrifice. Then the sacrificial attendants knocked the animal dead or
senseless, lifted its head back so that the god could look down from above
on its dead face. An attendant cut its throat, saving the blood, or some of it,
to sprinkle on the altar when the logs there had burned down to a red glow.
Animal, attendants, worshippers had themselves been sprinkled again with
water which was rendered holy by plunging into it a burning, sizzling
branch, drawn from the sacred fire on the altar, the closely fitted masonry of
which was built up to a convenient height.

The animal was now skinned and disembowelled and divided. Some
portions were set aside for the temple staff, some for the participants in the
sacrifice, some for the god. The god's portions were wrapped in the caul-
fat, and placed on the glowing altar coals. Wine was poured over these
packets of flesh and fat, they were scattered with incense of one kind and
another, and as they burnt away to ashes, the savour rose to the god. All
the while a woman would be playing on the pipes, and other women would
be singing choral songs to the god. These were professionals, and paying
them was an item on the bill.

Finally the worshippers, who had raised their hands in prayer to the god and made their requests or given their thanks for past favours, would get down to their feast, eating their portions of kid, pork, lamb, veal, their carefully roast kebabs off the altar, and washing them down with wine (perhaps the European habit of cooking meat with wine began in these ancient sacrifices). Then the god would be regaled with more song, and there would be dancing in his honour. A god had taken blood. A god and men had shared a meal—of the customary food animals.

The less expensive sacrifices, meal, cakes, apples, pears, olives, quinces, honey, milk, vegetables, etcetera, were not burnt on the altar, but laid on a table in front of the god's statue inside the temple—along with dedicated offerings, grand or humble, items of gold or silver, or terracotta images.

Aphrodite fared like the other gods of Olympos. Like them, she was given light-coloured animals (dark-coloured animals were sacrificed to the underworld gods and powers, who belonged to the night side of life). Like them, she probably preferred animals of her own sex, though in some places she was given males, including rams and bulls. White kids were customary sacrifices to Aphrodite. Pigs she refused as a rule, though pigs and wild boars were sacrificed to her on her special island of Cyprus, as if in vengeance for the death of Adonis. She was also given birds, her own doves especially (white doves, when possible?); and geese and partridges, both of which were also sacred to her. A goddess of flowers, she was given flowers and garlands, which might be burnt on her incense altar. In the Agora Museum below the Akropolis in Athens, there is a drinking bowl of the sixth century B.C. decorated with a vitally drawn *hetaira*. She is naked, and is laying a garland on a flaming altar, which no doubt belonged to Aphrodite.

Frankincense and Myrrh

Incense she liked, and perhaps with special cause, because it has been reasonably conjectured that the use of incense came into the Greek ritual of sacrifice with Aphrodite herself. There isn't a word about frankincense in Homer's frequent reference to sacrifices which were fragrant, but no doubt from the use of scented timber for the fire; and the middlemen, for its later supply to the Greeks, were Syrians and Phoenicians who imported frankincense (and myrrh and cassia, which also scented the altar fires) from Arabia.

The perfume of incense went well with Aphrodite Giver of Joy, and was no doubt considered to exercise the same emotional, pleasurable effect on gods as on men. It had the practical advantage certainly of sweetening the temples and the area surrounding the open air altar, the scent masking the stench of blood and the nasty sacrificial smells of burning meat. Moreover incense which was burnt at mealtimes in the home, was equally suited to a sacrificial meal for their gods; who had their smaller altars for incense in front of statues. On one of the two side panels of the Ludovisi Throne a married woman sacrifices incense to Aphrodite (Plate 25). And Horace in a poem wrote that his girl Glycera is burning extra incense to call Venus into her room:

> O Queen of Cnidos, Queen of Paphos,
> Give Cyprus up, though you adore it so.
> O Venus, Glycera puts more incense on
> And more, and she is calling you. Shift
>   To her sweet shrine.

> Quick, and bring your hot-blooded
> Boy with you, the Graces with their belts
> Undone, the Nymphs, Iuventas* who is not
> Quite kind without you, and
>   Mercurius too.

Empedokles, in the fifth century B.C., certainly seemed to think, if you recall that piece translated from him a few chapters ago about the offerings made to Aphrodite by the more sensitive worshippers of the Golden Age—before Zeus appeared with his strong arm and his thunderbolt, that bottles of scent and the smoke of myrrh and frankincense and outpourings of honey accorded more than bulls and slaughter and blood with a goddess of creativity, a goddess of flowers. That would be our way of looking at it too: love and incense or love and roses, not love and blood and ripping life into gobbets. But gods were like men, at least in some ways, and the Greeks would have supposed that as well as any of her fellow Olympians the goddess of love needed and expected the more nourishing diet that calves, lambs and kids provided. At Paphos, it is true, she refused blood. No blood might be spilt on her Paphian altar, but that only meant that one of the usual items in the rite of sacrifice was omitted at Paphos, where she enjoyed all the rest of the perquisites of slaughter.

As the centuries went by, the Greeks who came to be doubtful about sacrifice, questioned not its bloodiness, but the morality and propriety of bribing or softening up the gods in the old way. In Rome, inheritor of

*Goddess of the young men.

Greek beliefs and ritual, Lucretius looked round at the temples of his Greek and Roman universe, and rejected sacrifice—along with the gods— as mumbo-jumbo:

> How unlucky was the race of men, to have
> Ascribed such workings—and vindictive
> Anger also—to the gods! What groans
> That meant for them, and what calamities
> For us and tears for our posterity!
> Piety is not repeatedly to be observed
> Turning a cloaked head towards
> A stone, is not traipsing round to altar
> After altar, or flattening yourself
> Abjectly on the ground, or holding both
> Hands up in front of the temples of the gods
> Or sprinkling their altars with much blood
> Of quadrupeds, and joining vow to vow.
> Piety is to be able to look upon
> All things with an unworried mind . . . .

And then the early Christians rejected the eating in idols' temples of food which had been offered to the idols—see St Paul in 1 Corinthians viii. They rejected sacrifice—with cruel consequences to themselves, since this repudiation of the old ritual meant that they repudiated state worship, making themselves enemies of the state. When they replaced blood sacrifice with concepts derived from later Judaism, from the prophet Micah and the *Psalms*, when they accepted that their one god delighted not in burnt offerings, but cared instead for the sacrifice of a humble spirit—

> A broken heart thou wilt not despise—

that was the beginning of the end of paganism; and of Aphrodite.

In the second century the Christian philosopher Athenagoras, of Athens, wrote to the Emperor Marcus Aurelius, in his *Embassy on behalf of the Christians*, and assured him that the Framer and Father of this world required neither blood nor the odour of burnt offerings, nor 'even the sweet perfume of flowers and incense'. He was the perfect fragrance, and man's noblest sacrifice was to acknowledge him as the creator.

10

Her Statues

Matching Statues to Poems

What would a late Victorian or Edwardian devotee of high art and the Greek ideal have said of Botticelli's Venus, on her shell, among the roses? I suppose, that she was not 'Greek'. A Greek, a true Greek Aphrodite for the nineteenth-century idealist would have been that rather chill giantess in the Louvre, the Vénus de Milo; by whom most of us now are vaguely unmoved, I suspect, or even repelled.

Armless and off her pedestal, and heaped with other marble fragments to go into a lime-kiln, this statue had been found on Melos, in the Cyclades, in 1820, in time for the ideal evasions and elevations of the nineteenth century. She seemed 'classical' and she was nearly seven feet high. In her it seemed that at last the truly grand Aphrodite had been discovered and restored to Europe. The authorities of the Louvre were suspected of having destroyed the pedestal, which showed by its inscription—allowing that the statue and the pedestal belonged to each other—what was also shown by the style of the Vénus de Milo: that she wasn't 'classical' at all. She had in fact been carved late in the second century B.C. by a sculptor in Antioch. He was a revivalist, mixing old and later modes, after a lapse in sculpture; he was working perhaps to a robust, meaty, reactionary Roman taste. So his Aphrodite was more matronly than erotic: she was a heavy version, twisting and loosened, of the at once more graceful and solemn temple Aphrodites which Greek masters had produced 250 years before, in the time and in the mode of the great Praxiteles.

A young Oxford scholar, L. R. Farnell, well aware of the date of the Vénus de Milo, was still compelled by her fame to write, in 1896, of the way she combined 'natural truth with high ideal conception', in a style 'large and dignified', her countenance 'free from human weakness or passion' and 'stamped with an earnestness lofty and self-contained, almost cold'. A few pages earlier in his great book on Greek cults* this same classical

*The Cults of the Greek City States, Vol. ii, 1896.

idealist in the grip of his time had already wriggled out of the ambiguities of the nature of Aphrodite and her worship by saying, all in one paragraph, that while Aphrodite had less than most Greek deities to do with 'the arts of civilization or the concepts of advanced morality and law', her worship— on the whole—had been pure and austere.

What would such an idealist have done about all the stone phalluses which have been unearthed on the site of the temple of Eros and Aphrodite on the Akropolis at Athens?

Perhaps the momentum of the nineteenth century still makes this Venus in the Louvre the most famous statue in the world, the Venus of Venuses, on sale in white plastic in the gift shops of Athens and everywhere else. But it is the phalluses we have to account for and it is her image we have to get rid of, if we are to know what the Greeks came to feel about their goddess of loving, through most of her actively divine career. In sculpture, as soon as they developed the expressive skill, the Greeks matched Aphrodite to their lyrics, and made images of her which were voluptuous and enticing, images of the provocative and the not easily attainable—nearer in fact to the goddess as reconstituted by the youthful imagination of Botticelli.

Boulder and Log

Aphrodite, or visible Aphrodite, began a three-dimensional career as an unshaped natural stone, in Cyprus certainly, and may be on the Aegean islands and the Greek mainland as well. Her last great temple at Paphos must have been a Graeco-Roman affair of columns and entablature, shaken down eventually by earthquakes, its *temenos* filled with ex-voto statues of Aphrodite, of the late Greek or Graeco-Roman kind, which jostled each other on the inscribed bases now dustily stored in the museum below the ruins. But inside, the eastern style shrine may have survived. Cypriot coins of the Roman Empire were stamped with a rough view of the shrine, surmounted by Aphrodite's doves. Visible inside is the tall conical stone or betyl, which was Aphrodite, or in which Aphrodite had her being, and which her worshippers tenderly anointed with oil. Such betyls (the word comes from the Hebrew *Beth-El*, meaning 'house of god'), anciently described as 'ensouled stones', served for deities in the Phoenician cities over the water from Cyprus.

When Pausanias toured Greece in the second century A.D., he often found ancient stones (and pieces of tree trunk) which represented gods. For instance at Thespiai, in Boeotia, Eros had three images, famous statues by Praxiteles and Lysippos, and a boulder in its natural condition; and at Orchomenos the three Graces were worshipped in their old temple in the shape of three stones which had fallen from heaven. So perhaps Aphrodite at her first coming into Greece, was worshipped in the same rough form in all of her early temples.

But there was a difference. If Astarte or Aphrodite came to the Greeks from the Phoenicians, there came with her no expressive sculptural tradition. That wasn't the Phoenician line. In the Phoenician cities words on the whole were the conveying art—words, myths, invocations, hymns, poems conveyed the realness of Astarte or Baal, of which metal, clay or ivory figurines seem to have been no more than sacred indicators. It was as if a small bronze of a naked woman had been no more than an A for Astarte, a simple reminder of her divine personality and powers. With such little clay approximations, with hymns and invocations, with betyls in the shrine, the Phoenicians were content; whereas the Greeks learnt from the strength, the assurance and the sharp contours of the stone carving of the Egyptians.

Adept in words, the Greeks did not begin to carve in stone until the seventh century B.C., the century in which conquest by the Assyrians breached the isolation of Egypt and made it possible for the Greeks to set up their first Egyptian colony, their great treaty port of Naukratis in the Delta.

A concept forms in the mind. The concept Aphrodite projects itself into the roughest symbolization in the unshaped or scarcely shaped stone or tree trunk. The rough object draws to itself the emotions of worship, the oil, the offerings. Then gradually, as skills increase and as the concept of divinity elaborates and becomes clearer, the rough object has to conform.

It is as if the goddess in her beauty (a word we do not have to be afraid of, in this Aphroditean context) had to work her way outwards, from the inside of her first rough symbolizations on Hellenic soil to their surface, becoming in time the perfected goddess of that hierarchy in human form who had their mansions on the shining snows of Olympos.

Naukratis became celebrated for the worship of Aphrodite. Could the sculptural idea of a long slender Aphrodite, as finally realized, without clothes, have come via Naukratis, from the elegant reliefs of naked goddesses in Egypt?

The Lost Originals

More than 2,000 Aphrodites remain, in marble, heads and fragments included; and to them must be added many little Aphrodites in bronze, and thousands of little Aphrodites in terracotta, from temples, tombs and houses.

37 Figurine of Aphrodite from her city of Naukratis in the Egyptian Delta. Hellenistic terracotta, 1st or 2nd century B.C. British Museum, London.

A few of these were made anciently in the sixth or early fifth centuries B.C. Most are late Greek or 'Hellenistic', products of a Greek world which had extended further than Greece and the islands and the Italian colonies. The grand period lay in between, from about 480 B.C., the year in which the Greeks defeated the Persians under Xerxes in the sea-battle of Salamis, to the end of the fourth century, following the triumphs of Alexander and the overthrow of the free, independent city-states; and from this time there survives, in fact, not a single one of the great temple statues of Aphrodite. Not one original. We know about the Aphrodite statues which brought fame throughout Greek and Roman antiquity to this or that sculptor. We know about the poses and types of Aphrodite, and who established them, or some of them. It is those originals we don't know, those stony objects with the direct touch of the sculptor. And when we contemplate the later copies or variants, many of which came from inside vanished or ruined temples around the Aegean and the Adriatic and the Mediterranean, they are even then, as a rule, incomplete, Aphrodite minus arms, legs and attributes, Aphrodite minus head and face and tell-tale features and expressions, Aphrodite minus colour and golden or bronze adornments.

Scraps of Aphrodite which do survive from the fifth century, can be disappointing. We do not discover a face of divine loveliness in that early fifth-century relief of Aphrodite rising from the sea, that famous frontal relief of the 'Ludovisi Throne' (Plate 7), which was taken from somewhere in Greece to ornament the temple of Erycine Venus in Rome. Her breasts, her body, her outline are voluptuous, under her transparent dress; but in face—and it would be the same even were her nose undamaged—she doesn't seem extra divinely entrancing in a specific way—the way of the species Aphrodite—or so very seductive. Only the action, the occurrence, tells us who she is, only the birth from the waters, and the help given her by the two Horai, the two Hours, whose feet press on her pebbled beach— these things and the presence on the side-panels of a naked prostitute playing the pipes and a respectable married girl offering Aphrodite a sacrificial return for her favours. Aphrodite is sweeter—if dumpier—in little terracottas of the middle of the sixth century, which display a draped Aphrodite holding her dove, figurines of the type which worshippers offered at her shrines.

No free-standing temple Aphrodite, then, remains by Pheidias or Alkamenes or any other sculptor of the decades of that fifth century in which Euripides or Sophokles wrote their plays, in which Empedokles the poet-philosopher considered the nature of Aphrodite and the relationship of Love and Strife, the century of Perikles the statesman and the building of the Parthenon. It seems the sculptors were still providing statues of

Aphrodite which were heavily or monumentally and symbolically obvious, closer perhaps in their kind to one colossal head of Aphrodite of about 500 to 475 B.C., which has come down to us (Plate 11) and which images divine power and inscrutability, rather than the power and inscrutability and tenderness of love. Should we much care—supposing it were extant—for the Aphrodite of gold and ivory which Pheidias carved for her temple at Elis? With one foot on a tortoise, she seems to have been a solemn domestic goddess, the tortoise symbolizing Aphrodite's respectable role in marriage, since tortoises, Plutarch reported about this statue, don't talk, and stay at home, inside the house.

The sculptors were learning rapidly all the while to compel their human-figured, human-faced divinities to 'speak' for themselves less by attributes than in features, gestures, volumes and grace. In the next century, the fourth century B.C., the time of Praxiteles, Skopas and other masters of sculpture, and of Apelles in his pictures, the time also of Plato, Aristotle and at last Alexander the Great, Aphrodite began to emerge from her clothing in temple statues certainly imaging the irresistible power which the Greeks—back to Homer—discerned in the sweetness, bitterness and insanity, as it may be, of love, and which had already been so compellingly expressed by the poets. Here—if with some loss of majesty—was the Aphrodite whose invincible son was the winged Eros, no little cherub, but the male god—at first—to Aphrodite's essential femininity.

The later copies and the later variants—still there are no originals—tell us something of such fourth-century Aphrodites. So do a small number of genuine fragments, especially the marble head in the Boston Museum of Fine Arts (Plate 20), which in its pose, its features, its eyes, in the sweetness of the mouth, and its suggestion of enigma, of desire and the desirable, and tenderness, and also lack of mercy or consideration, corresponds to the Aphrodite of some of the poems I have quoted; to the Aphrodite who brings fire out of water, who is a force individually and universally, and who with Strife is the mover of existence.

Compare the two heads, this one from the fourth century and that colossal archaic head, remote, powerful and majestic, and primitive, of the earlier century (Plates 20 and 11).

Aphrodite in the Sea and at the Bath

Losing her clothes, or again and again letting them fall from her shoulders—it is that which marks the Aphrodites of the fourth century, and then of the Late Greek time. Aphrodite in her statues becomes fluid and pliant, and her popular types, or most of them, are by now established.

Alkamenes in fifth-century Athens may have invented one type, with his vanished 'Aphrodite in the Gardens', cult statue of the temple of Aphrodite and Eros on the northern slope of the Akropolis. It was to this temple that two girls, two children, paid a ritual visit every spring, bringing with them, from Athene's temple on the summit, loaves shaped like phalluses and snakes. In Aphrodite's temple the loaves acquired the power of fecundity. In autumn they were taken back to the Akropolis, and crumbled into the seed grain, to ensure a good yield after the next sowing.

Alkamenes' Aphrodite in the Gardens seems to have been of the form which the Romans knew as Venus Genetrix, Venus the Mother—for them the mother, by Anchises, of Aeneas, and so their own mother, their own ancestress. The Venus Genetrix was clothed, but her transparent chiton slipping from her left shoulder and revealing one of her breasts must have been intended more as an intimation of fruitfulness than a first intimation of the nakedness of loving.

Skopas, who came from Paros, in the Cyclades, where the sparkling Parian marble of so much Greek sculpture was extracted from underground quarries or stone mines (which can still be visited), was said to have made the first naked Aphrodite. But it is only possible to guess at the pose and attributes he gave her.

We know more of how Praxiteles the Athenian dealt with Aphrodite, either naked or naked to the waist. He was one of two artists who broadly dictated the forms in which the goddess was to be familiar in antiquity and afterwards. The other, painter instead of sculptor, was Apelles, who came from the Ionian city of Kolophon, on the Asiatic coast, north-west of the island of Samos.

Apelles painted Aphrodite rising from the sea. Praxiteles—in his Aphrodite, in one of her temples at Knidos, carved Aphrodite ready for the bath, an Aphrodite whose form we know at least approximately in the various ancient copies. Apelles' picture and Praxiteles' statue shared the most ecstatic praises of the ancient world. Tourists sailed to Kos, in the Dodecanese, to stare at the Aphrodite Anadyomene, which was exhibited, with other religious pictures by the master, in a small Ionic temple (it is still standing) which was one of the constituent buildings of the Asklepieion, the great sanctuary of Asklepios, the god of healing. They would remember the poem about her:

> Just rising from her mother the sea, look,
>   The Cyprian, whom Apelles has laboured to paint!
> How with her hand she takes hold of her tresses
> Damp from the sea! How she wrings out the foam

From these wet locks of hers! Now Athene and Hera
Will say, For beauty we no longer compete with you!*

Then they would sail over the strait from Kos to Knidos, a few miles away,
under the lofty blue, or black, frown of the Asiatic mountains, and climb
up to Aphrodite's temple above the two harbours of Knidos and walk
round the marble goddess of Praxiteles, examining her front, sides and back,
as Aphrodite herself was said to have done, in a poem, ascribed to no one
less than Plato:

> To Knidos, to examine her own likeness there, Paphian
> Kythereia came across the heaving seas,
> And stared at that statue which can be seen from every side,
> And cried, Now where was I seen naked by Praxiteles?

Lucian, or whoever wrote the discussion of love ascribed to him called the
Erotes, records a story about the statue which the woman attendant used to
inflict on visitors. One of Aphrodite's thighs was marked by what visitors
took to be a fault in the marble. No, the attendant would tell them, the
mark was caused by a young man who fell in love with the statue, and
managed to get himself locked in with it one night when the temple was
closed. Then he did his best to couple with Aphrodite, leaving the stain on
her thigh.

That was another story which Christian apologists chalked up in scorn
and disgust against paganism and Aphrodite and the Greeks. But then what
else was Aphrodite about?

What Apelles painted was Aphrodite's entry into life and mind, whereas
Praxiteles carved, more or less, her function, her role. Apelles painted from
Hesiod's poem. Praxiteles carved from Homer. It appears that in the picture
Aphrodite must have arisen half-length from the sea. A veil of drops of
water fell round her, and she raised her arms and her hands to wring her
wet hair. The Aphrodite of Benghazi (Frontispiece and Plate 24) is thought
to derive from the picture. In marble it shows precisely what Apelles had
imagined in paint, a figure finished across the thighs, as we see her, not a
fragmentary torso, a goddess who had risen only that far out of her maternal
sea.

As for the marble Aphrodite of Knidos, it was natural enough for
Praxiteles to have supposed that a goddess of love and beauty, in the shape
of woman, went to her bath after a night or an encounter of love. Hadn't
Homer described in the *Odyssey*—in Book VIII—how at once she had gone
to Paphos, after being netted in bed with Ares, and how in her temple she

*By Leonidas of Tarentum, of the ? third century B.C.

had been bathed by the Graces? When a Greek woman went to the bath, water was poured over her from a pitcher or ewer. Praxiteles included the pitcher; and Aphrodite's towel, on top of it.

What we see is that these two visions of Aphrodite crossed with each other. As if from the picture by Apelles, Praxiteles invented as well a naked Aphrodite Pseliumene, arms above her shoulders again, ornamenting herself with her bracelets (*pselia*) or necklaces, and a naked Aphrodite Stephanousa, raising her hands to put on a head-dress or diadem (*stephane*). In the late Aphrodite statues motifs are combined, changing the emphasis or adding emphasis to this or that particular. The Aphrodite of Knidos shielded her triangle of sex with one hand in a gesture of provocative timidity (adopted from Syrian or Phoenician reliefs). And of course connoisseurs and worshippers looked behind the hand. 'Those parts pressed inwards by either thigh—what an indescribably sweet smile they have!' exclaims one of the friends in the *Erotes*, as they stand and admire the statue, a trio of connoisseurs of sculpture. Aphrodite could be recreated now in a dozen related poses at once timid and suggestive or exciting, in this Praxitelean way. She could be designed with both hands in play, one shielding that nether smile, the other guarding a naked breast (Plate 38). Or Aphrodite's act of undressing could now be indicated in the extra grace of Aphrodite leaning forward to loosen one of her sandals (Plate 39). Or fusing the Knidian Aphrodite who has now undressed for the bath after her love-making, with the Aphrodite who is born of the sea and is worshipped therefore by mariners and passengers as well as lovers, sculptors could transform the *hydria*, the pitcher, of Praxiteles' statue into that symbolic dolphin, tail up, head and snout down, by the side of the goddess (Plates 31 and 47).

Intermediate between Aphrodite clothed and Aphrodite naked or unclothing herself are the statues in which she is naked to the waist, her chiton having fallen below the sweet gouge of her navel to her hips, or naked lower still to her thighs, or the statues such as the Aphrodite of Syracuse (Plate 40), and the Aphrodite from Zouaglia (Plate 41) and the Aphrodite of Horbeit (Plate 42), in which drapery enfolds and emphasizes her naked body or legs or is kept from falling by one strategically situated hand. Movement is arrested. Only wait and the clothing will fall, the nakedness will be revealed.

It is reasonable to suppose an Aphrodite half-undressed would have suggested undressing for the bed as well as for the bath. If Aphrodite goes to the bath after her performance with Ares, as in the *Iliad*, in the Homeric Hymn to Aphrodite she is bathed by the Graces in her sweet-scented temple

38 The Capitoline Venus. Graeco-Roman copy of a Hellenistic original of about 250 B.C., derived from the Aphrodite of Knidos. Marble. Museo Capitolino, Rome.

39 *Aphrodite loosening or fastening her sandal. Hellenistic bronze statuette, c. 200 B.C. British Museum, London. Photo by Edwin Smith.*

40 *Aphrodite from Zouaglia. Marble. Hellenistic, 2nd century B.C. Musée du Louvre, Paris.*

41 *The Aphrodite of Syracuse.*
Marble. Hellenistic, 2nd
century B.C. Museo
Nazionale, Syracuse.

42 *Aphrodite from Horbeit,*
Egypt. Marble. Hellenistic,
2nd century B.C. Musée du
Louvre, Paris.

43 and 44 Aphrodite crouching at the bath. Marble. Graeco-Roman copy of a lost variant of the Crouching Aphrodite carved c. 250–240 B.C. by Doidalsas. Museo Ostiense, Ostia.

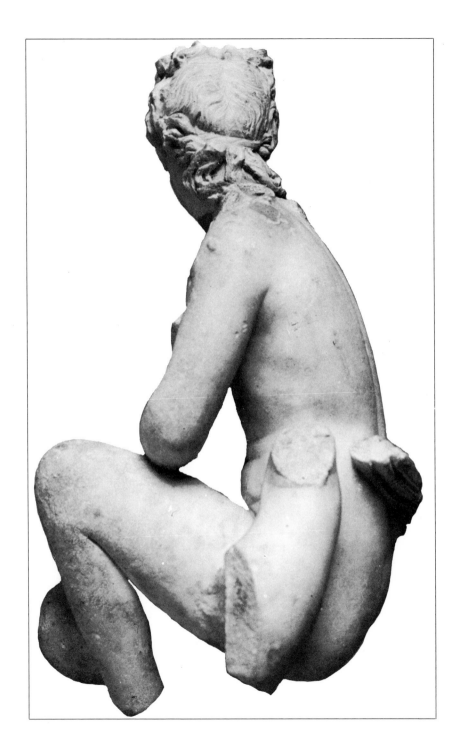

at Paphos—she enters by the glittering doors and closes them, and the Graces wash her and then smear her with the fragrant oil used by the gods; and she is off, in her fine clothing and golden jewellery, to Mount Ida, to find Anchises and seduce him.

When it comes to the point, or begins to come to the point, then Anchises on his fur-strewn bed acts like any Greek husband and looses the girdle or belt she wears around her waist. Custom demanded that a Greek (or a Roman) girl, when she married, should wear such a girdle, and that in bed her husband should unfasten it ceremoniously. If the girl slipped her chiton from her shoulders, it would fall over the belt and still be held up: the husband undoes the belt and the chiton falls to her feet, to the bed, or the ground.

It is just so in many of the statues, in their various stages between the goddess clothed and the goddess naked.

In conditions of dress or undress Aphrodite can tend her hair, regarding herself in a mirror, or she can look at the reflection of her beauty (the Aphrodite of Capua, Plate 18) on the polished surface of the shield of her divine lover Ares, which she is holding in front of herself with both hands; or she can appear to embody love and life in the gay advancing manner of the little Hellenistic bronze, 8 inches high (Plate 59), which was excavated from the cellar of a house—Aphrodite in the far north—at Verulamium, in Hertfordshire.

One of the last much imitated variants or developments of Aphrodite at the bath was Aphrodite, not ready or getting ready, but actually bathing or being washed, crouching, in the Greek way, as the water was poured over her by invisible attendants. This type was established in the first half of the third century B.C. by Doidalsas, who worked for Nikomedes I, king of Bithynia, a Hellenistic kingdom which extended to the eastern shores of the Bosporos and the Propontis (the Sea of Marmara). Nikomedes pressed the people of Knidos to sell him their Aphrodite, perhaps for his new capital Nikomedeia, which he established about 264 B.C. The Knidians refused, and it was possibly as a substitute that Doidalsas made his plump Aphrodite squatting and turning her head from the fall of the bath water.

It is part from Doidalsas, part from Apelles long before, that a Rhodian sculptor of the first century B.C. invented in his own manner the little marble Aphrodite of Rhodes (Plate 46), using Doidalsas's combination of triangular forms to fashion a more delicate, more slender and less pneumatic figure; who was still a goddess.

The Dolphin Aphrodites

Our own idea of the beauty of women, if not goddesses, is incorporated best in the late dolphin Aphrodites, unclothed, slender, elongated, and erotic—to use the adjective we derive from Aphrodite's son—and also 'decadent', as strict classical archaeologists used to complain, in their chargrin that classical modes had not lasted for ever.

These late Aphrodites are held to descend from a lost original by a sculptor of about 300 B.C., who produced his own variant of the Aphrodite of Knidos. The lost original would have resembled the Medici Aphrodite, now in the Uffizi in Florence (Plates 47 and 48). If this Florentine figure seems to have a certain compactness or stuffiness, even priggishness, of form, she is complete, she does tell us how the other dolphin Aphrodites held their lost arms and hands, as a rule, protecting one breast and half hiding their hairless triangles.

I prefer the Aphrodite in the Museo Nazionale Romano, in Rome (Plate 31), which comes from the ruins of the rich luxurious Greek city of Kyrene, capital of that Kyrenaia (Cyrenaica) which the Greeks also called the Garden of Aphrodite. It was discovered there in 1913 when the modern Libya had just become an Italian possession. Elegant, tall, slightly stiff, she has lost her head as well as her arms. Her dolphin had a fish in its beak. Eastward in Libya, there is another beauty of the kind in Lepcis Magna, the harbour-city of the ancient Tripolitania, which the Phoenicians founded for their trade with Africa. New York, too, has a dolphin Aphrodite, arms missing and most of her legs, but with a sweet head slightly turned and bent forward. Her rounded features are very suggestive of love.

Cyprus is unlucky. So far the soil of the island which fashioned Aphrodite, has not yielded any great full-sized statue of her. But Cyprus makes much in its publicity—and no wonder—of the little Aphrodite of Soli, a later, rather more human, rather less divine girl, or let's say a rather more humanly divine girl, of the first century B.C. (Plate 51). Her arms and her feet have gone, her dolphin too, though it was certainly there by her side; but she has kept her face, of a young powerful sexuality, touched with cruelty or indifference, as if tender—of course—only to the privileged; a face roundish and firm, matching the firmness of her breasts, her body, and its division into her thighs. She looks dangerous, and it would be an appropriate

45 (Overleaf) Crouching Aphrodite by Doidalsas of Bithynia. Roman-Greek copy of the lost original of c. 250–240 B.C. From Hadrian's Villa, Tivoli. Museo Nazionale Romano, Rome.

46 (Overleaf) The Aphrodite of Rhodes. Another variant of Doidalsas' Crouching Aphrodite. Marble. Hellenistic, 1st century B.C. Archaeological Museum, Rhodes.

surprise to see her parading one day, either gracious or aloof, along the sand of one of the carefully combed bathing beaches of Famagusta or Larnaca. At Soli, the city founded by Solon the Athenian lawgiver, she looked out over Morphou Bay, on the north coast of Cyprus. Soli had its temple of an Isis-Aphrodite.

Less known, less appreciated, is the Aphrodite of Italica, at the other end of the Mediterranean, at Seville, in the Museo Arqueológico; earlier, of some date between the goddesses of Kyrenia and Soli—no feet, no head, only half of one arm, but that arm holds a lotos leaf, making her, in the far west, another Isis-Aphrodite. This Aphrodite keeps a flush of her original pink colouring, a slim, silky, dimpled goddess, her marble unpitted and unroughened, an Aphrodite of the Sea who returned to the world in 1940 out of the ruins of Sevilla la vieja (Italica), birthplace of the Emperors Trajan and Hadrian, the city on the Baetis—the Guadalquivir—which exported, as Seville still does, quantities of the finest olives and olive oil, in ships which certainly required the maritime favours of Aphrodite.

She has a good home in her museum, which is more than can be said for the Kyrenian Aphrodite encircled by all the traffic and blue exhausts of modern Rome.

If you do visit her in Seville, you will see, outside her museum, white doves of the kind proper to Aphrodite, flying down from palm trees to coo and to be fed; and then, not so far away in this quiet park, three girls in marble crinolines, swooning for love, or for the death of the Spanish love poet Gustavo Adolfo Bécquer.

Experts on Greek sculpture have to say that the dolphin attached, rather on end, to the left leg of these Aphrodites was a clever structural device needed to add support to the slender legs of the new naked statues. But the art lies in what an artist makes of a device; and these sculptors turned the support into a dolphin, and the dolphin belonged to the goddess—and wasn't a vegetable marrow or a lump of nothing.

Something more of the tender way the Greeks or Hellenized people of the Mediterranean and Aegean cities regarded their Aphrodite statues may be felt, I think, in a poem by Kallimachos. He would have been rather younger than Anyte of Tegea, whose epigram on the Sea Aphrodite or the Headland Aphrodite I quoted earlier; a North African Greek born, about 305 B.C., in Kyrene; which means that with his own eyes he might have seen that Kyrenian Aphrodite now in Rome, in her entire beauty inside her shrine; before she was deprived of her arms and her head; and her shrine. Later on Kallimachos lived in Alexandria, on the staff of the great library founded by King Ptolemy Philadelphos, whose wife and sister Arsinoë was raised to godhead and identified with Aphrodite. Perhaps in

Arsinoë-Aphrodite's temple at Zephyrion, the 'windy headland', on the Egyptian coast, Kallimachos was intrigued by a nautilus shell, left there as an offering; or perhaps he saw the offering being made, and happened to know the girl, Selenaie, who made it.

It is the pretty Nautilus, or 'Sailor Shell', which speaks to Aphrodite:

> Zephyrite, Kypris, I am yours, an empty shell, Selenaie's
>   First offering to you, a Sailor Shell
> Which once moved on the seas, when the wind blew,
>   Stretching my sail-cloth on my cords, or
> Paddling strongly with my feet when Calm
>   Shiningly ruled—my action like my name.
> And then I fell on the Ioulidian sands, to become
>   A plaything loved, Arsinoë, by you;
> No more, my life being done, a floating chamber
>   For the watery halcyon's egg. But now,
> Show grace and favour to this virtuous
>   Daughter of Kleinios, traveller from Aiolian Smyrna.

It is no good complaining of the lightness or prettiness either of late Aphrodite statues or of late poems about Aphrodite; and it is only subjective, it seems to me, or classically prejudiced, to suppose that the Greeks, while paganism lasted, came scarcely to think of Aphrodite as divine, or as more than an image of sensuality and appetite. A goddess she remained. And love has its prettiness. Neither a religion of love nor the pursuit of love, if inclusive of pain as well as delight, would be genuine if the expression it found were always in solemn, earnest philosophical terminology, whether of words or forms. Never has love been taken exclusively or commonly in that way, whether in ancient Egypt, classical or Hellenistic Greece, T'ang China, Augustan Rome, Heian Japan, Ronsard's and du Bellay's France, or the England either of the madrigalists or of Robert Graves.

From the zeal with which the Christian Fathers so often railed at Aphrodite, it does seem that the Greeks worshipped her to the end, retaining perhaps more individual love for Aphrodite than for the rest of the old pantheon, able still to achieve that bright lyricism both in her statues and in poems about her.

Yet why? Because it was into such an Aphrodite that the old goddess and the idea of love had inevitably changed? Because 'the Greeks' at the close

47 and 48 (Overleaf) The Medici Venus, with a dolphin and two Erotes. Graeco-Roman copy of a Hellenistic original of about 300 B.C. Marble. Uffizi, Florence.

included all the hellenized who were not Greek by descent? Because the hellenized of Syria and Egypt and North Africa inherited as well an extra, more eastern sensuality?

Perhaps. But I do not know that *hellenized* or *hellenistic* has to mean decadent.

That Alexandrian Greek of recent times, C. P. Cavafy, wrote a poem 'Return from Greece' in which such a 'Greek' and his 'Greek' friend are coming back from a visit no doubt to Athens. The speaker remarks that they are back in their own seas, in

> the waters of Cyprus, of Syria and Egypt,
> cherished waters of our native lands.

He says

> We too are Greeks—what else are we?—
> but with the affections and emotions of Asia,
> with affections and emotions
> that hellenism sometimes finds strange.*

The blood of Syria and Egypt in them is nothing to be ashamed of: 'let us honour it, let us boast about it.' There we have something of the spirit in which the late Aphrodites need to be estimated. From the east Aphrodite had come, to the east she had returned.

About Aphrodites or Venuses in general, and I suppose he was thinking of the severer prototypes and the imitations of them in later sculpture and painting, Paul Valéry concluded sensibly, if obviously, that it is nearly impossible to make such a goddess of beauty attractive because she is meant to have all the perfections, and 'What captivates us in some being or other is not this highest degree of beauty; it is not a generality of grace, but always some special feature.'

If they had survived, I doubt if we should so much admire Aphrodites of the classical period, the cold Impossible Beauties. It is the best of the hellenistic beauties who have speciality in their grace, their nakedness and their attitudes, the Egyptian Aphrodites of the Louvre or of the Coptic Museum in Cairo, or the late Aphrodites which were carved in wealthy Rhodes. It is worth going to Rhodes, not for the few stones of her temple near the grand medieval harbour, but to stare and stare in the museum at the

*Translated by Edmund Keeley and George Savidis in C. P. Cavafy, *Passions and Ancient Days*, 1972.

49 and 50 (Pages 180 and 181) The Vénus de Milo. Marble. Hellenistic, late 2nd century B.C. Musée du Louvre, Paris.

small crouching Aphrodite (Plate 46), and at the nearly naked, more than life sized, if wave-washed Aphrodite of the Sea (Plate 28), who seems the proper goddess of an island of light, once a great centre of statue-making, the island traditionally of Rhodos, daughter of Aphrodite and Poseidon, mother of seven children by Helios the Sun God.

To be fair I should add that a Greek or hellenized postulant, who brought his gifts with prudence and regularity to one of those late dolphin Aphrodites, might have had more serious thoughts, on occasion; without being an Aischylos or an Empedokles. Since more Greeks had come to believe in an afterlife from which not all except heroes were excluded, mightn't Aphrodite and her dolphin give him, too, a fair voyage in death? Sometimes a dolphin token, a dolphin coin, was buried with the dead; and dolphins, before the end of Greek religion, came frequently to be depicted as symbols —a happy concept—of the oceanic journey of the soul to the Isles of the Blest, as ancient Hesiod had described them: isles where fruits as sweet as honey ripen three times a year, the Elysian Fields of Homer's *Odyssey*, where the air is fresh off the sea at the end of the world, and where there is neither wind, nor rain, nor snow.

51 *Aphrodite from the Temple of Aphrodite, Soloi, Cyprus. Marble statuette. Hellenistic, 1st century B.C. Cyprus Museum, Nicosia.*

II

Some of Aphrodite's Attributes

Her Doves

Aphrodite's scallop shell, her *kestos* and her dolphins have been accounted for in earlier chapters. But as goddess of love she had several more attributes which require to be explained and celebrated, birds, flowers, fruit, the goat, and the Evening Star.

An attribute is both object and symbol. It will have a quality in some striking way like the quality which it indicates or emphasizes in a divinity. The colour, the softness and the scent of roses—especially the scent, with its exciting power; the colour of wild anemones; the scent of myrtle and of quinces, the tenderness of doves and their quiet cooing and purring, the shape and the contents of a pomegranate, the actual or supposed habits of partridges or sparrows—associating any of these with a goddess of the pursuit of love filled out her personality. And if we look at them and experience them for ourselves, we can, I think, achieve some special rapport, after all the centuries, with the goddess and with the feelings and needs she personified.

Smell a damask rose, and you can turn yourself into one of those devotees of Aphrodite walking towards her temple in search of favours, some fine morning in April (her month) two thousand or two thousand five hundred years ago.

There is a reciprocity here: if the roses we pick in our own gardens, without going to Greece or Cyprus or the Lebanon, tell us something about Aphrodite, in her turn the contemplation of Aphrodite tells us something extra about roses, and why for so long now they have been the flowers most favoured by western men—something extra about ourselves. It is in her roses, her myrtle, her doves, her quinces, that we can experience that reciprocity most of all or most delightfully of all, not forgetting that she is differently present, also essentially present, let us say in her geese or her goats, or her temple prostitutes.

I shall claim priority for the doves of Aphrodite, and for her roses,

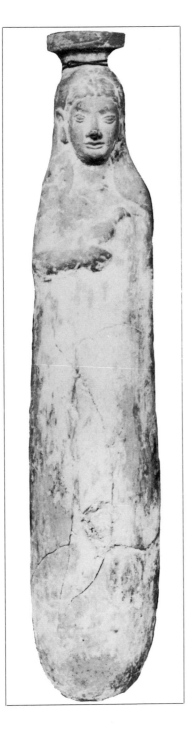

52 Scent bottle in the shape of Aphrodite with a dove, from Kameiros, Rhodes. Terracotta, c. 540 B.C. British Museum, London.

both of which mark the trail of this goddess from Asia into Greece and then
into the rest of Europe.

The Greeks liked to invent and tell stories of transformation, such as the
transformation of the nymph Daphne into a bay tree when Apollo had
almost caught up with her. Another transformation explained why doves
were sacred to Aphrodite. Aphrodite and her son Eros competed in picking
flowers. When it seemed that Eros was picking most and was going to win,
a nymph named Peristera ('dove', 'pigeon') helped Aphrodite to get the
better of him. Eros was so annoyed that he changed Peristera into a dove.
But Aphrodite was not the first—nor has she been the last—deity to be
attended by this most sacred of birds. She inherited the dove from her own
ancestors, the love goddesses, or fertility goddesses, of the Middle East
and the Phoenician cities (handing the dove, in turn, on to the Christian
Madonna).

Clay doves and fertility goddesses of the fifth millennium B.C. are known
from the city mounds of Iraq. Perhaps in Cyprus there was a meeting of
dove goddesses from east and west. Clay doves have been found in association with fertility goddesses in Crete, and from Crete have come clay
statuettes of such goddesses of the late second millennium B.C. who carry
doves—they can hardly be any other kind of bird—perched on their heads.
Then in the Near East doves—and especially white doves—fluttered around
the Astarte temples. Askalon (page 30), from which tradition brought the
Paphian Aphrodite to Cyprus, was only one of the Levantine cities which
resounded to the cooing of sacred doves. 'Why should I mention'—the
Roman poet Tibullus, in a travel catalogue in one of his poems—

> how the white doves the Syrians of Palestine
> Revere, flutter unharmed through every city?

These would have been domesticated doves, descendants of the rock-
dove. But we may suppose that doves of every kind belonged to Aphrodite,
including both the rock-dove (the commonest wild species in Greece
and the islands, resident there all the year round) and the turtle-dove, which
arrives in spring from its winter lodgings in Arabia and Africa.

Homer mentions wild doves in association with the divine—with Zeus,
not Aphrodite. Wild doves brought ambrosia to Zeus. He does not
mention tame doves; and it does seem that doves may have been first
domesticated in Middle Eastern temples. Hosea, a prophet of the eighth
century B.C. from Northern Israel, who married, or so it seems, a temple
prostitute, 'a wife of whoredoms', shows his familiarity with Assyrian

dove-temples by writing of the tribe of Ephraim as a 'silly dove without heart', and having his God declare that he will make Ephraim and Israel tremble 'as a dove out of the land of Assyria'. Cypriot coins show doves perched on Aphrodite's temple at Paphos: doves of fact and symbol, no doubt. But then to doves one temple would have been as good a home as another; and in Greece, as the grand stone temples proliferated, domesticated doves became temple birds, cooing and jud-judding and pursuing each other along the pediments and fluttering in and out of the colonnades. For instance, in the *Ion* of Euripides there is a part to be played by the tame doves which live around Apollo's temple, at Delphi. (Ion, as Apollo's temple attendant, shoos off the other birds which make messes round the stonework. But it looks as if the doves enjoyed a privilege they couldn't very well be refused.)

Haunting every temple, the dove remained Aphrodite's bird, all the same, the essence of that affinity having been that doves coo and are gentle and are publicly amorous, just as the essence of the affinity between swans and Apollo was that the swan has grace and dignity and snowy purity, flies high and delivers a grand and remote music with the slow beat of its wings. Doves croon, and are comfortable: their crooning to each other is a music of the preliminaries, their comfortable quality is the langour of afterwards.

Certainly the Greeks appreciated this tenderness of doves, and their beauty. They supposed that these birds of Aphrodite were faithful lovers, even that they mated for life (which may be true of turtle-doves). They knew that doves feed their young, in their early weeks of existence, with 'milk'— with 'dove's milk', 'pigeon's milk', which is the fatty lining of the crops of both the male and the female. It was not difficult to imagine that these birds of the goddess of love could also be love's messengers, a fancy which one celebrated Greek poem—author unknown—helped to popularize in European poetry. In answer to a question the dove in this poem explains that she is a slave of the poet Anakreon and that she is on the way with a message from Anakreon to the boy he is in love with (beginning with Thomas Stanley in 1651, English translators of the poem sedulously changed the boy into a girl):

> You breathe a delicate rain
> Of perfume on the air.
> Where have you flown from,
> Sweet dove, what
> Brings you here?

Anakreon sent me
To Bathyllos, the boy
Whom he loves most.
You see, he made a song
For Kythereia,
And, as quid pro quo,
She gave him—me;
So he's my master,
I'm his messenger,
And he declares that soon
I may go free.

But what's the point
Of flitting round
The fields and hills,
And perching on
Some tree and eating
Wild, when I can eat
Good bread
Upon my master's hand instead,
And sip wine
After him? Then
He plays, I dance—
A little tipsily.
I hide below my
Wings, and when
He sleeps, I sleep as well,
Perched on his lyre.

Now be good enough
To go. I might be
Some jackdaw,
Stopping here and
Chattering so.

That Anacreontic poem has been dated between about 50 B.C. and 50 A.D.,
so it would be coeval with the Aphrodite in the museum at Rhodes who
combs out her wet hair or separates it lock from lock (Plate 46) or with that
delicious Aphrodite of Soli (Plate 51), in the museum at Nicosia.

None of this respect or affection for doves kept them from fire and altar.
Young Greeks, young men or women, would seek to assure themselves

of Aphrodite's favour by offering her—among other things and creatures—
terracotta bottles full of scent, in her own shape, the cork fitting into the
top half of her head as if it were her customary citadel-like head-dress; or
brightly coloured statuettes, again of Aphrodite herself, carrying a dove
on her bent arm, against her body; or indeed actual doves, which were on
sale in cages near the temple.

> Taken from her mate the white dove
> Is often burned on the altars of Idalions

Ovid says in his *Fasti*. The doves had their necks wrung, and Aphrodite
snuffed up the savour—were the doves plucked?—of burning dove, as
of burning lamb or kid, or even pig.

Wild rock-doves and wild turtle-doves were no doubt luckier. There are
doubts in the matter of Aphrodite and the turtle-dove. We might think that
our familiar crooner or crooler from the deep summer hedge specially
images the tenderness of Aphrodite, in its soft colours of grey and wine, its
voice, its habits and its gentle way of being rather unsuspicious of man. It
was familiar to the Greeks, certainly. But Greek writers mention the turtle-
dove in a sententious way, as a rule; as a bird which is always chattering—
at both ends, through its mouth and its backside. So women in particular
were compared to turtle-doves.

I still believe the turtle-dove must have been included among the birds of
Aphrodite. The Greek writer Aelian, who lived *c.* 170–235 A.D., had been
informed that white turtle-doves were sacred to Aphrodite and Demeter,
while ordinary turtle-doves were sacred to the Furies and the Fates;
which is a little unexpected. But here is a bird which arrives in spring
—in the season of love—in all the high country north of the Himalayas,
and in Greece and Italy and Cyprus. Over Aphrodite's Cyprus the turtle-
doves arrive at the end of March and the beginning of April. Many drop
down to breed, on the plains, in the olive valleys, and up on the mountains.

There is one Aphroditean, or one Astartean story which must refer to
turtle-doves and their migratory habits, reported again by Aelian. Every
year, he wrote, there were two festivals observed by the people of Sicily.
One was called the Anagogia, the Festival of the Putting to Sea, because
Aphrodite then made a journey to Libya (i.e., Africa) from her rich prosti-
tution-temple on Mount Eryx on the toe of Sicily, accompanied by huge
flocks of doves. 'The Erykinians say that the doves are escorting Aphrodite,
and sharing the common belief about them, they call doves the "pets
of Aphrodite".'

Nine days later—Aelian would have been nearer the migratory interval if he had written nine months—a dove was to be seen coming back over the sea from Africa (which is about 100 miles from Mount Eryx). Unlike the doves which followed it in great numbers, this leading dove was of exceptional beauty, rosy-coloured, Aelian said, the colour of Aphrodite according to a description of her in a poem by Anakreon.

With this return of the doves, the Sicilians all celebrated the second of two festivals, the *Katagogia*, the Festival of the Coming to Land.

In these dove journeys back and forth Erykinian Aphrodite was said to be paying her yearly visit to another temple of hers in the African city of Sicca Veneria (El Kef, in Tunisia, about 100 miles south-west of Tunis), where girls earned their dowries by temple prostitution. But the legend must really be explained by migration: flocks of turtle-doves coming and going. Flocks of migrating turtle-doves are very noticeable, each bird flying along with quick, jerky, characteristic movements.

The Romans thought more kindly than the Greeks of the singing of turtle-doves. Or at least Virgil did, handing on his *Nec gemere aëria cessabit turtur ab ulmo*—'Nor shall the turtle-dove cease its moaning from the high elm'—to Tennyson, and eliciting in return Tennyson's 'Moan of doves in immemorial elms'.

Her Roses

To associate roses and love, roses and the loveliness of women, is an inheritance from the Greeks; and for them roses, above all, belonged to Aphrodite and her son Eros (sometimes pictured with a rose in one hand—Plate 14—as he goes about his business) and to the Graces who so often attend her. In Euripides' grim play *Medea* the chorus of women with one breath avert the fierceness of love from themselves and with another talk of Aphrodite always wreathing her long hair with odorous roses.

One fancy of the Greeks was that roses and Aphrodite were born simultaneously. At the moment when the young goddess took shape in the sea from the sperm of Ouranos a new shrub appeared on earth. The assembly of the blessed gods spilt drops of nectar on its scions, and each drop became a rose (so the roses in Botticelli's painting were doubly appropriate). Some Greek and then Latin poets favoured the different story (from Cyprus no doubt) that the first roses grew from the blood of Adonis, when he was killed by the boar, just as the first anemones sprang up at that moment, and in that story, from the tears which fell from Aphrodite.

It is as if the rose and Aphrodite came to Cyprus together, and then to Greece together, which is probably true. The garden roses would have spread from Persia to Syria and Asia Minor, and so into Greece of the islands and the mainland; and *rhodon*, the Greek for rose, was in fact a word from Persia, originally, an Old Iranian word, an exotic label for an exotic flower.

But then exactly what kind or kinds of rose would have been connected, first of all, with this new goddess of the Greeks—or at least of the Cypriots, both Greek and Phoenician?

The candidates are the roses we know as Gallicas and Damasks. In both groups there are roses assuredly pink enough to have sprung from the blood of Adonis, pink enough to have suggested the deep flush which spreads through a girl's features when she is suddenly embarrassed by love, a change of colour which was certainly in the Greek thinking about roses, Eros, and Aphrodite.

Aphrodite's primal rose might have been a *Rosa gallica*, which is the deep pink, sweet-smelling, single-flowered ancestor of the double Apothecary's Rose, the rose of medieval medicine, our Red Rose of Lancaster. But I doubt it. The likelier candidate is a Damask—a Summer Damask flowering in the season of love. The Summer Damasks (traditionally brought to Western Europe from Damascus, by pilgrims and crusaders returning from the Holy Land) are the roses grown in Bulgaria and in the Faiyum in Upper Egypt, and elsewhere, for distilling attar of roses. They are hybrids. *Rosa gallica* is one parent, and the other parent—bringing us nearer to Aphrodite and her island—is a wild rose which grows in Syria, a sprawling unremarkable species with small white flowers, named *Rosa phoenicia*. The autumn-flowering Damasks descend from *Rosa gallica* crossed with *Rosa moschata*, the Musk Rose.

Sometimes English and American gardeners are blessed with flowers of the original *Rosa damascena*, this *Gallica-Phoenicia* cross, without realizing it—on bushes of the *Rosa damascena variegata* which we know as the York and Lancaster Rose, from the Wars of the Roses. They expect flowers streaked with pink, and then find that on some branches, instead, the blossoms are a deep undivided pink—reversions, in fact, to *Rosa damascena*; to the rose with a fair claim, at any rate, to have come to Cyprus, and into Greece with the goddess of love. When I see these pink reversions in June, I have imagined girls wearing wreaths of Summer Damask on their way up from the shore to the great temple at Old Paphos.

Scent is important in the roses of Aphrodite, scent and its emotional effect. The three vegetal attributes that have most to do with Aphrodite are all sweet-scented, her roses, her myrtle, her quinces. Certainly the Summer Damasks emit that spicy, slightly sharpened sweetness which can be named aphrodisiac. One investigator of the scent of flowers and leaves says that sweetness of scent stirs 'the instinct of courtship'. Scent is a help towards the consummation which is personified and deified in Aphrodite.

53 *Venus on her scallop shell. Detail from* The Birth of Venus *by Sandro Botticelli (1445–1510). Uffizi, Florence.*

The fresh scent of roses and the fresh touch of rose petals suggest the touch and the perfume and the freshness of young bodies; and the scent suggests deity. 'La Rose est le parfum des Dieux,' wrote sixteenth-century Pierre de Ronsard in one of his Greek-inspired or Greek and love-inspired poems. And he was right. More gods than Aphrodite and Eros, in more religions than the Greek, have been imagined to have a scent of roses.

So there is the rose: it is scented, it is soft (for the Greeks suggestive also of the part of herself Aphrodite so ostentatiously hides or protects with one hand in her Hellenistic statues?), it blushes, it is fragile, transient, feminine; and stems of the rose have thorns or prickles, like the course of affairs of the heart. The rose comes in the Aegean and Mediterranean spring (Ovid says that the first roses of spring were offered to the goddess), and love comes in the spring. The symbolization is complete.

But then in spite of those first roses springing red from the blood of Adonis or from those drops of divine nectar spilled by the gods, why after all were some roses, including some of the wild ones, so evidently and obstinately white?

In mythology contradictory stories can happily and usefully co-exist without friction, each story answering its situation. Aphrodite was responsible. Roses were white to begin with. As she ran to keep jealous Ares (in the shape of the boar) away from her Adonis, Aphrodite was pricked in the foot by rose thorns, and her blood fell on the white petals.

That at any rate was what the Cypriots and the Phoenicians used to say, according to the Greek sophist of the third century A.D., Philostratos the Athenian, in one of his *Letters about Love* (this Philostratos, by the way, contributed to English love poetry, since another of his *Letters* gave Ben Jonson the substance of his 'Drink to me only with thine eyes'). Picking the rose thorn from her foot became an attitude for Aphrodite in her statues.

Another story is that Eros led the dance when the gods were feasting and overturned the bowl of nectar with his wing. It was in this way that the nectar fell to earth and changed roses from white to red.

To the possible history of Aphrodite and the Summer Damasks there is still a small postscript to be appended. In the last century a particular form of Summer Damask was recognized in Ethiopia, where it was grown in Christian premises in the province of Tigre, around the old holy city of Axum. It was named the Abyssinian Rose, the Holy Rose, or *Rosa sancta* (the modern name is *Rosa x richardii*). A wreath of flowers of this same Holy Rose was also found by Sir Flinders Petrie when he excavated a tomb of the second to the fifth century A.D., at Arsinoë, in the Faiyum.

Could this Holy Rose, this special Summer Damask, and not *Rosa damascena* itself, have been the rose of Astarte in Syria, the rose of Atargatis, and the rose of Aphrodite in Cyprus? And then have become a rose of the Christian churches in Syria, and so in Ethiopia? Dr C. C. Hurst, who investigated the cytology of the genus *Rosa*, and worked out the ancestry of this Holy Rose, spotted a plausible explanation. Ethiopia and Syria were linked in the fourth century A.D., when Ethiopia was evangelized by monophysite Christians from Syria, led by St. Frumentius, Bishop of Axum, who was a Phoenician, from the great city of Tyre.

Or perhaps—a more simple explanation—this Holy Rose had come first from Phoenicia to the hellenized Egypt of the Ptolemies, as a Phoenician or Syrian contribution to the goddess who was Astarte, Isis, and Aphrodite all in one; had then been cultivated around temples of the goddess in the Faiyum, passing eventually from the Faiyum to Ethiopia? In a sense the Faiyum, once named Arsïnoites, was Aphrodite's creation, having been colonized by Arsinoë, that queen of the second of the Ptolemies who was herself identified with Aphrodite (see page 176), and worshipped.

This possible rose of Aphrodite does have single, delicately pink flowers. If that seems appropriate enough to our Botticellian vision of the young goddess, perhaps it won't quite do for the deeper flush of love or for the blood-rose of Adonis or the rose from the drops of Aphrodite's blood.

Actually the roses in the air, in the breeze, in Botticelli's *Birth of Venus*, are some flushed form of *Rosa x alba* (our White Rose of York). This was another of the roses which the Greeks cultivated and then passed on to the western world; and again it has Syrian ancestry, by way of that small white-flowered *Rosa phoenicia*. Botticelli's roses seem nearly, but not quite, the favourite old rose, *Cuisse de nymphe*, the Nymph's Thigh, the rose which goes by the timider English name of Maiden's Blush.

Her Myrtle

Few trees or shrubs (it is really between the two) held so much significance for the Greeks, and then the Romans, as the myrtle. Scent was the myrtle's good fortune. This *Myrtus communis* is beautiful, evergreen and fragrant; it was cultivated by the Greeks in several varieties and it grows wild round the Mediterranean and Aegean as an element of maquis and garigue, and on the edges of watercourses or on rocks by the sea. Perhaps its liking for seaside habitats helped to associate myrtle with Aphrodite, as if it had welcomed her ashore, or been created with her, like the rose. Ovid has a thing to say about this in his *Fasti*, his long poem about the seasons and festivals of the year. In April, on April 1st, he tells wives, girls and tarts, you must wash the statues of Venus all over, put their golden necklaces on again, and give them roses and other flowers; and then, as the goddess commands,

you must wash yourselves, under the green myrtle—why? Because when
Venus-Aphrodite came ashore and was wringing the water from her hair
she saw that she was being watched by a coarse crowd of satyrs—

> And so hid her bodily parts with myrtle
> And was safe. Now she tells you to do the same.

Myrtle leaves shine. They are pin-marked with minute oil-glands. Their
scent rubs off on your hands, and a myrtle bush on a bright day envelops
itself in its own perfume. Then the flowers, white, more than half an inch
across, are also sweet-scented and crowded with yellow-tipped stamens:
they populate a thick myrtle bush in May and June with thousands and
thousands of scented stars.

Scent, wiriness, shape and habit—the long oval of the leaves, the way
they grow opposite each other up the branches and the way the flowers each
tip a long separate stalk, made the myrtle a splendid plant for wreaths,
which the Greeks wore publicly or privately on the least excuse.

Myrtle entered, in other ways, with other deities, into life and ceremony,
but its divine relationship with Aphrodite was much the commonest and
most intimate. For the Greeks, in a frank way, these scented leaves and
scented stems and scented flowers indicated love, and its pleasures, in
mutuality: brides wore myrtle for what was to come on the wedding night,
and afterwards; not as a modern white wedding symbol of innocence and
virginity. These might have been desirable qualities in a Greek bride, but
with the goddess of the act of love they weren't exactly the basic virtues.

Myrtle was no less important to the Romans, and a most moving celebration of myrtle and love comes in Virgil's *Aeneid*, in a coupling or con-
trast of love with death. When Aeneas goes down to the underworld, he
finds Dido, who had killed herself for love of him, in a place where myrtles
grew as a bitter-sweet reminder:

> Nearby extend the Fields of Mourning, as they call them,
> Where, lost in a myrtle wood, lurk along hidden
> Paths those cruelly driven by inexorable love
> To pine to death. Here even in death their
> Sorrows stay with them.

Long after Virgil's time, the fourth-century Ausonius, who came from
Bordeaux, wrote a *Cupido Cruciatus*—'Cupid Crucified'—in which he
imagined Cupid being unwise enough to fly down to these Fields of
Mourning. In the gloom he is recognized by the great ladies who have

died for love, they catch him, and string him up on one of the myrtle trees, and stick needles into him. Venus who had also suffered so from his activities, comes along and swears at Cupid, and beats him with her chaplet of flowers.

One special story of Aphrodite and this plant of hers was preserved by Athenaios. A merchant from Naukratis, the Greek city in the Nile Delta, touched at Paphos on his way home, and while he was there bought a small archaic figure of Aphrodite—no doubt because she protected sailors and was the goddess of fair voyages. When his ship was nearly home, it was caught in a storm. The sky blackened, the sea turned rough, visibility dropped to a yard or two; the ship's company crowded round the statuette of Aphrodite and begged her to save them. Aphrodite liked the citizens of Naukratis, who had brought her cult with them from Ionia, and suddenly when everyone was vomiting and desperate, a sweet smell filled the ship: they saw that everything round Aphrodite's image was covered with fresh, shining myrtle. Their ship was green with myrtle. The sun came out, and they made harbour. The merchant took his Aphrodite and her myrtle branches off to Aphrodite's temple in Naukratis, dedicated them to her, and then invited his friends and family to a feast in the temple, crowning each of them with a myrtle wreath.

That the religious uses and associations of myrtle were inherited by the Greeks from the Middle East is suggested by the fact that *murtos*, the Greek for myrtle, derives from one of the Semitic languages. Myrtle, too, was certainly valued by the Assyrians.

In Cyprus wild myrtle is common. Cypriots spread myrtle on their church floors at Easter time. Perhaps the island cult of Aphrodite survives in another Cypriot practice—boiling up myrtle leaves into a scented, water-softening bath essence.

Rose Campion, Lotos and Water-Mint

Aphrodite has another flower we grow still in our own summer gardens, the charming Rose Campion (*Lychnis coronaria*), which is a wild native of Greece and south-eastern Europe.

The Greeks called it *luchnis stephanotike*, the lychnis or lamp flower used in wreaths, for putting round the head. The story which Athenaios told, or quoted, about this rose campion, with its soft leaves and its wide-eyed solitary carmine flowers, opening in May, is that it sprang up wherever Aphrodite bathed after making love with her lame, sooty husband, the smith-god Hephaistos; and it was reckoned, according to the same Greek source, that the best rose campion grew around various cult centres of

Aphrodite and Hephaistos—as you would expect, in Cyprus and Kythera, and Eryx in Sicily, where Aphrodite's great temple overlooked the Sicilian Channel; in the North Aegean island of Lemnos (Hephaistos fell on Lemnos when Zeus pitched him out of heaven), and on the volcanic Strongyle (Stromboli), in Hephaistos's Lipari Islands, off the south-west coast of Italy.

Aphrodite with a lotos flower is the Greek goddess blended with the Egyptian Isis, goddess of nature, goddess of the earth and the waters, whose worship spread through the Mediterranean after Egypt had fallen to Alexander the Great in 332 B.C., and after the foundation and rise of Alexandria.

Isis wore the lotos flower on her head as a symbol of life and birth—and rebirth. There were Egyptian myths that a bud of lotos had risen out of the waters, opened, and released the infant sun. Indeed one item of the treasure discovered in the Pharaoh Tutankhamun's tomb in 1922 was a stuccoed and painted wooden carving of an infant's head emerging from the sharp blue petals of a lotos flower—Tutankhamun newly born as the sun god.

It is this blue-petalled lotos, the Blue Egyptian Lotos, *Nymphaea caerulea*, of the same genus as the yellow and white water-lilies of an English river, which is usually painted in Egyptian tombs, and has been found in garlands laid on the bodies of the dead (Tutankhamun included). Its pale blue flowers are scented, sweetly if not strongly; and it is still one of the common plants of the Delta, in ponds and ditches. Egyptian girls in tomb paintings prettily wear a single blue lotos flower on their foreheads, attached to a fillet or head ribbon. The connection between lotos flowers and birth and sun and life seems more likely to have been suggested first of all by the other, less common Egyptian water-lily, *Nymphaea lotus*. Its flowers are white and larger than the Blue Lotos flowers. Their white petals surround a tuft of golden stamens, and certainly suggest, to us, a sun surrounded by rays of light. The outer petals tend to pink, and there is no reason why this *Nymphaea lotus* should not be the water-lily of the Nile which Herodotus likened to a rose.

The white lotos flower isn't perfumed; but whereas the flowers of the Blue Lotos stay open three days, the flowers of the White Lotos come out in the evening and stay open till about noon the next day, when the sun beats down. Then they sink back into the water. It is as if, in alternation of day and night, the flower of the sun came up, opened on the waters, and then sank again to recuperate.

To complete the symbolism of birth in the primordial waters of life, these two Egyptian water-lilies form their fruit (which the Egyptians used to eat) under the water.

One of the reasons why Isis and Aphrodite so easily merged into a single deity when Egypt became hellenized, is that both the Egyptian and the Greek goddess protected sailors. Both gave favourable wind and weather (the Pharos, the great beacon-tower or lighthouse, which the Greek king Ptolemy Philadelphos built at Alexandria in the third century B.C., was dedicated to this Isis-Aphrodite: she was Isis Pharea, Isis of the Lighthouse).

It is a line in Ovid's *Fasti* which most clearly connects Aphrodite with water-mint, or at least with the plant the Greeks called *sisombrion*, described by the Greek physician Dioskorides as like garden-mint, with broader leaves and a sweeter smell (he mentions that it was used in garlands).

In the *Fasti* for April—which is Aphrodite's month—Ovid tells the prostitutes of Rome that they must always remember to make their offerings to Venus on April 22nd (the feast of the Vinalia, when the new wine of the previous autumn's vintage was dedicated to Jupiter). She looks after their earnings, so they must give her incense, myrtle, chaplets of roses and rushes and her favourite *sisymbrium*, and pray that she will keep them pretty and popular and charming.

Water-mint (*Mentha aquatica*) grows all over Europe and in Western Asia. Tread on it in a marsh, and the pungency of its scent comes up and hangs in the air. I should call it one of the most haunting and refreshing of plant perfumes—very fit for the goddess.

According to Pliny, in his *Natural History*, people took water-mint from the mountains and set it in their gardens. And it is true that it does transplant well, away from marshy ground, as long as you give it a place which isn't altogether too dry.

The Quince and the Pomegranate

A fragment by the Sicilian Greek poet Ibykos, of the sixth century B.C., describes how love comes down on us like north wind and lightning. Ibykos begins with quinces and vines and channels of water in a garden:

> In spring water flows in from the
> Streams, and the quinces swell,
> And the grapes, under the vine's
> Shaded tendrils, in the Maiden's
> Unplundered garden.

54 Venus Genetrix. Graeco-Roman copy, a Greek original of c. 430–400 B.C. Musée du Louvre, Paris.

But for me love is alert
In all seasons.
Love is a north wind
On fire with flashes of lightning,
Sent by the Cyprian.
It brings a withering madness,
It is black, it is shameless,
Our hearts through and through
Are wrung by its violence.

A Greek familiar with the poem would at once have understood why Ibykos began with quinces. It is the power of scent again—the swelling fruits ripening into perfume. Yet the first links between quinces or quince trees and Aphrodite are quince buds and flowers. In early spring, the beginning of the special season of love, the five sepals of each quince flower bend back from a remarkably firm bud, which is pointed, and at first less pink than brown. The bud swells and stands erect, opening to its rose-like shape of tender pink, each petal lightly netted and veined.

Little can have seemed more delicious in gardens in Sicily or on Samos, where Ibykos wrote his poem, than a quince bush or quince tree suffused with the tint of the buds and the open flowers. The flowers, too, have their scent; not very strong, yet sweet and piercing if you smell them close enough—the scent of narcissi.

From their shape and the soft grey bloom which covers their firmness, young quinces were likened to the breasts of young girls (Leonidas of Tarentum, in the third century B.C., wrote a poem on the famous picture of Aphrodite Anadyomene by Apelles. Apelles sees her new born, still bubbling with the foam: she wrings out her hair, her eyes gleam calmly with love, and her breast 'announcing her prime, is a quince'). The quinces swell, then ripen and turn yellow and develop a perfume of exactly that sharp-scented quality of the aphrodisiac, a heavenly smell so pervasive that a few ripe quinces in a bowl will scent a room.

Everyone knew that quinces meant love, that Aphrodite in her bird-powered vehicle carried quinces as well as myrtle and roses, and that eating quinces (which needed cooking and sweetening with honey, since they were so hard and tart—bitter-sweet, like love), increased appetite in bed. According to Plutarch, in some precepts he addressed to two young friends of his who had just married, Solon the great law-giver of Athens in the sixth century B.C. (he was a poet as well) advised newly married girls to eat a quince before sharing a bed for the first time with their husbands—it would make for pleasure and harmony. Plutarch came back to this eating of quinces in his life of Solon, slightly altering the story and saying that

Solon instructed both the bridegroom and the bride to eat a quince together in their bedroom, on their first night.

Aphrodite's quinces, like Aphrodite's roses entered Greek life from the east. It is true the Greeks called them Kydonian Apples, on the assumption that they came from the old city of Kydonia in Crete. In fact the quince is not a native of the Mediterranean region, but of Central Asia—Transcaucasia, Iran and Turkestan.

The apple—the ordinary apple—is said to be Aphrodite's fruit. But since the same word served for apples and other apple-shaped fruit, it does seem reasonable to conclude that Aphrodite's apple needs the colour, the scent and the breast shape of the quince. Quinces and love: the association endured. Long after the time of Aphrodite or Venus an Andalusian-Arabic poem about the quince and love was written by Shafer ben Utman al-Mushafi, who died in 982 and was vizir to Al Hakam the Second of Cordova, a poem of this Mediterranean world, this quince world:

> It is yellow in colour, as if it wore a daffodil
> tunic, and it smells like musk, a penetrating smell.
>
> It has the perfume of a loved woman and the same
> hardness of heart, but it has the colour of the
> impassioned and scrawny lover.
>
> Its pallor is borrowed from my pallor; its smell
> is my sweetheart's breath.
>
> When it stood fragrant on the bough and the leaves
> had woven for it a covering of brocade,
>
> I gently put up my hand to pluck it and to set it
> like a censer in the middle of my room.
>
> It had a cloak of ash-coloured down hovering over
> its smooth golden body,
>
> and when it lay naked in my hand, with nothing more than
> its daffodil-coloured shift,
>
> it made me think of her I cannot mention, and I feared
> the ardour of my breath would shrivel it in my fingers.

Isn't that Aphrodite's apple?

A more mysterious fruit than the quince, the pomegranate has as a rule less to do with Aphrodite than with Hera, the great goddess of motherhood and marriage, and Demeter, the corn-goddess, the Great Bringer of Seasons, and her daughter Kore or Persephone. And in Asia Minor it belonged to the cult of Kybele, counterpart of Demeter as the Mother Goddess of all fertility. Yet a pomegranate tree—again according to Athenaios— is the one thing which Aphrodite was said to have planted in her island of Cyprus. The flowers, of such glorious scarlet, open in May, but what mattered symbolically was the fruit, enclosed by the enlarged calyx—a womb with an opening, a womb packed with seeds of translucent pink, rather like tinted pearls (our word pomegranate comes from the Latin *pomum granatum*, 'fruit with seeds'). The pomegranate, then, is the physical secrecy and portal of the feminine, whether for Aphrodite, or any related goddess of fertility and the sexual.

The pomegranate, which was Hera's symbol of marriage, was also one of Demeter's fruits of the earth. And pomegranates were to be found also in the subterranean kingdom of the dead, where Kore or Persephone lived after Hades had snatched her from the field of flowers. Before Kore was allowed back to earth and light so that plants and crops might continue, Hades (all this is told in the Homeric Hymn to Demeter) slyly compelled her to swallow just one pomegranate seed. Having eaten of the fruit which symbolized marriage, she was now tied to Hades indissolubly, and had to return to his arms in his kingdom of the dead for part—the winter part—of every year.

Perhaps there is some link with Aphrodite the planter of the pomegranate as well as with Demeter and Kore in the Easter ceremonies which are still carried out in Cyprus and in Greece every spring. Into the country churches they bring wide flat loaves of bread and trays of wheat patterned over with pomegranate seeds. These are all laid in front of the ikonostasis, the screen holding up the icons of the saints. Candles are passed around, and there comes a moment when the candles are all alight, everyone holding them by the handful. The candles twinkle, their light glitters on the gold leaf of the ikonostasis, the priest shakes his censer and the perfumed smoke hangs over these symbols of food and life, of reproduction and growth, of the seasons of spring renewal and winter rest.

Aphrodite's Birds—and Goats

The eagle for Zeus, the peacock for Hera (spreading its tail of stars for the Queen of Heaven), the Little Owl for Athene, the duck for Poseidon, the

55 Aphrodite on a Swan. Attic lekythos. Ashmolean Museum, Oxford.

dove for Aphrodite—and for Apollo the raven and the hawk, to carry his messages, but above all the swan.

Why then is Aphrodite often represented, on vases, on bronze mirrors, etcetera (Plate 55), riding side-saddle, so to speak, on a swan—a swan flying through the air?

Swans served Apollo, god of inspiration, prophecy, poetry, music and the dance, as his special birds of song. Seven swans flew over Delos, singing to the rhythm of their wings, when Leto lay on the island and gave birth to Apollo. Swans are serene birds of rivers and lakes, they lived so contentedly as servants of Apollo, that when they knew they were going to die, they sang with great sweetness, but with a touch of sadness, according to knowing mortals who happened to hear them. Aristotle reported that this sweet sad music was once heard from a flock of swans over the Libyan Sea. They were singing in chorus, then when the song was over, some of them were seen to die (the swans which visit Greece are Mute Swans: the wings of this species, *Cygnus olor*, do make a marked and peculiar singing noise, audible as the birds pass overhead).

Swans also served Apollo by drawing his carriage through the sky. The poet Alkaios, who lived on Lesbos at the same time as Sappho in the sixth century B.C., wrote about his swan-carriage in an ode to Apollo. From the remaining stanzas it can be supposed that Apollo did not stay the whole year at Delphi. He would be drawn away by his swans to the land of the Hyperboreans, and he would stay with these more or less legendary people, these favourite worshippers of his, for the winter months, then in spring, in early summer, his swans would bring him home again to Delphi:

> It was summer and the middle of summer
> When you came back from the Hyperboreans,
> And nightingales sang and swallows sang
>   And cicadas chirped and announced your
>
> Arrival to man, and in silver Kastalia
> Ran down and great Kephissos let us know
> A god was no longer absent from home and
> Deepened and darkened his flow.

Aphrodite in her swan pictures, has borrowed one of Apollo's birds: she too has brought spring and summer back with the south-west winds, and she rides on the soft air to meet Apollo at Delphi. It is the rapprochement of love, song, and dancing, of Aphrodite, the Seasons, the Graces, the Muses and Apollo. Latin poets wrote of Aphrodite's carriage being drawn by swans or cygnets instead of sparrows. But that was a late idea, and not a Greek one. For the Greeks Aphrodite on Apollo's white swan is the return of the time for love.

Swans migrate. The peculiar thing is that in fact they breed up by the Black Sea, north of Greece and come down to Greece for the winter—the wrong way round according to the legend of Apollo, Delphi and the swans, if migration has anything to do with it. But it would have been the right way round, if Apollo's ancient home had been in the north—it is often argued that he was a god brought from the north into Greece—and if legend first of all had thought of the god and his swans going south for the winter, and then coming north again in spring or summer to some 'Hyperborean' centre of his worship, some original centre 'beyond the North Wind', which is the meaning of Hyperborean. But that is another matter, and nothing to do with Aphrodite riding Apollo's swan.

Is there much to be said of sparrows, vulgar house-sparrows, as birds of Aphrodite? For the best part of a millennium literate Greeks would have known that Aphrodite's carriage was drawn by sparrows, not swans. In Sappho's *Prayer to Aphrodite* (p. 105) Aphrodite was drawn from the golden house of Zeus, through heaven and through middle air, to the region of our black Earth, by beautiful fast-flying sparrows. And Sappho's readers knew why. They knew sparrows were lewd and lustful little birds. To set Cole Porter and Sappho together, they knew sparrows are always doing it, on paths, pavements, roofs, on the heads and shoulders of statues, without caring a straw about spectators; and 'doing it', after all, is Aphrodite, in high poetry or low comedy. The Greeks believed that eating sparrows, or sparrow's eggs, increased the appetite for love. One late Greek account of Egyptian symbolism, Horapollo's *Hieroglyphics*, perhaps of the fourth century A.D., explained why a sparrow on fire symbolized a man who fathered many children—'When the sparrow is troubled beyond measure by lust and an excess of sperm, it mates with the female seven times in an an hour, ejecting its sperm all at once.'

Partridges and geese—they as well were birds of Aphrodite, acceptable in sacrifice from those who wanted favours in love, and for the same reason. Partridges were reputed to tread their females on every possible occasion. Aelian calls them 'very lustful and adulterous', sneaking round after each other's females all the time. And he says that the females hid their eggs, because the cock birds destroyed them whenever they could, knowing that once the chicks were allowed to hatch, their wives would have no time for them: they weren't going to lose their fun. These insatiable birds were also accused of homosexuality: cock birds who lost their mates promptly abused each other; which wouldn't have worried Aphrodite, goddess also

56 Aphrodite riding on a goose, by the Pistoxenos Painter. Attic cup, c. *470 B.C. British Museum, London.*

of love between men; and between women, as in the poems, or fragments of poems, by Sappho.

Geese were reckoned—again according to Aelian—to be 'very hot and fiery in nature', which compelled them to paddle round in the damp and eat grass and other moist, cooling plants. So they also took pleasure in water, as Aphrodite took pleasure in the sea. There are terracottas of Aphrodite on a goose, as well as vase paintings of her conveyed through the air on goose-back. (Geese also belonged to Isis, who was compounded with Aphrodite.)

Perhaps it is relevant, too, that geese, clumsy, noisy, hissing, aggressive, can be very affectionate to each other, and to their owners as well. Anyone who has reared geese from the egg will agree to that.

And goats. Aphrodite was worshipped in one temple and another under a goat name, Aphrodite Epitragia, Aphrodite on the Billy-goat. An Aphrodite riding on a goat was carved by Skopas, master sculptor of the Classical Period, for her temple at Elis, on the western side of the Peloponnese.

Goats are proverbially lecherous. They smell of sex, so men have always thought. Aelian mentions goats in one sentence with baboons; he says they were supposed to couple even with women. Billy-goat scent, the scent of roses, the scent of quinces or of myrtle—Aphrodite's nature was to like them all. But then again kids are charming (so are goslings), and the large billy-goats they turn into, will behave in a very gentle, loving way with their owners, if they are treated properly. Sex and tenderness, lechery and tenderness—that was a combination approved by this Queen of Heaven.

Goats of course were sacrificed to Aphrodite. They no more escaped that, as we have seen, than her doves, her geese and her partridges. It was their privilege. Tacitus says that in her Paphian temple on Cyprus they put the greatest trust in the entrails of kids—i.e., when the creatures were offered to the goddess, and then opened up for clues to the future.

The Wryneck

Another bird linked with Aphrodite was the wryneck. Among her gifts to mankind was the use of this brown-barred, brown-mottled little bird like a small woodpecker, to excite love.

A wryneck was caught and fastened by its spread out wings and feet to a small coloured wheel with four spokes. The wheel and the wryneck were revolved, to an incantation, and an image of the person desired was thrown into a fire, along with other things to do with him. Irresistibly his love was roused and he was drawn to the wryneck-spinner.

Pindar says in one of his odes that Aphrodite brought the wryneck on a wheel down from Olympos and gave it first of all to Jason, so that he could compel Medea's love. Medea would then help him, in spite of her scruples, and in spite of her parents, to get his hands on the Golden Fleece, and would go back to Thessaly with him as his wife. The 'maddening bird', Pindar called the wryneck.

This magical and maddening wryneck-wheel twirls in the famous poem by Theokritos, in which Simaitha tries to regain her golden-bearded athletic lover Delphis, who has had her virginity and then deserted her for some boy or some other girl. She throws the necessary things on to the fire, which burns in the moonlight on the altar of a roadside shrine of Hekate, the witch-goddess of the Underworld (they include an image of Delphis and a piece of his cloak), and as the wheel spins she repeats

> Draw this man to my house, wryneck.

Theokritos calls this contrivance 'the bronze wheel of Aphrodite'. By his time a magic wheel served by itself, a 'wryneck' or wryneck-wheel without a wryneck, a bird-wheel without the bird—just as well, because how do you catch a wryneck, when it is required? Especially in Greece where wrynecks are about only in the winter?

A short poem by one of the unknown writers of *The Greek Anthology* also describes a 'wryneck' which an *hetaira* named Niko brings to Aphrodite as an offering:

> Niko's wryneck, which can draw a man
> To cross the sea, and boys from bedrooms,
> Set in gold, cut from translucid amethyst,
> Is here laid by you, Cyprian, a cherished
> Thing, hung by the middle on a purple
> Length of soft lamb's wool, given to you
> Gratefully by the Larissaian witch.

The earlier employment of Aphrodite's wryneck—a real wryneck—in this strange love magic perhaps has to do with the striking way a wryneck, if it is picked up or surprised in its nesting hole, twists its head and neck, 'wry' in the sense of distorted. The Greeks explained the wryneck's love role by the legend that Iynx (which was the Greek word for wryneck) was a nymph, daughter of Pan and Echo, or Pan and Peitho, 'Persuasion', one of Aphrodite's attendants, who tried her magic on Zeus and so made him fall in love with Io, priestess of Hera, the consort of Zeus, in her temple at Argos. For this Hera punished Iynx by changing her into the wryneck.

Loving and Dying

The Evening Star

Ishtar appeared in the Assyrian and Babylonian sky in the shape of the Evening Star (and the Morning Star). The emblem of that great ancestral goddess of love, war and fertility was, in fact, a star with eight points. The Greeks had no astral deities. Aphrodite descended to them from Astarte, and Astarte descended from Ishtar, but the Greeks did not look up and exclaim, 'There's Aphrodite!', when the Evening Star glowed over their houses and temples after sunset. For them the planet belonged to Aphrodite rather in the sense of belonging to love, or being suggestive of love, both thrillingly and agonizingly; which was not the same thing. They called it both the *hesperis aster*, the 'star of the evening', of the time for love, and the *phosphoros aster*, the 'star which brings light', or the *heosphoros aster*, the 'star which brings the dawning', whose appearance before sunrise warned lovers to go.

The Syrian-Greek love poet Meleager (*c.* 140–*c.* 70 B.C.) wrote a two-line poem on this astral union and parting of lovers:

> Goodbye, Dawn-teller, Light-bearer. Bring back to me quickly,
> In secret, Star of the Evening, the girl you are stealing.

It wasn't the Queen of Heaven he invoked, but a star which belonged to her. And it was so with other Greek poets, for instance Meleager's contemporary Bion (who is supposed to have written *The Lament for Adonis*):

> Hesperos, gold light of the Lovely One born from the Foam,
> Kind Hesperos, glory and blessedness of the blue night,
> Less bright than the Moon by as much as you're
> Brightest of stars, good evening, kind star. As I go
> To my shepherd, give me your light, for new
> Is the Moon and it goes down too early

Tonight. I am not a thief in the dark.
I shall not molest those around in the night.
I am in love. And helping a lover is right.

When the Greeks and the Romans came eventually to think that the planet
afloat in the tinted sky of evening or morning was also the goddess, and not
just her property, her sign, and when the Romans called the planet Venus,
it was a kind of re-identification, due to late contact with the religion of a
Babylonia which had become a Greek kingdom after the conquests of
Alexander; and Venus this star, this planet, has remained ever since.
However, myth having its agreeable inconsistencies and conveniences, the
Romans also followed the Greeks in distinguishing the two epiphanies of
this planet of love, Vesper and Lucifer, Evening Star and Morning Star,
allowing them as well their two separate mythic identities.

For ourselves I think it is the appearance or the reappearance of the
Evening Star which most directly recalls the goddess of love, although
powerful artificial light so often drives the first intimations of darkness out
of our heavens. Coleridge is one English poet who felt himself especially
affined to the Evening Star, ever since he watched it as a boy, from the lead
roofs of Christ's Hospital, his school; and in English there is more than one
fine poem to Venus as at once star and goddess, for instance, that invocation
by the monk John Lydgate which I quoted in the first chapter, or the
invocation by the Elizabethan poet and dramatist John Fletcher, which
expresses that doubleness of feeling, provoked in us when we suddenly
become aware of the Evening Star, that it is both the hunger and the food,
the desire and the satisfaction:

> O Divine Star of Heaven,
> Thou in power above the seven:
> Thou sweet kindler of desires
> Till they grow to mutual fires:
> Thou, O gentle Queen that art
> Curer of each wounded heart:
> Thou the fuel, and the flame;
> Thou in Heaven and here the same:
> Thou the wooer, and the woo'd:
> Thou the hunger, and the food:
> Thou the prayer, and the pray'd:
> Thou what is, or shall be said:
> Thou still young, and golden tressed,
> Make me by thy answer blessed.

Then in high Victorian times a passionate, egoistic, imperious, yet cautious poet, Coventry Patmore, could suddenly expose the passion underlying his respectable novel in verse about courtship, and marriage in four lines of force and colour:

> I drew the silk: in heaven the night
>   Was dawning; lovely Venus shone,
> In languishment of tearful light,
>   Swathed by the red breath of the sun.

Aphrodite and the Underworld

A goddess of life may also be expected to have something to do with death and the Underworld: life is responsible for death, life goes to death, and the dead to the Underworld, out of which life climbs again in resurrection. So the wheel revolves, and goes on revolving.

Aphrodite's eastern progenitors were concerned with the resurrection, the rebirth, of the plants; so was Aphrodite, in her relationship with the ill-fated Adonis, whose infancy and childhood she had shared with Persephone or Kore, Queen of the Underworld (page 56). Aphrodite, too, had her truck with Hermes, that very Greek god, that originally Arkadian god, of the fertility of beast and man; who also guided the souls of the dead, and took messages from Olympos to Hades in his dark kingdom.

Here and there Aphrodite does seem to have been worshipped under titles linked with death or rather mysteriously connected with a condition so antithetical—at first thought—to love. At Delphi we know there was worship, at least in the first and second centuries A.D., of an Aphrodite Epitymbia, an Aphrodite on the Grave. By her statue the dead were called up, eager for the libations poured into the ground. Elsewhere, in Argos and Lakonike, she was known—again in late times—as Aphrodite the Grave Robber, Aphrodite Tymborochos, perhaps because of the same practice, as if she had power to bring back the dead.

Then there is evidence of an Aphrodite Skotia, Aphrodite of Darkness, in Egypt and Crete; and an Aphrodite Melainis, Black Aphrodite, at Mantinea in Arkadia, at Corinth, city of foreign travellers and foreign merchants and foreign influences, and at Thespiai. On the outskirts of Corinth this Black Aphrodite's temple was in a small wood or plantation of cypress, the tree of death and mourning, sacred to Hades, alongside the grave of the elder Lais (page 113), that very beautiful *hetaira* who was so hard and sharp that men nicknamed her the Axe.

They are exceptional, these special Aphrodites. We know little about

57 Terracotta figurine of Aphrodite from Amisos (Samsun), on the Black Sea. Hellenistic, 2nd century B.C. Musée du Louvre, Paris.

58 Aphrodite risen from the sea, the 'Vénus du Mas'. Marble. Hellenistic, 2nd century B.C. Musée d'Agen, Lot-et-Garonne. Photo by Bernard Henras.

them. Aphrodite on the Grave, Aphrodite the Grave Robber—it isn't difficult to accept that the exquisite goddess, ever young, who excited desire and aided the yearly impregnation of the earth, could be called upon to defeat death, to which she gave rise by ensuring birth.

Black Aphrodite? In the museum at Limassol, in Cyprus, they have a small black figure of an Aphrodite paired with a similar white Aphrodite—two votive offerings perhaps from Aphrodite's long disappeared temple at Amathos, two miles away. The robe swathing the Black Aphrodite is embroidered with shapes which are either stars or roses—rosettes. She could be the Aphrodite of the night, the time of love, not death; Aphrodite of the Heaven, and of the Evening Star, from the Syrian coasts.

More likely—and perhaps the true explanation of Aphrodite Melainis, Black Aphrodite, elsewhere—she is an Egyptianized Aphrodite or a hellenized, or Cypriotized, Isis—goddess of love who absorbs into herself Egypt's great goddess of love, and the fruits of the earth, and the Underworld, and the death and the resurrection of her husband and brother Osiris. Egyptian influences were strong at Amathos.

The fascinating trouble about Aphrodite—as about all gods—is that she inherits, develops, absorbs; one Aphrodite, yet many Aphrodites, according to place and time.

13

Aphrodite into Venus

Venus, Venerem, Venia

How is it that Aphrodite of the Greeks has descended to us under the Roman name of another goddess? How did she become Venus?

Botticelli painted a *Birth of Venus*, not of Aphrodite. It is Venus, not Aphrodite, we link at once with a recollection or a mention of Adonis, Venus and Adonis, as in Shakespeare's poem—

> Full gently now she takes him by the hand
> A lily prisoned in a jail of snow.

And when the Louvre acquired its Aphrodite from Melos, the statue was at once, and has remained ever since, a Vénus de Milo. How has this Roman Venus—at least until the fairly recent recovery of the Greek world—overlaid Aphrodite?

Perhaps another question, or several other questions, should come first. Were the two divinities the same, more or less, at all times? Did the Romans, in Italy, accept this goddess of Greece, via their Greek neighbours to the south of Latium, their first territory, or via their Etruscan neighbours to the north, and then give her richer personality to a vaguer, less mythically endowed goddess of their own?

It was only a few miles from Rome, across the Tiber, to the nearest Etruscan cities, whose own strong culture, of still mysterious origin, absorbed so much from the culture of the Greeks. It wasn't so far from Latium, in the other direction, south-east, to some of the most ancient of the Hellenic colonies, down the leg of Italy, in Campania—to Kyme or Cumae, founded as early as 757 B.C., and then to Pythecusa (Ischia) and Neapolis (Naples) and Poseidonia (Paestum). For centuries Greek culture had seeped or poured into Campania, and Latium, as well as into Etruria. Rome would overcome these Greek cities of Campania, and the Greek cities of South Italy, and Sicily, and would be master of homeland Greece

as well by 146 B.C., herself, in the long process, overcome by the superior culture of the defeated.

So it came about that the sparer, and, as we look back to them, obscurer deities of Rome, closer fitted to practical requirements, doubled the deities of Greece, in approximate identification, Saturn and Kronos, Jupiter and Zeus, Juno and Hera, Ceres and Demeter, Proserpina and Kore, Minerva and Athene, Mars and Ares, Vulcan and Hephaistos, Venus and Aphrodite. The Roman counterparts to the Greek pantheon assumed the elaborate myths which filled out the personality of the man-figured gods and goddesses of Greece. Statues by the great sculptors and lesser sculptors were taken from the Greek cities to Rome, from Greek temples to Roman temples, once Rome was master, and worshipped there under the counterpart names. Rome spread its own power, its government, its language, its literature and architecture, and its Romano-Greek gods, to the west and the north and north-west. It was in its Roman forms that Europe received and later recovered a knowledge of antiquity; it was through Rome—

Time on horseback, under a Roman arch

—that Greece was at first, and then for a long time after, indistinctly appre-hended. Italy and Rome were close at hand. Rome was the centre of western Christendom. Byzantium, centre of Greek christianity, was far away to the east. The remains of Hellenic civilization in the homeland, in the islands, on the littoral of Asia Minor or of North Africa, were not only distant, but as time passed not so easily accessible in Turkish or Arab hands.

The aboriginal identity of Venus—the Venus of Rome or Latium—has been a mystery. The name Venus has been a mystery: a word of neuter form which was feminine, or the name of a goddess which was perversely neuter. There is no very sure sign of the early existence of Venus, no very sure evidence to suggest a divinity it was as natural or as simple to identify with Aphrodite as it was to identify Ceres with Demeter, or Ares with Mars. The Etruscans linked their goddess Turan with Aphrodite, but where did a Venus of the Latins come in? Was she a nature goddess? A goddess of the fertility and beauty of gardens? She came to be connected with gardens and spring, but that has been shown, with fair certainty, to be only a consequence of her later identification with the Aphrodite who was familiar from her worship and her temples in the Greek colonies, the Greek city-states in Italy.

59 Venus. Bronze statuette from Verulamium. 2nd century A.D. Verulamium Museum, St Albans, Hertfordshire.

The clue to Venus was found in her name. By itself that neuter word *venus* signified the force in spells, incantations, charms, prayers, which secured the attention and favours of a god. It is taken to go back to a base *wen-*, in the language ancestral to our Indoeuropean family of languages, which include Sanskrit, Greek, Latin, and no less German and English, a base meaning to win (the English verb has the same descent), to want, to strive for. And *venus*, with that meaning, had its other associates in Latin.

One was *venia*, signifying the grace or favour of the gods. Another was the verb *venerari* or *advenerari*, to obtain this grace divine by worship and the magic elements of worship. Yet another associated word was *venenum* (ancestor of our venom, and venomous), meaning not necessarily, or primarily, poison, but a magic philtre, a drug, a charm, a means by which this grace divine could be obtained.

This *venus* for practical, useful ends, this force of achieving a desire, neuter or no, became personified as a goddess, one who granted favours and fulfilled desires. And this goddess *Venus*, with her feminine accusative *Venerem*, worshipped at Lavinium, south of Rome, on the Via Appia, in a temple common to all the peoples of Latium, was soon associated or equated with the favour-granting Aphrodite, who answers our most intimate obsessive desires, who was the mother of Aeneas, by tradition ancestor of the Romans, and founder of Lavinium, in honour of his Latin wife Lavinia.

Rome itself first had a temple of Venus—*Venus Obsequens*, Venus who gratifies—in 295 B.C., but that may have been 150 or 200 years after Venus began to be worshipped in Lavinium. Half a century later, in 241 B.C., at the end of the First Punic War, the first great war against the Phoenicians of Carthage, the Romans took control of Sicily and captured Mount Eryx and its citadel and its famous Aphrodite or Astarte temple.

Here was a new Venus for the Romans—Venus of Eryx, Venus Erycina. Twenty-six years later the Romans gave themselves a temple of Venus Erycina, on the Capitol, the low hill above the Tiber which rose up to the grand temple of Jupiter and to the Citadel—a temple to the Sicilian goddess, though in Rome she lacked those prostitutes who gave such entertainment to high-placed officials and other visitors who went from Rome to Eryx. Venus of Eryx acquired another temple on the north of the city by the Colline Gate, and it was near this second temple, dedicated in 181 B.C., that the Ludovisi Throne (Plate 7) was discovered, as if that Greek treasure of the fifth century had been acquired to honour this Venus of love in a new home. The colossal head of an archaic Greek Aphrodite (Plate 11) may also have belonged to this temple.

60 Venus at the bath. Romano-British relief from the Roman station at High Rochester, Northumberland. 3rd century A.D. Museum of Antiquities of the University and the Society of Antiquaries, Newcastle-upon-Tyne.

Aphrodite, Mother of Aeneas

It was the parental relationship of Aphrodite to Aeneas that exalted Venus in the company of the Roman gods, all the more so when Virgil, in his *Aeneid*, towards the end of the first century B.C., had brought his hero to Eryx, and then to Cumae (where he consulted the Cumaean Sibyl and descended with his passport of a Golden Bough into the dark underworld, to meet with his father Anchises once more and hear Anchises tell of the future and of his Roman progeny), and then on again to Latium and to the site where Rome would be built, and where Augustus, descendant of Anchises and Venus, Augustus the first Emperor, and Virgil's patron, would renew Latium's golden age:

> Hic vir, hic est, tibi quem promitti saepius audis,
> Augustus Caesar, Divi genus, aurea condet
> Saecula qui rursus Latio, regnata per arva
> Saturno quondam—

Look, Anchises had told Aeneas, bringing the men of the future before his eyes,

> Look, here is that man whose coming has been foretold
> To you so often, Augustus Caesar, child of the gods
> Who will bring back her golden centuries to Latium
> Through all the land where Saturn used to reign.

Imperial propaganda; for which, after all, Venus from Eryx of the sacral prostitutes wasn't exactly appropriate. The official Venus of Imperial Rome remained, in fact, the more respectable Venus Genetrix, Venus the Mother, Mother of Rome, divine ancestor of the imperial line—Venus somewhat staidly figured in the mode of that still clothed fifth century Greek statue by Alkamenes (Plate 54).

For most Romans, in everyday life, Venus became and continued to be the Greek epiphany from the waters, the goddess of desire and the acts of love, whatever else might be added to her—the young naked goddess. So it was all through the Roman Empire, in the new countries, the new provinces of the west and the north, as well as in the Greek or hellenized provinces in the south and the east. Round Cologne—Colonia Agrippinensis, the capital of Germania Inferior—they made little clay

61 Venus risen from the sea. Gaulish bronze figurine from Neuvy-en-Sollias, Loiret. c. 230–240 A.D. Musée historique, Orléans. Photo by Serge Martin.

62 and 63 Venus, on the Virgil mosaic from Roman villa, Low Ham, Somerset. Venus, wearing her kestos, *between Aeneas and Dido; and Venus between two Cupids. 4th century A.D. Somerset County Museum, Taunton.*

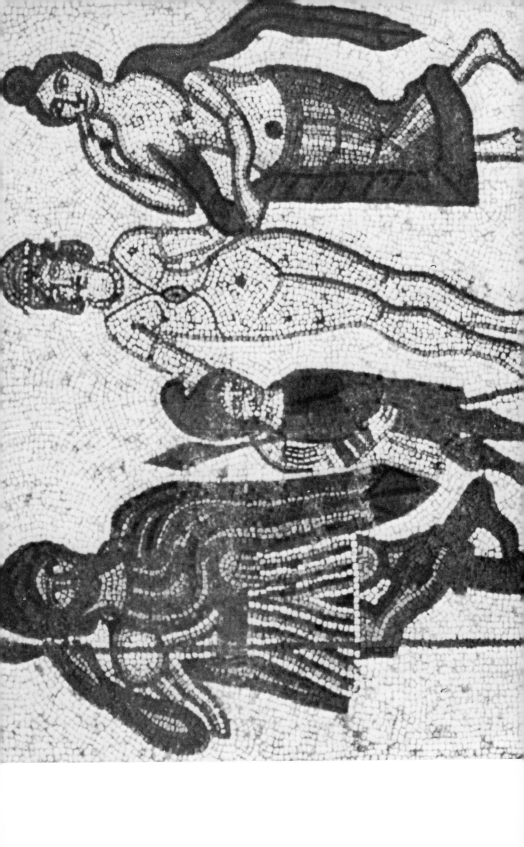

Venuses of one Hellenistic kind, left hand holding their falling clothes up at the waist, right hand to their hair. In the centre of Gaul, the centre more or less of modern France, in today's department of Alliers, the land of Vichy, Moulin and Bourges, which continues to be potter's country, the potters made little pipeclay Venuses of another Hellenistic kind, altogether naked, right hand to their hair, left hand to a shape which was once the water-jug or pitcher of Aphrodite at her bath, upholding her towel. These descend from the Aphrodite of Knidos carved by Praxiteles and from Apelles' picture of Aphrodite rising out of the sea.

They were traded to Britain, these little mass-produced Venuses of mid-Gaul. They have been found in York, in London, and especially in the south-east. They have even been found out in the Atlantic, at a Romano-British shrine in the Isles of Scilly. They have lost their colour, they don't look much in a case in some French or English museum. But think of their remotest ancestry, back beyond Greece, beyond Phoenicia, to the city-states and the divine observances of Sumer; and then again think of their descent from the sophisticated skills of Praxiteles and Apelles.

Archaeologists have claimed that these figurines up here in the north had most to do with health, and fertility, and life after death; that they were ex voto images of a Celtic goddess for whom the potters borrowed the shape of Venus or Aphrodite. But though they have been recovered, most of them, from graves and temple sites and from places where there was a spring and no doubt a shrine, surely they were still, to some degree, the goddess of love, in transit, so far from Paphos and Kythera, on the fringe of world? Surely they were touching the rough people of the Gallic and British tribal towns with something of an already ancient grace? Finding such Venuses, French peasants have taken them to be images of the Virgin Mary.

Mosaics of Venus

Naturally, in Britannia, as elsewhere round the edges of the empire, the native upper crust knew more of the myths and felicity of this goddess of desire who was also the ancestress of that Rome they adhered to. In Britannia, as elsewhere, wandering mosaicists from overseas were at work, ornamenting their *villa* mansions.

Such an itinerant Greek, a little rough in his formal skill, no doubt reached Somerset in the fourth century A.D.—as late as that—and made the floor for the Low Ham mansion (Plates 62 and 63), which illustrated Virgil's story of Dido and Aeneas. In two of his panels he fitted his red and green and ochre and grey *tesserae* into Venuses as naked as could be required. In one of the panels Venus lifts off her garment to reveal her nakedness, in the other she stands naked between Dido and Aeneas, the magic *kestos* hanging round her neck and between her breasts, much as she wears it in one painting from her city of Pompeii (in 80 B.C., when Pompeii was designated a Roman colony, it was placed under the official patronage of Venus—*Colonia Veneria Cornelia*), in which she leans naked against Mars.

On the floor of the Somerset *frigidarium*, the cold-dip room of the house, she was, if a reminder of the Trojan ancestor of Rome and the goddess who gave him birth, a reminder no less of the naked giver of joy whom they knew so well in Greece, Egypt, North Africa, and Asia Minor, and everywhere else in the hellenized portions of the Empire. (The boy in the panel with Dido and Aeneas, flanking the naked goddess, is Cupid in disguise: by his mother's plan he had taken the shape of Ascanius, son of Aeneas, the better to rouse love for Aeneas in an unsuspecting, and soon unhappy Dido.)

Venus, giver of joy, shows on other pavements in Britannia. One Venus, and a more seemly one (again of the fourth century A.D.) is to be seen in the Roman villa at Bignor in Sussex, head and shoulders only, accompanied with leaves and pheasants and *cornucopiae*, a goddess of abundant life, but also a goddess, or the goddess, of love, since she is surrounded by a frieze of cupids, small, warlike, and dangerous, playing at gladiators.

Love in Britain, Roman Britain, before the dark ages of Anglo-Saxony.

I prefer, no beauty as she is, the unseemly Venus from Rudston, in the Yorkshire Wolds, in the backward, not much Romanized territory of the Parisi, whom they have now taken away from under her tin shed (she was discovered only in 1933) and placed in a museum at Hull. Classical archaeologists are rude to her. Perhaps no more bizarre Venus has survived from antiquity. But there she is, in her museum, cavorting or seeming to; with one hand she holds her apple or quince, with the other she is about to pick up her mirror. She is naked, but for a bracelet on either arm. She is big-bellied. She has a red pubic triangle, and a white navel, and her eyes are outlined in red. A Triton with his fish-spear indicates that she is also a goddess of the sea, which flowed around Flamborough Head, only a few miles from Rudston. Huntsmen surround her, then wild creatures, leopard, deer, lion, and bull, surround the huntsmen, recalling, in the Homeric Hymn to Aphrodite, the wild creatures which followed her on Mount Ida and fawned on her, and coupled in the shadows, under her influence, as she passed in search of Anchises, the handsome father of Aineias or Aeneas.

Wilder love in semi-barbarian Yorkshire, in a vision surely by some native

64 and 65 The Rudston Venus. Mosaic from Roman villa, Rudston, Yorkshire. 4th century A.D. Kingston-upon-Hull Museum, Yorkshire. Photo 64 by Edwin Smith.

mosaicist, some British assistant or apprentice or slave, who had once carried the bags of *tesserae* around for his Greek employer or master?

Another Venus of the Sea in mosaic (now in the British Museum) comes from a villa at Witchampton in Dorset—Venus among scallops and fish and dolphins.

14

Aphrodite Afterwards

The Clerks of Love

In Constantine the Great's attack on the old religion, priests were ordered to bring their gods out of the darkness of the temples into the sunlight. People laughed and jeered, and Constantine's men stripped the statues of their ornaments 'and exhibited to the gaze of all the unsightly reality which had been hidden under a painted exterior'.

The unsightly reality was that of the statues we see and treasure in museums, mutilated torsos of bare marble. Some statues were roped and pulled down and dragged out. Imagine it, a delicate Aphrodite jogged and banged along the temple paving, losing arms, head, feet, dolphin, or water-jug, and all, leaving only a body to be thrown into the sea or into the foundations of a new building—a Christian basilica perhaps—or into a limekiln. Aphrodite into mortar.

Bronze statues of the finest workmanship—all this according to Eusebios*—were brought into Constantinople and set up in public places, to be ridiculed by the once 'deluded victims of superstition' who had honoured them with burnt offerings.

The destruction was not so complete as Eusebios seems to say, in scorn and virtue. Constantine, first Christian emperor, was tolerant; the two religions went on existing alongside each other, and even some two centuries later it was possible to see, in a gymnasium in the capital city of the East, a display of bronze statues of deities—and heroes. Among them were Poseidon, Apollo, Artemis, Hermes, and no fewer than three Aphrodites; all these statues were described in hexameters by the Byzantine-Egyptian poet Christodoros, who died in 518.

The fact is that Aphrodite—or at least Venus, since her pretty Greek name never triumphed in the western world, even when Greek studies were revived by refugee scholars from Byzantium—stood for something

***Life of Constantine*, tr. E. C. Richardson, 1885.

too important in our nature to disappear. Her worship vanished, of course (though there are stories of Venus transformed in France into a Christian saint. There is even a story that the member of her son Priapos was preserved as a relic in a chapel in the Hautes-Alpes, where it was libated by women, and where wax ex-votoes of male and female parts clattered against each other when the wind blew in through the chapel door). What remained were scintillae of her brightness. If to the Christian Fathers she had been a demon, and the 'overseer of intercourse', and the most shameful of the company of Olympian demons, she had still to continue swimming into the medieval sky as the Star of Love, she had still to be invoked as something more than a figure of speech by the poets of Europe. If the church had found naked Venus useful to teach morality, to represent Luxuria, the indulgent life of lust against chastity, to take the part, as in one of the huge Apocalypse tapestries at Angers, of the 'great whore' of *The Revelation of St John the Divine*, 'Mystery, Babylon the Great, the Mother of Harlots and Abominations of the Earth'; if Venus slipped into becoming the beautiful mermaid, mirror in hand, mortal danger to ships and sailors, a moralized embodiment of the wiles of the devil, in a thousand wall-paintings of St Christopher carrying Christ, never at any time was her Roman disciple Ovid overlooked entirely or forgotten. Ovid's poems were read through the Middle Ages. Chaucer, in his *House of Fame*, mentions how 'Venus clerk, Ovyde'

> hath y-sowen wonder wyde
> The grete god of Loves name.

Chaucer called himself, too, one of the clerks of Venus, one of her learned scholars, and in his retelling of the love-story of Troilus and Cressida (a medieval tale, from the twelfth century *Roman de Troie*, by Benoit de Sainte-Maure), Chaucer invoked her as both Evening Star and divine being, the very cause of health and gladness:

> In hevene and helle, in erthe and salte see
> Is fele thy might, if that I wel descerne;
> As man, brid, best, fish, herbe and grene tree
> Thee fele in tymes with vapour eterne.

He affirmed of Venus that

> in this world no lyves creature,
> With-outen love, is worth, or may endure,

and said to her

> And this knowe I by hem that loveres be,
> That who-so stryveth with yow hath the werse;
> Now, lady bright, for thy benignitee,
> At reverence of hem that serven thee,
> Whos clerk I am, so techeth me devyse
> Som joye of that is felt in thy servyse.

In the fifteenth and sixteenth centuries, the time of Botticelli and the poems of Poliziano and Lorenzo dei Medici in Florence, then of du Bellay and Ronsard in France, and Spenser and Shakespeare in England, increased delight in the divine arts and mythology of the ancients, and increase of knowledge of them changed the nakedness of Venus. Her at times starved pallid nakedness as the trap of lust became once more the acceptable, graceful and sufficiently ample nakedness of pleasure and beauty; accompanied—but that is not surprising in a Christian world—with speculative elaboration, with philosophical, spiritual, allegorizing justification. So it was to continue—if we think of all nudes in art as an extension of the Aphrodite subject—with equivocations, misgivings, hypocrisies and backslidings, and recoveries which in the end have advanced us towards frankness and a resumed wholesomeness.

With whatever subtleties Botticelli may have been programmed, willingly, by the young-minded Neo-platonists in fifteenth century Florence (especially by Poliziano, poet of the months of spring, humanist, Professor of Greek and Latin—of antique rediscovery—in the university of Florence), he still presented in his *Birth of Venus* a living body, a counterpart, improved, of the divine-featured girl whom Poliziano recreated, out of Hesiod and the second, fragmentary Homeric Hymn to Aphrodite, in the sensuous life of stanzas in which Aphrodite renews her birth, in a scene of action, colour, sparkle, flowers and music:

> And born of acts of loveliness and joy
> A girl with more than human face,
> Upon a shell, was pressed, gently, by zephyrs
> To the shore; which made the sea rejoice.

Intellectual 'angelical' love, human love and sensual love—these are all of them present in the living nakedness of Botticelli's divine girl, pushed to

66 Venus of Urbino by Titian (1488/90–1576). Uffizi, Florence.

land by Zephyr wound in the arms of Flora; and they are 'real' roses of spring which fall between Zephyr and herself. An object is necessarily and marvellously enfolded in its idea, an intricate idea enfolds the simple object which caused it and symbolized it. Yet for centuries we have been content with what is obvious in the picture; for centuries, as the captives of love, we have felt in it the earthly lyricism of love, and of being young— excellence, transience, pathos. Here Aphrodite is in the time of flowers. Everything passes, everything is renewed. For the time being—well, it is May, nothing is yet old:

> I' mi trovai, fanciulle, un bel mattino
> di mezo maggio in un verde giardino . . . .

> I found myself, maiden, one fine morning
> In mid-May, in a green garden.
> All round violets and lilies grew
> Where the grass was green and sweet
> Fresh flowers were white also,
> Yellow, bright red, and blue,

—which is from Poliziano once more, from one of his ballades. The time to pick the rose and include it in a garland is when it opens its petals, when it is sweetest and most welcome—

> Before its sweetness goes;
> So, maiden when it's full in flower,
> In the garden pick the sweet rose.

All this is poured again from antiquity into the present.

The naked image of Venus, of Aphrodite inside that Roman name, proliferated in paintings, bronzes and poems, contrived from the fifteenth century onwards with an expressive skill probably exceeding that of the artists for whom Aphrodite once lived as a veritable goddess who needed propitiation in turn for her favours and her mercies; certainly with an expressive skill which was more various within the shapes and situations stereotyped in antiquity—Aphrodite coming ashore, Aphrodite undressing for the bath, Aphrodite receiving the prize of beauty from Paris, Aphrodite with Mars, Aphrodite with Adonis, and so on; the central image always body, or body in relation to body, present always by sensuous objectification, yet distanced slightly by myth; in poetry as in paint—Shakespeare, for instance, on the bath of Venus: 'She bathes in water, yet her fire must burn', or Shakespeare on Venus contemplated:

> Who sees his true love on her naked bed,
> Teaching the sheets a whiter hue than white.

An art historian complains or explains that the naked Venuses of Titian, such as his Venus of Urbino, letting fall her red roses (Plate 66), are only the exquisite prostitutes of sixteenth-century Venice, painted for princes who could afford the pleasure of the pictures and the pleasure of the girls. But why not? And is it right to say *only*? Who modelled for Apelles in his Aphrodite Anadyomene and for Praxiteles in his Aphrodite of Knidos? Prostitutes. And Titian, devotee of women, painted his own 'Birth of Venus', his own 'Worship of Venus', his own 'Venus and Adonis' along with his prostitute Venuses, well up in the new knowledge of classical antiquity, well aware that Venus includes and unites and does not divide.

So it continues, with Cranach, Velasquez, Watteau, Boucher, Tiepolo, Goya, Ingres, Corot, Beardsley, Renoir (like Titian a long-lived devotee of the flesh), Modigliani, Matisse; artists painting sometimes a Venus, sometimes a nude that must be ascribed, all the same, to the tradition of the goddess, to the enigmatic and exciting and possessive and teasing qualities which she represented; her mixture of aesthetic and desirable, and her ability to confer mental conditions of more than *post coitum* peace and harmony.

To me it seems good that at last the charming syllables of her Greek name have come back. If you look up Venus and then Aphrodite, and their associated words, in a major dictionary, you find columns for the one, and for the other brief entries:

> *Aphrodite.* 1. The Grecian Venus.
> 2. A genus of marine
> worms with bristles of brilliant
> iridescent hues; also called Sea-mouse.

Even then, the *Grecian* Venus; although dictionaries do not define Venus as the *Roman* Aphrodite; which would be nearer the truth.

The Return of Aphrodite

In fact when do poets, as clerks of the goddess of love, begin to speak again of Aphrodite instead of Venus, at least in our own language?

A poet might be familiar with Greek, and yet stay contentedly, in this

matter, in the latinate clutch of Rome and convention. Such a cavalier poet as Thomas Stanley, in the seventeenth century, learned in Greek and Greek philosophy, translator of Anakreon, Bion, Moschos, and Aischylos, dedicated his poems to Love, and never let an Aphrodite escape him. Always Venus:

> Poor Venus! Thy Adonis murder'd lies!
> For every drop of blood he shed, her eyes
> Let fall a tear, which earth in flowers bestows,
> Tears raised' th'Anemony and blood the Rose.

Two centuries later, Shelley and Walter Savage Landor, lovers of Greece who never visited Greece, allow themselves now and then to say Aphrodite, though as a rule they remained Latinizers and utterers of persistent Venus. I think the change—and a significant change—came, in the 1860s of confident prudery and cautious sensualities, in those once scandalous poems of Algernon Charles Swinburne. I mentioned him in my first chapter, quoting his *Laus Veneris* and his *Hymn to Proserpina*, praise of Aphrodite still as Venus. He had written, savagely rather, of Aphrodite by actual name and nature in his *Atalanta in Calydon* (1865). There a chorus speaks of Aphrodite as an evil blossom of the bloody castration and the foam, a bitter flower of the sea, a perilous deity, yet a world's delight, and a flame

> Filling the heavens with heat
> To the cold white ends of the north.

His chorus asked her

> What hadst thou to do being born,
>   Mother, when winds were at ease,
> As a flower of the springtime of corn,
>   A flower of the foam of the seas?
> For bitter thou wast from thy birth,
>   Aphrodite, a mother of strife;
> For before thee some rest was on earth,
>   A little respite from tears
>   A little pleasure of life—

67 Venus Anadyomene by Titian. Duke of Sutherland Collection, on loan to the National Gallery of Scotland.

68 Detail of Venus, from the Allegory with Venus and Time by Giovanni Battista Tiepolo (1696–1770). National Gallery, London.

and went through a catalogue of her consequences.

But then this poet, writing also of Aphaka, Astarte and Priapos, thinks himself in his next book into the ecstasy of Sappho for her girls. In the *Sapphics*, appearing along with *Laus Veneris* and his *Hymn to Proserpine* and his *Anactoria*, he lets Aphrodite break again out of customary and tamed Venus—'white implacable Aphrodite'—in verses of such incantatory incandescent effect about the awe of her nature that I shall nearly, but not quite, end this book with them.

Swinburne is no longer the most quoted, or most read, of poets, yet the *Sapphics* say more than that most odd, fiery-headed, fiery-spirited poet is supposed to have been capable of saying. What he was capable of doing in the bed of Corporeal Beauty is another matter. If there he was an inadequate performer, according to his biographers, here in the line of Sappho, Anakreon, Ibykos, Meleager, Ovid, Catullus, Tibullus, Propertius, Chaucer, Wyatt, Ronsard, Shakespeare, Sidney, Drayton, Donne, Campion, Sedley, Clare, Christina Rossetti, Desbordes-Valmore, Hardy, Cavafy, Desnos, Eluard, Robert Graves, and any others you at once think of, not to run through all her painters and sculptors, Swinburne was assuredly one more of the clerks of this divinity of love:

> All the night sleep came not upon my eyelids,
> Shed not dew, nor shook nor unclosed a feather,
> Yet with lips shut close and with eyes of iron
>   Stood and beheld me.
>
> Then to me so lying awake a vision
> Came without sleep over the seas and touched me,
> Softly touched mine eyelids and lips; and I too,
>   Full of the vision,
>
> Saw the white implacable Aphrodite,
> Saw the hair unbound and the feet unsandalled
> Shine as fire of sunset on western waters;
>   Saw the reluctant
>
> Feet, the straining plumes of the doves that drew her,
> Looking always, looking with necks reverted,
> Back to Lesbos, back to the hills whereunder
>   Shone Mitylene;

VENUS.

69 Venus between Terminal Gods by Aubrey Beardsley (1872–1898). Frontispiece for Venus
and Tannhäuser. *Higgins Art Gallery, Bedford.*

Heard the flying feet of the Loves behind her
Make a sudden thunder upon the waters,
As the thunder flung from the strong unclosing
    Wings of a great wind.

So the goddess fled from her place, with awful
Sound of feet and thunder of wings around her;
White behind a clamour of singing women
    Severed the twilight.

Ah the singing, ah the delight, the passion!
All the Loves wept, listening; sick with anguish,
Stood the crowned nine Muses about Apollo;
    Fear was upon them,

While the tenth sang wonderful things they knew not.
Ah the tenth, the Lesbian! the nine were silent,
None endured the sound of her song for weeping;
    Laurel by laurel,

Faded all their crowns; but about her forehead,
Round her woven tresses and ashen temples
White as dead snow, paler than grass in summer,
    Ravaged with kisses,

Shone a light of fire as a crown for ever.
Yea, almost the implacable Aphrodite
Paused, and almost wept; such a song was that song.
    Yea, by her name too

Called her, saying, 'Turn to me, O my Sappho';
Yet she turned her face from the Loves, she saw not
Tears for laughter darken immortal eyelids,
    Heard not about her

Fearful fitful wings of the doves departing,
Saw not how the bosom of Aphrodite
Shook with weeping, saw not her shaken raiment,
    Saw not her hands wrung;

Saw the Lesbians kissing across their smitten
Lutes with lips more sweet than the sound of lute-strings,
Mouth to mouth and hand upon hand, her chosen,
    Fairer than all men;

Only saw the beautiful lips and fingers,
Full of songs and kisses and little whispers,
Full of music; only beheld among them
    Soar, as a bird soars

Newly fledged, her visible song, a marvel,
Made of perfect sound and exceeding passion,
Sweetly shapen, terrible, full of thunders,
    Clothed with the wind's wings.

Then rejoiced she, laughing with love, and scattered
Roses, awful roses of holy blossom;
Then the Loves thronged sadly with hidden faces
    Round Aphrodite,

Then the Muses, stricken at heart, were silent;
Yea, the gods waxed pale; such a song was that song.
All reluctant, all with a fresh repulsion,
    Fled from before her.

All withdrew long since, and the land was barren,
Full of fruitless women and music only.
Now perchance, when winds are assuaged at sunset,
    Lulled at the dewfall,

By the grey sea-side, unassuaged, unheard of,
Unbeloved, unseen in the ebb of twilight,
Ghosts of outcast women return lamenting,
    Purged not in Lethe,

Clothed about with flame and with tears, and singing
Songs that move the heart of the shaken heaven,
Songs that break the heart of the earth with pity,
    Hearing, to hear them.

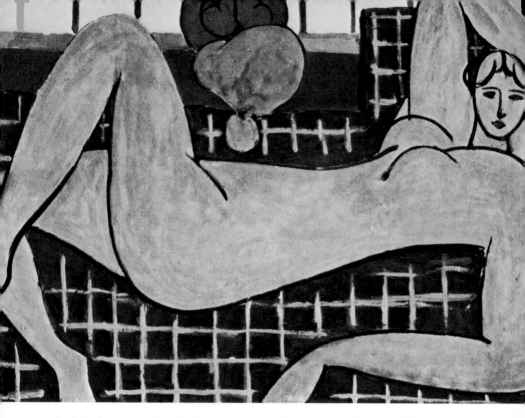

70 *Pink Nude, 1935, by Henri Matisse (1869–1954). Museum of Art, Baltimore U.S.A.*

71 *Love Crowning Death by Lorenzo Lotto (1480–1556). Duke of Northumberland, Alnwick Castle.*

Thomas Hardy wrote, of the first appearance of Swinburne's poems in 1866, that dropping irresponsibly from the sun in the 'formal middle time' of the Victorian age, it had been

> as though a garland of red roses
> Had fallen about the head of some smug nun.

No wonder.

And from John Morley, then climbing upwards as high guardian of the literary morals of the common run, Swinburne was famously denounced as 'the libidinous laureate of a pack of satyrs', who revealed 'a mind all aflame with the feverish carnality of a schoolboy over the dirtiest passages' in the then current classical dictionary.

He was a deliverer, extravagantly; and Aphrodite, conceptual Aphrodite, when understood—she also is a deliverer, even if she takes those who acknowledge her out of one captivity into another of her own.

In Auden's poem on the death of Freud, 'anarchic Aphrodite' is among those who mourn over the grave of 'one rational voice', of a man who looked into her ungovernable realm; about which we can again be as sensible and open at least as the Greeks, in their religious recognition of its extent, intricacy, dangers, and rewards, and beauty.

Bibliography

This is what may be called, I hope without causing dismay in scholars whose enquiry would have been far more systematic, an author's book-list, with a jackdaw quality, a list of books I have learnt from and raided, especially for out of the way topics. I have not, as a rule, listed sources in Greek and Roman literature. The names of poets, etc., will generally be enough for any reader wishing to track down original texts, with the quick aid of a classical dictionary.

Origins
Astour, M., 'Origins of the terms Canaan, Phoenician and Purple', in *Journal of Near Eastern Studies*, 24, 1965.
Barnett, R. D., *The Sea Peoples*, 1969 (fascicle for the *Cambridge Ancient History*).
Cox, Ian, ed., *The Scallop*, 1957.
Dhorme, É., 'Les religions de Babylonie et d'Assyrie', in *Mana, introduction à l'histoire des religions*, 1945.
Drower, M. S., *Syria c. 1550–1400 B.C.* Part 2, 1969 (fascicle for the *Cambridge Ancient History*).
Farnell, L. R., *The Cults of the Greek City States*, Vol. 2, 1896.
Fohrer, George, *History of Israelite Religion*, 1973.
Fraser, J. G., 'Adonis', in *The Golden Bough*, Vol. 1, 1890.
Harden, Donald, *The Phoenicians*, 1971.
James, E. O., *The Cult of the Mother Goddess*, 1959.
Jensen, L. B., 'Royal Purple of Tyre', in *Journal of Near Eastern Studies*, 22, 1963.
Moscati, Sabatino, *The World of the Phoenicians*, 1973.
Myres, J. L., 'Aphrodyte Anadyomene', in the *Annual of the British School in Athens*, 1940–45.
Ringgren, Helmer, *Religions of the Ancient Near East*, 1973.
Simon, Erika, *Die Geburt der Aphrodite*, 1959.

Cyprus
Bannerman, D. A., and W. M., *Handbook of the Birds of Cyprus*, 1971.
Blinkenberg, Chr., 'Le temple de Paphos', in *Kgl. Danske Videnskabernes Selskab*, 1924.

Catling, H. W., *Cyprus in the Neolithic and Bronze Age Periods*, 1966 (fascicle for the *Cambridge Ancient History*).
Cesnola, L. P. di, *Cyprus: Its Ancient Cities, Tombs and Temples*, 1877.
Chapman, Esther, *Cyprus Trees and Shrubs*, Nicosia, 1967.
Cobham, C. D., *Excerpta Cypria*, 1908.
Gardner, E. A. and others, 'Excavations in Cyprus 1887–88', in *Journal of Hellenic Studies*, IX, 1888.
Gunnis, Rupert, *Historic Cyprus*, 1936.
Hill, George Francis, *Catalogue of the Coins of Cyprus*, British Museum, 1904. *History of Cyprus*, 1940–52.
Hogarth, D. G., *Devia Cypria*, 1889.
Karageorghis, V., *The Ancient Civilization of Cyprus*, 1970. *Kition: Mycenaean and Phoenician Discoveries in Cyprus*, 1976.
Maier, F. G., *A Brief History and Description of Old Paphos*, Nicosia, Antiquities Department of the Republic of Cyprus, n.d.
Masson, Olivier, and Sznycer, Maurice, *Recherches sur les Phéniciens à Chypre*, 1972.
Matthews, Ann, *Lilies of the Field: A Handbook of Cyprus Wild Flowers*, Limassol, 1969.
Oberhummer, E., *Die Inseln Cypern*, 1903.
Polunin, O., and Huxley, A., *Flowers of the Mediterranean*, 1965.
Strand, W. E., *Voices of Stone: The History of Ancient Cyprus*, Nicosia, 1974.

Greek Religion
Burnet, John, *Early Greek Philosophy*, 1920.
Diels, Hermann, *Die Fragmente der Vorsokratiker*, 1903.
Farnell, L. R., 'Greek Sacrifice', in *Hasting's Encyclopaedia of Religion and Ethics*, XI, 1920.
Flacelière, Robert, *L'Amour en Grèce*, 1960.
Gernet, L., and Boulanger, A., *Le génie dans la religion grecque*, 1970.
Guthrie, W. K. C., *The Greeks and their Gods*, 1968.
Herter, Hans, *De Priapo*, 1932.
Horapollo, *Hieroglyphics*, tr. George Boas, New York, 1950.
James, E. O., *Sacrifice and Sacrament*, 1962.
Kerényi, Karl, *The Gods of the Greeks*, 1958. *Tochter der Sonne*, Zurich, 1944.
Licht, Hans, *Sexual Life in Ancient Greece*, 1932.
MacCulloch, J. H., 'Incense', in *Hasting's Encyclopaedia of Religion and Ethics*, VII, 1914.
Nilsson, M. P., *The History of Greek Religion*, 1949. *The Minoan-Mycenaean Religion*, 1968. *Greek Piety*, 1969.
Otto, Walter, *The Homeric Gods*, New York, 1954.
Page, Denys, *Sappho and Alcaeus*, 1955.
Rose, H. J., *A Handbook of Greek Mythology*, 1964.
Rouse, W. H. D., *Greek Votive Offerings*, 1902.
Séchan, L., and Lévêque, P., *Les grandes divinités de la Grèce*, 1966.
Yavis, C. G., *Greek Altars*, St Louis, Missouri, 1949.

Venus and Roman Religion
Coulon, M., *La poésie priapique*, 1932.
Ferguson, John, *The Religions of the Roman Empire*, 1970.
Galinsky, G. K., *Aeneas, Sicily and Rome*, Princeton, 1969.
Grant, Michael, *Roman Myths*, 1973.
Grant, Michael and Others, *Eros à Pompéi: Le Cabinet secret du Musée de Naples*, Paris, 1975.
Kiefer, Otto, *Sexual Life in Ancient Rome*, 1934.
Ogilvie, R. M., *The Romans and their Gods*, 1969.
Rudd, Niall, *The Satires of Horace*, 1966.
Schilling, Robert, *La religion romaine de Vénus*, 1954.
Witt, R. E., *Isis in the Graeco-Roman World*, 1971.

Venus in Gaul and Britain
Ashbee, Paul, *Ancient Scilly from the First Farmers to the Early Christians*, 1974.
Debal, Jacques, *Les Gaulois en Orléanais*, Orléans, 1974.
Hinks, R. P., *Catalogue of Greek, Etruscan and Roman Paintings and Mosaics in the British Museum*, 1953.
Liversedge, Joan, *Britain in the Roman Empire*, 1968.
Smith, D. J., 'Three Fourth Century Schools of Mosaic in Roman Britain', in *La mosaïque gréco-romaine (Colloques internationaux du Centre de la recherche scientifique)*, Paris, 1963.
Toynbee, J. M. C., *Art in Roman Britain*, 1963.
Twycross, Meg, *The Medieval Anadyomene*, 1972.

Temples and Sites, outside Cyprus
Akurgal, Ekrem, *Ancient Civilizations and Ruins of Turkey*, Istanbul, 1973.
Boulanger, Robert, *The Middle East*, Hachette World Guides, 1966.
Coldstream, J. N., and Huxley, G. L., *Kythera, Excavations and Studies*, 1972.
Eissfeldt, O., *Tempel and Kulte syrische Städte in Hellenistich-Römischer Zeit*, 1941.
Galinsky, G. K. (see above)
Melas, Evi, ed., *Temples and Sanctuaries of Ancient Greece*, 1973.
Pausanias, *Guide to Greece*, tr. Peter Levi, 1971.
Rossiter, Stuart, ed., *Blue Guide: Greece*, 1973.
Scully, Vincent, *The Earth, the Temple and the Gods*, New York, 1969.

Statues, Terracottas and Other Representations of Aphrodite
Bieber, Margarete, *The Sculpture of the Hellenistic Age*, New York, 1955.
Boardman, John, *Greek Art*, 1970.
Charbonneaux, J., Martin, R., and Villard, F., *Hellenistic Art 330–50 B.C.*, 1973.
Christodoros, in the *Greek Anthology*, tr. W. R. Paton, Vol. I, 1969 (Loeb Classical Library).
Clarke, K., *The Nude*, 1957.
Curtius, L., *Die Wandmalerie Pompejis*, 1929.
Higgins, R. A., *Greek Terracottas*, 1967.
Jones, H. Stuart, *Select Passages from Ancient Writers illustrative of the History of Greek Sculpture*, 1895.

Marinatos, Spyridion, *Crete and Mycenae*, 1960.
Mingazzini, P., 'Apelles', in *Encyclopaedia of World Art*, Vol. I, 1959.
Pliny, *Natural History*, XXXIV–XXXVIm in Vols, 9 and 10, *Loeb Classical Library*, 1968, and 1962.
Pollitt, J. J., *Art and Experience in Classical Greece*, 1972.
Reinach, Solomon, *Répertoire de la statuaire grecque et romaine*, 1897–1931.
Richter, G. M. A., *Greek Art*, 1967. *The Sculpture and Sculptors of the Greeks*, 1957.

Aphrodite, Temple Prostitutes, and the Early Christians
Arnobius of Sicca, *The Case against the Pagans*, tr. G. E. McCracken, 1949.
Athenagoras, *The Writings of Justin Martyr and Athenagoras*, Anti-Nicene Christian Library, Vol. 2, 1867.
Clement of Alexandria, *The Exhortation to the Greeks*, tr. G. W. Butterworth (*Loeb Classical Library*), 1968.
Eusebios, *Life of Constantine* and *Oration in Praise of the Emperor Constantine*, tr. E. C. Richardson, 1885.
Farnell, L. R., *Greece and Babylon*, 1911.
Justin Martyr, *Discourse to the Greeks*, in *Writings of Justin Martyr*, tr. T. B. Falls, New York, 1948.
Nilsson, M. P., *Griechische Feste*, 1906.
Peckham, B., 'Notes on a fifth-century Phoenician inscription from Kition, Cyprus', in *Orientalia*, 37, 1968.
Socrates Scholasticus, *Ecclesiastical History*, tr. in *Select Library of Nicene and Post-Nicene Fathers*, 2nd series, Vol. 2, 1891.

Roses, Doves and Dolphins
Gault, S. M., and Synge, Patrick, *The Dictionary of Roses in Colour*, 1971.
Joret, Charles, *La rose dans l'antiquité*, 1892.
Thomas, Graham, *The Old Shrub Roses*, 1955.
Glueck, Nelson, *Dieties and Dolphins*, 1965.
Stebbins, E. B., *The Dolphin in the Literature and Art of Greece and Rome*, Baltimore, 1929.
Thompson, Sir D'Arcy, *A Glossary of Greek Fishes*, 1947. *A Glossary of Greek Birds*, 1936.
Gubernatis, Angelo de, *Zoological Mythology*, 1872.
Toynbee, J. M. C., *Animals in Roman Life and Art*, 1973.
Post, G. E., *Flora of Syria*, 1932.
Richard, Achille, *Tentamen Florae Abyssinicae*, 1848 (in T. Lefebure's *Voyage en Abyssinae*, 1845–54).

Venus after Classical Antiquity
Adhémar, Jean, 'Influences antiques, dans l'art du Moyen Age français', in *Studies of the Warburg Institute*, VII, 1939.
Gombrich, E. H., *Symbolic Images*, 1972.
Poliziano, *Rime*, ed. Natalino Sapegno, 1967.
Seznec, Jean, *The Survival of the Pagan Gods*, New York, 1961.
Twycross, Meg (see above).
Wind, Edgar, *Pagan Mysteries in the Renaissance*, 1967.

Index

OGILVIE AND THE MEM'SAHIB

OGILVIE
AND THE MEM'SAHIB

Philip McCutchan

Severn House Large Print
London & New York

This first large print edition published in Great Britain 2004 by
SEVERN HOUSE LARGE PRINT BOOKS LTD of
9-15 High Street, Sutton, Surrey, SM1 1DF.
Regular print edition published 2003 by
Severn House Publishers, London and New York.
This first large print edition published in the USA 2004 by
SEVERN HOUSE PUBLISHERS INC., of
595 Madison Avenue, New York, NY 10022.

British Library Cataloguing in Publication Data

McCutchan, Philip, 1920 -
    Ogilvie and the Mem'Sahib. - Large print ed. – (A James Ogilvie novel)
    1. Ogilvie, James (Fictitious character) - Fiction
    2. India - History - 19th century - Fiction
    3. Historical fiction
    4. Large type books
    I. Title
    II. MacNeil, Duncan, 1920-. Restless frontier
    823.9'14 [F]

    ISBN 0-7278-7368-7

Printed and bound in Great Britain by
MPG Books Ltd, Bodmin, Cornwall.

Author's Note

The section in this book dealing with the delimitation escort for the High Commissioner owes its birth to the germ of an idea that came into my mind after reading a most interesting factual account by Mr J.E.G. Hodgson late of the Border Regiment (now amalgamated with the King's Own Royal Regt. to form the King's Own Royal Border Regt.). This described an action in which the 2nd Bn. The Border Regiment rendered distinguished service in Waziristan in the mid 1890s when ordered to march as reinforcements in the pursuit of native forces who had attacked the escort. All my characters are of course fictitious as is the way in which I have portrayed the development of the action.

One

The woman lay inert across the horse, held in place by the sinewy arm of an Afridi tribesman, one of six riding like the wind itself away from the Nowshera cantonment. The woman was unconscious and blood dripped from a wound in her left shoulder. There was no pursuit: behind them the officers and men of the British garrison slept soundly under the protection of the sentries and barrack guards. The penetration and the attack had been carried out brilliantly and in total silence, the tribesmen mere shadows in the night as they had approached the bungalow, their naked bodies oiled so that they would, if caught, slip easily from the strongest grip. Firearms had not been used; *thuggee* was the safer course, and four privates and a lance-corporal of the 1st Dorsetshires lay dead in the cantonment with cords drawn tightly around their necks, as did the *chaukidah*, the night-watchman, the old retainer responsible for keeping undesirables from the sahibs' domestic quarters.

The Afridis rode north of Peshawar and its

7

garrison, ultimately towards the Khyber Pass and the watchful sentries of the Khyber Rifles, high up in Fort Jamrud that guarded the eastern extremity; but well short of Fort Jamrud the riders turned off for the south, crossing the track leading out of Peshawar, to enter Waziristan by ways known only to the men of the tribes, and were soon lost in the hills and the maze of little-used passes into one of the world's wildest areas of savagery. No one saw them go: only the eyes of the hungry jackals and of the scavenging vultures watched, the latter hovering and swooping as the smell of the woman's blood came to them as earnest of a possible meal.

The evening before, James Ogilvie of the Queen's Own Royal Strathspeys had attended a brilliant reception along with his brother officers: a stupendous feast provided by His Highness the Maharajah of Amb for the benefit of the officers of the Raj. Much drink had been available for the guests. Ogilvie, a glass of whisky in his hand, was chatting with the lantern-jawed and voluble wife of a Surgeon Colonel attached to Brigade when he was borne down upon by his cousin Hector, carrying a glass of lemonade with some difficulty through the throng of brilliant dress uniforms.

'An extravanganza, James.' Hector bowed to the Surgeon Colonel's lady. 'Your pardon, ma'am. I'm interrupting.'

'Not at all, Mr Ogilvie, most certainly not.' The horse-faced woman gathered up her dress and made for an unoccupied major-general who for no apparent reason had turned up on the North-West Frontier from Calcutta.

'An extravaganza,' Hector repeated gloomily.

'As ever in India. The princes are lavish, and generous.'

'In their own cause, my dear chap, yes.'

Ogilvie lifted his glass and grinned at his owlish cousin. 'You mean, I'll scratch your back if you'll scratch mine?'

'An expression I don't care for,' Hector Ogilvie said in a distant tone, 'but I don't doubt it'll do. Frankly, I'll be glad enough when my duty in India comes to an end,' he added, causing James to reflect that the pleasure would not be Hector's alone. 'Have you seen Angela? I've mislaid her.'

Ogilvie waved his glass towards a corner of the immense, pillared apartment that formed His Highness's throne room. 'Over there. Talking to Lord Brora.'

'The devil she is!' His face flushed, Hector hurried away looking possessive. Once more, Ogilvie grinned: Major Lord Brora, second-in-command of the Royal Strathspeys, was an arrogant man but could also be a gallant one with the ladies ... and was a much more

9

prepossessing figure than poor Hector, a Civilian from the India Office in London currently condemned to a year's tour of Indian duty so that he could the better fit himself for his Imperial task of administering the sub-continent from afar. Hector Ogilvie, unlikely son of James's uncle, Rear-Admiral Rufus Ogilvie, was a man of much complaint. He didn't like the climate either in winter, which it was now, or summer; he didn't like the varied smells of Peshawar and he turned up his nose at the natives, from Maharajah to Untouchable – he had had an uncomfortable time in Calcutta, which according to him was full of Untouchables, of which low and smelly class he was to a large extent mercifully relieved in Peshawar. He disliked strong drink, and was appalled by the parties in the various regimental messes as well as by those in the native palaces. He was appalled, too, by the easy way in which officers in garrison drifted into relationships with married women whose husbands were absent, and since his arrival in Peshawar had stuck like a leech, whenever possible, to Angela. Ogilvie wondered, as he had wondered before now, why cousin Hector had ever entered the splendid portals of the India Office in the first place: it was something of an enigma, but was perhaps explained by Hector's love of power and prestige and his preference for the halls of

10

Government rather than the bloody field of action. Ogilvie watched him regain contact with his wife of a little under a year, saw the almost savage glare given him by Lord Brora as Angela turned with a smile of welcome for her husband. Hector's young wife seemed to have that sort of effect upon other men – Ogilvie had noted it more than once in the short time she had been on the Frontier, and was convinced she was innocently and totally unaware of it. Meeting her eye over Hector's shoulder – she was taller than he, almost of James Ogilvie's own height – he saw the response to him in her clear eyes and was stirred uneasily. He frowned: another enigma – why Angela had married cousin Hector! Certainly she appeared fond of him if subdued by him; she looked like a bride still, young and fresh as a flower, and wide-eyed with wonder at all she was seeing along the warring North-West Frontier, the out-posts and garrisons of which formed the last defensive line between the Afghan hordes and the British Raj, almost the farthest and certainly the most glittering pearl in the Imperial crown of Her Majesty the Queen-Empress ... lost in his own thoughts Ogilvie started when he felt the weight of a hand upon his shoulder and turned to find Andrew Black at his side. The Adjutant was looking dour.

'Fiddling while Rome burns, James.'

'This?' Ogilvie waved a hand around the expensive throng: there was enough metal in the orders, medals and campaign stars to build a battleship, while the officers' ladies collectively wore a small fortune in gold and rubies, diamonds and emeralds, to say nothing of the romantic splendour of the Maharajah's retinue and of His Highness's own exalted, sky-blue-turbaned person. 'It's nothing new or out of the ordinary, Andrew, and nothing's burning that I know of!'

'Maybe. But I smell trouble.'

'Where, for God's sake?'

'As yet I cannot say, and I'll thank you not to blaspheme in my presence—'

'I was not blaspheming.'

'Or to argue either. My words are a warning, and will be offered to all our officers with special intent for the company commanders such as yourself.' Black paused, his dark face somehow menacing as the light from the chandeliers was taken from it by a thick marble pillar inlaid with gold. 'The Colonel has seen fit to have a word in my ear. I expect to see sober officers in the morning, Captain Ogilvie. Do you take my meaning?'

'I think so, Captain Black, and I shall abide by it so long as it affects you also. If you take my meaning?'

Black glared, muttered something about insubordination, and turned away sharply, the tartan of the Royal Strathspey swirling around bony knees above legs like spindles. For the third time that evening, Ogilvie grinned. He finished his whisky and set the empty glass down on a side table of solid gold. Andrew Black was a more lucrative prospect than he for the whisky distillers of Scotland, and in the mornings was as ill-tempered from his occasional bouts of abstinence as he was when suffering the effects of over-indulgence. Ogilvie wondered what was in the wind now, if anything; Andrew Black tended to rush towards bad news, and often enough that news had turned out to lie in his mind alone. Ogilvie was not left long with his thoughts: he was approached by a bosomy young lady with a fan and a beaming smile and a heady scent that would have been stimulating had she been of slenderer proportions. As it was, she closely resembled her distinguished father, a portly major-general commanding a division of native cavalry, an officer known to irreverent regimental subalterns as Pigsgut Pomeroy.

'Dear James, I would so like to sit on the verandah, wouldn't you? It's so *nice* under the moon and really it's not awf'ly cold, is it, do you think? I haven't seen you for simply ages, James, in fact Mother was saying only the other day...'

She prattled on; prattle was another of her attributes, but she was a wallflower and

Ogilvie felt sympathetic, and also under-standing of her mother's guile: as a captain in a Highland regiment of panache, as a single officer, as the only son of Sir Iain Ogilvie commanding the Northern Army in India from Murree, James was a catch and couldn't help but know it and regret it. Few relationships with young women could ever be wholly spontaneous: behind each lay inevitably the web of intrigue and match-making that meshed in the social, and often enough the military, life of the garrisons and the hill stations. Only on patrol or in the isolation of an outpost fort or upon the march with one's regiment could one be really at home and at ease ... James obeyed the young lady's wishes and led her out on to the verandah, and spent some half an hour in study of the moon and the low-slung, myriad stars that hung like so many lamps in the night. He felt the keen edge of a cold wind coming down from distant Himalaya, across the foothills to bring the smell of the sub-continent to his nostrils as the sweat of the Maharajah's palace interior dried from the starched shirt beneath the scarlet jacket of his mess dress. Miss Mary Pomeroy evidently had blood less thinned by Indian service than had he.

'Did Andrew speak to you, James?'
'He did.' Ogilvie lay back against the

leather upholstery of the carriage that, in company with Robin Stuart of E Company, was taking him back after the Maharajah's roisterings to the cantonment on the far side of Peshawar. His mind had not been upon Captain Andrew Black but upon an entertainment presented by His Highness for the gentlemen only: much dusky female flesh had been on erotic display and some exceedingly curious acts had taken place while the drink had flowed freely for the guests – though the Scots officers, mindful of Black's words, had not over-indulged. The atmosphere had been hectic, with a background of throbbing music, and colourful with the varied uniforms of the British and Indian Army units; the Scots tartans, the blue of the gunners, the green of the rifle regiments, the red of the infantry had all added their lustre to the diaphanous and highly-coloured veils of the dancing women as they pranced and pirouetted. Ogilvie's mind was still full of the spectacle, but now he gave thought to Stuart's question. 'Do you know what's in the air, Robin?'

Stuart shook his head. 'Probably just Andrew fantasising again, old man.'

'Shouts of war are heard afar...?'

'Possibly. It's what we're here for, isn't it?'

Ogilvie yawned; little more was said as the carriage rolled on beneath the stars, passing through the native city with its drains running sluggishly in their stench along the rutted streets, passing sad bundles of humanity wrapped in rags to slumber the night hours away, passing the odd barking dog, its jaws slavering for food and its eyes bright in the moon. There was an occasional oil lamp burning to light the doorways of the hovels, light that glinted on the shining steel of knives or the dull metal of antiquated rifles. Peshawar at night was a place of potential danger for the traveller and men on foot kept well clear of its alleys; but mounted or carriage-borne officers of the British Raj in uniform were normally allowed to pass unmolested: the risk of vengeance was potent in the native mind, for the great Queen-Empress in Windsor Castle was immensely powerful and extended full protection to her armies overseas; though she might turn a blind eye to the robbing of a drunken private soldier who had asked for it, any attack upon authority passing upon its lawful occasions would bring down much wrath and many bullets. So the carriage passed in safety through Peshawar and on to the British cantonment some three miles westward towards the frowning sides of the Khyber Pass.

Ogilvie awoke bleary-eyed to the strident voice of the bugles blowing Reveille throughout the cantonment, bringing men awake in

16

the barrack-rooms to tumble out and wash and grumble their way to early-morning parade to be inspected by the section sergeants and corporals, to show clean rifles and shaven chins. Ogilvie lay in his *charpoy*, listening to the sounds from the square – the rattle of equipment, the stamp of feet, the shouted commands. When his native bearer brought hot water, he got up and walked in his dressing-gown on to the verandah and stared out into the cold and freshness of the pre-breakfast hour. Across the square he saw Lord Brora pacing the parade with the Adjutant: those two were up bright and early! Something must be in the air after all. As Ogilvie watched, Mr Cunningham, the Regimental Sergeant-Major, came briskly from the direction of his bungalow, marching as straight as a ramrod with his pace-stick beneath his arm. As the RSM gave himself an eyes right and snapped to the salute on passing the second-in-command and the Adjutant, he was hailed by Brora and altered course to halt before the officers, slamming his boots into the ground and saluting again. The three men were still in conference when Ogilvie turned away and went back into his room: water could grow cold, and the morning was undoubtedly a chilly one. Breath steamed from the parade-ground. At breakfast there was, as usual, silence except for the discreet movements of the Corporal of Mess

17

Servants and his native staff, offering food and coffee from white-gloved hands. Most of the officers were in fact invisible behind newspapers, many of them ancient ones that had travelled the long sea route from home and acted as shields to morning privacy rather than as purveyors of news. Captain Black finished his breakfast just as Ogilvie entered, and nodded a good morning as he passed. At one end of the table the great bulk of Lord Brora loomed, solid and scowling as he glared over the top of an old *Morning Post* to seek out more marmalade.

'You.'

Ogilvie lifted an eyebrow. 'Me, Major?'

'No, blast you. You!'

The Corporal of Mess Servants hurried across and stood at attention. 'Yessir?'

'*Yes, My Lord*. Don't you ever damn well *learn*, man? My Lord in the Mess, sir on parade. Next time you'll go before the Colonel.' Brora tapped the sticky silver pot before him on the table. 'Marmalade. See that it's kept filled. And wipe the damn thing.'

'Yes, My Lord.' The Corporal snapped his fingers at a bearer. '*Jaldi*!' His tone was fierce; the bearer salaamed twice, once towards the Major sahib, once towards the Corporal sahib. The silver vessel was filled with trembling fingers and set before the Major sahib, who sat in a frigid silence, glaring from angry accusing eyes. Breakfast

18

proceeded to a sound of munching and coffee-drinking. The start of one more day in India ... but before the meal was finished the Corporal, who had had words with a runner in the pantry, had approached each officer and had bent respectfully to deliver a message.

'Beg pardon, sir. The Colonel's compliments, sir, and he'd like to see you in the battalion office at nine-thirty sharp, sir.'

In the battalion office there was a buzz of conversation while Black, having counted heads, went off to report to the Colonel. Talk was stilled when Lord Dornoch entered with Brora and Black. The three officers walked to the Colonel's desk and arranged themselves on chairs behind it. Before sitting down, the Colonel wished his officers good morning and then pulled out his pipe. 'You may smoke, gentlemen,' he said. He filled the bowl and puffed to the strike of a match. Many other pipes and a few cigarettes were lit: the air grew thick as Dornoch went on, 'I'll be brief and to the point, for you're about to be busily employed.' He ran a hand over his moustache. 'Last night, at the Maharajah's palace, Captain Black acquired some information that may or may not be genuine, but which has already been passed to Brigade and is being forwarded by the telegraph to Murree. At this moment, we

19

await the GOC's reaction and possibly his orders.' Dornoch paused. 'Captain Black overheard two kinsmen of His Highness ... it seems that word has leaked through the grapevine, at any rate to native ears in the first place, that a serious boundary dispute has occurred in Waziristan – in the vicinity of Mana to be precise. I think you all know what that means, gentlemen. It can be put in a nutshell: trouble. Trouble that will initially be our concern, since we're the stand-by battalion...'

As Dornoch continued speaking, giving his orders for the battalion to be brought to instant readiness to march out if required, Ogilvie felt a shiver of excitement mixed with apprehension run along his spine. Waziristan, that remote and mountainous country to the south and west of Peshawar, was wild, desolate, a terrible place for a winter march, a land of many feuding tribes such as the Afridis and the Mahsuds who were ever individually at each other's throats and collectively at the throats of the Raj. A sizeable boundary dispute would not be easily settled and the regiment would be likely to mourn many deaths by Christmas if they were ordered out to exert the interest and authority of the Raj. Mana was around a hundred miles as the crow flew – longer via the high passes, with the Tochi River and its tributaries to cross. This would be no ordinary patrol and could lead to a confrontation with tribal power that might involve the whole Peshawar garrison if things went ill for the Raj in its mediation attempts. Much would of course depend on the mood of the *maliks*, the local headmen, and that mood was always unpredictable except in so far as it was seldom friendly towards the Raj. Lord Dornoch was not as brief as he had promised: Surgeon Major Corton of the Medical Staff caused delay. There were a number of sick and a number of those recuperating were on light duties, and there was a shortage of medical supplies such as would be needed on the march into hostile and cut-off territory. These had of course been indented for to Brigade but had not yet arrived ... Brora was heard to remark loudly that here was a case of damned inefficiency if ever there was one, and it was clear that he was metaphorically pointing the finger of blame at Corton rather than at Brigade. Lord Dornoch took the fuse from an explosive atmosphere.

'We all know what the supply situation's like. I shall have words with Brigade at once. I—' He broke off as the door opened and a subaltern saluted. 'Yes, what is it, and who are you?'

'Second Lieutenant Roberts, sir, Probyn's Horse ... from Brigade, sir. I have despatches, sir.' At Dornoch's nod, the subaltern

21

marched forward and handed a sealed envelope to the Colonel. Frowning, Dornoch slit it and read, then looked up. He appeared shocked.

'Thank you, Mr Roberts. I have despatches in return, and you shall wait.' The Colonel got to his feet. 'Orders, gentlemen, and the speed with which they have come from Murree indicates their urgency. Sir Iain has had similar information from the Political Department that confirms the word to Captain Black, and the High Commissioner is proceeding into Waziristan to sort out the dispute. He will take a Delimitation Escort, and we are ordered to form part of a brigade that will provide that escort.' He turned. 'Captain Black, we're ordered to be ready to march by noon. We move south by way of the Kohat Pass, at the southern end of which we'll rendezvous with the remainder of our brigade who'll march out from Kohat to join us under Brigadier-General Norris. We're to be brigaded with a battalion of the Punjab Frontier Force and one of Ghurkhas, and I'm told we're required as stiffeners for the native troops.'

'I trust that guns and cavalry will be provided, Colonel?'

'Yes, yes, the Kohat contingent will join with a cavalry squadron provided by the Guides, and a battery of mountain guns.' Lord Dornoch paused, his face serious.

'Thank you, gentlemen, that's all. Make your reports as soon as possible to the Adjutant, if you please.' He lifted a hand to Ogilvie. 'Captain Ogilvie, I'd be obliged if you'll remain behind a moment.'

'Yes, Colonel.'

The officers left amid a buzz of conversation: the general feeling was that Dornoch's manner had been unduly sombre. When they were alone Lord Dornoch pulled at his moustache, an expression of extreme gravity on his face. 'I have bad news for you, James. Family – though not immediately close, I hasten to add. The fact is, the despatch brought other news. There was an attack upon the Nowshera cantonment during the dark hours after the palace reception – five bodies, six with the *chaukidah*, found when the guard changed, all killed by *thuggee*. A British subject was taken – or at any rate is missing, and there were signs of a struggle and some blood.'

'My cousin, Colonel?'

Dornoch shook his head. 'Not your cousin, James. Your cousin's wife ... a lively and like-able young woman to be sure. I'm very sorry.'

Ogilvie's face was white. 'And the reason, Colonel? Has any reason emerged?'

'No, but there's a very clear connection. Your cousin ... the Government in Calcutta had in fact decided already to appoint a commission to enquire in general terms into boundary matters in Waziristan, and your cousin was to have been one of the commissioners. Word may have leaked, and the result is kidnap.'

'To put pressure on Hector, Colonel?'

'Very possibly, and on the High Commissioner too, for a woman's life can't be held lightly. It's nasty, James.' Dornoch gave him a direct look. 'Well, what's your wish? I'm prepared to excuse you escort duty if you feel you can be of assistance in Nowshera. It's up to you.'

Two

James Ogilvie rode out alone for Nowshera while the regiment prepared to march south. Hector was family and would need his support: his father, indeed, would expect no less than that he should give it. At Division in Nowshera he reported to a staff captain and was admitted to the presence of the Lieutenant-General Commanding Her Majesty's First Division, Lieutenant-General Francis Fettleworth. With the Divisional Commander was Hector, his face white, his eyes red as though from weeping. All Hector's pomposity was gone: Ogilvie saw him as he had seen him as a small boy, visiting the Ogilvies' home at Corriecraig Castle in distant Scotland: a small boy, plump and sailor suited, who had lost a toy boat on Loch Rannoch and had howled his head off.

'Well, Ogilvie. A sad business and a serious one for the Raj.'

'Yes, sir.' Ogilvie turned to Hector. 'I'm sorry, old chap. I don't know what more to say ... except that I'm here to help in any way I can.'

There was no response from Hector other than a nod: he seemed completely distrait. Fettleworth blew through the trailing ends of a white walrus moustache and said, 'Patrols, Ogilvie, search parties. They're being organised. Care to go with one?'

'Whatever is most useful, sir. My Colonel has released me from regimental duty.'

'So I understand. Well, you've been in India a long time, Ogilvie, you know the Frontier better than many of the officers in my Division. What do you suggest may have been the course of events since Mrs Ogilvie disappeared? Mr Ogilvie, I think perhaps you should explain all the circumstances as you found them, to your cousin.'

'Yes.' Hector's voice was low and thick. For a moment he put his face in his hands, then seemed to stiffen a little and looked up at his cousin with pain-filled eyes. In a halting voice he told his story: after their return from the Maharajah's palace he and Angela had gone straight to bed in their adjoining rooms, which gave on to the bungalow's verandah. The doors and jalousies had been closed, but he had heard no sound of their being opened by any intruder: he was a heavy sleeper and was tired. Nothing had been known until the guard-change, when the bodies had been discovered, and then he had been at once awakened by the Sergeant of the Guard and had gone with the orderly officer to Angela's room. The door from the verandah had been open, swinging slightly in the dawn breeze. The bed was awry, with the sheets trailing to the floorboards, and there was a trace of blood on the ground, and some of the furniture had been displaced and a chair overturned. That was all. There had been an immediate search of the bungalow and the go-down where the native bearers and sweepers lived, and of the vicinity. Nothing had been found: Angela had gone, leaving no clues.

'We'll find her,' James Ogilvie said.

Fettleworth nodded. 'Indeed we shall. No stone left unturned, Mr Ogilvie, I promise you. Especially where a woman's concerned, the Raj responds quickly.'

'It'll be too late, General.' Hector's tone was flat.

'Upon my word it will not!' Fettleworth said stoutly.

26

'She'll be tortured ... she won't stand that for long.'

'Even the tribesmen respect women,' James said, with a glance at Fettleworth as though appealing to him to support a necessary untruth. 'She won't be harmed physically, Hector.'

Hector's eyes blazed and his white face flushed to an unhealthy colour. 'I don't want stupid palliatives, James. You've always thought I knew nothing of India, haven't you? I'm not as green as you imagine ... I know what the natives are capable of. We're not all wrapped in cottonwool in Whitehall, and since I've been out here I've heard more than you think. I'm not a damn—'

'Yes, yes, Mr Ogilvie.' Fettleworth gave a loud cough and made a rasping sound in his throat. 'India's India, of course, we'll not deny that.' He stopped and once again blew through his moustache as though suddenly conscious of having uttered a non-profundity. 'Everything that can be done will be done, you have my word. I feel what has happened to be my own responsibility and matters will be put right. And while we await the results of the patrols, Mr Ogilvie, we must also await something else.'

'Something else?'

Fettleworth got to his feet and walked over to a wide window overlooking the green patch of grass in the centre of which the

Divisional standard flew from its flagstaff; turning again, he looked upwards and met the stern, framed gaze of Her Majesty the Queen-Empress, staring down at him from the wall opposite. As ever, that imperial gaze affected his emotions. He cleared his throat. 'We must await word from the persons who have removed your wife, Mr Ogilvie. Soon they must utter, and tell us their demands.'

'You think they'll have demands?'

Fettleworth tugged at the neckband of his scarlet tunic. Mr Ogilvie was a fool. 'Of a certainty they'll have demands! These things are never done without reason behind them, you may be sure. When the demands come, then we shall have more to go on.'

Hector stared. 'What do you suppose the demands might be, General?'

Fettleworth pulled for a moment at his moustache, his eyes cold and bleak. 'You are about to sit on a boundary commission, Mr Ogilvie, and I'm bound to see a link.' He paused. 'What would be your reaction ... if your wife's kidnappers put pressure upon you and your colleagues to find in favour of some persons as yet unknown?'

James Ogilvie and Hector walked alone in the grounds of Divisional HQ. Hector's response to Fettleworth's question had been indirect; he had said, properly enough in his cousin's view, that it was now his duty to ask

Calcutta to remove him from the boundary commission. Fettleworth had at first been dubious, saying that to do such would be to play to some extent into the hands of the kidnappers, to admit their power to control events and to admit it pointlessly since the effect would be much the same whether or not Hector remained a member of the commission: the pressure would still be upon the Raj. But he had eventually agreed, for it was obvious Hector would not only be useless but would also be a confounded nuisance and an embarrassment. Hector's request would be passed via the Army Commander in Murree who was already, as it happened, hastening in person to Nowshera by the railway for words with his nephew – this had been intimated by the telegraph from Rawalpindi where Sir Iain had been about to inspect the troops in garrison. Walking beneath some trees that gave a degree of shelter from a cold wind, James Ogilvie did what he could to offer hope and comfort. Certainly the Frontier was a big area to cover, certainly the kidnappers could have ridden north or south, or west into the Afghan hills, though it was unlikely they would have risked entering the Khyber Pass with its many forts friendly to the Raj. But Peshawar and Nowshera were strongly garrisoned and more troops could be sent speedily from Murree and Rawalpindi and Mardan. Ogilvie did not add that no general would too far deplete the northern garrisons by sending out patrols in sufficient strength and numbers to weaken his base; nor did he add that patrols could be cut up to a man and never return to Peshawar to report. It had happened before and would happen again in this wild land where the bullet came without warning and the knives sprang like magic from the scrub and the sides of the passes, and the cord of *thuggee* could be whipped around even a horseman's throat before he had heard a sound or felt a movement from the man who had dropped upon his horse from a tree or overhanging jag of rock. Although all this remained unsaid, Ogilvie had the uneasy feeling that his cousin was possessed of much more imagination than he had suspected.

'Find her, James,' Hector said in a tight, too-controlled voice, a voice that was in basis as brittle as the morning frost. 'She's like a child ... and not strong. Not strong at all. So – thin.' And so trusting too, James thought to himself, remembering her eyes of the night before. Wherever she went she saw no evil, but God alone could tell what she was seeing now. He felt a lump in his throat and his vision misted. Find her he would.

The 114th Highlanders, The Queen's Own Royal Strathspey, marched out of cantonments at noon precisely behind the pipes and drums, kilts a-swing round knees still brown from the blazing suns of the last summer season, rifles at the slope until the order should be passed by Lord Dornoch to march at ease. The side-arms in their brightly polished scabbards bumped the pleats of the kilts as the step was called by the section sergeants. From ahead of the Colonel and Lord Brora, riding with the High Commissioner, Sir Lawrence Bindle, the wail of the pipes swept back upon the marching files, stirring and haunting, warlike yet sad, as the cantonment and the troops in garrison who had turned out to cheer them on faded away in the dust behind. The tune was 'The 79th's Farewell to Gibraltar'; it beat out strongly as Captain Black came riding down the line from the van, face haughty, eyes sharp for any slackness of dress or marching. The NCOs and men were ready for the expected, and Black could find no fault. He spurred his horse back towards the van, where he joined the Colonel.

'All well, Andrew?'

Black saluted. 'Yes, Colonel.'

'A devilish business!'

'And a damn pretty filly,' Brora said.

The Colonel turned his head. 'I dislike your choice of word, Major.'

'Never mind the choice of word, my dear sir, if I find her I'll slit the damn guts of the

31

buggers who laid a hand on her last night! And I'll tell you something else as well: I realise that our orders are for Mana and a peaceful exort, but *balls* to our orders if we should happen to raise the scent of the wench – which is a word I trust you'll like better than filly, my dear sir!'

'Thank you, Brora. I think you've said enough.'

'If you say so, Colonel.' Brora's eyes flashed, and he exchanged a look with Black. Black thereafter avoided the Major's eye: he was unsure of his ground as between the Colonel and the Major, who were ever at loggerheads since Brora's brief and unfortunate command of the battalion in the absence of Dornoch in hospital some months before. It made it hard for an Adjutant to please both at once, and often Black sighed for the return from the dead of John Hay, an ineffective Major but an easy man to deal with, and a mild one. Brora was an aristocratic swashbuckler, and Black, with his background of moneyed trade, felt more ill-at-ease with him than he did with Dornoch, equally an aristocrat but not by any means a swashbuckler. Brora, Black felt, would have made a first-class buccaneer in the days of ocean piracy ... meanwhile the advance on the Kohat Pass continued and after a few more minutes Lord Dornoch passed the word for the battalion to march at

32

ease. As the order went down via the Adjutant, the company commanders, the Regimental Sergeant-Major and the colour-sergeants, rifles left the shoulders and were hung from their blanco-ed slings, the neck-bands of the khaki-drill tunics were thankfully loosened and voices lifted in song: at first, bawdy song, and loud. A roar from Mr Cunningham almost reached the van.

'Stop the filth, d'ye hear me? This is no' an ordinary march, it's a Delimitation Escort and we have the High Commissioner wi' us.'

There was some muttering, but the song changed. In the van Dornoch suppressed a smile and thanked heaven for his RSM. Sir Lawrence Bindle wore almost continually pursed lips, and was in truth little different from Hector Ogilvie. As the afternoon shadows lengthened the air became colder with the sun's westerly decline over the stark Afghan hills. A halt for resting of men and horses was called soon after the column turned southwards and came into the Waziri heights, and under the care of the scouts and picquets pipes were lit and smoke rose blue over the fallen-out line and feet were eased from heavy boots. The respite was brief, for there was yet much distance to be covered to the vicinity of Kohat, but it was not too long before the battalion went into their night bivouac before entering the Kohat Pass which the Colonel preferred to traverse in daylight hours.

The single shot came like the crack of a whip, shattering the night's brooding silence. From the hillside the body of a picquet tumbled, head-over-heels, sliding down and bringing small boulders and stones with it in a cascade of debris. Everywhere men came awake, rubbing the sleep from their eyes and seizing the rifles which were ever at their sides. Mr Cunningham, who seldom seemed to sleep when on the march in hostile territory, was the first to reach the body. He bent for the heart and found no flutter.

He straightened. 'Dead,' he said. He looked around, saw nothing. There were sounds from the hillside as the picquets still on post searched for the man who had fired.

Brora came stalking up, a revolver in his hand. 'What is it, Sar'nt-Major?'

'Private MacFarar, sir, C Company, shot dead.'

'How d'you know he's dead, Sar'nt-Major?'

'Why, sir, I—'

'You're not a medical man, Sar'nt-Major, rouse out the Surgeon at once.'

'But I—'

'Do as you're told.' Lord Brora swung away abruptly, peering about and lifting his revolver. Cunningham, an angry man, shouted for a runner. In the meantime, the company officers and colour-sergeants were forming the men up for the defence of the bivouacs and for a search of the hillsides; and while this was going on a flaming torch was seen to be descending from a lofty crag on the eastern hillside, a torch that swung out widely to drop between the bivouacs. The moment it was seen an intensity of rapid fire was opened on its spot of origin by the rifles and the Maxim detachment, who had their gun ready assembled for night fighting. There was a loud cry and another body tumbled, crashing down the slope to lie with spread arms and legs and a turban soaked in blood from a split skull. Several men ran towards where the torch had landed and was still sputtering. It was attached by a long cord to a stone, and to the stone was tied a square of goatskin. As a lance-corporal removed the goatskin from the stone, Lord Brora appeared.

'Hand me that.'

The lance-corporal saluted. 'Sir!' He passed over the skin, and Brora bent to examine it in the light of the native flare.

'By God!' he said, and straightened. He said no more, but made at the double towards the Colonel. 'A message from the damn natives, in English.' He shouted for a guard lantern, and one was quickly lit. In the guttering yellow light Dornoch read out the words burnt with red-hot iron into the skin.

'To the British High Commissioner and escort. The woman will die if you advance further.' Dornoch balled the skin in his fist, and looked up. In the lantern's light his face was strained and old.

'Well, Colonel?'

Steadily Dornoch said, 'We must continue. We are under orders from Murree, not from Waziristan.'

'It'll be the High Commissioner's decision.'

'I am the military commander here, Brora.'

'But his is the mission. He may consider it more prudent to abandon it. Nevertheless, I agree with you, Colonel. We should not be dictated to and be seen to give in – that way lies eventually the end of the Raj.'

Dornoch seemed dazed. 'But that poor young woman—'

'My arse to that, Colonel,' Brora broke in loudly. 'The filly's safe for a while yet. These buggers are wily and artful – they won't throw down their own wicket by killing their hostage so early. Let us go to Sir Lawrence and put our views with force.'

In the late afternoon, with all plans made as far as they could be at this stage, James Ogilvie had ridden out westerly from Nowshera with a reinforced cavalry patrol found by a squadron of the Bengal Lancers. With him

36

went two mountain guns, stripped down with their parts distributed with the ammunition on the backs of the mules. Further patrols had been sent out to north and south; the easterly direction, which was not considered a very likely route for the kidnappers to have taken since it led into British garrisoned territory, would be covered on the off-chance by units from Army Command at Murree. Ogilvie's task, outlined to him by Brigadier-General Lakenham, Fettleworth's Chief of Staff, was to follow the westerly track through to Fort Jamrud and look for any spoor that might yield up a clue and, if he found such, to follow it up after sending back a mounted runner with a report. He had carte blanche to pursue any track anywhere north or south of the Peshawar to Fort Jamrud route and even, if he thought fit, to enter the Khyber Pass itself. The word had gone out that Angela Ogilvie was to be found at all costs; no effort in terms of men or animals, ammunition or supplies was to be spared. Her safety was vital for the Raj and any patrol that picked up her trail would have the fullest backing from Murree and the other garrisons by way of reinforcements to be despatched immediately their need was notified. Available at this immediate notice were full battalions of the Dorsetshires, the Duke of Cornwall's Light Infantry, the Manchesters, Hampshires, and

Middlesex together with half-a-dozen Indian Army infantry battalions plus three cavalry brigades, guns and support columns including signal companies, engineers and field ambulances.

'Enough to have pleased the Duke of Wellington himself,' Sir Iain Ogilvie, who had arrived shortly before his son's departure, had said. 'But the tribes can still win so long as they can keep hidden. It's touch and go, James. Do your best.'

'I shall, sir.'

His father's eyes had been a trifle moist. 'Damn it, she's only a child. It's a filthy country at times, James. Her father's one of my and your Uncle Rufus's oldest friends.' He had said no more, had simply given his son a firm hand-clasp. But when James Ogilvie glanced back as he rode away with the squadron he was aware of a blank look on his father's face. He thought: the old man's suddenly aged ... he's getting long in the tooth for the strain of high command, and it doesn't help when it comes so close to home.

Three

In his bivouac, Sir Lawrence Bindle, his holstered revolver laid across his knees, looked shaken and undecided, cheeks puffy and pale behind the stubble peeping through. 'I'm not a man of action,' he said. 'You are, Colonel. What d'you advise?'

'My instinct's to go through, Sir Lawrence.'

'And mine,' Brora said loudly. 'We have the strength, and we shall join our brigade the other side of the Kohat Pass.'

'But that's not quite the point—'

'The orders from the GOC were clear enough: a full effort. And full backing.' Brora's voice rose even higher. 'It's permission to slaughter the damn natives willy-nilly and teach 'em a lesson they'll not forget!'

Sir Lawrence lifted a hand. 'Please, Lord Brora, allow me to continue. You must not lose sight of my special mission, which is essentially one of peace. I enter Waziristan simply as an adjudicator, to settle a dispute between two opposing tribes, two opposing aspirations for land. The military power represented by yourselves is here only as an

39

escort, at any rate in the first instance. And, of course, there is the lady who is the subject of this communication—'

'Precisely!'

'I cannot put her in danger of her life, Lord Brora.'

'You'll not do so any more than she is already, and has been since the moment she was taken.'

'The message reads that Mrs Ogilvie will die if we advance. In my experience of India, which is longer than yours, Lord Brora, the natives do not make empty threats – especially the Frontier tribes. You would agree, Colonel?'

Dornoch nodded heavily, shadows passing across his face as the light from the guard lantern flickered. There was a stir of wind, a sound of desolation, and from the distance came the mournful hooting of some night bird that had found its prey and was making a kill. Killing was the very essence of this lonely land ... Dornoch said, 'Yes, I agree in general, but I think not on this occasion.' He put the point Brora had made earlier: the natives would not precipitately despatch a valuable hostage. He put another point as well: his battalion was currently and undeniably under orders to act as the Delimitation Escort for the High Commissioner, but such did not relieve him of his duty to act in accordance with the spirit of the overall order from Murree, which was to spare no effort to find and rescue Mrs Ogilvie.

'Who could well be not far away, Sir Lawrence.'

'Not far?' Bindle raised his eyebrows. 'How likely is that proposition, d'you suppose?'

Dornoch shrugged. 'Not very likely, I admit, but it's a possibility I can't ignore.'

'You would see no conflict with your orders to act as my escort?'

'No, Sir Lawrence, I would not.'

'Then I'm sorry, but I do. The two cannot be compatible.' The High Commissioner lifted a hand as Brora attempted to interrupt. 'Suppose you send out search parties, Colonel ... suppose they become involved in fighting? What happens to my mission then, if my escort fires perhaps on one of the parties with whom I am here to negotiate? What will be my use then, as an adjudicator?'

Dornoch said quietly, 'I'd not propose to detach patrols specifically to search, Sir Lawrence. Others are doing that, and I would certainly not wish, for instance, to delay your arrival at Mana—'

'Then what *do* you suggest?'

'Simply that we continue, and disregard the goatskin – in Mrs Ogilvie's interest. I'm convinced they'll not carry out their threat yet, and I believe that if we advance as ordered they'll in fact take pains to preserve her life until she can be of more use to them than she can be at this moment. Also, if she is being held in the vicinity, then there's a chance she'll continue to be near us.'

'Possibly, possibly. A difficult situation, gentlemen, a difficult decision ... I would like guidance from Calcutta.'

'Calcutta's a long way off,' Brora said tartly.

'The telegraph—'

'Is also a long way off, at Peshawar, and we have not laid a field telegraph for the simple reason that the natives would have cut it the moment we were out of sight along what's an unprotected track. And a runner would delay us for too long.' Brora turned to the Colonel. 'I have pre-empted, no doubt, what you were about to say yourself, Colonel. I apologise.'

Dornoch, who had in fact made up his mind as to his course of action, had been fully prepared to enforce his decision and to over-rule the High Commissioner; but some further persuasion did the trick. The orders were passed for the regiment to move towards the Kohat Pass at first light, with picquets out and scouts extended ahead. As the sky lightened, the bugles blew and the Scots eased themselves from their bivouacs and after a hastily-taken wash in a stream, and breakfast from the field kitchens, they were fallen in and formed into column for the march. The pipes and drums played them on towards the high sides and sinister gloom of the pass. There was no sign of human life and no repetition of the previous night's goatskin threat; but just before moving out Lord Dornoch had sent back three mounted men, a lance-corporal and two privates, each of them carrying copies of a despatch for Division. As the van of the advance came beneath the shadows of the pass, the pipes and drums continued playing, giving heart to the marching files as the heights took away the climbing sun and the wind blew cold along the rock-strewn track beneath. Still no one was seen; but there would be watchful eyes along the peaks and behind boulders on the steeply-sloping sides where the picquets doubled to protect the column from flank attack, doubled until they reached the sanctuary of rough *sangars* from which they could watch the hillsides behind the sights of their rifles. The unseen native eyes would be reporting their progress, sending the word on from peak to peak that the Raj was coming through. When the column was deep into the pass, something happened: as in the night before, there was the crack of a rifle, quickly followed by another. From half-way up the hillside a turbaned figure rose, clutching at its throat; its back arched and, screaming, it toppled and rolled down towards the track, bounding from the boulders in its path. From a *sangar* one of the picquets looked down, his rifle smoking still. The native fetched up almost at the feet of Black's horse, and as the Colonel lifted a hand to halt the column the Adjutant dismounted and bent over the bloodied, trembling figure.

He looked up. 'Alive, Colonel – just.'

Lord Dornoch turned in his saddle: the Surgeon Major was already coming up. Corton carried out a quick examination. 'He hasn't long, Colonel.'

Dornoch, his face stiff and drained of emotion, nodded. 'The Sar'nt-Major – quickly.' A runner was sent down the column at the double, and within the minute Cunningham was puffing up and slamming to the halt and the salute beside the Colonel's horse.

'Sir!'

'Mr Cunningham, that man – that native. He's to be made to talk – you've had success at that in the past. You haven't long. Find out what he knows of Mrs Ogilvie.'

'Sir!' Another salute, and Cunningham turned about, his face set like the Colonel's. Then he squatted on his haunches beside the dying man, looked up at the waiting runner, and gestured for the man's bayonet. Drawn from its scabbard, the gleaming blade was handed down. Pointing it at the face, Cunningham began talking in Pushtu, rapidly, urgently and with threat in his tone. After a while the bayonet moved and there was a cry that ended in a throaty bubbling. There was a bloody froth. Corton, who had turned and walked away during the questioning, turned again as he heard the sound and came hurrying back. He bent, then looked up. 'All right, Sar'nt-Major. Enough's enough.' There was a silence, then Corton looked up once more. 'He's dead, Colonel.'

'Thank you, Doctor. Well, Mr Cunningham?'

'Not a word, sir.'

'I see. Thank you, Mr Cunningham – a distasteful job, I know.' Dornoch glanced at Lord Brora. 'Move out, if you please, Major.'

The order to resume the march was passed; the pipes and drums sounded again, to beat off the rocky slopes and fill the pass with martial sound. No one enquired as to the body's burial: such was unnecessary. The bones, when left bare by the vultures already clustering in a black cloud overhead, would be of themselves a warning message to the enemy. Without further incident the Royal Strathspey continued through the Kohat and came unscathed to the southward and into more open but still rocky and desolate terrain with high mountains all around in the great distances, peak upon peak, range upon range to every point of the compass. Ahead there was an immense cloud of dust

45

and as it was seen, so also was a subaltern from the scouting party seen, riding back to make his unnecessary report.

The rider halted. 'The brigade, Colonel, out of Kohat.'

'Thank you, Mr MacTaggart. Captain Black, the signallers, if you please. There's sun enough for the heliograph. My respects to the Brigadier-General, and an identification of my column.'

'Very good, Colonel.' A runner was despatched and shortly after he had doubled away the mirrors of the heliographs began their winking. The columns converged, and Brigadier-General Norris was seen to be cantering ahead of his troops with his Brigade Major and a subaltern. Riding ahead himself, Dornoch saluted and said formally, 'Colonel the Earl of Dornoch, sir, joining your brigade with the 114th Highlanders.'

There was a friendly nod. 'Delighted to see you, Colonel, though I fear it'll not be for longer than it takes me to pass your orders.'

Dornoch was surprised. 'You have fresh orders, sir? I was to accompany you to Mana.'

'Yes, indeed. Army Command's changed its mind – I shall take over the High Commissioner, with yourselves replaced by the 2nd Border Regiment who will join from Dera Ismail Khan when I reach Mana.'

'And us, sir?'

'You're to be detached to back up the Kohat garrison and join the search for Mrs Ogilvie, Colonel—'

'Good God, we might just as well have been left in Peshawar to probe south from there!'

'Not so. There's a need for you in Kohat. The garrison's depleted and it's considered a likely area.'

'To find Mrs Ogilvie?'

The Brigadier-General nodded. 'Fresh information has come to hand, it seems. You'll be fully informed by the Political Officer ... feller called Blaise-Willoughby, sent down from Nowshera a few weeks ago.'

Ogilvie had ridden the day before with his cavalry patrol along the whole route to Fort Jamrud: an officer of the Khyber Rifles had come down to greet his arrival in the lip of the pass. There was little to report on either hand: no unidentified persons had entered the Khyber below Fort Jamrud, and for his part Ogilvie had picked up no leads. The rifle subaltern, however, had a piece of information that might be worth following up: a Pathan had ridden out of the pass a few hours earlier from Afghanistan with two other horsemen. Riding apparently in peace, he had not been interfered with. Many of the tribesmen from the Afghan hills had relatives inside the Frontier, and it was customary to

47

allow latitude for their visits; but on this occasion the NCO of the native guard had been curious enough about the man's splendid accoutrements, and impressed enough by his imperious bearing, to talk about it after being relieved.

'And the result?' Ogilvie asked.

'A very clear description. He wore gold earrings with medallions dangling, medallions bearing a boar's head motif – like a crest. The same motif appeared on the haft of his dagger. He was tall – exceptionally tall. And he didn't wear the usual filthy goatskin coat, either. He had a cloak of some sort of maroon cloth, with gold thread worked into it—'

'And you identified him?'

'Yes, I did. Murrum Khan, basically a horse-thief and gun-runner—'

'Who would have been better arrested?'

The subaltern shrugged. 'I suppose so, but in point of fact he's done nothing against the Raj specifically and I doubt if I'd have arrested him even if I'd been there myself and recognised him. Most of the bloody Pathans are horse-thieves and gun-runners, aren't they?'

Ogilvie grinned. 'Well, that's true! What's different about Murrum Khan?'

'I didn't know this at the time, as it happens, but he's a kinsman of Dostman Khan, the chap that's behind the boundary dispute

48

down Mana way.'

'Is this on your file?'

'No. My NCO recognised the name when I told him. He has a second cousin – I think I'm right in saying – who's married to the aunt-in-law of Dostman Khan's wife's niece. Something like that. My NCO has never met him, but he's heard of him via the family.' The subaltern paused. 'There's something else as well: *badal* may come into it.'

Ogilvie's eyes narrowed: when the Pathan invoked *badal*, the tremendously important concept of ultimate revenge, then murder became inevitable. The subaltern elaborated: Dostman Khan's father, now dead, had killed Murrum Khan's elder brother in a dispute over a woman. Ogilvie asked, 'Have you reported this to Peshawar?'

'I was about to. I'd only unravelled my NCO's story just as you came in sight.'

'Then I suggest you report at once.'

'I'll do that, providing the field telegraph's not cut again—'

'If it is, send a runner. I'd advise your Commanding Officer to treat that as an order from Division, and waste no more time.' Ogilvie spoke harshly: in his view there had been an appalling slackness, a lack of proper vigilance on the part of Fort Jamrud's garrison. He went on, 'Murrum Khan ... which way did he ride from here?'

'Along the track for Peshawar—'

'I didn't meet him.'

'There's a pass to the south, the Rahkand Pass—'

'Yes. I shall ride along it, into Waziristan. The message to Peshawar quickly, please.'

'You think there's a connection with Mrs Ogilvie?'

'I don't know, but I do know this: if she's got mixed up in *badal*, if she's going to drop between two factions looking for revenge for wrongs – or trying to avoid its results – then it's going to go hard for her and she's likely to be killed the moment British troops approach wherever she's being held.' Ogilvie swung his horse and rode towards the Squadron Commander of his patrol; after they had had words Ogilvie and the Bengal Lancers turned away, back in the direction of Peshawar, and rode fast for the Rahkand. Ogilvie's heart was like lead: his words to the rifle subaltern had been only too true. *Badal* was always a killer, and was the one thing that precluded all attempts at reason. Angela could well become a helpless pawn in the dreadful game of *badal*...

The Royal Strathspey marched with their drums beating into the native city of Kohat, to be met by an Assistant Provost Marshal who directed them to the British encampment beyond the outskirts to the east. Awaiting them in camp was the familiar figure of

Major Blaise-Willoughby of Lieutenant-General Fettleworth's divisional staff. With him on his shoulder, Dornoch saw, was his pet monkey, disrespectfully named Wolseley after the Army Commander-in-Chief in Whitehall. As Blaise-Willoughby approached in unmilitary fashion, Wolseley nibbled at a nut and scattered fragments of shell over Blaise-Willoughby's appallingly crumpled suit of *mufti*.

'What's in the air now, Blaise-Willoughby?'

'A smell of monkey, sir. Wolseley needs a bath – but I digress and apologise for it.'

'For the smell?'

'For the mention of it, sir, in an ungentlemanly way. I suggest your battalion makes camp, and that we talk in privacy while they make it.'

'With my second-in-command and my Adjutant.'

'Oh, by all means,' the Political Officer said in a distant voice, sounding put out. He stared at the other two officers, a touch of disdain noticeable. 'Captain Black, isn't it?'

'Yes,' Black answered shortly: he disliked monkeys and unsmart officers who had defected to the ranks of the Civilian establishment. 'We have met, Major Blaise-Willoughby.'

'Yes. And?' Blaise-Willoughby raised an eyebrow at the second-in-command.

'Major Lord Brora. It's not only your

51

damn animal that needs a bath – so, by God, does that suit of yours!'

'Colour-Sar'nt MacTrease!' The Regimental Sergeant-Major's voice was a bellow that seemed to strike against the Waziri hills and come back in loud thunder. 'A word in your ear, if you please.'

MacTrease marched up smartly and stood at attention. 'Sir!'

'You will have words with your company, Colour-Sar'nt, and tell them to modulate their voices when referring to the Divisional Political Officer.'

'Aye, sir—'

'He is a *gentleman*, Colour-Sar'nt, even though he serves now in a Civilian capacity, *not* a whatever it was I overheard loud and clear. Mr Oscar Wilde is not a subject I wish to hear spoken of, do you understand?'

'Aye, sir, I do that.'

'Very well, then.' Cunningham relaxed a little. 'I don't deny the accuracy, just the stressing of it in a loud voice. Major Blaise-Willoughby has a job to do and I for one wish him luck with it, bloody monkeys not-withstanding!'

'So do I, Sar'nt-Major—'

'*Sir* on parade, Colour-Sar'nt MacTrease, and we are on parade now, a parade to make camp. It will be done smartly. There are native units adjacent, and I will not be made a laughing stock before natives. Straight lines, Colour MacTrease, and dead even spaces – you'll pass the word round. I'll be checking distances myself, with the RQMS. Understood?'

'Aye, sir.'

'Very well, then.' Cunningham turned about smartly and marched off, back straight as a rod, free arm swinging from the shoulder. MacTrease stared after him thoughtfully: old Bosom was being unusually unfriendly. It was, MacTrease thought to himself, the atmosphere ... the kidnap by thugs of a young lady with regimental connections was having its due effect on tempers and reactions. The regiment was a family in its own right; so, in a much larger sense, of course, was the Raj itself, and this sort of thing diminished the Raj and its power. That affected them all, from the Viceroy down to the newest joined recruit from the home depot ... MacTrease shrugged, and marched away with his pace-stick to haze the section sergeants and junior NCOs, who in their turn would harry the poor suffering privates into precise tent placement. It wasn't only Bosom Cunningham who had the good name of the regiment at heart.

Four

It was an unhappy conference, one that brought bad news for Lord Dornoch: Blaise-Willoughby reported that word had been received via the telegraph from Division of Ogilvie's contact with Fort Jamrud, of the entry into India of Murrum Khan – and of the fact that subsequently Ogilvie and his patrol of the Bengal Lancers had, apparently, vanished.

'Easily enough done,' Dornoch said, frowning. 'Why your seeming inference that harm's come to them?'

Blaise-Willoughby laughed and stroked Wolseley's hairy back. 'Harm's easily done, too! But the facts are these: Captain Ogilvie was known to have the intention of entering the Rahkand Pass into Waziristan. When this news was to hand, General Fettleworth ordered out a regiment of cavalry with attached guns to ride to his assistance—'

'Had Ogilvie asked for this?'

'No, I gather not,' the Political Officer said, 'but we all know what Bloody Francis Fettleworth is like, I think. Can't resist a show of force ... anyway, the cavalry found no sign of him right the way along the Rahkand or in

54

the vicinity of the Waziristan end of the pass—'

'Understandable, surely?'

Blaise-Willoughby shrugged. 'True, it's a big area, but Bloody Francis's reinforcements couldn't have been all that far behind Ogilvie, and there was one suspicious circumstance reported back to Division by a mounted runner: there was a cast shoe on the track inside the Rahkand.'

There was no need for elaboration: no cavalryman, indeed no mounted infantryman who understood horses, would have ridden on in the circumstances. If the refitting of the shoe was impossible, the horse would have been walked all the way back to base if necessary; but no dismounted trooper had been seen.

'Man could have been intercepted by a Pathan and killed,' Brora said.

'Yes, he could. I'm not saying positively that harm's come to Ogilvie's patrol.'

'I take it,' Dornoch said, 'it's not because of the possibility that it has, that my orders have been changed?'

'Not directly. You're here – you've been as it were checked in your southward advance – to cover the Waziristan end of the Rahkand and parts adjacent and find Mrs Ogilvie.'

'This is on account of the man Murrum Khan?'

'Correct, Colonel.'

'I think you'd better tell me about him, Blaise-Willoughby, before we go any further.'

'Right, I will.' Settling Wolseley comfortably, the Political Officer proceeded with his exposition. Murrum Khan, who should undoubtedly have been apprehended before passing easterly of Fort Jamrud, was a man of great influence amongst the tribesmen, a stirrer of trouble wherever he went, a ruthless man dedicated to self-aggrandisement and to harassment of the Raj whenever he saw the chance. It was, Blaise-Willoughby declared, a certain wager that if he was not already the mainspring of the boundary trouble in the Mana area, then he would be seeing to it that he became such; Brigadier-General Norris had been informed of the man's entry into India and of the inherent dangers. Murrum Khan, Blaise-Willoughby said, would in the process of thrusting his fingers into the pie adding to his personal dimension in the esteem of the tribesmen of at any rate one of the opposing sides – and, if he could outwit and outmanoeuvre the Raj, possibly of both.

'And the outmanoeuvring's to come via Mrs Ogilvie?' Brora asked.

'It's very possible – indeed likely.'

'Then it's a case of find this Murrum Khan, find the filly?'

Blaise-Willoughby's smile was enigmatic.

'Never assume the native's simple, my dear Brora. There's no black and white out here – in a metaphorical sense, of course—'

'For God's sake,' Brora snapped, 'talk English! What's all that supposed to mean?'

'It means, if I must put everything into words of one syllable, that Murrum Khan's much too wily to be close to his hostage, if that's what the lady's to become, and frankly I'm working only on guesses so far. She'll be held somewhere distant, yet handy.' Blaise-Willoughby waved an airy hand. 'Your oyster's a large one, Brora. You haven't the world, but you have a sizeable chunk of Waziristan.' He paused, eyeing Brora mischievously: the two were poles apart in character and approach, already full of mutual dislike. 'I know you've not been long in India, my dear chap. You'll learn much in the next few weeks—'

'Not from you, at all events.'

Blaise-Willoughby shrugged. 'Be naive if you wish, it's not my funeral. I only try to help by attempting to instil a *soupçon* of guile into regimental officers—'

'Bosh! If an officer can't be forthright and honest, what does he become, what's he worth to an army in the field? Guile my arse.' Lord Brora got to his feet, breathing hard. 'I am Lord Brora. I insist on fighting clean. Guile's not for the field, it's for pimps' parlours. I wish you good-day – with your

57

permission, Colonel, I have duties to attend to.'

Dornoch, the twitchings of a smile playing about his mouth, nodded. 'By all means, Major.'

Brora turned for the tent-flap; as he bent to leave, the Political Officer, his face pale, spoke venomously. 'I shall not forget your words, Lord Brora—'

'I am unrepentant.'

'I have a long memory ... like the elephant. I trust you enjoyed your sojourn with the Supply and Transport, Lord Brora?'

Brora straightened. His face had gone a deep red and his eyes bulged, bright blue anger signals flashing at the Political Officer; but he caught the warning stare from Dornoch and contained his temper with an effort. Without a word he turned away and thrust his large frame through the flap and out of the tent. He seethed away: the past was back with a vengeance, the recent humiliation when at Sir Iain Ogilvie's instigation, no less, he had been temporarily seconded to the S & T, a damn lowly bunch, to superintend the journey of a contingent of elephants to the domains of the Rajah of Rangapore, a sop arranged by Captain Ogilvie to bring a rebel back within the Raj! It had been a shameful business and a direct result of his having done his duty in arraigning Captain Ogilvie before a General Court Martial that

58

had had the crass stupidity to reject his charges almost out-of-hand ... Lord Brora, smelling nepotism all the way, had suffered an appalling journey to Rangapore. As for Political Officers, they could give themselves fancy titles if they wished, but they were no more than damn spies in reality.

The cave-mouth was well hidden: across its entry stood a hefty boulder, screening the black hole from all passing sight but allowing the ingress and egress of persons prepared for a tight squeeze. Inside little light penetrated, and the air was foul. Immediately behind the boulder, just within the cave, a man stood guard with a curved dagger thrust into a cartridge belt and a bayonetted *jezail* sinister in the crook of his arm. Though he stood where he could get, as it were, first sniff of such air as came through, he seemed not to mind the stench too much. The stench would get worse, far worse: it came mostly from death. The cave was deep, running back into the hillside's rocky strata for more than a mile, penetrating far below the summit like the great system of caves and pot-holes beneath Ingleborough in the West Riding of Yorkshire; and there was much room in its cross-passages and extensively-opening caverns to house the dead as well as the living. A squadron of cavalry of the Indian Army consisted of three British officers, four Viceroy's Commissioned Officers, a hundred and ten native other ranks and seventy-two followers, with one hundred and eighteen riding horses, sixty pack mules and two riding camels. True, the special patrol that had been ambushed and heavily out-numbered in the Rahkand Pass had not been of such great size: there had been no followers and no transport train attached, while the squadron itself had not been up to strength. Nevertheless, the knives and the *jezails* had been busy and all prisoners save the one had been despatched most expeditiously and the bodies of men and animals rolled down a slope that led to a wide surface hole connected to the main cave system. Reaching the bottom, they had been dragged by sweating Pathans with hooks and ropes into the side passages and caverns; what the sentry's nostrils picked up now was the smell of blood: soon the putrefaction would set in. But for now just blood, and the metal of the guns, which had been dismantled to seal the total disappearance of the British patrol and had been cast down the slope behind the corpses. All this, James Ogilvie knew: he had seen much of it and had heard the rest after he had been manhandled to the slope, tied hand and foot and lowered down the shaft on the end of a rope. Once down, he had been seized by four armed Pathans in stinking garments and carried to a recess at the side of the main passage where he was thrown down, still bound, to lie under guard of two men. The only sounds now were of their movements and voices as they exchanged occasional words of Pushtu but said nothing of any help to their prisoner.

Time passed: how long, Ogilvie could only guess. He lay in pain from wounds received and from the binding ropes that were drawn over-tight, in misery approaching despair as he went over and over the massacre, blaming himself, wondering how long it would take Bloody Francis in Nowshera to react to the non-return of his patrol.

At sundown that day Lieutenant-General Fettleworth was enjoying a *chota peg* in his private quarters with his Chief of Staff and complaining of the lack of news from all the various probes that he had ordered.

'Someone must have found something, Lakenham.'

'There was the cast shoe, sir.'

'Yes! I know. And then what? Damn silence, that's what! What's become of the unit I ordered out to reinforce young Ogilvie?'

Lakenham stifled a sigh. 'They were the ones who reported finding the cast shoe, sir.'

'Ah, yes. And they were who?'

'Probyn's Horse, sir.'

'H'm.' Fettleworth took a mouthful of

61

whisky and lifted the glass to study the golden glow against the lamp on a table beside him. 'Don't know what we'd do without the Scots, hey, Lakenham?'

'Fine regiments...'

'Well, yes, them – but I was referring to the whisky.' Fettleworth frowned, and eased his stomach a little in the chair. 'Talking of Scots regiments, what about Dornoch's lot?'

'I told you, sir, Blaise-Willoughby's spoken to Lord Dornoch—'

'Yes, so you did. Yes, indeed. Well, they're the right regiment in the right place at the right time – what? We can be sure they'll do their best – after all, the name of Ogilvie ... d'you follow me?'

'I do, sir, but—'

'When I've the time, I'll write a memo on security of married quarters, *all* married quarters, not just the military. Remind me of that, Lakenham. Damn Civilians! Blasted inefficiency, losing that poor young woman – and just look at the hoo-ha it's put me to!' Fettleworth scratched his chin, lifting his face like a bulldog to do so. 'Before long I'll have everyone on my back – the Commander-in-Chief, HE, Whitehall and the Prime Minister, even Her Majesty I dare say.' Fettleworth turned as a bearer came in and made a low salaam. 'What is it?'

'Dinner, General sahib.'

Disregarding the native, Bloody Francis

spoke again to his Chief of Staff. 'Drink up, Lakenham, and we'll fill the inner man. I'm dashed hungry – *dashed* hungry! It's all the pressures, y'know...' He heaved himself to his feet and ushered Lakenham towards the dining-room. Conversation at dinner was limited: Fettleworth was ever a hearty trencherman, and his wife, who could normally be relied upon to entertain guests with chatter, was away, somewhat unseasonably to be sure, in Simla. Fettleworth concentrated therefore on the food and cleared his mind of the worries of command: he'd done what he could.

A man came at last to Ogilvie, a tall man though far from splendidly dressed. He stood in silence, smiling down, teeth very white in a dark, handsome face, clearly visible in the light from a lantern set on a pole beside Ogilvie's recess.

'Murrum Khan?' Ogilvie asked.

The man shook his head, his smile disappearing. 'Not Murrum Khan, sahib. I am called Razjah Shah. But you shall tell me what you know of Murrum Khan.'

'I know nothing of Murrum Khan beyond his name.'

The smile came back. 'Yet you ask if I am he. I am not a fool, sahib, nor am I a fat and slothful Hindu. I am a Pathan, a warrior. Our way is to strike, and strike hard as I have

63

already done. If you do not speak of Murrum Khan, I shall strike again, and this time at you.' From the folds of his garment he brought a long knife, and drew the end across Ogilvie's cheek, not deeply but enough to sting. 'Now, sahib. Murrum Khan.'

No harm, perhaps, would come of the truth. Ogilvie said, 'He has ridden out of the Khyber, and is believed to have entered Waziristan.'

'By way of the Rahkand Pass, and you were in pursuit of him?'

'Yes.'

'Why, sahib?'

Ogilvie didn't answer. The Pathan's smile was still in place, and he shook his head slightly as he said, 'I shall tell you: because you believe he knows the whereabouts of the Englishwoman, Ogilvie mem'sahib. The wife of your cousin of the boundary commission.' He paused. 'I see surprise in your face that I know your name, Ogilvie sahib, but you must realise that men can talk, and some did so before they died.'

'Under torture.'

'Yes. War is war, Ogilvie sahib, and exists only to be won. Now I shall tell you more, which perhaps you do not know: Murrum Khan has not the woman in his own hands yet, but soon will have unless I can prevent the happening, the transfer—'

64

'You?'

'I, Ogilvie sahib.'

'You are yourself friendly to the Raj?' Ogilvie asked, lifting a sardonic eyebrow.

The smile widened. 'That you shall find out. So often events dictate our loyalties, for we are largely nomads, and must do as needs be at the time. More I shall not say, except this: soon now you will move from here, since this place may be known to Murrum Khan, who is no stranger to this side of the Afghan frontier.'

He went away; the guards and the lantern remained, and after a while food was brought, and water, and Ogilvie's wrists were untied. While he ate the guards stood with their *jezails* pointed at head and stomach, the sharp ends of the rusty, snaky bayonets only inches from his nose. The food was scanty and the meal was soon finished and another period of silence and inactivity began, and once again Ogilvie's wrists were bound with the rope. He thought of Hector's wife: so far there were no clues but he had a feeling he was close now to learning more and that soon there might even be a contact with her; that gave hope. He wondered continually how Angela would be standing the strain of captivity and perhaps brutality. James Ogilvie had first met his cousin's wife in Simla, whilst on local leave at the hill station; though her father and his own father were old friends, Angela had been a child when James had last been at home at Corriecraig, and he had no recollection of a visit from her – a matter for regret, he had felt when Hector had arrived with her in Simla. She was friendly with everyone and was a favourite with the elderly officers to whom she seemed to bring back a touch of their youth: many gallantries had been accorded her. Yet, in spite of this and in spite of the propensity of Simla tongues to wag in gossip over even the most innocent of friendships, the ladies of the hill station had nothing but good to say of young Mrs Ogilvie, and this James considered a major triumph on Angela's part. Almost every other woman in Simla had had her reputation shredded by Mrs Colonel This and Mrs Major That: jealousy was Simla's watchword, and gossip the inevitable outcome of sheer boredom in a way of life in which there was no work whatsoever to be done. Angela had enjoyed her first experience of Simla, but James was certain that its new delights would fade quickly if she had to be there for long; Hector's duties, however, had taken him back to Calcutta and then on to Nowshera. James Ogilvie had missed Angela after she had left in the bullock cart for the railway junction at Kalka; and had somewhat moodily cut short his own leave and returned early to rejoin his regiment and expend some of his energies in polo and pig-sticking, envying his cousin his luck in the marriage stakes. There were few females of interest in Nowshera and Peshawar, or in Simla either: those bored, sharp-tongued military wives and their jolly daughters who almost knew more about their regiments than the husbands and fathers did ... James, however devoted to the army, had no wish to marry it.

His thoughts of Angela were roughly interrupted when Razjah Shah returned, striding into the circle of light from the lantern. He said, 'The time to move has come, Ogilvie sahib.' He gave an order in Pushtu and the guards bent and hoisted Ogilvie to his feet, untying the ropes from around his ankles but leaving his wrists secured. A smelly but concealing goatskin coat was thrown over his uniform. The lantern was taken from the pole and Ogilvie was marched away down the main cave towards the entrance. Squeezing round the great boulder, he emerged into darkness to find more ready *jezails* with bayonets fixed.

A voice said in Pushtu, 'Come, follow me.' Urged on from the rear by the bayonets Ogilvie moved behind the man who had spoken. There was a cold wind; the night was icy. Through the darkness Ogilvie made out horses, some score of them waiting in a semi-circle around the boulder-hidden entry. Ogilvie was led to one of these horses and swung up into the saddle along with a rangy Pathan who put strong arms around him after tying a filthy rag in place as a gag. More Pathans mounted and then Razjah Shah emerged from the cave and swung himself into the last remaining saddle. He lifted an arm and called out, and the cavalcade got on the move through the night, descending swiftly to the track below and riding towards the south. The horses' hooves had been muffled and there was scarcely any sound, and no sign of life but for their own. Ogilvie sat helpless with his wrists still tied and the sinewy arms of the Pathan holding him close to a stinking body.

In the Kohat encampment, patrols of the Royal Strathspey had been detailed and had marched out by nightfall to scour the inward end of the Rahkand all the way from the Kohat Pass itself, leaving the Scots' lines depleted and too open to surprise attack for Lord Brora's liking. Blaise-Willoughby had left during the afternoon, remarking to the Colonel that he had matters to attend to in the city of Kohat.

'More spying, no doubt,' Brora said that night in reference to the Political Officer's intentions.

'Bad blood doesn't help, Major,' Dornoch said mildly.

'Nor does rudeness. Feller's a boor, a cad

and a damn bounder. Within the hour he'll be rootling about in the brothels of Kohat like a pig in its sty.'

'Live and let live, Major.' Dornoch, his voice quiet and level still, raised a hand as Brora began to interrupt heatedly. 'That is an order, and you'll do well to heed it. Do you understand me? Major Blaise-Willoughby has an important job to do and we must be of mutual help.'

'Firmness is needed now, Colonel. Not guile and jiggery-pokery.'

'Then how would you handle this?' Dornoch asked.

'Mount a counter-threat. Threaten somewhere – Kohat city if you like – with the guns. Blow it to smithereens if Mrs Ogilvie's not handed back unharmed.'

Dornoch smiled. 'The idea's not without its attractions for me, Brora, I admit, but it would in fact be fatal and we must both recognise it—'

'Why so, Colonel?'

'Because the area's like tinder, that's why. We should light no sparks. To destroy – even to threaten to destroy – a native city that may have no connection with the kidnappers would cause the trouble to spread throughout India, far beyond—'

'Villages are laid waste from time to time, are they not?'

'Occasionally, yes, as part of a punitive

expedition.'

'Then it's simply a difference of scale.'

'I disagree,' Dornoch said. 'Along the North-West Frontier the infrequent burning of a village is seen as an expected punishment for some specific act against the Raj. To shatter a town by gunfire before there has even been a death would be viewed quite differently—'

'But if that death should come, it will be too late!'

Dornoch spread his hands. 'True. We must bank on it that the death won't come – we must wait, and keep our powder dry until more is known, and in the meantime search as diligently as we can. We must do nothing to make harder the High Commissioner's task, either – that's important.'

'But the filly—'

'What happens or does not happen to Mrs Ogilvie is wholly dependent upon the fate of the boundary dispute, and that means the High Commissioner, Brora. Don't lose sight of that, and remember something else: India's changing – not fast, not much, but change is in the wind and some of it has settled on the land already. Our footing here has never been entirely sure since the Mutiny. The Political Officers today are possibly more germane to our problems than the soldiers are!'

Lord Brora made no reply but turned away

rudely and pushed through the tent-flap into the darkness, thinking slanderous thoughts about such as Blaise-Willoughby. Sighing in frustration, Dornoch set about drafting orders for the morrow, which was likely to be a repeat of today: patrols and more patrols, and very probably nil reports coming back when they marched in again. After a while the Colonel drew his watch from a pocket and threw down his notes. He went outside the tent and stood in silence as the bugler sounded Last Post. Then, a moment later, he heard the first wail as Pipe-Major Ross blew air into the bag beneath his arm, and squeezed. In accordance with regimental tradition, the Pipe-Major marked Lights Out with the gut-twisting strains of 'The Flowers of the Forest'. A lump came to Dornoch's throat as he listened. That same tune had been played by the regiment over the Heights of Abraham within sound of the closing ears of Wolfe; it had stolen over the bloodied battlefield of Waterloo. But it was Scotland that came back tonight to Dornoch, Scotland that he had not seen for many years; Scotland and the men of the 114th Highlanders who had fallen in action under his command throughout the long years of Indian service, men who would not march back again to the depot at Invermore when at last the regiment took the troopship for home. Sad thoughts and nostalgic ones:

71

Dornoch was almost glad when the pipes had finished playing.

Into the smelly alleys of Kohat a man came furtively: slinking along by the running sore of the open drain, keeping in the shadows of the hovels as the moon's light stole down. He was thin as a rake and poorly clad for a cold night; the face was cadaverous, the nose hawk-like, the eyes piercing as they met the moonbeams now and again. The man carried no *jezail*, no firearms at all, but a knife was handy in the folds of his clothing and would be used if necessary. As he made his way along he heard regular footfalls and a clink of equipment and then, fortuitiously, the moon lit upon marching men, and khaki, and Lee-Enfield rifles: a patrol from a British regiment, ensuring the peace of the native city – at any rate, on the surface of the public face. The man saw the entry to a cross-alley ahead, and moved for it swiftly and silently. Unseen, he dived down into obscurity, and the British soldiers moved on past, their sounds fading behind in the night. The man continued his journey, only to be impeded again: Kohat had its share of persons anxious to rob even those who appeared of little wealth. Those with wealth did not move around at night alone, and the choice of victim was thereby restricted, and even a poor man might possess an *anna* or two. The footpad struck swiftly from a black hole that passed for a doorway, but the hawk-nosed man was quicker. The knife came out and thrust upwards into the throat, and there was a gurgle and a fountain of life-blood, and the man pulled out the knife and moved on. The body fell in a heap, the head drooling into the open sewer, to lie there until the city's sweepers should be prevailed upon to remove it from human sight, and its stench from human nostrils. The hawk-nosed man vanished again into the shadows, and went by way of many alleys and cross-passages until he stopped by a thick wooden door bound with brass.

Here he knocked three times and waited, his eyes casting glances all around as though attack might come before he was admitted. The door was opened to him by Major Blaise-Willoughby.

Five

'Hold!'

Razjah Shah's voice was not loud but it carried back; his upraised hand was faintly seen, at any rate by the forward riders. The cavalcade halted, the breath of the horses steaming in the chill night air. They were on high ground and open to the wind. Ogilvie could make out nothing ahead but the scrub and rock of a barren land looming through the night. The leader rode back and faced his followers.

'It is below us now. I have seen lights. Here we part for a while.' He spoke in Pushtu. 'The British officer sahib comes with me and will be guarded by the three men as already told. The rest of you will ride on and take our horses with you.'

No mention of where they were to ride to, no mention of what it was that lay below with lights: Ogilvie's guess was a native village, or perhaps a bandit camp. He found himself lifted down from the horse and set on his feet, once again with bayonets close. Figures loomed through the darkness: the leader spoke again, this time in English. 'It is near to journey's end, Ogilvie sahib. There is to be no sound if you wish to live.' The men moved closer with their *jezails* and Ogilvie was pushed ahead along a sloping track, and a moment later he saw what the tall man had seen: lights below, just a handful of them but widely scattered: the place they were coming to was clearly bigger than a mere camp. More than the lights he could not see: there was no moon now. Heavy cloud lay across the sky, moving fast before the wind but being backed up by more rolling cloud out of the north.

The downward journey was taken carefully, with hands holding fast to the prisoner. As the ground levelled out they came to some isolated hovels; they went on past these and began to enter what seemed to be a small town nestling behind its walls at the foot of the mountain range, a small valley community. Here the wind was less, but the air as cold with a hint of snow to come out of the wind blowing across the peaks from the foothills of Himalaya. The men moved swiftly, like fleeting shadows, deeper into the town; at the corner of an alley a man met them.

'Come...'

He turned away and was followed. At the end of the alley was a crumbling building, its windows gaping, its stone broken and jagged, a staircase bare to the elements. The party was led into this semi-ruin, tramping through dust and debris and decay. The disturbance brought fragments down like rain, with larger pieces of masonry that fortunately fell free of the intruders but made noise enough to waken the dead, Ogilvie thought. In a place that had been a room the guide stopped in the darkness and swept debris aside with his foot until a square had been cleared and a trap-door lay revealed. The foot tapped twice, then once, then twice more: the trap-door swung open on a counter-balancing weight, and steps were seen.

'Down, Ogilvie sahib.'

Ogilvie obeyed; all the men came down behind him except the guide; when the trap-door had been shut his feet were heard again, scuffing the concealing debris back into place.

In the Kohat morning, after the Union Flag had been hoisted to the flagstaff and the colour guard marched away with the pipes and drums, Major Blaise-Willoughby and Wolseley the monkey rode out again from the city and, passing the guard tent to the salutes of the sentries, were met by Lord Brora, who was on a tour of inspection of the regimental lines.

'Ah, Lord Brora. A very good morning to you.'

Brora looked the Political Officer up and down. 'I trust you've come from your damn spying to apologise for your remark of yesterday?'

'No.'

'It was in filthy taste,' Brora stormed, his face red, 'and I *demand* an apology. If I don't get it, I shall make representations to Division and have you damn well recalled out of my sight!'

Blaise-Willoughby smiled and shifted Wolseley to a more comfortable position on his

76

shoulder. 'How will you do that, I wonder?'

'Via the telegraph from Kohat, of course.'

Blaise-Willoughby's eyes narrowed. 'To use my name on the telegraph would be foolish, but I believe you're fool enough to do it all the same. As for me, I have my duty to consider. You have my apology, as abject as you'd like.'

'And for your remarks just uttered.'

'And for my remarks just uttered. Where's your Colonel?'

'In his tent.'

'Thank you.'

The Political Officer rode on, wearing an expression that Brora considered supercilious and impertinent. At Dornoch's tent Blaise-Willoughby dismounted and took off his hat to the sentry's salute. Hearing sounds, the Colonel put his head from the flap and once again Blaise-Willoughby removed his hat.

'Good morning, Colonel. I come with tidings.'

'Do you indeed? Come inside.'

Blaise-Willoughby entered and was bidden to a canvas camp stool. Dornoch asked crisply, 'Well?'

'Last night,' Blaise-Willoughby said, 'a man came to me. As a matter of fact, I was expecting him – if not his news.'

'A native?'

'One who passes as such,' Blaise-Willoughby answered obliquely. 'I prefer his identity to remain with me.'

'Your privilege, Major.'

Blaise-Willoughby leaned forward and spoke quietly. 'This man has been in the field – in the field in *my* terms, that is – for some weeks past. He's learned some interesting facts, Colonel. He has learned that a bandit by name Razjah Shah is concerned in the boundary dispute around Mana. More recently, in fact only yesterday, he learned that your Captain Ogilvie and his cavalry patrol had been ambushed and taken by this man Razjah Shah – I hasten to add that Ogilvie is alive and kicking. I'm sorry to add that his patrol was slaughtered to a man after the ambush.'

'Good God!' Dornoch's face had whitened beneath its sunburn. 'What ... where is Ogilvie being held, Blaise-Willoughby, do you know that?'

'No. Only where he *was*, as last known by my man. He was to be moved. My man didn't know where to.'

'No clues?'

Blaise-Willoughby shook his head. 'I'm afraid not, Colonel. Frankly, I can't even make a guess. Waziristan's an easy enough place to vanish in – as don't we all know! However, I'm able to make certain conjectures in the broad sense.'

'Well?'

'This bandit, Razjah Shah, is known to the Political Department and so, of course, is Murrum Khan. Now, Razjah Shah, although a Pathan as is Murrum Khan, is of the Mahsud tribe. Murrum Khan is an Afridi.' Blaise-Willoughby paused. 'You follow, I think, Colonel?'

'Indeed I do. Murrum Khan and Razjah Shah are on opposing sides of the boundary fence – of the current dispute? Is this the fact?'

'Yes,' Blaise-Willoughby answered. 'And more than that: if Murrum Khan has a hostage in the form of Mrs Ogilvie, then so now has Razjah Shah in the form of her husband's cousin! And I don't like it one little bit. Young Ogilvie and the girl are going to be somewhat nastily played off against each other as counters, I fear ... and somewhere in between is the greater consideration of the security of the Raj.'

Dornoch, who was lighting his pipe, looked sharply over the bowl. 'Do I understand you right, Blaise-Willoughby?'

'I fear so, yes. There must never be a breach ... the administration can never allow any thin ends of wedges, Colonel, such that could become levers.'

'I'd prefer plain language, if you please, Blaise-Willoughby.'

'Very well, Colonel.' The Political Officer got to his feet. 'The considerations of the Raj must come first. You'll not disagree with that, I know. Unless a double rescue can be brought off, it may become necessary for one or other of the parties to be—'

'To be left to it?'

'To make a sacrifice, Colonel. Even both of them. I'm sorry.' Blaise-Willoughby put a steadying hand on Wolseley's rump. 'I shall be making my report to Division at Now-shera, and no doubt there'll be a reaction from General Fettleworth. Good-day to you, Colonel.'

Blaise-Willoughby left the tent; Dornoch listened to the hoofbeats as man and monkey rode away towards Kohat. Dornoch felt a shake in his hands; Blaise-Willoughby was a cold-blooded man, as cold as a fish, and a schemer ... but that was not fair, of course. Political officers had to be schemers, to be such was part and parcel of their trade, a trade that Dornoch in fact liked as little as did Brora. Of course the Raj must come first: that was why they were all in India. Ogilvie would realise that as well as anyone else, and would make no complaint about it, but the young woman was in a different category. And Bloody Francis Fettleworth? What would be that reaction when it came? Dornoch believed he could sum it up in advance: it would follow precisely along the lines of Blaise-Willoughby's recent utterance. But of one thing Dornoch felt positive:

Fettleworth would still use every endeavour to get the woman at least to safety, and if he failed he would mount the biggest punitive expedition ever seen upon the Frontier – for what that would be worth after the event.

Dornoch left his tent and stood looking along the precisely-spaced regimental lines, at parties of men going about their work at the ammunition and supply train, at men cleaning rifles, at the Farrier-Sergeant and his section tending the hooves of horses and mules, re-shoeing where necessary, while the menial tasks that in military stations in white countries would be performed by fatigue parties were carried out by the lowly natives of the camp followers. A peaceful, workaday scene, with a wintry sun shining down from a clear sky to bring a touch of warmth to the northern chill. But all around stood India, the immensity of the great sub-continent brooding in its age-old silence, brooding as though biding its time ... Blaise-Willoughby was right! Dornoch's own words to Brora came back to him starkly: India was changing, and no person would be more aware of that than the officers of the Political Department whose ears were ever to the ground. New ideas were stirring, new faces of native power were emerging with clamouring voices, voices that spoke in the bazaars and in the hills against the British Raj and to whom each small victory would be manna from heaven. Certainly no breach must come! The integrity of the Raj must stand four-square or it would go piecemeal.

Dornoch braced his shoulders and turned to his native runner, standing obsequiously by the sentry. 'Go to the Adjutant sahib speedily. I wish all officers and the Regimental Sergeant-Major sahib to attend outside my tent.'

The word spread fast after the conference: Dornoch had given no orders that it should not, and in fact preferred his men to know the facts rather than be misled by rumour. The mood of the Scots was grim and determined; James Ogilvie was a well-liked officer and this business had now come even closer home. Vengeance was firmly in the air, and the opinion was freely expressed that Northern Army Command in Murree should draft in more troops and saturate the whole area. More cautious voices suggested the truth: that Waziristan was much too vast a territory for even the total strength of the combined Murree and Ootacamund commands to cover in such a way that every hole, every crevice and every town hide-out could be found and searched. The natives were as ever wily, and would contrive to keep one jump ahead. Wiliness was better met by wiliness, a task that no regiment was equipped to carry out; which put the matter firmly in the hands of the Political Department, whom not a man amongst the Scots trusted. They were a dodgy lot, and too clever by half, and had opted for the Political as being a softer billet than the field and the cantonment.

In the meantime the patrols continued, fresh ones going out as tired men marched or rode in with their nil reports.

In the cellar below the derelict building there were three apartments, damp and dirty and smelling of all manner of unpleasantness. In one sat three Pathans with knives and *jezails*, and a crone, as old as the surrounding hills, dressed in black that was green with an age that came close to rivalling her own tally of years. Her face was seamed, the eyes coal-black and bright in the beams that struggled through the oily fumes from a lamp set on a chair. She sat against the wall like a carven image of Methuselah, her bottom on the damp bare earth, seeming scarcely even to breathe. In the next apartment were heaps of sacking that did duty as makeshift beds, also set on the bare earth, and a young woman, modestly veiled, with a baby in her arms being gently rocked and crooned to sleep. It was to the third apartment that Ogilvie had been taken; still with his wrists tied behind his back but the goatskin garment now removed, he looked around in the flickers of a kind of Aladdin's lamp, a wick in a boat-shaped vessel containing tallow. The apartment was quite large, and in the centre was sunk a pit the bottom of which he could not see from where he stood. Over the pit a beam ran, just below the ceiling, and on this beam was rigged a runner with a pulley and hook dangling from it. As Ogilvie waited at knife-point the pulley was hauled along the runner, a rope was placed around his chest and pulled taut under his bound arms, the slack was taken up by two of his escort, and he rose in the air. He was then pushed along the runner until he was positioned over the pit.

Then the lamp was brought closer and set in a niche in the wall close to the pit. Ogilvie looked down: at first he could see nothing but thick blackness. The pit was deep. Then he made out smooth sides, sides with no purchase anywhere – they could almost have been of polished rock. Razjah Shah lifted the lamp from its niche and held it over the lip of the pit.

'Look,' he commanded.

Ogilvie looked downward again. He could hear a curious rustling now and could begin to see something heaving and undulating: snakes, very many of them, small but no doubt deadly, writhing, some of them attempting to climb the smooth sides, and failing, and dropping back, and trying again.

This was not an unusual ploy of the Frontier tribes but it was nonetheless scarifying for that. Ogilvie clamped his teeth, and felt a horrible crawling in his flesh.

Razjah Shah smiled, his teeth shining in the lamplight. 'It is my hope you will not become their meal, Ogilvie sahib. Such would be an ungallant ending for an officer of the great Queen-Empress.' He gestured to the two tribesmen on the end of the rope; Ogilvie was lowered until his head was below the rim of the pit, and then the rope's-end was turned up around the beam and secured. Restless sounds came from below, louder and closer now, and stench arose. It was warm in the pit. Fear of the revolting gripped Ogilvie. His throat went dry, his tongue seemed to swell in his mouth. As if from a great distance above him the voice of Razjah Shah came again: 'Ogilvie sahib, here you shall remain until my negotiations are finished. If success comes, you will be free to live and to rejoin the Raj. If there is no success, you remain. Before we leave this place, the rope will be cut, and you will fall to the snakes.'

When the voice stopped, sounds of departure came down followed by the slam of a heavy door and then the creak of locks and bolts. The light remained to flicker in its oily fumes from the niche in the wall.

★ ★ ★

85

The night's calm broke under the impacting clamour of horse's hooves moving at the gallop: in the Royal Strathspeys' camp the Sergeant of the Guard ran full belt towards the sound as a shout came from the picquet on outpost duty. The sergeant himself made the challenge.

'Halt!' His voice carried strongly; the hoof-beats slowed and stopped in the darkness.

'Who comes there?'

'Friend!' It was a breathless, urgent shout.

'Advance, friend, and be recognised.'

Two men rode forward, tattered men whose uniforms were dark with sweat as they came under the light from the guard lantern held aloft by the sergeant: the uniforms of the Raj on native bodies, a lance-*duffardar* and a *sowar* of the Guides. Up behind the sergeant came the Regimental Sergeant-Major as the camp began to stir.

'Sar'nt Anderson, what have we here?' Mr Cunningham turned to the lance-*duffardar*. 'Let's have it quickly.'

'Yes, Sergeant-Major sahib. We come from the brigade that is marching on Mana, sahib. There has been very heavy attack ... we are the only men remaining of the squadron, which was destroyed when great shells exploded in our midst, sahib.' The man's eyes were still wide with shock. 'The position is most serious, sahib, and the Brigadier-General sahib wishes reinforcements speedily.'

The Regimental Sergeant-Major gave a brisk nod. 'You'll come with me at once to the Adjutant, the both of you. Carry on, if you please, Sar'nt Anderson.' He turned and saluted as the Subaltern of the Day came up at the double; he reported what had happened. 'Will you deal with it, sir, or shall I?'

'You took the report, Mr Cunningham, so I'll leave it to you while I check the outposts.'

'Sir!' Cunningham saluted again, then raised his voice. 'All you men, there, back to your tents and get some sleep. It'll maybe turn out the last you'll get for a while.' Marching smartly to the Adjutant's tent, he shouted Black to wakefulness.

'What is it, Mr Cunningham, for heaven's sake—'

'Begging your pardon, Captain Black, sir. We must go immediately to the Colonel.' Cunningham explained briefly, and Black grumbled himself to his feet and pulled on shirt and trews, tunic and boots. When awakened in his turn, the Colonel's response to the lance-*duffardar's* full report was fast.

'A message to Division via the telegraph at Kohat, Captain Black. You'd better ride yourself – and report also that I must wait for my extended patrols to come in before I move. Mr Cunningham, see the men from the Guides are examined by Dr Corton and then fed and bedded down till morning.'

'Sir!'

'Warn all companies at first muster, to prepare to move out if so ordered by Division. And my runner to Lord Brora. I'd like words with him at once.' Dornoch had scarcely finished when the tent-flap was thrust aside and the Major entered, hair tousled and an open dressing-gown flapping about his large body. The RSM left the tent with Black and the two cavalrymen and Dornoch said, 'Bad tidings, Major. The column's been cut up en route for Mana. Among other things, they're left with no cavalry.'

'And we're wanted as infantry replacements? That's—'

'As reinforcements in the action. The Brigadier-General's holding on.'

Brora stared. 'Then had we not better get on with it at once?'

'Not until the patrols are in, and I think not until we're ordered out by Division.'

'You mean we sit on our arses while a British brigade's cut to pieces?' Brora's voice was loud and angry. 'Balls to that for a start, Colonel! I'll not have it said that the 114th refused to fight!'

'There is no refusal to fight and I object most strongly to your insinuations. I shall not march without my patrols, which leave me currently with so little strength as to render me useless to any brigade—'

'You—'

'And I have to remember our priority orders, which were to extend patrols to locate and rescue Mrs Ogilvie.' Dornoch was white with anger. 'You will hold your tongue from now on, Major, or you will be relieved of your duties as my second-in-command and held in arrest in Kohat while we march out – if that is what we're ordered to do. Do I make myself quite plain, Major?'

Brora's face suffused, but he held his tongue. Swirling his dressing-gown, he turned and stormed out of the Colonel's tent. For a moment Dornoch put his head in his hands; to be up against one's second-in-command was a devilish trying experience and one that was of no help to discipline or the conduct of a regiment in the field. Then he stiffened; difficult subordinates were part and parcel of the tribulations of command and had to be accepted as such, and no man among his Scots was in any doubt as to who commanded the regiment.

Andrew Black waited in Kohat while Dornoch's message was transmitted to Division, waited while Bloody Francis Fettleworth was awakened from his slumbers and pulled his thoughts together and sent post-haste for his ADC and Chief of Staff. Waiting, Black dozed. When he was roused with the Divisional Commander's reply the dawn was breaking. Black mounted and galloped back to camp, where he handed Fettleworth's orders to Lord Dornoch. Those orders held a touch of not unprecedented ambiguity: on the one hand Lord Dornoch was told to march to the assistance of Brigadier-General Norris as soon as he had re-mustered his patrols, and was to attempt to rendezvous with the 2nd Border Regiment who had already reached Kajuri Kach on the Gomal River en route for Mana; their Colonel would be contacted by the field telegraph laid from Dera Ismail Khan – if it had not been cut by the men of the tribes – and ordered to deviate and force-march north towards the map reference of Norris's brigade. So far, so good and clear: but Fettleworth thereafter was covering himself nicely and in effect contradicting his own orders: Lord Dornoch was to bear in mind that the withdrawal of his regiment would leave an important part of Waziristan uncovered in regard to the search, which was also an urgent matter. Units currently in the Nowshera district could not be spared as replacements. Dornoch was to use his discretion and act as he thought best after taking into account all the circumstances. There was an informative footnote to Fettleworth's orders: as of the time of origin of his message, there had been no approach made by any persons who might have either Mrs Ogilvie or Captain Ogilvie in their hands.

Six

One way of complying with Fettleworth's ambiguous orders would be to march out towards Brigadier-General Norris whilst at the same time leaving enough men behind to maintain patrols on a skeleton basis; this Lord Dornoch rejected the moment it came into his mind. To march on relief with a depleted battalion, to go against what he had himself said to Brora during the night, would be to fail the Brigadier-General and also to leave no backbone for the patrols should they come back to camp with information that would need following up. To split one's force was, to say the least, inadvisable and would serve neither objective properly. Dornoch made up his mind speedily: he would obey the first part of the orders, and march. To allow a British brigade, and even worse the High Commissioner, to be cut up by rebels would most certainly set the Frontier alight in the present situation. But even as he made the decision in his mind, he was uncomfortably aware that he might to some extent have allowed Lord Brora's insubordinate remarks to affect his judgment.

He faced the Major squarely as he gave his orders.

'We shall move out, gentlemen. When the last of the patrols reports back, they are to be given a meal and allowed one hour's rest. Then the battalion will be paraded in marching order and formed into column of route.' He pulled out his watch and addressed the Adjutant. 'I shall speak to all officers and senior NCOs in ten minutes' time, Captain Black.'

Ogilvie's chest was sore from the rope's pressure as he hung over the pit, waiting helplessly. Above him in its niche, the oil lamp flickered, casting yellow light that penetrated a little way down the walls of the pit, just enough for its loom to show the ever-moving surface of the horror below, the undulations as the snakes heaved and twisted and reared their scaly heads. After a while the light dimmed, gave a few hiccoughing flickers, and died.

The darkness made Ogilvie's flesh creep, as though the snakes were already upon him. He was enveloped in their curious smell, like a smell of death and decay and corruption. It was all he could do not to cry out; he clamped his teeth and sweated. After a long, long time as it seemed, he heard the sound of the door's bolts and lock, and it opened, and light stole in behind it. It remained open and he heard footsteps retreating and a minute later returning. More light came in: above him the oil lamp was lifted and oil was poured in and it was re-lit. Bending his head backwards he was able to make out a figure, and then he heard a creaking noise and found his body moving slowly upwards, inch by inch: he was being wound in by a handle, as though he were a bucket down a well. When his head came level with the lip of the hole, he saw the young veiled girl whom he had noticed on his first arrival. He could see little of her features, but was aware of a slim body behind the voluminous garment she wore.

In Pushtu she said, 'Food, sahib. Eat.'

'How?' he asked.

'I shall feed you.' She squatted by the edge, and he saw the bowl in her hands. With slim brown fingers she picked out meat – chicken, it tasted like, with rice which she crammed into his mouth. Then she turned aside and reached for a pitcher, and poured water into her cupped hand and tilted it towards his mouth, and he drank, one handful after another, gratefully.

'You have had enough, sahib?'

'Yes, thank you. How long have I been here?'

'I do not know, sahib.'

'And Razjah Shah – when will he return?'

'This also I do not know.'

'Do you know where he has gone?'

'No, sahib, this I do not know.'

Like hell you don't, he thought. He tried once more. 'The English mem'sahib ... do you know where she is?'

'I know of no English mem'sahib.' The girl got to her feet with a swift, graceful movement. 'Now I go.'

By devious ways Razjah Shah had entered Thal on the Kurrum River and had gone alone to the house of a kinsman on his mother's father's side. This kinsman, a small, dark man with glittering eyes, knew well enough why he had come and wasted no time.

'You seek the woman, cousin, the mem'sahib from Nowshera.'

'Yes. Do you know where she is?'

There was a shrug of indifference. 'It is possible. There have been rumours.'

'Of Murrum Khan?'

The eyes flickered, and discoloured teeth showed in the lamplight. 'Of Murrum Khan, unloved of Allah.'

'And of me also. And of you.'

'Yes. Praise be to Allah.'

'Praise be to Allah.' Razjah Shah bowed his head in reverence. 'Where is Murrum Khan, cousin?'

A dreamy look came into the glittering eyes, and for a moment they shifted away

94

while the thin shoulders shrugged: Razjah Shah recognised the signs easily enough. The small man said apologetically. 'In Waziristan is much poverty, also hunger. Not enough crops, not enough goats. I have much need of a hundred goats, cousin.'

'A hundred goats?' Razjah Shah laughed, a sound of scorn. 'Never have I heard such a thing! You are my mother's father's nephew ... one's kin does not make demands such as this, cousin.'

'Yet there is the need, cousin. I am sorry.'

'I cannot spare a hundred goats.'

'You are a rich man, cousin. Your kin suffers much poverty and deprivation—'

'Because of the British, not because of me.'

'Because of the British, yes, this is so. Yet there is talk of possible happenings at Mana, and I believe you to be concerned. If matters go as you wish, you will become a richer man.' A touch of steel had crept into the tone. 'Without your help, your kin in Thal will grow poorer.'

Razjah Shah made an impatient gesture. 'Very well. Forty goats.'

Hands were raised to Allah. 'Forty goats!'

'Some in kid.'

'Cousin, forty goats is far from enough even if all were in kid.'

'Fifty goats...'

A compromise was reached at sixty goats with ten nannies guaranteed to be in kid, delivery to be made after Razjah Shah had satisfied himself that Murrum Khan was indeed at the place yet to be revealed by his kinsman. 'Now, cousin: where is Murrum Khan?'

'Murrum Khan is to be found in a disused fort belonging to the Raj ... one mile north-east of the village of Takki, which is—'

'Takki I know, and the fort. Murrum Khan is both daring and brazen, to make such use of a British fort!'

'The British go there no longer, cousin.'

'Even so...' Razjah Shah stood up and laid a hand on the haft of his dagger. 'May Allah look with favour upon you, cousin. You have been helpful and I shall not forget.'

The small man bowed his head meekly. 'More help will come, more information if there are more goats ... word of the movement of British soldiers...'

After further satisfactory haggling, Razjah Shah rode out of Thal and outside the town he rendezvoused with his followers. Takki, which was some forty miles due north of Mana, was no more than twenty miles west of Thal and could be quickly reached, though not before the dawn. Razjah Shah deemed it more prudent to approach the fort during the hours of darkness and made his plans accordingly. For now it was back to the cellar; and at the next night-fall he would ride for Takki.

* ★ ★

Sweat poured from Ogilvie as he became aware of a shift in his position: his midriff, as he had seen when looking down, had moved just a little relative to the slant of the oil lamp's beam. A little more of himself was outside the direct rays.

He was very slightly lower, very slightly closer to the probing horror below.

There was only one conclusion: the rope was tending to stretch under the continuing pull of his weight. Either that, or it had been damp and now was dry. His sweat blinded him, running into his eyes. He called out loudly: they would not want him to die yet, his potential use was in being still. No one came: the pit itself held down his shouts and muffled them. There was increased movement below, an extra surge, he believed, in the hideous undulations. Very gradually the lamp's shadow moved up his body: the skirt of his tunic could be seen no longer now. He bent his knees, lifting his feet clear, and held his posture while he shouted again and again, and no one came through the locked and bolted door. Minutes passed, his legs grew heavy ... heavier until he could hold them up no more and the muscles relaxed in instinctive desire to ease the agony. As his body swayed a little on the rope he felt the scrape of his feet across moving things, and a dry sound of rustling, and something fell across his boots.

He screamed: and then lost consciousness.

The regiment had moved out of camp as ordered, towards the map reference as indicated by the lance-*duffardar* from the Guides. This reference put Norris's brigade in a mountain pass about half-way between Kohat and Bannu – thirty miles approximately of appalling terrain south-west from the encampment. With forced marching Dornoch reckoned he could arrive by noon the following day; but, as he remarked to the Major as they rode together in the van, he would arrive with exhausted troops that might be little succour to a heavily engaged brigade.

'They're Scots, Colonel.'

A frown passed across Dornoch's face. 'I'm well aware of that. Even Scots can tire.'

'Not when brought alive by the pipes.'

Dornoch made no response: there was, in fact, a good deal of truth in Brora's dogmatic-sounding statement. The pipes often enough wrought miracles, but Dornoch failed on this occasion to see them as sufficient to rally men dog tired from slogging all night and next morning through the rocky passes. If he was to arrive even as late in the day – and in the engagement – as noon, there would be scant time for rest en route, and horses as well as men needed rest...

Brora spoke again. 'Colonel, have I your permission to speak to the company commanders personally?'

'To what end, Major?'

Brora blew out his cheeks. 'To what *end*, my dear sir? Why, to ensure the men put their best foot forward and that there are no damn slackers and drop-outs – *that's* what end!'

'Then it's not necessary—'

'But—'

'They know the facts. They don't need to be reminded, Major. I'll not have them hazed.'

'Colonel—'

'Save your breath for the ride, Brora. I have first-class men and the best NCOs in the British Army, under the best Sar'nt-Major. Hazeing is not officers' work, Brora. Mr Cunningham can be relied upon to do all that's necessary.'

'So you do not give your permission?'

'No.'

'Then,' Brora snapped, 'upon your head be it, if we fail to reach Brigadier-General Norris in time!'

Dornoch turned and stared at the Major. 'I am the Colonel,' he said simply. 'Everything's upon my head, is it not?' For a moment Brora met his eye, then turned angrily aside, blowing through his drooping moustache, and rode on in silence. Dornoch felt immensely depressed and even felt dislike for his own class. Money and privilege ... not a poor man himself, his wealth could not bear comparison with Brora's. Perhaps there was something wrong with the system after all ... whilst the possession of wealth made for independence of spirit, which in itself was no bad thing and prevented a weak toadyism sullying the army, it could work the other way also, which was a bad thing when it came to officers like Brora who were impetuous and in Brora's case too often stupid in addition. Private means could be a two-edged sword, breeding arrogance as well as independence. Dornoch sighed; it had to be borne and for the sake of the regiment his hand upon the Major would need to be firm when they came to action. The Colonel's thoughts moved on: a lot would depend upon the Border Regiment, the men from Carlisle and England's north-west corner already on the march to Mana from Dera Ismail Khan. If the diversionary order from Division had failed, as fail it easily could, to reach them and deflect them northwards, then the Royal Strathspey must needs go in alone and the casualties must be heavy. In the meantime, however, there were heartening sounds coming from the marching Scots behind as in the last of the daylight their voices were lifted in song.

★ ★ ★

Opening his eyes, Ogilvie found himself lying on his back beside the pit, free now of the rope from which he had hung. Faces peered down, among them Razjah Shah's. There was a smell of gunsmoke, and there was some pain and blood, as though a bullet had grazed his right thigh, as in fact was the case.

'We were just in time, Ogilvie sahib,' Razjah Shah said. 'I myself shot the snake that had climbed, then you were at once hauled up. One more minute, perhaps ... that would have been sad.'

'Indeed it would,' Ogilvie said sourly. 'You, no doubt, would have wept like a woman over the loss?'

The native smiled. 'You are brave enough, which is a thing I admire. No, I would not have wept, though I might well have thrown my watchmen to the snakes for not being wakeful, since I assume you would have called for help when the rope stretched.'

'I did.'

'But now all is well for you.'

'For how long?'

'That shall be your decision, Ogilvie sahib. The snakes wait still.' Razjah Shah squatted beside Ogilvie. 'I seek your help. I believe you will give it ... not only because of the snakes that wait.'

'Then why?' Ogilvie attempted to sit up, but was pushed flat by one of the men. A knife was brought out and held with the point towards his throat.

'You will wish to assist the Raj, Ogilvie sahib.'

Ogilvie laughed. 'As you yourself do, Razjah Shah?'

'Perhaps so, perhaps not. Or perhaps this: for certain purposes the welfare of the British Raj runs parallel with my own. Do you understand, Ogilvie sahib?'

Ogilvie narrowed his eyes, staring thoughtfully at the native leader. 'It's possible, Razjah Shah. Do you refer to Murrum Khan and—'

'And the mem'sahib, the wife of your cousin – yes, that is so. I know where Murrum Khan is hidden, and the mem'sahib will be with Murrum Khan. Progress has been made, and with your help more can be made.'

Ogilvie asked, 'Is the mem'sahib alive, Razjah Shah?'

'I have not heard otherwise. Why do you ask?'

'Because I have been told that *badal* is involved in the boundary dispute, that Murrum Khan seeks revenge for an elder brother killed by the father of Dostman Khan who is behind the Mana dispute. This you knew?'

Razjah Shah nodded. 'All this I knew. Why should the mem'sahib suffer on account of the father of Dostman Khan?'

'When *badal* is involved, as of course you know, many die. Many become involved who were not involved in the first place. Dostman Khan will know by now that Murrum Khan is in Waziristan and seeks vengeance. Dostman Khan will protect himself. Does your information say if there has been any attack upon Murrum Khan?'

'It says nothing of that, Ogilvie sahib, but I realise that there is much truth in your words. It is partly because this is so, that there must be no delay.'

'You intend to attack yourself, Razjah Shah?'

'Yes—'

'And take over the mem'sahib?'

'Yes. I understand your quandary, Ogilvie sahib, but the mem'sahib will fare no worse with me than with Murrum Khan and will be protected from *badal*. I ask you to show me your trust.'

Again Ogilvie laughed. 'Why should I do that, Razjah Shah?'

'Because you have no alternative. Think, and you will realise. The snakes wait ... and the mem'sahib is in more danger where she is than if she were here.'

'And the snakes?'

Razjah Shah seemed to understand. He met Ogilvie's eye steadily and his tone was solemn when he went on, 'She will not go to the snakes. You have my word, this I swear

103

upon the Prophet and upon the souls of my fathers. I shall make a bargain with you, Ogilvie sahib. Do you wish to hear?'

'Go on.'

Razjah Shah got to his feet and stood looking down at Ogilvie. 'When the mem'sahib is in my hands and has been brought here, an exchange will be made. For her – you! The mem'sahib will be escorted in safety to the track running from Fort Jamrud to Peshawar, and left to ride in peace to your British garrison. You shall remain as my hostage – and the teeth of Murrum Khan will be drawn. Are you agreeable to this?'

There could be only one answer; Ogilvie nodded. He believed that in this at all events Razjah Shah could be trusted. The advantages to the native of depriving Murrum Khan of his bargaining power vis-à-vis the Raj were clear and obvious, and there was another point that Razjah Shah had not mentioned: the release of Angela Ogilvie would go much in his favour when the Raj came to consider the distribution of land should new boundaries be agreed in the district of Mana. Ogilvie said, 'You asked my help, Razjah Shah. Have you more to ask?'

'I have. Let us go more comfortably to consider this.' Razjah Shah gestured to his followers. They moved back, and Razjah Shah himself assisted Ogilvie to his feet, and they went through the door, away from the horrors of the pit, into the adjoining room where chairs were set. Razjah Shah faced Ogilvie across a table. He said, 'I have been given certain tidings of your British soldiers, Ogilvie sahib. Do you wish to hear?'

'Yes.'

'Between this place and Mana there is an engagement of a British brigade of foot-soldiers and cavalry and the forces of Dostman Khan. With this brigade is your High Commissioner. The battle has not gone well for the Raj, and from Kohat is being sent a battalion of the men in skirts, the men who fight like devils. It is possible that these men are of your own regiment, Ogilvie sahib. So much I know or conjecture. It is necessary that I know more, since Murrum Khan may move to a new hiding-place if the troops of either the Raj or of Dostman Khan should threaten to come too close. In that would lie continuing danger for the mem'sahib, and for my own future plans. You understand?'

'What is it you ask of me, Razjah Shah?'

'Your knowledge of the dispositions of the Raj, Ogilvie sahib. As accurately as possible ... I must know the places beside Kohat whence reinforcements may be sent for your High Commissioner, also the strength of forces in your garrisons in Waziristan, and the likely tracks along which your patrols will be operating. If you do not know all this in detail, you as a soldier will be able to make estimates. Such will be of help.'

'To free my cousin's wife from Murrum Khan?' Ogilvie's tone was sardonic.

'That is so.'

'I think you take a sledgehammer to crack a nut, Razjah Shah! The men of the tribes such as yourself are well accustomed to sneaking through the British lines and snatching persons and arms away – just as the mem'sahib was snatched in the first place from the Nowshera cantonment.' Ogilvie paused, and leaned across the table. 'There is something else, is there not, something further that you seek? I shall make a guess at what this is: you seek information so that you can assemble your own tribal warriors from Afghanistan, who will filter through the passes and over the mountains and form your army in Waziristan! Is this not so, Razjah Shah?'

The native smiled blandly, and nodded. 'Your guess is good. What you have said comes near perhaps to the truth. It is for you to consider, and come to a decision. This decision must be made quickly in the mem'-sahib's interests.'

As he had done in the pit, Ogilvie broke out into a sweat. He was in something of a cleft stick: the information sought by Razjah Shah, if given, could lead to a charge of rendering assistance to the enemy if ever he got back again to Peshawar. But Angela counted also, and might well be under torture for all he knew: Hector, her husband, as a highly-placed Civilian from Whitehall, knew many things about the administration of the Raj, more than the military knew about future policy, and Murrum Khan might well try to pick the brain of a hostage so close, or least by proxy of marriage, to the seats of power in the land of the Queen-Empress. Nevertheless, duty and training and upbringing held: officers did not part with information, and in this instance to attempt to fob Razjah Shah off with false information must rebound upon him soon enough, and very likely upon Angela as well.

'I'm sorry, Razjah Shah,' Ogilvie said quietly, looking the native in the eye. 'You ask the impossible. For my part, I believe you both can and will find the mem'sahib without my answers to your questions.' He paused. 'If there is any other help I can give ... if you will tell me where Murrum Khan is hidden, then perhaps I can advise you on a more restricted basis, by indicating any danger in the vicinity, perhaps?'

Razjah Shah frowned and his eyes shone with anger; but he said, 'To tell you cannot be of harm, I think. Murrum Khan is occupying an abandoned fort to the northeast of Takki, which is—'

'A British fort?'

'Once a British fort, Ogilvie sahib, yes.'

'Fort Canning, named after a former Viceroy.'

Razjah Shah's eyes widened. 'You know this fort?'

'I have served there. I know it well.' Ogilvie's voice held sudden excitement. 'I know how it can best be attacked, and with a small number of men such as you have here. My knowledge—'

'Will for the time being prove more helpful, I think, than the broader information! I can trust you, Ogilvie sahib?'

'In regard to the mem'sahib, yes. Further than that, no.'

Razjah Shah gave a deep chuckle and his eyes sparkled. He reached forward and laid a hand on Ogilvie's shoulder. 'You shall be most closely watched, I promise you! You shall ride with us tonight, Ogilvie sahib.'

Seven

The regiment had so far made good time, but the resulting effect upon men and animals was plain to see: as the dawn came up in the east it lit the straggling column, the stumbling, weary men, the sagging heads of the horses and the transport mules as they plodded on between the boulders and the desolate scrub. The pipes and drums were silent; by now the regiment was not many miles from its objective, and there was no point in sending ahead the warning of their coming; even though they had probably been reported onwards by the enemy's scouts along the high peaks, Dornoch would not take an additional chance. As that dawn broke, the Colonel turned in his saddle to look along the column, shading his eyes against the first rays of a hard sun.

'We must rest them, Major.'

'We must consider the time, Colonel.'

'I do not propose to send them into action on empty stomachs,' Lord Dornoch said curtly. 'Captain Black, I shall halt the column for long enough to take breakfast. Pass the word for the field kitchens to be set up the moment the men fall out.'

'Sir!' Smartly, Black saluted and turned his horse. As he rode down the column, Dornoch lifted a hand high, then brought it down. The long column shambled to a halt and without waiting for the order the men fell out, many of them collapsing on their faces beside the terrible track, feeling some of the weariness drain away as they gave themselves up to the comparative comfort and relief of the hard ground. The Regimental Sergeant-Major took the opportunity of sprucing himself up with the aid of his bearer, and of using a pool of water between some rocks to shave. Thus tidy, he marched along the column giving words of encouragement to the men. Meeting the Adjutant, he slammed his feet to the halt and gave a swinging salute.

'Good morning, Sar'nt-Major. The men are a mess.'

'Not surprising, sir, not surprising at all.'

The Adjutant pointed with his riding-crop. 'That man. His kilt's around his waist. It's not decent. Take his name, Sar'nt-Major.' Black rode on, slowly and haughtily, looking down his nose. Cunningham, breathing hard, approached the miscreant, a lance-corporal.

'Don't chance your stripe, Corporal Mathieson.'

'Sir!' Mathieson started to get to his feet, but Cunningham gestured him back. 'What is the trouble, sir?'

'Your kilt, man! Now rectified. The Adjutant wants no public demonstration of what highlanders wear or do not wear beneath the kilt – that's all.' Cunningham passed on, leaving a softly swearing Scot; the name would be conveniently forgotten and Black could do what he bloody well liked about it. Cunningham liked a smart regiment, but there were limits, and pinpricks could become bayonet thrusts when men had been pushed to their full extent. Always with a Scottish regiment the hand of command and discipline had to be sensitive to atmosphere: Scots could never be driven stupidly, and Black could often be as stupid as the Major if not as rude ... the RSM blew out his cheeks as he marched along, left-right-left to his own internal voice of command. Warrant officers such as himself had much to sort out between officers and men and as a result were frequently the butt of both, but he could take any amount of that. What matter-ed was the regiment; and by this evening's sunset the regiment might well be sadly mauled and there might be many graves to dig in the hard Waziri hills, many hastily-constructed crosses to be planted to mark a sacrifice in the Queen's name. Cunningham gave himself a shake: action was action and they were trained to it and would acquit themselves as well as ever.

There was a sound and a smell of frying, a welcome one. There were steaming mugs of tea, and after a while there was conversation and some laughter from the men as smoke rose from pipes, trailing upwards, blue in air that was almost dead still as the wind was taken away by the high, rearing mountain peaks. Trestle tables were set up for the officers, with deck chairs to sit upon. Coffee was brought by the bearers, and fried eggs and bacon. With his coffee Lord Brora lit a cigar and slumped back in his canvas chair, his long legs stretched out before him. As he puffed at the cigar there was a sharp crack and the end of it seemed to explode in his face. A ball of smoke was seen from one of the peaks as Brora leaped to his feet and shook a fist in the air. Down the column the NCOs shouted the men off the track and into such cover as they could find, while the sharpshooters took post behind boulders and opened on the spot where the smoke had been seen.

'I'll be buggered!' Brora said loudly. 'Where the devil are the damn picquets?' He glared upwards. The picquets in the *sangers* had in fact fired only seconds after the shot, but the sniper seemed to have got away with it: a *jezail* was brandished from the peak and a jeering shout came down. Fire was opened again, but the Pathan dodged back into cover and the bullets pinged uselessly off the rock. A moment later there was another shot from above, though the man had not re-appeared, and one of the cooks at the field kitchens spun round, knocking over a pan of fat. There was a shout for stretcher bearers, and two men ran up with a *doolie* into which the wounded soldier was lifted: the bullet had entered his shoulder. While Surgeon Major Corton sterilised his instruments and began the unanaesthetised extraction, the orders came down by bugle to prepare to march. The field kitchens were packed away and quickly the regiment was once again on the move: Lord Dornoch's decision had been to join the main action as soon as possible rather than be pinned down and wait for more bullets. For a while there was no more firing, but as they moved along the pass the odd isolated *jezail* cracked, and the picquets were kept busy on the hillsides as they ran and scrambled ahead to clear the slopes for the advance.

Brora looked towards the Colonel. 'The pipes, I think?'

'Not just yet, Major.'

'Why not, my dear sir? Damn it, we've been spotted, have we not, the buggers'll know we're coming!'

'The effect's better when held to the last moment. Major, I've had years of Frontier fighting and I know the Pathan as well as anyone. The pipes will remain silent until I give the order, and Pipe-Major Ross knows my mind as well as I do myself.'

They rode on, Brora looking stiff and angry and with a sneer twisting his lips. Dornoch speculated on the current position of the Border Regiment, pushing north from Kajuri Kach on the Gomal. They were going to be most mightily welcome if they turned up in time: one battalion would help, two might decide the outcome. Might: the Pathan was always a tough fighter, and this time the prize was great. As the advance continued the sniping from the heights died away altogether. To Dornoch it was almost as though the Pathan saw no point in wasting ammunition on a column that night in any case be marching to its extinction.

'Here we halt, Ogilvie sahib.' Razjah Shah, riding up alongside in the night, laid a hand on the bridle of the horse that carried Ogilvie, who was tied as before. His uniform was once again hidden by the goatskin. 'We shall dismount and go forward on foot, and in silence. The horses will remain here, with four men to guard them.'

'Will you detach the frontal assault party now?'

Razjah Shah nodded. 'Yes. They will ride on farther yet, then converge on the fort dismounted.'

Ogilvie was set on his feet, his wrists remaining bound. With no time lost the horses of the dismounted men were led into the lee of a cleft in the hillside, and the fifteen men who would ultimately approach the fort on their stomachs rode off. The remaining half moved forward, mere shadows in the dark, behind Razjah Shah and Ogilvie. For many past miles a careful watch had been kept for any sign of men extended by Murrum Khan as sentries – though in fact Ogilvie, who had picked up remembered landmarks and bearings some way back, had not expected any watch to be set so far out from Fort

114

Canning. Now, as they began to close the perimeter of the area which, when directly under British control, had been regarded as the outer defensive line, the watch was even more painstaking and the men moved like ghosts, careful to make no sound at all as they trod the rough ground, careful to keep in the shadow of the hillside and out of the moon's beams.

After an hour's slow progress they came within sight of the mountain track's end: from some quarter-mile ahead, as Ogilvie knew, that track left the hills and started the precipitous descent into the broad valley in the centre of which lay Fort Canning. He was about to whisper this information to Razjah Shah when the native leader put a hand on his arm, lightly.

'Stop, Ogilvie sahib, and keep very still and silent.'

'What is it?'

'On the peak to the left ... a man. Stay here.' As Razjah Shah moved invisibly away, making no sound, Ogilvie screwed up his eyes and searched the peak. He could see nothing, though the rocky jags stood out fairly clear in the hard moonlight. Nothing but those jags ... certainly a man could as it were melt into the rocky outlines if he were able to remain still enough, but the smallest movement could betray his presence to sharp eyes. Razjah Shah must have very sharp eyes indeed ... Ogilvie shrugged and waited with the others, none of them stirring but remaining like carven images in the darkness. There was a sigh of wind, a cold wind that eddied along the pass and rose now and again to a whine as it curled its icy fingers around the high places to bring a reminder of Himalayan snows. A timeless part of the globe, and time tonight seemed to merge into past centuries ... when Razjah Shah at last returned, he returned as silently as he had gone, making Ogilvie start as his whisper broke the intense stillness.

'All is well, Ogilvie sahib, and we go on.'

'What did you find?'

'Two men, both now dead. I believe the way is clear.'

'There'll be more at the entry – I warned of this.'

'True. They also will die.'

'You sound confident,' Ogilvie said. There was no response. The tribesmen moved on again behind Razjah Shah and Ogilvie, as slowly and as carefully as before, taking no chances. They approached the break in the hills, the point where the track descended, and in so doing came to the point of most danger. At a word from Ogilvie, Razjah Shah ordered his men down on to their stomachs and himself brought out a knife and cut the rope away from Ogilvie's wrists.

'Now there must be full trust, Ogilvie

sahib,' he said. They crawled on, a painful process over the hard, stony track. Ahead now, they could see the stark outlines of the fort below, far below, its walls and battlements and its guard tower silvered by the moon that spread a blanket of light over the entire valley and the surrounding peaks. With difficulty they moved down the sloping track until, rounding a bend between rocky sides, they came to more open ground where, at a signal from their leader, they moved aside into boulder-strewn scrub that would give them a degree of cover and prevent an over-swift descent that might well alert the men they expected to find farther down. When they had moved some three hundred yards towards the valley, Ogilvie reached out for Razjah Shah's shoulder.

'Ahead now – you see? The upstanding rock. That's it.'

Razjah Shah stopped and spoke a few words of Pushtu to his followers. At once a sideways movement began, the men fanning out to right and left. When they had gone down far enough, they would converge on the rock and mount an attack from either flank. Razjah Shah and Ogilvie moved on behind, still flat on their stomachs, clothing and skin ripped by stones and thorns. There was a rattle as some rock debris was loosened to fly down the hillside: there was a savage intake of breath from Razjah Shah. Ogilvie, watching out ahead, saw, or fancied he saw, some movement at the right-hand edge of the great rock beside the track. A man, alerted by the small give-away sound?

There was no turning back now.

As they crawled painfully on, the man below was confirmed as such: a figure moved out from the rock's lee, tall and ragged, garments blowing out along the wind, his *jezail* and its snaky bayonet clear in the moonlight. Then something seemed to be hurled from the shadows like a rocket, and the sentry vanished. There was a short scream that ended in a gurgle, and on its heels another man came out from the rock, moving fast, but not moving for long: from the left flank Razjah Shah's men came in quickly with moonlight glinting on their knife-blades. The second man died as quickly as his comrade.

Razjah Shah gave a sound of triumph. 'Now the way is clear,' he said. 'Come!'

With Ogilvie he rose from his stomach and together they covered the last stretch to the rock on their feet but bent double: it was possible, though Ogilvie thought unlikely, that they might be seen from the fort. In safety they reached the rock where they were rejoined by the men of the flank attacks.

'The bodies?' Razjah Shah asked.

'Already dragged into the entry.'

The leader nodded and followed Ogilvie

behind the rock; on the side facing the valley there was a wide hole, large enough to admit a man with bowed head. The two went in, and Razjah Shah struck a flint and lit a torch that flamed and smoked foully in the enclosed space. The bodies of the dead sentries lay huddled in a corner; stones and debris were being piled on them. The walls, black shiny rock, reflected back the torch light; at ground level there was another hole, a smaller one, and beyond it a smooth downward slope that seemed to travel into the very bowels of the earth.

'It looks difficult,' Ogilvie said, 'and it is, but it can be done. When you're half-way, Razjah Shah, it will be well to remember what I told you: that I myself have made the whole passage in safety.'

Razjah Shah laughed. 'You think I am frightened, Ogilvie sahib?'

'No. But I think you may come to believe that the tunnel has no ending! The way is long.'

There was another laugh, a sound of scorn and confidence. The leader gestured Ogilvie to enter the inner hole, and, once again on his stomach, he did so, feet first. Next came Razjah Shah himself; the others followed, some of them looking not so ebullient as Razjah Shah, their eyes rolling as they committed themselves and their fate to the unknown. Behind them the loom of moonlight faded from the entry, as did the smoky fumes of Razjah Shah's torch, now extinguished. For a while they moved fast, finding the value of the British officer sahib's strictures that their feet should go first and their bodies follow: that way, they had more control of their movement and could check their sliding progress over smooth rock when it became necessary. It was an unnerving and totally helpless feeling as they sped willy-nilly to the earth's fiery stomach, leaving behind them the good fresh air and open skies.

Towards the previous noon, not far to the southward of Fort Canning as it happened, the Royal Strathspey had seen the advanced scouts of the warring levies ahead, natives highly situated atop the pass, armed with *jezails*. As these men were engaged by the picquets, the Colonel in the van saw the rising blobs of smoke as word of their coming was signalled onward. He turned to the Adjutant.

'Sound the Stand-to, if you please, Captain Black.'

Black saluted. 'Sir!' He called to the bugler; a moment later the strident, brassy voice spoke loud and clear, echoing out along the pass.

'And my compliments to the Pipe-Major. The pipes and drums to commence.'

'Sir!' Black passed the word by runner, and the Colonel glanced quickly at Lord Brora, who was muttering something about it damn well being time ... Brora's face was alight and savage, and already his revolver was drawn. A moment later that revolver was thrust back into its holster, and Brora reached down for the leather scabbard that bumped along his horse's flank. He drew his highland broadsword, its blade flashing in the sunlight as he whirled it exultantly around his head. In the marching files behind bayonets had been fixed and the rifles, with their slings tightened, had been removed from the 'march-at-ease' position and were ready for the order to open. In the centre of the advance the Maxims' crews had their guns ready to blast into the native hordes when the column extended, with plenty of ready-use ammunition boxes broken open and at hand in the limbers. At the tail and in comparative safety the commissariat and transport mules plodded on ahead of the rearguard; along the flanks the colour-sergeants of companies encouraged and exhorted and kept the step going with their shouts and their pace-sticks, their crimson sashes bringing touches of brilliance to the humdrum khaki mass of men, khaki that was itself lightened a little by the tartan of the Royal Strathspey as the kilts swung to the step. That step lightened noticeably, and chests swelled boastfully, as the pipes and drums beat out along the pass, thrown back upon the marching column by the rock sides, a very real sound of war and glory. In accordance with regimental tradition the first tune to be played as action approached was 'Cock o' the North'. The battalion swung on defiantly to the rescue of the brigade and the High Commissioner; and as the sound of the embattled guns blazed down from ahead Pipe-Major Ross changed his tune to 'Highland Laddie'.

Oh where and oh where,
Is your Highland laddie gone?
He's gone from bonnie Scotland
Where noble deeds are done,
And it's oh, in my heart,
I wish him safe at home...

Once again Dornoch gave a brief glance at Lord Brora. The Major's lips were moving: he was singing to himself and his eyes were shining. Dornoch smiled slightly; he loved the pipes himself. So far he had not seen his second-in-command in action: in the Mess, in cantonments in general, the man was a boor and a bully. But he had the air of a man whose best side would show itself in action, and for that Dornoch was truly thankful. Compactly, the column moved on: Dornoch had the feeling that in a sense they were

122

moving into a situation not unlike that faced years before in the Crimea by Lord Cardigan and his light Brigade. However, what was to come was inevitable: the pass, as indicated by close study of the maps, was the only approach from easterly to the brigade's position, and once in it there was no turning aside to the flanks, and there was no cover. And currently there was no sign of the Border Regiment, whose field telegraph, it now seemed confirmed, must have been cut before the message came through from Bloody Francis in Nowshera. Such was the luck of the soldier. As Dornoch turned to look back along the column, there was a shout from the Major.

'Scouts coming back, Colonel!'

Dornoch turned again, eyes front: the subaltern with his scouting party was pounding back at the double, and as he came rushing on he fell in his tracks, his body crashing into a boulder and blood spurting like a fountain from his neck. All at once the peaks along the sides seemed to sprout men, and a sustained fire was poured down, while from ahead came the roar and blast and flame of heavy gunfire.

Eight

After that first sliding descent, the tunnel flattened and the going became a good deal harder and disadvantages were found in the feet-first progress. The air grew thick, and bodies grew wet with sweat that ran into the eyes and blinded them with muddy grit. It began to seem as though their journey really was into some red-hot interior of the planet; even Ogilvie, with his knowledge that the end of the tunnel must come in time, began to feel a kind of desperation brought about by the enclosing walls of rock and the fact that there was not room enough to reverse his mode of progression. If one of the Pathans should panic, all hell would be let loose; but Pathans did not panic easily – not, that was, on the surface. Allah or the Prophet alone could tell what the effect of subterranean confinement might bring to the superstitious mind! Ogilvie tried to concentrate his thoughts ahead as he dragged himself along: the objective was all that mattered and somewhere, not far ahead by now, Angela would – he hoped – be found alive and well. He prayed that she might be;

and hoped that Allah also was playing his part in keeping Razjah Shah's powder and flints, charges and explosives dry and intact for journey's end. When the journey ended, it would end in a wall built during the British occupation of Fort Canning to seal off the tunnel. This had been built partly in order to keep out any tribesmen who might penetrate and partly to permit the construction of a chamber below the fort for combined defensive and disciplinary purposes: the chamber had been divided into an underground armoury and magazine on the one hand, and cell accommodation on the other. There was a heavy wooden door, and danger would lie in the blowing of it if the charge should be too big. Ogilvie, however, was reasonably confident that he could prepare a safe charge and tamp it well down; Razjah Shah had agreed with him that it was unlikely Murrum Khan would yet have assembled enough weapons and explosives to need the use of a magazine. Nevertheless, much of this was, of necessity, based upon hope and guesswork; and one of the imponderables was whether or not the explosion would alert the natives in the fort above before the infiltrators were ready for the next move. The one defence against that was sheer speed after the event.

Razjah Shah's voice came from the total blackness: he was suffering acutely. 'May a thousand asses defecate upon Murrum Khan. It will give me much enjoyment to slit his throat!'

'Try to discipline yourself not to, Razjah Shah. It is important that he should live to talk.'

'For the Raj?'

'For the Raj, perhaps. Also for you.'

There was a grunt. They moved on as fast as possible. The air was growing foul and there was an immense lethargy in their aching limbs; to push and drag was a tremendous effort and every part of their bodies was lacerated and grazed by the unevenness of the walls and floor once they had come to the flat section. It was akin to medieval torture; but they held on in the knowledge that to go on was considerably easier than to retreat. Ogilvie listened abstractedly to the scrape of the Pathans' ancient rifles along the floor of the tunnel, at the clank of the heavily loaded bandoliers. The time factor was much on his mind. It was to be hoped that by now Razjah Shah's surface party would have completed their stealthy crawl towards the fort. Everything would depend upon the co-ordination of the attack on two fronts.

They crawled on, closing their objective inch by inch. At long last Ogilvie felt the tunnel widening out, and he passed the word to the others to keep as quiet as possible.

126

Soon he was able to stand up, a process that he took carefully in the pitch darkness. He heard the small sounds as the rest of the party emerged, heard Razjah Shah's whisper in his ear: 'The light now, Ogilvie sahib?'

'Yes.'

A flint was struck and a tallow candle was lit. The resulting shadows were eerie, scarifying. There was a total silence but for the breathing of the Pathans. Ogilvie looked around: the end-chamber was as he remembered it, a circular cavern of some fifteen feet diameter, with the one door leading into a passageway between the cell accommodation and the armoury. He put his ear to the door and listened: he heard no sound – but the door was thick.

He turned to the native leader. 'The explosives, Razjah Shah.'

Razjah Shah reached into his voluminous garments and brought out gunpowder in four goatskin bags; one of his followers produced more bags, this time filled with workable clay; another brought out pieces of goatskin and canvas in strips and squares and oblongs. Ogilvie set to work preparing the blasting charge, a tricky process with the flickering candle held close to the explosive material. When he was ready, and when another man had prepared the clay, he set the charge on the rock floor at the door's foot, against the woodwork: to blow the lock would be pointless, for at any rate under British occupation there had been bolts at top and bottom and a heavy beam set across the middle. With the charge in place and a short powder-trail laid into the cavern, the clay was applied, packed in tight, and then the layers of goatskin and canvas were placed across.

Ogilvie beckoned to four of the Pathans, and spoke in Pushtu. 'All the rubble and loose rock you can gather,' he said. 'Lay it against the skins, and build it up well to cover them and help contain the explosion when I light the fuse-trail.'

They set to, their lean dark faces devilish in the candle's glow. They worked fast, keen enough to be above ground again; quickly, as effective a casing as possible was run up, and the pieces of skin and canvas vanished, leaving only the powder-trail visible. Ogilvie took the candle from Razjah Shah. 'In a moment,' he said, 'I shall touch the flame to the powder. We shall have ten seconds, no more. Much rubble will fly ... there may be injuries. You must all go into the tunnel and crouch on the floor and cover up your heads as well as you can. Your heads to the tunnel entry, your rumps to the explosion. Go now, and go quietly.'

The men moved hastily into the tunnel. When the last man had vanished, Ogilvie gave it fifteen seconds more, then bent with the candle to the end of his fuse-trail, and touched the burning wick to the powder. It caught first time; as soon as he saw the spark move, Ogilvie ran for the tunnel and got down on hands and knees. He had scarcely done so when the charge blew: in the confined space the noise was tremendous, battering at the ear-drums like an artillery barrage in the field. Debris flew everywhere, and the acrid powder-smoke spread from the cavern along the tunnel. Back through the smoke crawled Razjah Shah's men, cannoning into one another as they came into the cavern. The smouldering edges of the hole in the door gave them their bearings. Razjah Shah struck his flint again and the candle was re-lit. They got to work like demented men with knives and daggers and bayonets, expecting a rush of the fort's defenders at any moment. The hole was quickly widened out enough and Ogilvie pulled his body through and stood up in the passageway. The others came through behind, and Ogilvie gestured towards a flight of spiral stone steps at the end of the passage. As he did so he felt Razjah Shah's hand on his arm. Looking down, he saw the British Army revolver in the Pathan's other hand.

Razjah Shah passed the revolver to him. 'You shall lead, Ogilvie sahib, and you shall not lead unarmed.'

'You trust me, Razjah Shah?'

'You have given your word as an officer sahib. You will not break it. When the need to be armed ceases, the revolver will come back to me.'

Ogilvie held out a hand and shook that of Razjah Shah. He said, 'Now we must not delay. Remember, at the top of the steps, we come to the stables and through them to the open courtyard.' He went for the steps, the Pathan's revolver in his hand with the hammer drawn back, and climbed fast. There were sounds from above, becoming audible as he climbed: the movement of horses in their stalls, and some whinnying, and the pull of halters against ring-bolts. The climb was a long one, but was taken in short time, and all the men had ascended into the stable area when human footsteps were heard, and gruff voices came, and then a lantern was seen, held high above a man's head and guttering in a wind blowing coldly in from the courtyard. Razjah Shah dropped to the ground and Ogilvie and the others followed his motion. The Pathan leader crawled silently through the mixture of straw and droppings, the noise from the horses increasing as they became more uneasy, concealing the approach of the infiltrators come from the depths of the earth.

The man with the lantern halted just behind the row of horses, the light bringing up his puzzled frown as he looked to right and left. But not for long: like a striking snake Razjah Shah rose behind him and plunged his dagger centrally between the shoulder-blades, twisted it and withdrew it dripping blood as the man fell with no sound beyond a harsh cough that sent more lifeblood gushing from the mouth. The guard lantern had fallen with him, and the glass had shattered. Flame was already curling into the straw and taking hold. Razjah Shah called out to his men, and at once they freed the horses and gave each a stinging smack on its rump. As some of Murrum Khan's men appeared, entering the stables, the terrified horses plunged out with forelegs a-flail, some of them rearing up with flashing hooves, at least one of which found a target and smashed a head like an egg-shell. Razjah Shah seized one of the horses and quietened it; mounted, he rode out into the courtyard, a scimitar whirling around his head, a figure of sudden vengeance that had sprung from nowhere, his wild tribesmen behind him with their bayonetted *jezails*. At a shout from Razjah Shah, just as the fire took a firm grip of the stables and began to billow smoke and flame, one of the Pathans raised his *jezail* and loosed it off into the air. Immediately from beyond the high walls of the fort a sound arose in response to the expected signal: high shouts of war and of determined

131

men, accompanied by a fusillade of bullets that smacked into the outer walls by the guardroom or snicked over to break slivers from the stonework inside. Razjah Shah, bent low over his horse as fire came from the defenders emerging from the one-time barrack-rooms, spurred for the gate where he dismounted. Scimitar in hand, dripping blood from men hacked at as he went along, he lifted the great beam that secured the gate, throwing the latter back on its hinges. As he shouted his internal attack force aside, his surface party stormed in through the gate behind a hail of bullets.

It was all over very quickly: surprise, as ever, was proved the best of weapons, and the burning of the stables helped as it spread throughout the fort. It was victory, but one of doubtful value: a thorough search of the fort revealed no British mem'sahib, no prisoners at all, and no Murrum Khan. Razjah Shah, his face grim and forbidding, had one of Murrum Khan's chief lieutenants brought before him, held fast by two Pathans. Outside the burning fort now, he glanced at Ogilvie's face in the red glow. 'Your pardon, Ogilvie sahib. The man is now to be made to talk.'

'Torture?'

Razjah Shah nodded. 'You are not a part of British India at this moment, Ogilvie sahib.

It is my fiat that runs now, and for all our sakes I must have the truth, but I shall save your face.' He gave an order in Pushtu and the captive was dragged away. Razjah Shah rode after him, still holding his scimitar. The group faded into the shadows. Soon screams came back, screams of torment and agony that chilled Ogilvie's blood. Then silence, followed by groans, then further screams and after them silence again. Razjah Shah came riding back; there was a strip of flesh hanging from the tip of his scimitar, and there was no captive. He met Ogilvie's questioning eye.

'Food for the vultures,' he said. 'But before he died, he spoke! We ride again, Ogilvie sahib, as soon as my horses rejoin us.' He swung towards the north, and put a hand to his mouth. A long cry rang out, high and vibrant like the call of some great bird, a cry that carried into the distance of the hills to be answered by a similar one from afar where the reserves had been held behind with the horses.

Razjah Shah turned back to face Ogilvie. 'Our ride will be to the south. Murrum Khan left many hours ago for the town of Mana itself, with the mem'sahib. It will be a long ride and must needs be a fast one, or I fear much for the life of the mem'sahib once the bargaining starts.'

★ ★ ★

133

The Royal Strathspey, marching as it were into the very mouths of the guns, had suffered badly in the first assault: before the ranks had scattered by order of the Colonel to find what cover they could where there was virtually none, the rebel artillery had caused upwards of two hundred casualties all told, including forty-three blown to pieces as the pounding shells exploded to scatter case among the Scots. All around them when they had had the time to notice had been the remains of the shattered squadron of the Guides Cavalry, men and horses lying in blood and spilt guts and brains. Here and there an arm or a leg hung upon a bush or a jag of rock; an appalling sight in which to engage the enemy. But morale and discipline had held, and from somewhere along the line the pipes had played on to give heart to the sorely struck battalion. The Maxims had gone into stuttering action immediately, pumping and swinging over the Scots to find targets amongst the enemy gunners, whilst the picquets had been strongly reinforced by men who climbed towards the heights to bring rifles to bear more closely upon the attacking native infantry along the peaks. Support had come from the Brigadier-General, whose force was evidently in being yet: his guns had opened down the pass, sending shells into the rebel artillery positions, but it had been a sadly depleted bombardment and had not lasted long, though in fact the native guns fell silent afterwards.

'I think Norris has not many guns left,' Dornoch said breathlessly to his Adjutant, his face showing pain: his left arm hung by his side, limp and bloody.

'No, Colonel.' Black added, 'I'm fearful of the outcome, I must confess—'

'And your suggestion is?'

'A strategic retreat, Colonel.'

'From an impossible position?'

Black nodded. 'Yes, Colonel.'

Dornoch's voice was brisk, though there was a wince in it as his arm swung to a sudden movement. 'No situation is totally impossible, Andrew, certainly not this one, and in my view there is no such thing as a strategic retreat. A retreat is a retreat and in this case it would leave the brigade in the lurch.' Dornoch stared ahead along the pass to where it was effectively blocked by the rebel gunners. 'They've ceased firing, which probably means a parley. In my view there's nothing to parley about, but it gives us a breather.'

'Yes, Colonel, and—'

'Send Mr Cunningham to me, and Lord Brora. And all company commanders. At once!'

'Very good, Colonel.' Black shouted at the runner waiting beside his horse, and the

135

man went off at the double. The Regimental Sergeant-Major was the first to come up and salute.

'Sir!'

'Mr Cunningham, how are the men?'

'In good heart, sir.'

Dornoch's eyes narrowed. 'You're wounded, Mr Cunningham.'

'It's nothing, sir.'

'You'll have that shoulder seen to nevertheless.' The Colonel turned as Lord Brora rode up, to be followed by the company commanders. They made a tattered, blood-streaked band of officers but there was no defeat in their faces. Dornoch said, 'Gentlemen, we have a respite. It'll not last long. While we have it, we shall act. I intend to scale the heights and get the battalion beyond the ability of the rebels' guns to bear. Action will be carried on atop the pass. Mr Cunningham, you'll split the battalion in half, one to scale the northern side, one the southern.'

'Sir!'

'It'll be a hellish job, but will be done. I shall command the southern half, Lord Brora the northern. You, Sar'nt-Major, will come with me. Captain Black goes with Lord Brora. All understood?'

'The wounded, Colonel—'

'Yes, indeed. They'll have to be carried in *doolies*. I'll not leave any man behind. I'm afraid the dead must wait.'

'Until after victory?' Brora asked.

'Until after victory, Major.'

Brora gave a loud laugh. 'You are over hopeful, I think, Colonel, but damned if I don't admire your spirit!'

Dornoch stared, sensing a kind of impertinence, but said nothing; in any other subordinate the remark would indeed have been impertinent, but Brora seemed to be a law unto himself and probably considered his words polite enough. Dornoch said abruptly, 'Very well, gentlemen, make your dispositions immediately. A to D Companies south, remainder north. You have three minutes precisely, then I shall sound the Extend, and that will be the signal to advance from the flanks. And good luck and success to you all.'

Salutes were exchanged, and the officers broke up to move at the double for their companies. Dornoch sat on his horse like a ramrod, watching his men, casting a glance towards the enemy whose guns remained silent still. It was an almost uncanny silence in the middle of an action, and Dornoch was puzzled: something odd was in the air, and it might prove to be the emergence of a flag of truce and a demand for surrender or it might not. Certainly the enemy must be thinking the British were in that impossible position claimed by Andrew Black! As a medical orderly came up, Dornoch dismounted and allowed his arm to be splinted and bandaged. This work was in progress as the three minutes ended by Dornoch's watch and he gestured to the waiting bugler. The notes echoed out harshly and at once the battalion moved to the flanks and sprang up to climb, moving nimbly with ready rifles and the bearers with the *doolies* coming on much more slowly as they lifted the wounded onward. As the movement was seen the gunfire started again and shells whined down the pass. Dornoch urged the medical orderly to hurry and as soon as his arm had its bandage in place he went at the double for the southern flank, leaving his horse with the other animals. Case and fragments of rock and earth flew everywhere and there were many more casualties. Along the peaks the rebel levies were again in action, pouring down their rifle fire on the climbing Scots. Men rose in the air, arms flung wide, to come off the steep slope and fall outwards, plunging down into the pass below. First to reach the top, a colour-sergeant died with a bayonet through his throat, the blade coming out bloody the other side so that for a moment he hung like a rag doll speared by a sadistic child. Dornoch, in much pain from his arm, sweated and climbed. By dogged determination not to be bested, by guts and courage, the Scots on both sides pounded and dragged themselves to the top, and re-formed; disciplined rifle-fire now battered at the enemy, while in the pass the artillery stood helpless to intervene, their barrels unable to elevate so far. Dornoch, advancing in the van of the southern flank force, looked across to the north: Brora was running ahead in great leaps like a stag, his broadsword awhirl about his head. Even over the rifle-fire Dornoch could hear his shouts and yells as he encouraged his half-battalion on, his big body a prime target that yet seemed impervious to the native fire. As the advance continued amid the highland oaths and cries, the rebels began to press back. Coming farther westwards, Dornoch caught a glimpse of the brigade below in the pass: they had been caught in the worst possible sector, a place where any flank movement was sheerly impossible: the rock sides, if anything, leaned outwards, their tops overhanging the deep cleft in the hills. There seemed to be an enormous number of dead men and horses, Dornoch noted, and shattered guns and limbers: the brigade had been almost cut to pieces – but it was fighting still. Two guns were firing down towards the rebel artillery, and the rifles were in action too. Dornoch turned his attention back towards his own regiment: their progress was slowing as rebel reinforcements came in to join their fellows on the heights, and the Scots' casualties were mounting.

Dornoch found the Regimental Sergeant-Major beside him. He said sadly, 'We're hard pressed, I fear. Perhaps I was wrong to try.'

'You were not, sir. You were not! There's not a man who'd agree with that, sir!'

Dornoch sighed. 'I think the dead would, poor fellows ... but I appreciate your remark.' He held out a hand and speaking again addressed the RSM by his regimental nickname. 'We've served together for a long time, Bosom. I appreciate all you've done for the 114th.' There was a lump in his throat as he shook Cunningham's hand, and he couldn't go on.

Cunningham pressed the hand warmly. 'Never say die, sir.' All at once he stiffened and said, 'Wheesht, Colonel! Listen, sir. D'ye hear what I hear?'

Dornoch listened, then picked up the distant sound. Over the thunder of the guns below and the sharp crackle of rifle-fire he identified the sounds of a British regiment on the march, the notes of the fifes and drums sweeping down from ahead – the Border Regiment marching in from a westerly approach to form a pincer movement on the rebel hordes. Dornoch stopped and beat time with his cane as the fifes and drums came up more strongly to the tune of the regimental quickstep:

D'ye ken John Peel
At the break of the day,
D'ye ken John Peel
When he's far, far away
With his horse and his hounds
In the morning ...

Nine

With the arrival of a second British battalion
to reinforce the brigade, much of the heart
had seemed to go out of the rebel infantry
attack. The heights were thereafter quickly
cleared by the Scots, the natives melting
away into the hills and leaving their com-
rades still in the pass to fight it out with the
newcomers. As the men of the Border Regiment halted and opened fire with rifles and
Maxims, with their attached battery of
mountain artillery quickly assembling their
pieces and opening in support, Lord Dornoch was already leading the left half of his
battalion back to the point where they had
climbed out of the pass. The Scots scrambled down the hillside like goats, slipping
and sliding, to engage the rebel gunners
from the rear as their artillery was turned on

Norris's still beleaguered brigade. The Scots charged along the pass with bayonets fixed, yelling and shouting like demons as the pipes and drums played them on. From the northern heights Brora's half battalion poured down a concentrated fire on the gun teams, and by the time Dornoch's companies had reached the gunners, half lay already dead behind the breeches. Hand-to-hand fighting started, a murderous business and a bloody one as the knives and bayonets grew red in the sunlight. Looking up at one moment, Dornoch saw Brora leading his men back to come down into the pass and join the action at closer quarters. Such of the rebel infantry as had not fled from the peaks was pouring down now to the assistance of the guns, and no doubt Brora had seen this from his higher position, and no doubt also saw the difficulties of finding the right targets in the mêlée below him. Brora came down the hillside like an avalanche, picked himself up and ran like the wind towards the fighting. He came up and joined the Colonel with his broadsword whirling and as Dornoch looked round he saw a turbaned head roll and bounce from the rocks littering the floor of the pass.

'He was about to have you, Colonel. With that splinted arm you're not safe, and I suggest you retire to the doctor's care.'

'I'm all right,' Dornoch said briefly, 'and

the doctor has other things to do. What's the situation ahead, did you see?'

'The Borderers have matters nicely in hand.'

Dornoch nodded: tactically, everything was now to the British advantage. With the main body of the brigade in the centre, the rebel force was now hemmed in on both sides of it and it must be merely a matter of time and attrition. At the Scots' end, the guns now stood silent; but not for long. As the native crews were killed or captured, the Scots took over. Though not artillerymen and with only a basic, rudimentary knowledge of heavy guns, they handled the pieces well enough. As the shells from their own guns landed amongst them, the rebel infantry, massing for a charge down the pass, wavered and then turned and ran, yelling, back into the ready barrels of Norris's brigade. Dornoch waved his broadsword ahead and called for the bugler. The Royal Strathspey, advancing once again as a battalion, ran for the enemy's unprotected rear.

Twenty minutes later, as the defeated natives fled from a scene of appalling carnage, Dornoch and the Colonel of the Border Regiment closed the Brigadier-General from their opposite sides. Norris's tunic was blood-soaked and his face was white, but he was still in command as he shook the hands of the two colonels.

'Thank God,' he said, and turned to his orderly officer and Brigade Major. 'Sound the Cease Fire.'

'No pursuit, sir?' Brora demanded loudly.

Norris lifted an eyebrow. 'Pray who are you, sir?'

'I, sir, am Major Lord Brora, second-in-command of the Royal Strathspey—'

'And not long on the Frontier, I assume! In these hills pursuit is useless, and I have to reach Mana with the High Commissioner.'

'Is he all right, sir?' Dornoch asked.

'Yes,' Norris answered briefly. 'And your battalions, gentlemen?'

'Badly cut up,' Dornoch said.

'Colonel Hinde, your Borderers?'

'As the Scots, sir – there'll be a sad count.'

The Brigadier-General nodded. 'I don't need to say how sorry I am. My own casualties have been very heavy, I'm afraid, and the burials ... this ground's too hard in winter. We've not far to go to clear the pass westwards – you'll confirm that, Colonel Hinde, I think?'

'Yes. Four miles, no more. The natives chose their ground well enough!'

Norris swayed a little; his Brigade Major put out a steadying arm. 'My apologies, gentlemen, I think I have lost blood. The men will rest for half an hour but the picquets must be maintained, of course ... after that time the dead will be placed on the mules and camels and the column will march out with them. As soon as we come clear of the pass they'll be buried in open ground where there is less rock. Carry on, if you please.'

The colonels saluted. As they turned away to their battalions, the Brigadier-General slumped on to a camp stool opened for him by his orderly officer. Dornoch walked slowly towards his Scots and passed the orders. What he saw around him was terrible: the dead lay everywhere, both British and native, loyal man and rebel, with the clouds of vultures gathering, black above the pass. The very earth seemed red; and in the pass was gathering gloom as the sun declined. Dornoch walked on, hearing the cries of wounded men, of men with arms and legs severed by the rebel blades, of men on the point of death, men for whom the medical parties could do nothing. He walked down to the place where for the Scots the action had started that day, the point where he had split the battalion for the climb to the heights. All along the track lay bodies. Going sombrely back towards Brigade he met the Regimental Sergeant-Major.

'A sad day, Bosom.'

'Aye, sir, but when all's said and done, sir – we won.'

Dornoch nodded. 'Yes, we won.' His voice was bitter. A high price had been paid, but it was no more than a deposit on somebody's land holding – and they had yet to reach Mana for the High Commissioner to hold court and make his decisions on that! Dornoch said heavily, 'The British soldier is the world's maid-of-all-work, Sar'nt-Major. Sometimes I wonder he puts up with it all!'

'Aye, sir. But – it's a matter of pride, sir, is it not?'

During the half-hour's rest, rum was broken out and issued, a quarter of a mug for each man. It was warming and it helped, so did the words of praise from the Brigadier-General, who cast aside medical advice and rode along the pass to talk personally to the men. He was proud of every one, and said so, adding that he believed the way would now be clear for Mana, that the enemy had expended his force and lost it in the place most propitious for him, and would be in no position to strike again along a less amenable part of the route. After this Norris assembled the officers and announced that interrogation of the prisoners had revealed that the attack had come from the Afridi tribe: although the prisoners didn't know, or wouldn't reveal, the whereabouts of Murrum Khan himself, it was fairly clear that his were the forces and that he was attempting to assert his strength and settle the boundary dispute favourably to himself by despatching the High Commissioner to his Maker in advance of mediation.

'Somewhat foolishly,' Norris said, 'since High Commissioners can be replaced, but it's well in line with the Pathan outlook that sees military victory as decisive.' He smiled wanly. 'I suppose we do too, but at least we're able to look beyond it, and see that the element of decisiveness is often illusory.' He pulled out his watch. 'Time passes, gentlemen. I shall sound the Advance in fifteen minutes.'

The officers dispersed and the men, having had their half-hour's respite, were fallen in and sent about the business of gathering the dead on to the transport animals and manning the *doolies* for the carriage of the wounded who could not walk. In fifteen minutes precisely the bugles sounded from Brigade and the regiments moved out with their silent burdens, led by a solitary drummer of the Borderers, a poignant beat to keep the step going. From the centre, behind the Brigadier-General and his staff, Pipe-Major Ross blew a haunting highland lament, a sound that brought a prickling to the eyeballs of the Scots as they marched in sad procession out from the enclosing walls of the pass. Once into open country it would become a matter for the pioneer sergeants and for all men capable of wielding pick and shovel or of fashioning with the bayonet's blade rough crosses from any pieces of wood that could be mustered after the cairns of stones had been set in place.

Razjah Shah had said the ride for Mana would be a fast one: it was. They rode in silence, concentrating all their energies on their objective. Ogilvie's wrists had been left free: he was a firmly trusted man now, one who had kept his word and had brought about victory over the holders of Fort Canning. For his part Ogilvie was willing to trust the Pathan leader, and had no doubt that in his turn Razjah Shah would honour his side of the bargain and allow Angela to go free once he had got her away from Murrum Khan. All help Ogilvie could give, that he would give, and never mind that Razjah Shah was as sworn an enemy of the Raj as was Murrum Khan himself.

Good progress had been made by the time the sun came up; they halted a while to rest the horses and to eat a frugal meal of berries and mushy rice that had been brought ready boiled from the cellar hideout, now many miles to the north. Water-bottles were re-filled from a stream and then they mounted and rode on; there was some deviation resulting in a loss of time when the necessity arose to ford a tributary of the Indus River. As that afternoon the sun went down the sky, they entered a narrow defile, filled with rock and much overgrown with scrubby trees. The men were forced to dismount and lead the horses on. Razjah Shah brought down curses upon the delay, savagely: there was, he said, no other way through the mountains at this point and the track they were using was in fact one that had been disused for many years except by bandits such as himself, and that only rarely.

'Where does it come out?' Ogilvie asked.

'In the plain which we must cross to reach Mana by the fastest route.' With his men, Razjah Shah hacked away at the scrub, forcing a passage. The horses could scramble through behind only with great difficulty; there was much time lost. Working desperately, Ogilvie thrust through with the others, using a heavy-bladed, very sharp knife to hack away at the branches that seemed covered throughout their length with some of the worst thorns he had ever experienced, thorns that ripped at his flesh and uniform and brought a good deal of blood. An hour passed ... two hours, three hours, the men taking only brief rests. From Ogilvie sweat poured freely though the air was bitterly cold; at last he saw, or thought he saw, the end of the defile ahead. There was more light and he believed open country was in view. He turned and called back to the Pathans behind him, then went on hacking at the scrub. A last effort and he was through, and standing on high ground just outside the defile, looking down a steep track to the plain – and seeing something that brought a mixture of emotions: a swirl of dust extending for something like a mile, a snake making its way along the track ... a military formation of perhaps brigade strength, men and guns and animals on the march.

He stood there with thoughts crowding ... a moment later he heard the sound, sweeping up towards him as an unheard order was given, the unmistakable sound of the pipes and drums. Fresh sweat broke out. Unless there was an almighty coincidence around, the Royal Strathspey was down there with the marching column! No more than perhaps a couple of miles distant ... with luck he could make it, or at least attract attention.

But to what end? It would scarcely help now for Razjah Shah to be taken by the British, or for time to be spent in questioning and in making decisions afterwards. In Ogilvie's view Razjah Shah in freedom offered the fastest route to Angela's safety; and besides there was the clinching factor anyway: he had given his word. That word held until his cousin's wife had been set upon her way back to safety in Peshawar.

Ogilvie turned away and went back into the defile.

★ ★ ★

Lord Brora lowered his glasses with a savage movement. 'He's gone, Colonel. Turned aside. I tell you it was Ogilvie. A kilt, below a filthy goatskin jacket! I have not a shadow of doubt.'

'Then he will show again, Major. Of that *I* have no doubt ... unless he's under duress.'

'Duress my arse. He's got free! He was entirely alone. I had a fine view!'

'Which no one else had. The distance is too great for certainty.'

'Am I to be blamed for sharp eyes, Colonel? Is no blame to be given to those with blinkers when they should be keeping watch on the flanks? Damn it, that's no way to conduct a column in hostile territory—'

'Thank you, Major, that's enough said. The light is none too good, but you are convinced you saw Captain Ogilvie. Very well! I am *not* convinced yet—'

'For God's sake, Colonel, how many kilted officers do you expect to find wandering about Waziristan and turning their backs upon British troops and buggering off into cover?'

'Major—'

'It's damned fishy, Colonel, damned fishy. I'd like to know how you explain it away.'

'I shall make no attempt to do so until Ogilvie rejoins—'

'Which I think he will not!'

'Or until he at least reappears, Major,

when I can see for myself. In the meantime you may send a runner to Brigade with a report of a sighting on the right flank.'

Brora snorted and called up a runner. As the man doubled away Brora and the Colonel rode on in a tense silence, with Black hovering on the flank. Time passed; there was no reappearance of the kilted figure. Brora began to make ominous sounds and Dornoch said, 'Well, I agree there's to be no reappearance, Major—'

'Quite! And much time wasted, if not by you then by the Brigadier-General.'

'For whose order we must still wait.'

Brora's mouth closed like a rat-trap. They rode on; within the next few minutes the orderly officer was seen riding down from Brigade. He pulled up his horse beside the Colonel and saluted.

'The Brigadier-General is about to halt the column, sir. Will you please detach a company to form Mounted Infantry on mules and extend to the right flank to investigate the sighting?'

Dornoch nodded, and turned to the Adjutant. 'Captain Black, detach Ogilvie's own company. Major, if you wish to satisfy yourself once and for all, you have my permission to ride yourself in command.'

Brora's arm rose to the salute; it was a somewhat ironic gesture, and he was smiling in a sneering way as he gave it. 'My thanks,

Colonel. I shall not be long.' He turned his horse and rode down the column towards B Company a little way behind the Adjutant. The mules were led up from the transport section at the rear of the battalion and, clumsily in their kilts, the NCOs and men mounted and were reported ready by the Colour-Sergeant.

'So many sacks of potatoes, Colour Mac-Trease,' Brora said disagreeably. He pointed with his riding-crop. 'That peak there, some two to three miles away by my estimate. We are to close it as fast as possible – I hesitate to use the term gallop in connection with mules, but gallop we must try to do. Understood, Colour MacTrease?'

'Aye, sir.' MacTrease hesitated. 'And when we get there, sir?'

Brora stood in his stirrups, his eyes challenging and angry. 'When we get there we dismount and climb and we carry out a search for no less a person than Captain Ogilvie, whom I happened to see briefly through my field glasses a long enough time ago to make our task doubly difficult. Carry on, Colour MacTrease.'

Brora swung his horse and touched spurs to its sides. He went off fast to the flank, the animal's shoes striking sparks from the stones in the track as it obeyed the prick of the rowels. He had soon well outpaced the obstinacy of the flap-eared mules behind.

* * *

Ogilvie had made his report of British troops below, and in return Razjah Shah's handclasp had been warm. 'Your word is an honourable one, Ogilvie sahib. I am grateful.' His eyes were sharp and searching nevertheless. 'Were you seen by the soldiers?'

'I don't know,' Ogilvie answered. 'I saw no reaction from them, but something may have been seen and they may investigate.'

'Truly they may do so, Ogilvie sahib—'

'So what will you do now?'

Razjah Shah shrugged. 'One thing only is left to do! The defile is cleared, and we can go back much faster than we came.'

'But then what? You said this was the only way for Mana.'

'And I spoke truly, for it is. There must now be more delay. We shall go back along the defile, and hide, and when the British have gone away we shall move again and descend into the plain, and follow behind them at a safe distance into Mana.'

'But if they investigate, and overtake us in the defile?'

'What I have said is all that is possible, Ogilvie sahib.' Razjah Shah paused. 'Perhaps your eyes saw that a quarter of the way back from here there is a cave in the side of the hill?'

'I didn't see it.'

'It is well hidden and my hope is that the

154

British will not see either. I saw it and I looked inside. It is deep, and we can cover the entrance even more than it is presently covered. Come!'

The Pathan turned away; Ogilvie and the rest of the bandits followed, making their way with the horses, back through the cleared passage in the scrub. When they reached the mouth of the cave Ogilvie failed to find it even though he now knew it was there: smiling, Razjah Shah moved some scrub aside and showed him the opening. The men and horses moved in, penetrating well back though slowly in the pitch dark. When they stopped there was complete silence, a silence broken only faintly by the plop of a water-drip coming through the rock from above. They waited in as much silence from outside as there was inside. But after a while the outside silence vanished in the sound of men making heavy weather of their search, and the sound of a truculent voice raised in exasperation that verged on fury when after passing on the sounds came back. For a second time the sounds faded. The men in the cave remained as still and silent as carven images for a long time after they had gone. Then they relaxed as Razjah Shah's voice broke the stillness.

'All is well, Ogilvie sahib. While the British were here, I could feel the rope about my neck ... but they have gone, and we are safe.'

Brora was in a savage mood when he rode in to report.

'No one, Colonel. That is, no one I could find.'

'You still think—'

'I *know*, Colonel, I do not *think*. The signs were plain to see. Scrub hewn down, and horse manure in plenty – and recently dropped. But no horses and no men.'

'And your construction, Major?'

There was a loud laugh, a contemptuous and dangerous one. 'My construction, Colonel? Why, I smell treachery, by God! The filly that was taken ... who's to say Ogilvie doesn't lust for her flesh? Who's to say that if pushed to the point he wouldn't put her before the Raj – or even throw in his lot with the damn Pathan and decamp into Afghanistan and thereby put her before his cousin, her lawful husband, as well? Who's to answer with certainty, Colonel?'

Ten

While Dornoch utterly rejected the Major's insinuation, and said so unequivocally, it remained in his mind as an accusation, not against Ogilvie, but against Brora himself. Brora's arrogance and egotism had caused almost the whole regiment to fall foul of him from the start; Ogilvie had never been the sort to put up with bullying either of himself or of his men, nor injustice to boot. And whilst earlier in the year Dornoch had been on the sick list and the command of the battalion had passed temporarily to Lord Brora, the latter had managed to make a considerable fool of himself. His conduct at the Court Martial proceedings against Ogilvie on a charge of cowardice in the field had been a sorry exhibition. This episode Brora had not cast from his mind, and it looked as though he never would. In Brora's view, James Ogilvie in particular would never put a foot right.

In the meantime Brora's remark, uttered in the Major's usual hectoring and ringing tones, had been overheard by the rank and file. There was a good deal of adverse comment on Brora when the word spread like lightning down the column, and the colour-sergeants turned deaf ears to mutinous rumbles: Captain Ogilvie was a well-liked officer, and the Major was a bastard...

When the nil report was made to the Brigadier-General, he passed the order for the column to move out. There must be no more delay for wild-goose chases now: the safe delivery of the High Commissioner to Mana was of paramount importance and the arrival was to be made before the situation could deteriorate further.

At dusk the British brigade had vanished into the distance. Razjah Shah announced that the time had come to move out behind; with Ogilvie he led the way down the steep track to the flat ground, walking the horses so as to relieve them of their burdens. As he said to Ogilvie, they must not make too great a speed yet, but must remain well behind the British column.

'Yet, Razjah Shah? Will there, then, come a time when we can move faster?'

'There will, Ogilvie sahib, but not tonight and perhaps not tomorrow. Many miles ahead there is another track, another pass through the hills. By using this we can outflank the British force.'

'And overtake? But won't they use it themselves, Razjah Shah?'

'No. It is narrow and twisting for most of its length, and while it will not delay us, it would be almost impossible for a large force with guns. Never fear, by taking this track we shall reach Mana on horseback before your Brigadier-General sahib.'

Ogilvie nodded. The need to linger for the time being was hard to endure, for he felt in his bones that the arrival of Sir Lawrence Bindle to start his duties in Mana would prove the time of real danger for his cousin's wife. He believed that pressure would be put upon the High Commissioner to make his decision in Murrum Khan's favour at once, rather than to delay in order to hear all the pleas and arguments of the various *maliks*, the headmen with fingers in the pie of land division. The *jirgahs* at which these local leaders would talk so endlessly could go on for many months, as they had done in the past. Angela Ogilvie was there to ensure that they did not. Ogilvie spoke of her once again to Razjah Shah. The Pathan said, 'You should not think too much, Ogilvie sahib. It does not help. The mind should be clear for action to come.'

Ogilvie gave a short laugh. 'That's when I'll stop thinking! Without action—'

'Without action it is hard. I know this. I wish to be reassuring, but also I must not raise false hopes. We men of the hills know much about false hopes ... perhaps as a result we have grown hard and bitter—'

'Against the Raj?'

'Against the Raj many times, yes, but not of necessity against the officer sahibs, many of whom are such as you – honourable men and accustomed in their own land to a high station, such as gives them an inherent quality of mercy and compassion for those not so fortunate as themselves. You understand me, Ogilvie sahib?'

Again Ogilvie laughed. 'We call it noblesse oblige ... yes, I understand very well! We don't all follow it, I must confess,' he added, thinking of Lord Brora. 'Something of the same thing applies to the Pathans, I fancy? I believe you to be a good man, Razjah Shah. Murrum Khan is a Pathan of a different sort.'

Razjah Shah spat on the ground. 'An Afridi! Yes, a different sort, and that is why I cannot in honesty be reassuring.'

They trudged on in silence, Ogilvie's thoughts growing gloomier and harder to bear. At dawn Razjah Shah called a halt, and they snatched some sleep under the watchful guard of a man who remained awake as sentry. Then more rice was eaten, and more berries. In a grey cold day they moved on; there was a bitter wind blowing free across the mountains as they began to climb, and ahead there was a covering of snow on the hills, lying red beneath an angry, cloud-strewn sun that hung large and watchful like the eye of the Prophet. All that day they trudged with the horses, not yet daring to move too fast, the ragged Pathans striding out hard-faced and with rangy limbs that seemed not to feel the terrible cold of the stark Waziri hills. Shortly after the next night had come down to bring out the stars to hang like lanterns close above, and as the air grew wickedly colder and sharper, good news came from the leader.

'The side pass, Ogilvie sahib. It is now but two miles ahead of us.'

Ogilvie let out a long breath of relief. 'Thank God! Shall we mount now?'

'If you wish, Ogilvie sahib.' Razjah Shah turned to his men and passed the order. Legs were swung over the horses' backs and there were happy grunts from the bandits as the weight was transferred from sore feet. Now there was no more delay: they rode for the pass as fast as the rough ground would allow and within the next few minutes were inside its high walls and making good speed towards Mana. By the next nightfall, Razjah Shah said, he expected to reach the city and come within striking distance of Murrum Khan.

'But do not hope too much, Ogilvie sahib,' he said warningly. 'If Murrum Khan should get word of our coming in time, he will move to another hiding place.'

'Or stay and fight.'

'I believe not,' the Pathan said sombrely. 'Murrum Khan is a warrior indeed, but has never been eager to cross swords, as you would say, with myself.'

'And *badal*, Razjah Shah?'

'Murrum Khan's brother was killed by the father of Dostman Khan, Ogilvie sahib, not by one of my family. *Badal* is not directed against me.'

'But Dostman Khan—'

'I understand your mind. Dostman Khan is also an Afridi. Nevertheless he may be of assistance to us against Murrum Khan. Of this I am hopeful.'

Ogilvie, though full of questions, forebore to press: all along, Razjah Shah had been unwilling to elaborate much, and to that extent Ogilvie felt that the Pathan did not trust him fully but had reservations when it came to outlining plans in any detail. This was fair enough in one respect at least: matters could easily go wrong and if captured by an enemy, he who knew could be forced to reveal. That was a fact of life along the North-West Frontier that had constantly to be borne in mind, and the hill tribes were ever suspicious, confiding usually only in their own close family or in their brothers-in-blood, a status which Ogilvie had not remotely attained with Razjah Shah, though there was undoubtedly a mutual respect as between men of war.

They rode through the night, battered by the wind blowing cold and eerie, sighing along between the hillsides, the horses stumbling now and again over the rocks in their path.

Twenty-four hours after they had entered the side pass Mana lay visible ahead, a city set in a surround of jagged peaks, starkly silhouetted beneath the moon: it was a romantic sight and a beautiful one, but also currently a foreboding one, since the city held the crux of the present trouble. As they came within sight of the clustered buildings beneath the minarets, Razjah Shah halted his followers and sat for a while looking down deep in thought, as though only now at this late stage formulating his final plan for the approach, the infiltration and the attack. After his thought he reached out and laid a hand on Ogilvie's bridle.

'The moment for decision, Ogilvie sahib.'

'I wait your word, Razjah Shah.'

There was a silence; the Pathan's eyes seemed to glitter in the moonlight. 'I have your trust, as you have mine?'

'Yes, Razjah Shah, you have my trust.'

'Then you will follow orders without question, taking me as your leader?'

163

'Without too much question, yes!'

'Here, then, is my decision.' Razjah Shah spoke quietly but with firmness and an expectation of obedience. 'For all to ride down into Mana would be foolish. The moon is such that we must be seen, and I find no approach uncovered by the moon's light. Therefore one man will go, and he shall be followed by one more. These men will go on foot – there is cover enough as far as the outskirts for two widely-spaced men moving carefully. Do you agree?'

'Perhaps.'

'Then you shall be the first to descend, Ogilvie sahib, and I shall—'

'Why me? On my own, I'll stand out a mile in uniform – even under the goatskin!'

'You have answered your own question,' Razjah Shah replied with a low laugh. 'Ogilvie sahib, you are the target, the magnet that will attract the attention of Murrum Khan. When he gets word of you, as undoubtedly he will very quickly, he will know who you are and why you come to Mana—'

'And he'll have me taken to him?'

'Exactly, Ogilvie sahib! And my man shall follow discreetly, and then return here to tell me where you have been taken. You are willing? I shall come fast to you, I give you my word.'

There was a pause; the breath steamed from the horses' nostrils as they snorted, their hooves pawed impatiently at the ground. All the men waited for Ogilvie's answer, their gaze upon him expectantly. The British were brave, sahibs had no fear in their minds or bodies. Ogilvie looked Razjah Shah in the eye.

'It shall be as you say,' he told him. 'I'll go.'

Razjah Shah reached out his hand and took Ogilvie's. 'I shall come. I have promised. You will say nothing of me to Murrum Khan. You have made your way alone from your regiment to seek the wife of your cousin. Murrum Khan will not believe this, but it is all you will say to him.' The leader reached into a leather holster attached to his horse's harness and brought out the British Army revolver that he had lent Ogilvie for the assault on Fort Canning. 'This you shall take again. It will be expected of an officer sahib who has come from his regiment.'

'Thank you, Razjah Shah.'

'Now go. My man will be behind, though you will not be aware of him.'

Ogilvie dismounted, handed over the horse to one of the tribesmen, and turned away, making down the track beneath the moon. As Razjah Shah had said, it was easy enough for him to keep in reasonable cover on his own. It was a long descent through scrubby ground dotted with rock, a progress similar to their earlier route. There was no indication at all of the man who would be following him down: the Pathans knew well how to shadow. As he entered the sleeping city Ogilvie felt the presence of watchful eyes, of men lurking in the alleys and the doorways, or watching from the minarets with the special purpose of reporting any movement of strangers to Murrum Khan in his hideout. It was an eerie advance into the cluster of mean dwellings, into the varied smells of the city, into the enclosed spaces of the filthy alleys and their few nocturnal wanderers. As in all cities of the sub-continent, there were many sleepers in the open, the men and women and children who could find no abode and must needs use their pitiful scanty garments as bed and bed-clothes while the cold wind blew through to the bone. None stirred as he passed by them: they could have been the corpses of the dead. Now and again a mangy dog scavenged or cowered from Ogilvie's approach in avoidance of the anticipated heavy kick or the wielding of a stave. There were few lights: no more than one or two flickering oil lamps behind the glassless holes in the walls that did duty as windows to admit air and release smells. Two Indias, if not three, Ogilvie thought as he passed: the India of the great princes, the rajahs and maharajahs, the gaekwars and the nabobs with their unmeasurable wealth in diamonds, rubies, gold and emeralds; and this India of the natives who lived in poverty and deprivation and stinking squalor, diseased and in constant fear of death ... and superimposed on both lay the third India, the India of the British Raj and Her Majesty the Queen-Empress and her armies and administrators who did their best in an impossible environment to hold some sort of balance, however rough and incomplete, between high and low. At least if the British had not been there, matters would be far worse and the sub-continent would be continually in a state of turmoil and murder and civil war...

Ogilvie became aware of footsteps padding the earth behind him. He was about to turn and confront the follower when from a doorway a little ahead of him a man materialised, a curved dagger in his hand, and stood in his path.

Ogilvie stopped. He asked in Pushtu, 'What do you want?' Behind him, the padding footsteps also stopped, and he felt the second knife-blade press against his spine. He smelled dirty flesh and clothing, an appalling smell to add to all the others. He repeated his question, adding that he came in peace to Mana.

'Peace,' the first man said, 'yet you come dressed as a soldier of the Raj. Why is this?'

Ogilvie shrugged. 'Soldiers of the Raj can come in peace as well as in war. Why do you stop me?'

'I stop you only to move you in another direction. Come.' The man moved to his side and thrust the dagger close. Razjah Shah's revolver was removed from him. The knife in his back remained in position as the walk proceeded. They went ahead, then turned down one of the alleys, and after that they twisted snake-like so that soon all sense of direction was lost. They passed only one other wakeful man, a man who stared briefly and then vanished, presumably lest harm should come to himself. They stopped at last outside great gates of iron worked into strange shapes and topped by massive balls that could have been solid gold. Inside a man stood guard, a man who appeared to be of some private army, a man who at a word from Ogilvie's escort opened the gates to admit them. Two more men came from a guardroom inside the gate and held Ogilvie at rifle-point while his captors spoke in low voices to the sentry. A moment later, after handing over Ogilvie's revolver, the men went away and the gates were shut behind them. Ogilvie was pushed ahead of the rifles, through another gateway and into a large square courtyard around which a building like a palace rose in majesty, its towers seeming to probe the bright clusters of stars and to challenge the moon itself. Ogilvie was pushed up a flight of steps carved out of marble and from there into a magnificent

168

hall, filled with light from oil lamps and candles burning in crystal chandeliers that hung from a ceiling patterned in gold with clusters of jewels sparkling red and green, white and blue and purple in the lamplight. Great marble columns climbed to this ceiling, and from one end of the apartment a staircase rose with wide, deep steps covered with a crimson carpet. Ogilvie was marched across the hall and through another door where, abruptly, the scene of splendour changed. Here he was in a bare, functional passage with dirty walls of rough stone and an uneven stone floor. Ahead of the rifles he went to the end of this passage, through yet another door, and down a greasy flight of steps that spiralled into the depths of the palace. At the bottom was another passage, at its end a trap-door.

Events had come full circle, though the venue had changed: the trap-door was lifted and Ogilvie was pushed to the brink of a black hole from which a vile smell rose. The goatskin coat was torn from him. Then a heavy blow landed in the region of his kidneys, a smashing blow from a rifle-butt, and he doubled up in pain and dropped like a sack through the hole.

As snow began to fall Razjah Shah's man threaded his way back through the maze of alleys and reached the perimeter in safety.

He left the city, heading for the track into the hills, moving at a loping run as soon as he was away and clear, unseen and unremarked as he had been throughout. He was breathless when he reached the heights and answered the challenge, to be brought to Razjah Shah. 'Ogilvie sahib has been taken to the palace of a merchant friendly towards Murrum Khan,' he reported. 'I followed all the way, but was not seen.'

'And you can find this palace again?'

'With no difficulty. It is big, and I have the way in my mind, Razjah Shah.'

'You have done well and I am pleased.'

'Then we go down again to Mana, Razjah Shah?'

'I have given my word that I shall come to Ogilvie sahib, and come I shall, but not yet. We must wait and find out more things first, and when the dawn comes I shall go alone into Mana.'

When the first streaks of morning lit the peaks, now snow-covered, around the silent city, Razjah Shah was as good as his word. His orders given, he rode alone down the track, out of the hills to the flat lands. He rode openly and arrogantly, and swaggered his way into Mana, riding slowly through freezing alleys already starting to teem with native life, heading for the bazaar quarter, where he dropped the word that he wished a meeting with a one-armed man, a *fakir* named Zulifiqar. As he waited beneath the snowflakes' fall for the *fakir* to be found, he heard a sound from the distance, a sound that slowly swelled and, as it was heard by the towns-people, brought conflicting emotions to the dark faces around him: the evocative and often terrible sound of the wailing pig, the stirring warlike sound of the instrument beloved of the soldiers with skirts like Captain Ogilvie sahib, a sound that also stirred the hearts of the Pathans themselves. As this sound grew louder a thin man approached Razjah Shah's horse and caught his attention, bowing low.

Razjah Shah stared down. 'Well?'

'The *fakir* Zulifiqar waits, Razjah Shah sahib.'

'Where does he wait?'

The thin man bowed again. 'I will take you to him.'

'Then quickly! Time passes, and the sounds of war beyond the city tell me that certain threads may cross to the disadvantage of many people.'

The wind had died, but now the snow had come in earnest; it lay white and deep over the peaks and drifted down to cover the countryside, the great plateau in which Mana was situated, to bring more discomfort at the end of a long and weary march, a march that had seemed to bring all the varied fortunes of the Frontier. Hunger and thirst and cold, and the fording of rivers during which in some cases men had had to wade through rushing waist-deep water with their rifles held above their heads. The guns had been sent across on rafts while the transport mules were made to plunge in and swim with their loads, and the camels pushed through with dignified faces above the bow-waves at their breasts. The wet clothing had to dry as best it could on the soldiers' bodies as they marched on, and the soaked kilts brought chafing and sores to the thighs. Now the marching feet lifted and came down soggily in the snow's muffling silence, making it almost impossible to keep the step despite the exasperation of Captain Black who rode down the column like a snowman on horseback, snapping at the colour-sergeants. As the covering deepened the order was passed back by the Colonel for the battalion to break step; much relief was brought thereby. The pipes and drums continued, sending their message ahead towards Mana that the High Commissioner was approaching under escort of the power and panoply of the Raj to see justice done in the name of Her Majesty Queen Victoria.

From Brigade, the orderly officer came riding down the marching, weary line with orders for all commanding officers to report to the Brigadier-General for briefing. The orders were concise: the brigade would make camp two miles outside Mana to the north and never mind the snow. It would be warm enough inside the tents. Full defensive precautions were to be taken: the perimeter to be strongly protected by a rampart faced with a ditch, the guns to be posted along the perimeter itself with the horses, mules and camels held in the centre with the camp followers. Guards and sentries would be maintained all along the perimeter, with warning posts established a hundred yards outside for the shoot-and-skedaddle men.

The Brigadier-General pointed ahead with his riding-crop, indicating a ravine that ran out across the plateau from the mountains. Along it marauders could descend in cover from the heights and lie nicely concealed until the moment came to spring out and attack. 'I don't like that *nullah*, but it's going to be difficult to avoid unless we skirt the town and come up round the southern side. I don't like that either! It puts Mana between us and our line of communication to the north.' He frowned. 'What d'you think, Brigade Major?'

'I'd risk the *nullah*, sir. Provided we make camp so as to leave enough space between the perimeter and the *nullah*, we should not be easily surprised.'

Norris agreed. 'Very well, gentlemen, but see to it that your sentries are vigilant.' He turned to the High Commissioner, who was in fact only just visible beneath an immense fur coat that covered his horse's rump as well as his own body, and a heavy fur cap with ear-flaps. 'There'll be a fluttering in the dovecotes of Mana now, Sir Lawrence, and I expect a visit shortly from a representative *malik*. When do you wish to start your business?'

'As soon as possible,' Sir Lawrence Bindle answered through chattering teeth and blue lips. 'I shall be ready for the *maliks* whenever they wish, and propose to hold a *jirgah* in the first place.'

'Talking-shops!' the Brigadier-General said with a snort.

'A very necessary preliminary, I fear, General.'

'Well, Sir Lawrence, I trust you'll not lose sight of two facts: the bayonets are ready if and when you want them, and the men of my brigade are made of flesh and blood – and both can freeze in this damnable climate!' The Brigadier-General turned back to his colonels. 'Thank you, gentlemen, that's all for now.'

Salutes were exchanged and the officers rode back to their battalions, where the temporarily halted men were stamping feet and blowing through mittened fingers to keep the horrors of frostbite at bay. The brigade moved on, to be halted in their appointed position below the hills now white and bleak with the falling snow, some of them bearing the dark green of pines that were becoming invisible as the flakes drifted down. As the order to halt was given, the pipes and drums fell silent and the men were fallen out and at once set to the task, a busy one, of making camp. Parties were marched away to dig the perimeter trench and throw up the rampart while other men shook out the tents from the backs of the mules and under the direction of the Regimental Sergeant-Major and the Regimental Quarter Master Sergeant began to peg them out in their strictly measured lines, scooping the snow from underneath with shovels. It was a warming task and the men had no objection to that, and in all conscience it was little colder than the depot at Invermore in Scotland, little worse than the route marches through the wild Monadhliath Mountains or the Grampians...

Cunningham, marching about his duties, was hailed by the Adjutant. He halted, making a personal snow-flurry beneath the swirling pleats of his kilt, and saluted.

'Sir!'

'Tents up – but we must still consider warmth, of which there will be little enough. What there is must be self generated.' Black stared down from a greyish face, the dark moustache flecked with snow that, melting, ran into his mouth. 'Do you take my meaning, Mr Cunningham?'

'I think you mean drill, sir.'

'I think I do too, Mr Cunningham. See to it that the drill-sergeants are instructed.'

'Aye, sir. Begging your pardon, sir, the men will be kept busy with guards and sentry duties and providing the outpost—'

'Not all the time, Sar'nt-Major. When not employed on guard, they are to drill. Sleep will take second place – in their own interest, as advised by the Surgeon Major.'

'Aye, sir.' Cunningham hesitated. 'Is there any word yet of Captain Ogilvie, sir?'

'None.' Black swung his horse round and moved away, his trewed thighs damp with the snow. The Regimental Sergeant-Major marched off to inspect progress at the perimeter ditch and reflected sardonically on drill in two feet, maybe more, of snow ... not that he disputed the doctor's dictum, for sleep could bring the frostbite if the temperature fell low enough – but drill! The men would be better employed shovelling the snow than tramping it into hard-packed ice, and Cunningham made a guess that drill was not the doctor's panacea but one hatched up in his name by the Major and the Adjutant. Meanwhile, what in God's name was Captain Ogilvie undergoing?

The holy man, the *fakir* named Zulifiqar,

was as brown as a nut, as bald as a coot, as thin as a stalk of wheat, and, despite the cold, almost as naked as a baby. Dressed only in a dirty white loin-cloth, he sat cross-legged in a fireless room into which blew eddies of snow through the hole in the hovel's cracked wall. It was a desolate and unpropitious sight, but it was somehow warmed and lightened and made to glow with hope by the eyes of the *fakir*. Holiness and goodness shone like a lantern in the darkness of a mountain pass, and gladdened Razjah Shah's heart.

'Whence do you come, Razjah Shah?' the *fakir* had asked.

'From Afghanistan.'

'And your purpose?'

'To watch boundaries, O Zulifiqar, holy one. And in watching, to frustrate the schemes of another, an Afridi who would bend affairs to his own ends to the detriment of not only myself and my tribe of Mahsuds but also to the detriment of the townspeople of Mana.' Razjah Shah paused, watching the *fakir* closely. 'I think you know to whom I refer, O Zulifiqar, holy one, beloved of the Prophet and of Allah.'

The eyes shone with benevolence. 'This is possible. The one to whom you may perhaps refer is of the faith, a believer, and is beloved of Allah also, as much as you, Razjah Shah.'

'Neither Allah nor his Prophet is blind or

deaf, O Zulifiqar. Because of this he loves some less than others.'

'We do not presume to know the mind of Allah,' the *fakir* said with a hint of a reprimand.

'But we are permitted to guess.' Razjah Shah shifted slightly on the earth floor, which was abominably cold when a man kept his body so still, and his attitude of obeisance was uncomfortable also. 'This man is rich, and rich men are not beloved of Allah so much as poor men. In addition he is a murderer, and the son of a murderer—'

'All Pathans kill, my son.'

Razjah Shah was momentarily nonplussed: what the *fakir* said was the truth. But he turned the statement neatly. 'When the cause is good,' he responded with equal truth, 'the crime is less heinous in the eyes of Allah.' He said no more; a case could be too strongly pressed and he needed, urgently, the help of the holy man. Humble silence was better now, and the *fakir* could be left to his digestion of utterances made. Digestion took a long time; Razjah Shah, growing restless, became seized with impatient and unworthy – and unholy – thoughts. The holy one was a holy old faggot, an old idiot to whom all men were in basis good – a stupid philosophy and demonstrably, at any rate in non-Prophet terms, a false one. Razjah Shah shifted again, anxious to interrupt the processes of thought with further evidence of Murrum Khan's many iniquities, but fearing still to do so. At length patience and humility were rewarded. The *fakir* spoke.

'Razjah Shah, all men are brothers and must be treated as such. Yet within the family are the unruly ones together with the obedient and peaceable ones.'

'Your words are true, O Zulifiqar, O holy one.'

'The wise father admonishes the unruly sons for their own good.'

'Yes. This is what the wise and good father does, O Zulifiqar.'

There was another pause, a lengthy one again, and cruel for the spirit to bear in abjection. And prostration was becoming most painful ... before Razjah Shah was forced to groan aloud, the *fakir* spoke once more. 'My son, we must follow the teachings of the Prophet and the good example of his holy master's fatherhood.'

'And admonish the unruly son, O Zulifiqar?'

The bald head inclined slightly. 'So. You must tell me more, and then I can consider the admonishment, and how much of it there should be.'

'Your wisdom is great, O holy one, beloved of Allah, seer of seers, in touch with heaven, doer of much good in the name of the Prophet Mahomet. The man of whom I speak has seized an officer sahib, a white officer of the powerful Raj ... and also a mem'sahib, wife of a high official of the civil power, one who in India speaks for the white queen who presides over the world from the great castle at Windsor. This will bring much trouble and the shedding of rivers of blood to Mana, the more so since British soldiers now sit waiting outside the city. I, Razjah Shah, an unworthy man in the eyes of Allah but a loyal one and one well disposed towards Mana and its people, offer help. This help will not be enough without your help. O holy one, O great thinker, O man of much humbleness and goodness...' Razjah Shah most mightily abased himself, speaking almost automatically whilst his mind roved busily over more mundane matters: the *fakir*, who was of the *Ba Shara* class, and therefore one who was "with the law" according to the faith, was undoubtedly good, undoubtedly holy and wise; but he was also practical, and his poverty was more apparent than real. Zulifiqar could help much; Zulifiqar was a power of his own, with call upon the services of many, many men and guns in the name of Allah, and was indeed something of a rabble-rouser whom almost one might call a lost *mullah*. After the help had been rendered, Zulifiqar would not be found unwilling to receive a reward. His price would be high, even if it were never mentioned in so many

180

words, but it would prove well worth a large number of sheep and goats laced with just a little virgin gold, and a promise that Razjah Shah would, if ever called upon to return favour for favour, be at the holy one's call beyond the mountainous border of Afghanistan...

Razjah Shah reached the end of his submission.

'You argue well, my son.'

'You speak with kindness, O Zulifiqar.'

'Unruly brothers disturb the family...'

'Truly they disturb it much, O holy one.'

'I shall help as you ask, and you will be grateful.'

'I will be very grateful, O Zulifiqar.' With a wince, Razjah Shah straightened his aching body.

In its long journey on the wings of the wind from the peaks and foothills of Himalaya in the north, the snow had passed over the splendid buildings of Division in Nowshera, and over Peshawar. It had whitened the cantonments and the garrison lines, the roads of communication, the Quissa Khawani Bazaar or Street of the Story-Tellers, the Mochi Lara with its dazzling displays of embroidered sandals, and all the spider's-web of alleys of the old native city. It had ceased its fall when the horseman out of the south, a wild man out from the Waziri hills, rode in;

but the flakes lay thick upon the ground and the hoofbeats were muffled as the rider cantered along the alleys, scattering the townsfolk who stared up at a wild and haggard face, dark with almost frozen and congested blood. The man, who was clad in a long cloak and wore a green turban, was well armed with knives and daggers and a *jezail* that lay ready to hand across his saddle. The rider turned aside quickly when a British military patrol came into view ahead, a corporal and four privates from a line regiment keeping the peace in the city, a peace that the lone rider seemed likely enough to shatter. But he passed through Peshawar keeping his weapons to himself, and no peace was shattered until he began to approach the outskirts on the Nowshera side and found a fat man squatting on a cushion in the doorway of a hovel that announced itself by a sign as being the shop of Sajjad Athar, trader in leathern commodities.

The rider pulled up his horse, and lying snow flew. He seized and waved his *jezail* and its rusty bayonet. 'You!'

Politely, the fat man clambered to his feet, holding his stomach and a bubbling *hookah* pipe. 'You wish harness, perhaps?'

'I wish you, fat trader. Come!'

The man approached a little fearfully. 'What do you wish, friend?'

'You are Sajjad Athar?'

'Yes, I am he—'

'Good! And as a trader in Peshawar, one who gets his living from his shop, you will wish no interference with your custom. Do not trouble yourself to answer. I know your answer before your mouth opens. Catch this, fat trader.'

He lifted his hand and threw something: a goatskin bag, rimmed with brass and with a hasp and small padlock, landed in the snow. The fat man bent and picked it up, staring at it in increasing fear and wonder.

The rider said, 'The bag you will take unopened to Nowshera, and you will deliver it to the Lieutenant-General sahib commanding the First Division of the British Army. If there is any failure, your trade will vanish in the burning down of your shop and the removal of your tongue, fat trader. You have a horse?'

'Yes—'

'Then mount and ride, but not before two hours have passed. In the meantime remain as usual in your shop and communicate with no one.' The wild man brought his horse round, its hooves slipping and sliding on the packed snow. He rode away, leaving the fat man to stare after him and quake for his family and his living.

Eleven

In Nowshera Bloody Francis Fettleworth raised his eyebrows at his Chief of Staff. 'A trader, from Peshawar?'

'With this, sir.' Lakenham held out the goatskin bag.

Suspiciously, the Divisional Commander took it, laid it on his desk and stared at it. 'What is it, d'you suppose, Lakenham?'

The Chief of Staff explained the circumstances of the bag's delivery to Sajjad Athar, and added, 'I take it as containing a message, sir.'

'Then we'd better look inside! But it's padlocked.'

'Allow me, sir.' Lakenham took possession of the bag again, brought out a pocket-knife with an attachment for removing stones from horses' hooves, and inserted this steel probe into the hasp. He twisted, the hasp parted company with the brass rim, and he upended the bag. A piece of parchment, covered with thin spidery writing, fell out upon the General's desk. Fettleworth picked it up, his expression distasteful, stared at it doubtfully as he had at its container, then laid it on the desk and told his Chief of Staff to smooth it out; which was done.

Fettleworth then read the words aloud: 'I have in my power the mem'sahib from Nowshera also her kinsman Captain Ogilvie, son of the Lieutenant-General sahib at Murree. Both will die unless the British High Commissioner is ordered to decide the boundaries as drawn on the other side of this parchment.' Fettleworth pulled a red silk handkerchief from his pocket and mopped at his face: he had begun to sweat badly, and his eyes were staring. 'It's signed Murrum Khan. God in heaven! What do we do now?'

'It's not unexpected, sir, when all's said and done—'

'No, but—'

'I suggest we turn the parchment over for a start, sir, and see what the actual demand is.'

'Yes, yes.' With shaking fingers, Bloody Francis turned the parchment over and swore again. 'Good God, Lakenham, just look at that! The bugger wants all the damn territory from a little north of Mana to the damn Afghan border! All the way north to the Kurrum River and the damn railway line from Kohat to Parachinar! It's monstrous, Lakenham, absolutely monstrous!'

Lakenham took up the roughly-drawn map and studied it. 'I agree, sir. What do you propose to do about it?'

'Do?' With glassy eyes, Fettleworth stared.

'For a start, reject the bugger's impudent demands, of course! He must be mad! What does he think I can do for him anyway? I'm the military. It's not for me to attempt to sway the High Commissioner's judgment, is it?'

'No, sir. I suggest Murrum Khan will be expecting you to pass on his message to quarters that would be in a position to accommodate him ... if they were so minded.'

'Which of course they damn well won't be!' Fettleworth said energetically. 'Damn impertinence, I've never heard the like! I suppose you mean the Government in Calcutta, don't you, Lakenham?'

'Naturally,' Lakenham answered with a touch of impatience. 'But you'll have to go through the proper channels first, sir.'

'What?' Fettleworth seemed dazed.

'The Army Commander, sir. And Sir Iain's going to be mightily concerned in a very personal way, is he not?'

Fettleworth sucked in breath and rose to his feet, his large stomach, scarlet-clad, rising over the edge of his desk. He went across to the wide window and stood looking out at the lying flakes and the Divisional flag drooping from its staff, its colours lost in a covering of frozen snow. However expected the demands had been ever since the disappearance of Mrs Ogilvie, their actual arrival was still a shock and the more so since the son of the Army Commander was also now a prisoner of the damn heathen: much trouble would now fall upon the luckless Divisional Commander at Nowshera, and Bloody Francis, not so far off retirement, had no wish to have his copy-book blotted at this late stage. Fettleworth stood and quaked, felt a shiver in his spine and a queasy visitation of his stomach: Sir Iain Ogilvie was far from being an easy man to suffer under, and never mind that their military ranks were the same – the Army Commander was his superior and that was that. The loss to the evil machinations of the Pathan of not only his nephew's wife, but also his own son, would certainly not incline Sir Iain towards reasonableness ... but as Fettleworth turned from the window and his protuberant blue eyes met, across the long room, the portrait of Her Majesty the Queen-Empress, he stiffened himself. That stern, autocratic face, the down-the-nose look, the neat bun sticking out a little way behind the lace cap, the plump and motherly breast, the firm rat-trap mouth the utterances of which scared the bowels out of the Prince of Wales ... it all added up to a tonic, a sort of distillation of the enormous power of the British Raj. Fettleworth's chest went out: Murrum Khan was nothing but a damn native, an ill-kempt Pathan ridden out from

187

beyond the Khyber, an upstart with crazy demands upon British territory, scum that would shortly be despatched with his brigands back whence he had come, unless his head first rolled bloodily in battle or his wretched body dropped limp from the scaffold in the civil jail in Nowshera! How could such scum dream that they could challenge the might and authority of Her Majesty Queen Victoria! Really, there was no cause at all for alarm.

Fettleworth once again seated himself behind his desk. 'That trader, whatsisname. Better send him in, Lakenham. Lily-livered bugger should have raised the alarm before the damn messenger got away.'

The Chief of Staff went to the door and beckoned. In came Sajjad Athar, trader in leathern commodities, a frightened fat man cringing between an armed escort of a corporal and two privates of the King's Regiment. His eyes were closed, so great was the glory of the Commander sahib of Her Majesty's First Division in Nowshera and Peshawar, Her Majesty's own representative, very God of very God to poor traders whose service to the Raj was but humble. Sajjad Athar quaked but began in a high voice to justify himself: his business, his living were at stake, so was his family of a wife and fourteen children and a mother and a mother-in-law and many aunts, uncles and cousins and cousins' children. All would have suffered, and in an agony of remorse he had obeyed the wild-looking nomad and had remained in his shop for the appointed time. He was most humbly sorry, he was abject, prostrate and most loyal to the Raj.

'Take him away, for God's sake, Lakenham, he makes me sick. Not a thought for the Raj! Get a description of the damn Pathan, for what it's worth, and notify Brigade at Peshawar. Then you shall inform Northern Command – and I'd better have a word with Mr Hector Ogilvie, I fancy...'

All night Ogilvie had lain in the hole's blackness, assailed by the terrible stench of drains and putrefaction, and by more: by the attentions of rats and smaller things that crawled and bit, and by puddles and trickles of water, and at one moment, a terrifying moment, by something cold and smooth that wriggled across his neck – a snake, but one that had not attacked. After that, the place held sheer horror and Ogilvie scarcely dared to breathe unless he should attract the snake. But as all things come to an end, so did this: as he began to give up all hope he heard the opening of the trap-door above, and yellow light came down, and in the glow he saw a man's face, evil and bearded and scarred with the cuts of knives or bayonets.

A moment later a rope's-end was trailed

down and the man said, 'Come.'

Ogilvie grasped the rope and climbed. As he came through the hatch his body was seized by two pairs of hands and he was set on firm foundation. The lantern's light gleamed on three men, well armed. Not another word was said; the point of a knife in his back gave him his marching orders, and he went ahead along the passage which he had traversed the previous evening, up the spiral steps and along the second passage; but not through the door at the end that led to the richly-decorated state apartments. Instead he was halted at a door half-way along, and one of the men knocked with the butt of a *jezail*. From inside heavy bolts were drawn and the door was opened.

Ogilvie was pushed in. Entering, he was at first blinded by sudden brilliant light, light from what seemed like thousands of candles burning in crystal chandeliers and reflecting off polished silver that surrounded many mirrors built into the walls of a great room. As his eyes became accustomed to the glare, Ogilvie saw that this was no ordinary room: at one end was a raised dais, and on this dais stood a number of gilded chairs like thrones, only one of which was occupied. Along the side walls stood benches; it was like a court-room or an auditorium. Running almost the length of the room, and some twenty feet wide, was water. By the look of it, deep water

– a kind of sunken bath of vast proportions. The atmosphere was warm and humid. Across this curious pool, some half-dozen feet from the far end, ran a barrier, a wooden boom with a strong wire-mesh net stretching down from it, a net that seemed taut as though it were held fast at the bottom. From beyond the pool, from the single man seated on the dais, there came a laugh that echoed round the high walls, a hand flashed, something flew through the air, and landed with a splash in the water beyond the barrier. On its heels there was a sudden flurry in the water, then a larger disturbance that made small waves run, and from a dark round hole just below the water's surface a thing emerged at speed, long and scaly and with enormous snapping jaws and big eyes: a crocodile.

Ogilvie shivered, a prey to sudden hopeless fear, but clamped his teeth hard. Behind him, the knives pushed him towards the dais and the seated man whom he guessed to be Murrum Khan. The description as given him at Fort Jamrud fitted in every detail: the gold-worked cloak of maroon cloth, the exceptional height of the man, the gold earrings with dangling medallions. Ogilvie could not see the boar's head motif but had no doubt that it was there. Halted by his escort, he stared upwards at the Pathan, and there was another laugh.

191

'How neatly you have dropped into my hands, Ogilvie sahib!'

'Not for long. The Raj never sleeps, Murrum Khan.'

'So you know my name.'

'As do others. I think your time will be short, Murrum Khan, now that you have transgressed the law of the Raj.'

The man gathered saliva and spat. The gob landed on Ogilvie's tunic and drooled down. 'That is what I think of the Raj. That is what I think of your Queen-Empress, who is fat with age and inactivity and who has reigned for too long, and who is greedy, and who must now shed land to those who dwell upon it. When the news that you are in my power is told in your garrisons of the Raj, especially those of the north, then I believe negotiations will start. Do you not agree?'

Ogilvie said, 'The Raj always negotiates, Murrum Khan, but from a position of justice. The High Commissioner is coming for that purpose, as you know well, but there will be no shedding of land on the part of the Raj—'

'I spit on your High Commissioner as I spit upon the Raj itself,' Murrum Khan said, and again spat. 'It is not your High Commissioner who concerns me, but the General Officer Commanding your Northern Army of the Raj.'

Ogilvie nodded. 'I expected that, naturally.

192

But I think you misunderstand the Raj and underestimate my father. What would you do, if your son were held as hostage by the Raj, Murrum Khan? Would blood weigh more heavily than what you saw as your duty?'

Murrum Khan smiled. 'I answer that it would not, Ogilvie sahib.'

'Exactly! On the other hand, you would use all your strength to get your son back. That's what my father will do. I am not so much a hostage, Murrum Khan, as a millstone round your neck, and your neck is a fragile thing when set against the regiments and brigades and divisions of the Raj.'

'Brave talk,' Murrum Khan said sneeringly. 'It is you who fail to understand *me*, not I you. I do not expect the General sahib to urge surrender on the Government in Calcutta for his own sake or yours, but I think the Raj will accommodate my wishes nevertheless. What is a mountainous track of land when set against a man's life?'

'Frontier land is much valued for defence against the Afghan tribes, and in any case it's a matter of principle, Murrum Khan. If a thing is done once, it can be done again. That is why there will be no surrender, no matter how many men's lives are threatened.'

The Pathan lifted an eyebrow. 'Then a woman's life?'

Ogilvie caught his breath: that Angela was in this man's hands he knew, but the utterance of the threat was hard to take. He asked, 'My cousin's wife?'

'The same.' Murrum Khan got to his feet, and stood tall and commanding. He clapped his hands twice. 'Turn round, Ogilvie sahib,' he said.

Slowly, feeling as cold as death, Ogilvie turned. The door was thrown open by a man standing just inside. Something like a procession came through, led by a man with the holy air of a priest. After him came two young women, heavily veiled in accordance with the teachings of the faith of Islam; after them two armed men in ragged garments, looking strangely out of place in the mirrored room with its chandeliers. Behind them Angela Ogilvie, calm seemingly, but with a face like ashes. Behind her two more guards and finally a bent and shambling old beldame, veiled like the young women, and clad in deepest black all over so that she looked like a slow-moving, earth-bound crow.

Ogilvie opened his mouth to call out to Angela, but the words stuck in a dust-dry throat and mouth. As for the girl herself, she seemed not to be registering or to have even recognised her husband's cousin; her eyes were dull, lacking all life. As the procession came forward and halted at the doorward end of the pool of water, Ogilvie turned on

194

Murrum Khan, fists clenched, and took a step forward. At once he was seized by his escort and a knife-point nicked his throat, drawing blood, while another pressed against his side. Again the words would not come: there was little point in the utterance of them in any case.

Murrum Khan spoke: 'The way out is open. It calls only for the compliance of the Raj. Let this be understood.'

Again he clapped his hands, and there was a stir behind Ogilvie, and then a cry of terror and despair. He swung round. Angela had been lifted high by the guards and was being borne past the veiled women. A moment later her body was swung, and thrown, and spread-eagled she splashed down into the water of the pool. Immediately she touched, and for a moment sank, the flurry came again from behind the barrier and an armoured tail was flailed, battering at the net, and cruel jagged teeth in the long jaw cracked harshly at the wooden boom and splinters came away. There was a violent thrashing, and as Angela, screaming in terror, put up her hands to grip the sides of the pool, the guards moved towards her with their knives. Blood trailed in the water thereafter and the scaly creature, which Ogilvie recognised as *crocodilus porosus*, a native of India, a species known to be capable of growing to a length of thirty-three feet and to have a voracious appetite for flesh, hurled itself again and again at the net, almost lifting the boom in its sockets and bringing a terrible hollow sound to echo about the apartment.

Twelve

The cold in Mana was intense: the wind bit to the bone and the snow lay to freeze the feet. But the *fakir* Zulifiqar seemed possessed of an inner fire. His nakedness covered only by a white cloth like a sheet that fell from his bald head to enfold his body, he went out into the alleys seated on a board carried by four men, pausing at corners and in the wintry bazaar to talk. His words spread; men gathered in groups in the alleys, or sat huddled in hovels out of the snow's searching wet fingers. The *fakir's* words were pondered: the great one in the palace, Murrum Khan, was about business that would bring much trouble to the city, and the Prophet would be displeased thereby. Already outside the city – and this they knew without assistance from the Prophet or his henchman Zulifiqar – the power of the Raj was manifest in the presence of many soldiers and weapons. Soon there would be discussions between the Raj and the *maliks* from the neighbouring tribes, and it would be well if these were peaceable. The British were on the whole just, and at times were merciful, but there were the other times when they reacted with fire and sword and put entire communities to the flame of the torch by way of punishment for crimes committed against the almighty Raj. Murrum Khan was of course powerful, but on a much more localised scale than the Raj that stretched from Cape Comorin to Himalaya, from Karachi to the Bay of Bengal and the Sundarbans of the Brahmaputra, embracing Muslim and Hindu, Sikh and Jain and many other religions, and enjoying the support of all the great princes of India. Against this, so said the *fakir* Zulifiqar, Murrum Khan was no more than the flea upon the dog. Yet Murrum Khan was here in Mana, while so far the main power of the Raj was not ... a problem existed, and many were the mutters as the dictum of the *fakir* spread.

Lieutenant-General Fettleworth's urgent despatches sped to their destinations and Hector Ogilvie was summoned to Division and given word of his wife: Fettleworth promised that everything possible would be done, but refused to be drawn on specifics. The matter, he said, was moving out of his hands and the orders would now be given by the Army Commander after decisions had been made at Viceregal level in Calcutta with the advice of the Commander-in-Chief. Hector, almost distraught by now, unable to eat or sleep since his wife's disappearance, demanded audience of his uncle, who had remained on in Nowshera; but found little help from that quarter.

'My dear boy,' Sir Iain said sympathetically, 'I'm as worried as you are, but what more can I do than send out patrols to cover as much territory as possible?'

'It can be settled easily enough, Uncle Iain—'

'Pray tell me how!'

Hector's lips trembled. 'The message to General Fettleworth. It offered a way out.'

'I disagree,' Sir Iain said frostily. 'It did no such thing.'

'But—'

'The integrity of the High Commissioner cannot possibly be compromised, and will not be by any order of mine. I hope that's clear, Hector.'

'Your own son!' Hector put his head in his hands.

Sir Iain caught Fettleworth's eye and read understanding: it was always the very devil when one's own flesh-and-blood became involved, and it was when such happened that those who held high command were put to the ultimate test. Sir Iain, who had already faced his own wife, James's mother, stiffened himself. He said quietly but formidably, 'Yes, Hector, my own son. I know. And I'm very fond of Angela as well. You must never doubt that. But you must remember my responsibilities. I have the whole future of the Raj to consider.'

Hector burst out, 'One wretched little boundary dispute, a parcel of barren land ... how can anyone be so damn stupid!'

'Barren land yes, but strategically vital. It must be held by those the Raj can trust. It can never pass to a border bandit such as Murrum Khan. Wretched it may be, but little it is not! You of all people, Hector, should know the balance for the Raj is knife-edged ... that there are many dissidents waiting their chance—'

'In other words, Uncle Iain, the integrity of the High Commissioner doesn't exist!'

Colour mounted in the GOC's cheeks. 'I beg your pardon?'

'It's already biased, isn't it? His decision must be acceptable to the Raj—'

'As must that of a judge be acceptable to the law. I see no difference. The Raj must remain faithful to its friends or it is lost. I shall not aid its enemies, Hector. I'm sorry, but if you've come here to persuade me to use my command for personal ends, you're wasting my time and yours.'

'Then you'll do nothing?'

Sir Iain's mouth opened, then closed again. He turned away and walked to the window, where, like Fettleworth earlier, he remained staring out at the symbol of the Raj, the standard of the First Division hoisted to the head of the flag-staff. There was a massive lump in his throat and he wished himself back as a regimental officer in the Royal Strathspey, a position where it would not be inconceivable that he could make a personal foray against the tribesmen, strike some personal and private blow in support of his own kin without it becoming a matter for rising murmurs in headquarters and messes and barrack-rooms as well as in the places of civil power and the echoing halls of government. As General Officer Commanding, the envy of many of lower rank, he was hamstrung, tied up in his own conscience and his own appointment, as it were the unfreest soldier in all Northern India after the Commander-in-Chief himself. Without turning, he spoke: 'I shall do all possible, Hector. Extra patrols, wider probes ... someone shall be taken, and will talk of Murrum Khan. He'll be found, never fear!' He had control of himself now, and he turned to face Fettleworth. 'I believe the most likely area is the Afghan border itself, Fettleworth, the area where Murrum Khan's interest lies.'

'From Jamrud down to Mana?'

'Yes. These bandits prefer to keep within the limits of their own influence – where their support is. I suggest you saturate the area and if necessary deplete the Nowshera and Peshawar garrisons, the others too. I've already asked for reinforcements from Southern Army, and don't tell me they'll take the devil of a time being trooped by the train from Ootacamund – I know it! It's the best we can do.'

'And Mana itself – and Sir Lawrence Bindle?'

'Bindle has Norris's brigade as escort and I consider that force enough, though you'd better hold some cavalry in reserve to reinforce if necessary. Norris may have reached Mana by now – we must await further word before we make more dispositions.' Sir Iain put a hand on Hector's shoulder and said kindly, 'It's hard to bear, Hector, but be assured everything's being done that can be done. I suggest you occupy yourself in work – it's the only way.'

Andrew Black made for the Colonel's tent, returned the salute of the sentry, and ducked down through the flap. 'Your pardon, Colonel. There's a mounted party approaching from the town, under a flag of truce.'

'Brigade's been informed, Andrew?'

'I understand so, Colonel.'

Dornoch reached for his Sam Browne and

buckled it on. As he took up his glengarry the bugle sounded from the brigade tent, ordering the stand-to. No chances were being taken, it seemed, and never mind the flag of truce. With the Adjutant, Dornoch left his tent. He looked towards Mana, as white as the surrounding hills. The air was bitter, with a rising wind blowing the lying snow and the falling flakes into whirls and flurries. There was quite a procession coming out: a troop of native horsemen, wild and ragged so far as could be seen beneath their covering of snow, twenty riders escorting a party of old, bent men, the *maliks* coming out for the *jirgah*.

'They appear as old as Methuselah, Colonel,' Black said.

Dornoch laughed. 'Then they should have much collective wisdom!' He turned and strode through the regimental lines towards the perimeter and its ramparted ditch. There was bustle outside the brigade tent, where Brigadier-General Norris was mounting with his Brigade Major and orderly officer to ride to greet the *maliks*. Around the perimeter the soldiers waited with rifles and bayonets, British and Indian together, fingers half frozen as they gripped their weapons, bodies a-shiver beneath the greatcoats. Inside the entry to the camp, where a drawbridge of wooden planks had been thrown across the ditch, a ceremonial guard found by the Border Regiment waited with rifles at the slope. Snow settled upon their helmets, edged the shining bayonet blades with white. The Brigadier-General rode through, behind a mounted *sepoy* of the Punjab Frontier Force bearing a white flag. A hundred yards from the perimeter he halted, and waited for the *maliks* to ride up.

Dornoch was joined by Lord Brora.

'Good morning, Colonel. Here beginneth the verbal diarrhoea. There'll now be delay ... the damn natives'll be here till next week and beyond!'

'Possibly, Major. Decisions can't be arrived at in haste.'

'With respect, Colonel, I think they can and should.' Brora waved a hand around. 'I don't like that damn *nullah*. It gives too much cover for attack, especially after dark.'

'I agree with you there,' Dornoch said, 'but it's out of our hands, and Brigade knows the risk.' He turned as a runner approached, with orders for all commanding officers to attend at Brigade for a ceremonial meeting with the *maliks*. Black and Brora stood watching as the Brigadier-General formally saluted the native party and spent some minutes in apparently friendly conversation, then turned his horse back for the encampment with the newcomers. As the party rode across the makeshift bridge, one at a time and carefully, the guard was ordered to the

Present: the *maliks* were to be treated with respect. Into the camp rode the motley collection of tribesmen and elders, old men with wizened faces like nuts, many of them bearded, all of them armed to the teeth.

'Some truce!' Brora said in a loud voice. 'I'd not trust the buggers with a dead nanny goat!'

At the brigade tent the *maliks* dismounted and went inside to meet the High Commissioner while their escort remained upon their horses, forming a warlike force by the entrance. As the guard was fallen out and marched away, the bugle sounded again to disperse the men from the stand-to position, and the normal routine was taken up again, parties returning to complete the defences before night should fall and bring the time of danger, though it was unlikely any attack would come while the *maliks* were present in conference.

Ogilvie was held under guard, sitting in the middle of one of the rows of seats by the side of the water. Angela was still immersed, the ravening scaly brute at the other end still thrashed in frustration behind the mesh barrier. Murrum Khan had departed; before leaving he had told Ogilvie that the water was warm from fires that burned beneath its stone base and the mem'sahib would come to no harm by remaining in it. He expected word before long as to the British response to his message; if that word was favourable, then the mem'sahib and himself would both go free. Should it be unfavourable, the barrier would be lifted. As for Ogilvie himself, he would accompany Murrum Khan into Afghanistan by a devious route; in Afghanistan a resistance to the Raj would be organised, and Murrum Khan would lead an army against the Raj, with Ogilvie still a hostage. Word would be sent to Peshawar of the fate of the mem'sahib, as a terrible earnest that Murrum Khan kept his word and carried out his threats, and Ogilvie himself would testify in writing as one who had been a witness. In the meantime Ogilvie was not left for long with his cousin's wife: soon after Murrum Khan's departure men came for him and once again he was dropped through the stinking hole below the palace, back to the utter darkness of the cell and its crawling, slithering denizens. Here all hope seemed at an end, and Ogilvie was left with his last image of Angela, of the appeal in her eyes as he was taken away leaving her without even the small comfort of his physical presence. Razjah Shah, it seemed, had let him down after all, though in all conscience there must be little the Pathan could do against the solidity of Murrum Khan's palace and his watchful guards.

★ ★ ★

The *fakir* Zulifiqar was back in his hovel, bald and bony and bare but still, apparently, not cold. The inner fire burned yet and his eyes gleamed at Razjah Shah. His words, he said, had borne fruit: the townspeople of Mana were anxious, fearful of the British brigade that waited below the hills. Without Murrum Khan, perhaps, the British would go away. Without Murrum Khan their wives and children would not be put to the sword.

'Yet they are a warlike people as are all Pathans, O holy one,' Razjah Shah said with a touch of disbelief in the *fakir's* confident words.

'True. But when the Prophet speaks...'

'And the Prophet has spoken?'

'Yes. He has spoken. He has uttered a warning, and his people will heed. It is written.'

'What has the Prophet advised, O holy one?'

'That the faithful of Mana turn their hands and their weapons against Murrum Khan and that the hostages be released and returned to the British, who will then heap rewards upon Mana and its people.'

'They will attack the palace of Murrum Khan, O Zulifiqar? In that I am ready to assist, since I gave my promise, the word of my honour, to Ogilvie sahib. You have only to say and I shall bring my men.'

The holy man lifted a hand, and smiled.

'Do not leap ahead of events, Razjah Shah. Your help is needed, but not yet. My ears have been assailed by other tidings, which are these: in the hills is Dostman Khan, and with him his men in much strength.' He stared at the Mahsud quizzically. 'You have heard of the paw of the cat, Razjah Shah?'

'The paw of the cat, O holy one, leader of the faithful?'

Zulifiqar inclined his head. 'To draw from the fire the nuts for others is thrust the paw of the unsuspecting cat, who burns while those whom he benefits remain unscathed.' He closed his eyes for a moment. 'Dostman Khan, the sworn enemy of Murrum Khan his kinsman, shall be the paw of the cat. A message will be sent, and down from the hills will come Dostman Khan with his armed men.'

'To attack the palace of Murrum Khan!'

The *fakir* gave no direct answer to that; he smiled enigmatically and said, 'I return to the unfortunate cat, of whom there are said to be more ways than one of killing when desired. There will not be an attack on the palace of Murrum Khan by his kinsman, for if that should be allowed, then the hostages might merely change hands, and much trouble would still come to Mana and its faithful. Better ways are known to the Prophet, my son, and you shall give ear to his wisdom...'

Razjah Shah bent a ready ear, and was

soon open-mouthed in wonder at the *fakir's* inspired strategy, and his fingers began itching for the fight even as his mind roved busily over the necessity of retaining the hostages, not for Murrum Khan nor for Dostman Khan nor yet for the British, but for himself and the grinding of his own axe. When the *fakir* had finished Razjah Shah's praises were many. Leaving the hovel he made his way, silent in the snow, out of the city and back into the hills to rejoin his patiently waiting men. When he made his contact in the heights he lost no time in briefing his followers; already the night was falling, dark and ghostly yet because of the lying snow not entirely dark, and already a message would be on its way to Dostman Khan, lurking with ready knives and rifles in the hills behind the British brigade encamped and in conference below. The Prophet's strategy, though of course wise beyond worldly wisdom, was simplicity itself: Dostman Khan was to be urged to mount by stealth a raid on the British and capture the arguing *maliks* who the *fakir's* message would say – were known to be about to settle against his interests. Razjah Shah's task was equally straightforward: he was to mount his own attack upon Dostman Khan before the latter had reached the British perimeter. True, his available force was small compared with Dostman Khan's, which was a strong one of a size that should give it the capability of cutting right through the camp's defences before the British had collected their wits; but Razjah Shah's sudden foray would deprive Dostman Khan of the vital element of surprise – and the delighted British, Zulifiqar had said with obvious truth, would return his loyalty with much good will. More importantly they would be certain, as a result of his submissions, to march at once upon the palace of Murrum Khan and release the hostages. It was this last part of the plan that had given Razjah Shah food for thought, thought that had proliferated during his journey back into the hills and, by the time he had reached his tribesmen, had crystalised into firm if dangerous decision: *fakirs* were not to be trifled with, but the prize was great, and afterwards much abasement would be made to Allah in propitiation of his wrath; and Allah's mediator the Prophet, who by virtue of his very calling must ever take the long and broad view of worldly events, would surely proclaim the wisdom of his, Razjah Shah's, act of deviousness ... if one thing was certain, it was that neither Allah nor the Prophet would wish to assist the infidel British.

'Gather round me,' Razjah Shah adjured his followers. 'Our difficulties are all but over, so long as our knives are sharp, our rifles loaded, and our wits keen.'

The argument in the brigade tent had been long, and was still continuing. Each *malik* in turn had harangued with passionate conviction for his own cause. Each was in conflict with his neighbour, each had his own territorial demand that must be resisted by all the others. Knives had been produced in support of argument and on three occasions troops had had to be summoned to restrain the headmen and avert the shedding of blood.

Through it all Sir Lawrence Bindle, representative of the Queen-Empress, sat almost motionless but for a head that either nodded or shook as the arguments were presented, sometimes many arguments simultaneously since the *maliks* were not susceptible to the disciplined approach. His mind wandered as the affair grew more and more tangled: long experience of his office as High Commissioner had taught him that tribal arguments could never in fact be untangled and that it was pointless even to try to do so. Before his eyes, as before the eyes of Lieutenant-General Fettleworth, there was ever an image of Her Majesty in the dignified, secure fastness of Windsor Castle: hers was the glory, hers the way all decisions must eventually go. The Raj was paramount, and the judgment of the Raj, like the cleaving of one of Her Majesty's ships of war through the restless seas, was sharp and clear and must cut cleanly through all the arguments, imposing a just solution to all problems. None of the *maliks* would be satisfied as a result of Sir Lawrence's judgment, but all would be dissatisfied together so that in a sense none would be the loser. Why, then, strain oneself by listening? Sir Lawrence listened in fact for one thing only: a mention of the hostages. None came.

The interminable hours dragged past, the atmosphere in the crowded tent became thick and smelly, a horrible cold fug that was oppressive to the senses, senses already battered by the excited, passionate voices of dissent. From outside the ordinary sounds of an encamped brigade followed one upon another; the shouted commands of NCOs, the crunch of marching feet on crisp snow as details and guards and picquets moved about, the notes of the bugles sounding the men to supper and the officers to dinner; and then, as Sir Lawrence yawned mightily, the sad notes of Last Post followed by the solitary piper of the 114th Highlanders. Sir Lawrence pulled out his watch surreptitiously, and sighed. It looked like extending all through the night, but he must not be seen to be hurrying justice yet: the *maliks* must be given their say in the hope that very many words would ease pressures. It had not been unknown in the past history of the Raj for

211

the tribes to talk themselves through un-
aided to a settlement ... Sir Lawrence's white
head sank to the prop of his left hand, and
his eyes gently closed as the waves of argument washed over him like a lullaby. He had
had a very tiring journey and he was no
longer young.

The first shot shattered the peace and calm
of the mostly sleeping camp. For a moment
it seemed to hang in lonely suspension, to be
somehow unreal, then it was followed by
others, and by shouts of war, and pande-
monium seemed to break loose as a rush of
feet crunched through the lying snow. In the
brigade tent the High Commissioner awoke
with a start to find the court in utter confusion, the assembled headmen trying to fight
their way out while a guard of the Punjab
Frontier Force under a *havildar* tried to push
in through what had already become a mob.
The *havildar* shouted at the High Commissioner sahib, but his words were lost. Sir
Lawrence left his seat of judgment and bur-
rowed through the mass of natives, largely
on the ground like an urgent mole, his chest
heaving and his eyes staring and a cry of
alarm forming in his throat. As he reached
the exit he was yanked to his feet, uncere-
moniously, by the *havildar*, and taken outside. He heard bugles and shouts and rifle-
fire and looking towards the south-eastern

perimeter he saw men outlined against the snow, leaping and bounding like stags over the defensive rampart and the ditch.

Thirteen

Lord Brora's face was almost black with fury. 'I damn well told you so, Colonel! That damn *nullah* was made for the purpose! By God, the Brigadier-General shall lose his balls over this!'

Dornoch took no notice of the Major's outburst. He ran ahead for the breach in the defences, the spot where natives were pouring into the camp undeterred by the rifle and Maxim fire. There was noise everywhere, and a degree of confusion as the various regiments tumbled out with their rifles. Ready dressed and armed as they were, it yet took some minutes to deploy them for the counter-attack, valuable minutes that were a gain for the enemy. Already, and in silence, the perimeter guard and the shoot-and-skedaddle men in the warning outposts had seemingly been attacked and overcome: at any rate they had given no warning of the assault, which had come from the point where the *nullah* ran closest to the perimeter.

As Dornoch watched, his revolver in his hand, the whole of the south-eastern defence line became alive with dark bodies that poured across the ditch to hack and stab. Dornoch lifted his revolver and emptied its chambers point-blank into a horde of men closing him, then went down with blood spurting from the shoulder of his already wounded and splinted arm. Feet trampled him as he lay, and he was aware of Brora cutting into more men with his broadsword. Dornoch staggered to his feet and sent out a rallying cry to his Scots: the Regimental Sergeant-Major, running past, checked when he saw the bloodstained figure.

'You'll be best taken to the medical tent, sir.'

'I'm all right, Mr Cunningham. Unless Brigade orders otherwise, fan the battalion out along the attack sector – concentrate the Maxims there too. Where's the Adjutant?'

'Coming up now, sir.' Cunningham went off at the double as Black approached, wild-eyed and covered with snow.

'Colonel, they've come in like the tide—'

'I realise that—'

'The Gurkha battalion's being cut to pieces. Their tents were facing the wind, so they laced them up, and were caught like rats. The Pathans have cut the guys ... the Gurkhas are being slaughtered beneath the folds.'

Dornoch swore. 'What's Brigade doing, I'd like to know!' A moment later Brigade appeared to react: from the mountain batteries star shell sped into the air, and burst, and in the sudden brilliant light the extent of the attack was seen clearly. The whole camp was alive with tribesmen out of the hills, and with bodies and much blood. A tight formation was moving towards the tent where the High Commissioner had held court; the *maliks* were bunched together, jabbering in terror, while their own guards attempted to fight back but were clearly about to be overwhelmed by sheer numbers. Dornoch shouted into Black's ear above the noise. 'Pass the word to all company commanders, Andrew: the battalion to fall back on the southern perimeter and then form into line. They're to move through the camp with bayonets fixed, and clear the ground as they go. No quarter, Andrew. Send a runner to Brigade to inform the Brigadier-General.'

Black doubled away, sending out blasts from the whistle on the lanyard round his neck. As the fighting continued in the centre where the Gurkhas and the men of the Punjab Frontier Force were still under heavy attack that amounted to bloody slaughter, the Scots companies began to withdraw to the ditch. They were joined by the Borderers led by their Colonel, who had assessed Dornoch's intentions and had reacted swiftly.

When both battalions had formed line with their backs to the defences, Lord Dornoch gave the word, blood pouring down from his shoulder. On a grim, long front the Scots and Borderers advanced at the double behind the shining steel of their bayonets, sweeping the camp from side to side, ready to return slaughter for slaughter. As the tribesmen continued their hacking at the helpless, canvas-bound Gurkhas, the bayonets took them from the rear, slicing savagely into writhing bodies, to be twisted cruelly and withdrawn and sent plunging into the next man.

All through the history of the Raj the Pathan had been a brave fighter against the guns and the rifles, but always the naked steel of the bayonet had been a different story and one that struck dreadful fear into the native mind, and as close upon twelve hundred bayonets came down upon them, they broke. Pursued by a savage vengeance, they ran screaming for the far side of the camp, falling along the way in scores as they were overtaken. Behind the advancing line of Scots and Borderers the *sepoys* of the Indian Army re-formed and were ordered by Brigade to outflank the centre fighting and mass along the tribesmen's escape route. As the attackers flung themselves across the ditch and up the rampart, rifle and Maxim fire stuttered out, tearing into the mass of bodies and sending them in heaps into the ditch as they fell in mid air or slid dying down the slope of the rampart. The rout was total. The last remnants fled before the gunfire, and then there came a curious silence; almost one of thanksgiving for deliverance. This silence was broken by an outburst of cheering, and in the middle of it the Brigadier-General was seen riding towards the Scots line. Dornoch, his face white and pinched in the light of the guard lanterns, saluted.

'Well done, Dornoch.' Norris was himself wounded, a wide patch of blood showing through his tunic. 'Your order was the right one, and I'm to blame for not having given it sooner. Had I done so ... there might have been less slaughter.'

'I doubt it, sir.' Dornoch swayed, feeling faintness overcome him. A corporal took him and supported him, and the Brigadier-General himself passed the order for the medical orderlies and a *doolie*.

As Lord Brora came up still brandishing his highland broadsword dangerously close, Norris addressed him. 'Major, you must take over as battalion commander for the time being. Your Colonel's to be placed on the sick list.'

'Very good, sir.' Brora smiled, and in the lanterns' light the smile was somehow devilish. He flourished his sword. 'Your further orders, if you please?'

'First of all, kindly control your broad-sword, Major. It's an instrument out of hell—'

'One that has proved effective, sir.'

'I dare say! But I am not the enemy. All battalions to muster their men and report casualties as soon as possible, and then remain standing-to until further orders.'

'Standing-to, sir? May I ask why?'

'You may, Major. The attack was not in fact unsuccessful. The prisoners we took during the attack in the pass have been released, and more importantly all the *maliks* have been cut out from under our noses. For a British force to fail to provide protection for the headmen will not be popular with their tribes, and I expect a reaction. That's all, gentlemen.' The Brigadier-General turned his horse, then paused and spoke over his shoulder. 'One thing more: the tribesmen, the dead and wounded. They are to be sorted out and the survivors are to be questioned. I wish to know by whom the attack was mounted and what is intended for the *maliks*, and I also wish as much information as possible as to the hostages, of whom we have so far heard nothing. Lord Brora?'

'Sir?'

'I am not disposed to be squeamish. Are you?'

'I am not, sir.'

The Brigadier-General, his face grim,

nodded. 'Then I shall leave the details to you, Major.'

He rode away to Brigade, leaving a somewhat tense silence behind him.

Razjah Shah had started down the hillside earlier, in dead silence, in the lead of his well-armed tribesmen, at about the same time as Dostman Khan's hordes had started their creep along the concealing *nullah*. As he reached the snow-covered plateau he heard the sounds of fighting from the direction of the British camp, and soon after this he saw the bursting shells and their brilliant stars falling over the embattled Dostman Khan. He smiled, and led his men on for the sleeping city, putting distance between himself and Dostman Khan, putting his deviousness into effect. Into the city like ghosts rode his bandits, the horses' hooves muffled by deep snow. They were not to be anonymous for long, as Razjah Shah had known and had indeed bargained for. The noise of the fighting was loud, the star shell was bright, the night had come alive. Men emerged from doorways to crowd the streets of Mana, and to wonder – and to fear. Razjah Shah, moving among them, fed their fear with clever and appropriately chosen words, words that inflamed and fanned. As the *fakir* Zulifiqar had said already, the hostages of Murrum Khan were likely to

219

bring much trouble to Mana. If the hostages were found by the British, as of a certainty they would be, Mana would suffer cruelly, for it would be held to have tolerated Murrum Khan and even to have offered support and succour to him in his wickedness. Already the sounds of war held overtones of great foreboding. The British were under attack; when the attack was over and the British were victorious, they would seek revenge – and Mana was handily placed for the wreaking of revenge. Much blood would flow from the British bayonets, for when roused they were far from being merciful fighters, and the men in skirts and with the music of the unhappy pig were always without exception wild. All this Razjah Shah's audience, a growing one, could comprehend well: *badal* was a wholly natural thing, a very proper thing, and was always exacted...

'I, Razjah Shah, shall save you all in the name of Allah.'

Murmurs rose round the tribal leader and his followers. 'How can this be – you, one man with a few other men?'

'I shall take away the hostages held by Murrum Khan.'

'And you? What will then become of you, Razjah Shah?'

Razjah Shah laughed. 'I shall be helped by Allah, who is great and powerful and wise, also good, and I shall take the hostages far from Mana, and thus draw the British fire. It shall be easily done. The attention of Murrum Khan and his guards will be upon the plateau and the fighting, and a mob can help much if it be determined to work the will of Allah. What say you, my friends?'

The murmurs grew louder, and swelled mightily, and fists were shaken, and the mob grew as the sounds spread.

Inside the palace the fighting had indeed been heard; Murrum Khan had climbed to his battlements to look out upon the plateau as the star shell burst. He didn't linger; he was deep in thought as he descended, and called down curses upon the head of whoever had attacked the British camp. He had received word that Dostman Khan had rallied forces in the vicinity, and ten thousand goats upon it that this was Dostman Khan attacking now! His ruminations ran closely along the lines of Razjah Shah's words to the mob in the streets: the British would seek vengeance and would mount a punitive expedition that would almost certainly attack Mana along with the isolated mountain settlements in the area. Panic, however, was not to be indulged in; the British would have suffered casualties, and they might well decide to send riders for reinforcements before moving further towards war. That, perhaps, was something that could be taken care of, and Murrum Khan gave his orders accordingly: risking the depletion of his palace guard, he sent a strong force riding fast for the hills, to outflank the British camp and come down to ambush the passes farther along and to cut any field telegraph wires that they might find, although the probability was that any such wires would have been cut long since, for few of the Waziri tribesmen could resist the cutting of British telegraph lines.

Thirty minutes after Murrum Khan's descent from his battlements, Ogilvie's trap-door was opened and once again the dim flaring light showed the rope's-end coming down. Ogilvie grasped it and climbed; he found it an effort, for he was weak now from lack of food. This, however, was to be remedied: at the top a meal of a sort awaited him – rice and mashed corn, some goat's milk, and some unidentifiable fruit preserved in sugar. He ate under the watchful eyes and the rifles of two Afridis, and he ate in silence, his questions remaining unanswered. When he had finished he was taken again to the great chamber with the pool of water. Angela was there still; not in the water, but standing with a rough garment thrown round her shoulders, under guard beside the pool. The crocodile was sluggishly inactive behind its mesh barrier, visible just below the surface with its humped nostrils awash and its eyes like lamps, waiting for human movement.

On the dais at the end Murrum Khan stood, a hand on the haft of a jewelled dagger thrust into a crimson sash.

'Ogilvie sahib, the time approaches and I am ready.'

'Ready for what, Murrum Khan?'

'I have told you. Now I tell you more: outside the city to the north is a British force. A brigade, I believe it to be. And there is fighting in their camp.'

Ogilvie's heart beat faster: the brigade, then, had arrived ... the regiment was not far away, and that was truly wonderful news that brought a sudden surge of hope; though Murrum Khan would scarcely have told him, of course, if the hope had been a high one. He asked, 'Fighting? Your men have engaged?'

Murrum Khan shook his head. 'Not my men. There has been an attack, and I believe it comes from Dostman Khan. I believe also that the British may come here. If they do, they shall find neither me nor you, but we shall not move too soon – not until I have word that the British are on their way. Nevertheless, I must be ready from this moment so that when the word comes, if come it does, you and I can be away on the route for Afghanistan.' He paused. 'That leaves the mem'sahib, whose fate also you know.'

Ogilvie looked at Angela. She was deathly white and shaking all over, and still her eyes were dull and without register; she seemed almost to have stopped caring, as though already she had gone past the coming agony and had stepped behind the veil ... Ogilvie said in a strained voice, 'You'll be hunted down, Murrum Khan, never doubt that. You'll hang in the civil jail as a common murderer.'

There was a sneer in Murrum Khan's voice. 'The British cannot find me when I go, Ogilvie sahib! I have known the hills and the passes all my life, as my father and my grandfather knew them before me. I know ways that the British would never find in a thousand years. I have no fear of being taken in the open by the Raj, Ogilvie sahib.'

'I would not be so confident if I were you, Murrum Khan.' Ogilvie licked at dry lips. 'Why cast away a hostage who could yet be useful to you?'

'You I shall have yet. You refer to the mem'sahib, but she will not be cast away before her time – you shall see. For now, you wait, and so does the mem'sahib.' Murrum Khan turned away and stalked through a door behind the dais, which was closed behind him with a thud, a sound of foreboding and doom. From the other door, the one through which Ogilvie had been brought, more men filed in – bandits carrying modern British Army rifles and many knives, and with bandoliers of cartridges across their chests. Ogilvie was made to sit on a bench at one side of the pool, and Angela at the other, each of them well guarded, and the wait began, a wait in enforced silence. Ogilvie tried to assess what might be in the air at Brigade, what the Brigadier-General might decide to do. A march into Mana was a possibility, if not to attack then at least to mount a show of strength, to show that the Raj was not going to have a snook cocked at it again. On the other hand the British presence was for talk and negotiation, not war. Norris might decide one way, he might decide the other, and a good deal would depend on the advice he was given by his colonels, Lord Dornoch in particular since he had many years of Frontier experience. And the High Commissioner would have his viewpoint: this was fairly certainly to be for the other cheek to be turned. One way and another it looked like being a long wait, and if the brigade made no move within, say, the next twenty-four hours, then Murrum Khan might put haste into reverse and maintain his low profile inside the security of his palace to await, as he had at first intended, some response to his message to Fettleworth in Nowshera.

Meanwhile Ogilvie, wishing desperately that he could talk to Angela and try to bring her hope, had to be content to believe that his physical presence might of itself be some comfort.

He had fallen into a kind of reverie from sheer weariness when he heard the rifle-fire, and he came to in an instant to sit up fully awake. The guards looked at each other in alarm, while keeping their weapons closely upon the two prisoners. The firing seemed close; within minutes Murrum Khan came back into the chamber, his face furious.

'The brigade?' Ogilvie asked.

'No. A mob! There has been treachery.' Murrum Khan shouted at his bandits in Pushtu and they ran from the room, hastening to their stations to repel the intruders, leaving two men each to guard Ogilvie and Angela. On the heels of his Pathans Murrum Khan departed again. Now there was considerable change in the air; much shooting came from outside, and there was the stutter of what sounded to Ogilvie like a Maxim, probably captured from the Raj on some raiding expedition for arms, or taken in the field. Which side was using it, he couldn't tell; but soon the sounds came closer and the fighting seemed to be taking place in the corridor outside. The guards were growing restive, anxious, beginning to show fear.

Ogilvie felt excitement rise in him. He was fairly sure now that the intruder was Razjah Shah, honouring his word that he would come to his assistance. Now, then, was the time ... once Razjah Shah's men were crowding the doorway, maybe sooner, the guards might shoot the hostages, for Murrum Khan would never allow them to fall to Razjah Shah, that was certain. Ogilvie took a deep breath and chose his moment when one of his guards had moved, rifle pointed, for the door. Lunging sideways, he took the other man with a heavy blow straight into the gut. There was a shout of pain and as the man doubled up Ogilvie wrenched away his rifle, took cover on the ground behind the benches and aimed at the man who had turned to run back from the door. He fired. The native fell with the top of his head blown off, and from his cover Ogilvie swung the rifle on the two natives guarding Angela.

He spoke in Pushtu. 'Move away from the mem'sahib. Then the rifles into the water or you die. I shall give you a count of five.'

Staring back at him, the men moved aside and Ogilvie scrambled to his feet. The rifles were thrown into the pool. Ogilvie, catching a flicker in the eye of one of the men, looked round just in time. The man who had taken the fist in his stomach was back on his feet and moving for him. Ogilvie, with no time to take aim, swung the rifle viciously and its heavy steel muzzle caught the man in the mouth, tearing the lower lip from his face and smashing blackened teeth. The man yelped and staggered sideways with both hands to his mouth, then fell, slipping on the greasy edge of the pool, unable to stop himself before his legs went in beyond the mesh barrier. Screaming, he tried to drag himself clear but he had no hope. There was a flurry in the water, a sudden dash at immense speed, and the great jaws snapped. There came a crunching sound and the screaming grew more dreadful and the body slid further in. As Angela stared with every drop of blood drained from her face, Ogilvie brought up the rifle and put the man out of his agony. Blood coloured the water, drifting down in long streaks past the barrier. The great tail thrashed, sending up a red spray. Ogilvie instinctively emptied the magazine on to the armoured back with no effect at all: the bullets richocheted harmlessly away. Meanwhile the two remaining guards were running around the pool towards him, knives ready. As Ogilvie stood four-square with the rifle clubbed, the door at the end went back on its hinges and men crowded through, bringing with them the smell of smoke. One was Murrum Khan, carrying something in his hands, something that he threw towards Ogilvie as the two guards stood back. Along the floor of the chamber rolled the bloody, severed head of Razjah Shah until its own matted black hair halted its progress and it stopped with the sightless eyes seeming fixed upon Ogilvie's face. Murrum Khan gave a sign with his hand, the rifle was wrested from Ogilvie, and its butt was brought down in a wicked blow on his head. As he fell there was another commotion from outside, shouts and cries and gunfire, and Murrum Khan, showing incredulous fury, shouted an order for the woman to be removed under guard, then turned away himself and ran from the chamber. The shouts and gunfire continued in the courtyard. Ogilvie was still unconscious under two Afridi rifles and was about to be removed when, ahead of thickly billowing smoke, the mob poured in tumultuous and victorious noise into the room.

Fourteen

A dozen mahsud riders sped swiftly out of Mana, heading back into the hills whence they had come. Across the saddle of one of them lay James Ogilvie, still unconscious and with a large lump on his skull. During the ride no one spoke; it was a grim and sorry ride without their leader, who would of a certainty be revenged another day. Murrum Khan's partial victory would not last for many more suns to rise on the Waziri hills. Below those hills now, part of his palace smoked still, though the flames had subsided. The fire had not been a big one, though its spread had served to allow the cutting-out of Ogilvie sahib and the escape of the survivors of the raid. It was to be hoped that the Prophet would now intercede to protect the wretched townspeople of Mana, and the *fakir* Zulifiqar ... Murrum Khan's raging fury would be terrible to behold!

In the comparative safety of the hills the riders halted and Ogilvie at last came round to a sick and dizzy headache. It was some while before he could understand his situation, and the tribesmen waited in patience until his head cleared enough for him to be told. He recognised the speaker as Razjah Shah's chief lieutenant, a Mahsud named Mohammad Yusuf.

'When Razjah Shah was killed, we grew more angry, Ogilvie sahib. Fire was set to the palace, and in the confusion many men fought their way into the room with the great bath, where you lay as if dead. You were lifted and taken from the palace. Not easily ... many men died, but those of us who are here brought you safely into the alleys and then here into the hills where Razjah Shah had ridden with you from Takki, from the fort—'

'The mem'sahib? You have her too?' Ogilvie tried to sit up.

The answer was grave. 'There was no sign of the mem'sahib, only of you.'

'But she was there with me!'

Heads were shaken. 'Not so. Not upon our arrival in the great room. We found the head of our leader Razjah Shah, and we found you, Ogilvie sahib, with guards whom we killed. But not the mem'sahib.'

Fear expanded, exploded in Ogilvie's head: could Angela have gone into the pool? This was doubtful, however; in the adverse circumstances of the sack of his palace, Murrum Khan would surely have felt it prudent to keep her alive for future use. He asked, 'And Murrum Khan himself?'

'Sahib, we did not linger to find out. He was not then in the room of the bath. Razjah Shah had ordered that we take you from Murrum Khan, and this we did—'

'He also ordered you to take the mem'-sahib, Mohammad Yusuf?'

'Undoubtedly, but I have said ... although we searched as best we could, the mem'sahib we failed to find.'

Ogilvie nodded dully; his head swam, he felt sick and parched. He asked for water, and it improved matters a little. 'And the

British?' he asked. 'What are they doing now?'

'They are still in their camp, Ogilvie sahib. They have sent out patrols, no doubt to locate those who attacked them earlier, and that is all.'

'You can see the camp from here?' The sun was well up now, and the sky was clear of snow.

'Yes, we see them well.'

Ogilvie raised himself on one elbow, but the effort worsened his head and he fell limply back to the ground. 'I must rejoin them. I must find the mem'sahib—'

'Sahib, with us you will be better able to search the city for her. The people of Mana may have heard whispers from the palace—'

'No! Murrum Khan spoke to me ... he will have gone from Mana into the hills, towards Afghanistan, for now most assuredly the brigade in which I serve will move in. An attack on the camp, then a fire and fighting in Murrum Khan's palace ... they must march, and Murrum Khan will know this.' Ogilvie pressed a hand to his aching head. 'If she's alive, the mem'sahib will not have been left behind now Murrum Khan has lost his other hostage.'

'Then we are still the better guide, Ogilvie sahib. We know the hills better than the British soldiers.'

'There is much truth in that, but it is my

duty to rejoin and give the Brigadier-General sahib full information. Of this there is no doubt. Besides, you will want your revenge on Murrum Khan for the killing of your leader—'

'*Badal* is much on all our minds, this is true.'

'And I understand it. The brigade is strong, and also wants Murrum Khan – for murder now. We shall assist *badal*, and we shall succeed quickly where you might take many years. You must let me rejoin my regiment, and I give you my word that I shall not act against you.'

There was a pause, then, with some reluctance, the new leader said, 'We trust your word, Ogilvie sahib.'

'There's yet a better way.' Ogilvie looked up solemnly at the assembled, haggard faces. 'If you throw in your lot with us, with the British brigade ... if you also join, and act as guides ... then Murrum Khan may be found the quicker. Is this not so?'

Below on the plateau, the bugles sounded to fall in the brigade by regiments. After due consultation with his colonels and his Chief of Staff, and with the High Commissioner, Norris had made his decision. With the heavy and callous hand of Major Lord Brora in the background, the prisoners taken had talked: although they knew nothing of

Ogilvie, they revealed that Murrum Khan was present in Mana. That was good enough in all the circumstances; the brigade would march but would not strike camp. With the possible reprisals in mind from the villagers of the captured *maliks*, the Brigadier-General ordered that the Punjab Frontier Force together with the remnant of the Gurkhas should remain behind as camp guard while he took the Royal Strathspey and the Border Regiment into Mana. Thus the battalions of the British Army formed column of route behind the Staff and marched away through the lying snow, with sloped rifles and fixed bayonets and the pipes and drums sounding loud and clear in the still air, marched to possible action and a warlike, rather than a peaceful, solution to the boundary problem. Only the High Commissioner had objected, and had been overruled on the grounds of present military necessity. As the pipes and drums at the head of the column came within the shadow of the city, the officer of the advanced guard came riding back to Brigade with something in his hand.

He saluted the Brigadier-General. 'A body on the track, sir – an Afridi, dead but recently I believe. This was skewered to the body with a knife.'

He handed up a large piece of skin, a square into which words had been crudely burned with an iron. The reading took some

minutes and when he had read the Brigadier-General's face was hard. He folded the
message, and beckoned to his ADC. 'The
commanding officers to Brigade at once.
The column will halt.' The ADC saluted and
rode away and the bugle sounded. Wondering what was in the air now, the column
halted and the men were stood at ease. From
the Borderers Colonel Hinde rode towards
Brigade, with Lord Brora from the Scots.
The Brigadier-General lost no time. 'A
message from Murrum Khan, gentlemen.
Mrs Ogilvie will be killed if we advance upon
the city.'

'So she's positively there!' Brora stood in
his stirrups, a scowl on his face. 'We must
make all speed to her rescue, sir!'

'I don't think you took in the purport,
Major—'

'Oh, yes, I did! Are we to be made lily-
livered by a damn native's threats?'

Norris reddened. 'It's scarcely a case of
that. I have Mrs Ogilvie's safety to consider.
I wish no bulls at gates, Lord Brora.'

'What, then, do you propose to do, sir?'

Norris said, 'The regiments will stand-
to but will not march. I shall ride ahead with
an escort and with my staff, and seek a
parley—'

'And bargain with a woman's life?'

'It's what we've been doing all along, in
essence. Melodrama won't help us, Major.

We must face the situation as it is, and the situation happens to be that currently Murrum Khan has the whip hand.' The Brigadier-General turned to the flank and was about to pass orders for an escort when his attention was caught by some movement below the hills to the south-east. Frowning, he pulled his field glasses from their case around his neck. Brora followed suit, and it was Brora who spoke first.

'A flag of truce ... a bunch of damn tribesmen ... and by God it's young Ogilvie with the buggers!'

There had been much explaining to do; Ogilvie felt that it was fortunate that the Brigadier-General was present in person when he rejoined. Norris, if with some difficulty, had a restraining effect upon Lord Brora, and Ogilvie was given a peaceful hearing as briefly he outlined the whole sequence of events since he had ridden back from Fort Jamrud in the Khyber many days earlier. He brought Razjah Shah's bandits before the Brigadier-General, saying that they had been of much service to the Raj and that he had given them his word that the Raj would not now lift arms against them.

'A somewhat large pre-emption of authority, Captain Ogilvie?'

'Yes, sir.'

'And the immediate future?'

'They'll assist further, sir. They know the hills, and the routes into Afghanistan, where we believe Murrum Khan to have gone.'

The Brigadier-General raised his eyebrows. 'I think you're wrong, Captain Ogilvie.' He quoted the recent message. 'The man's still in Mana, evidently.'

'With respect, sir, I doubt it. The message could be a ruse, a delaying tactic. Murrum Khan told me himself, when he had me prisoner and thought he could talk safely – he told me he intended going into Afghanistan to raise an army against the Raj. He intended taking a hostage with him.'

'Mrs Ogilvie?'

'Me, sir. My cousin's wife was to die at once if the British came.'

'As the message says.'

'Yes, sir. But I still don't give the message much credit. I believe that in the changed circumstances Murrum Khan will have taken her on into Afghanistan in my place, as a continuing hostage ... a continuing inhibition against our movement.'

'Yes, I see.' The Brigadier-General blew out his moustache, looking baffled. 'You appear to have been at the seat of affairs, Captain Ogilvie, at the nub. What would you do now if you were in my shoes?'

Ogilvie said, 'I'd first check the palace, sir, entering Mana in strength to make quite sure there were no prisoners—'

'And Mrs Ogilvie? If she *is* there as the message suggests, what happens to her then?'

Ogilvie bit his lip and felt the blood drain from his face: what would happen was clear enough and the mere thought was like a knife in his guts. But he said steadily, 'I'd bank on it she's not there, sir. In any case...' He didn't finish: he had meant to say that in any case a British force could not be held indefinitely from its duty, but the words would have seemed like a betrayal. The Brigadier-General seemed to understand, however; he said, 'Very well, what would you do after that, assuming nothing was found?'

'I would hold the brigade in camp, sir, and despatch someone who knew the hills, with a small and fast escort, to find Murrum Khan, and bring him back before he could muster support.'

Norris smiled. 'I think I know who you'd send!'

'Yes, sir. With Razjah Shah's men, I'd have a fighting chance. I could get through much faster than the brigade.'

Norris glanced at Lord Brora. 'Major?'

'A fool's errand, sir.' Brora seemed nettled that a junior officer should be consulted at all. 'We should not forget the attack upon us last night. You made the point yourself, that the villages would be up in arms about the loss of their *maliks*. The whole of the damn hills will be alive with men looking for vengeance.'

The Brigadier-General nodded. 'A point indeed. Well, Captain Ogilvie? What d'you think?'

'I take the point, sir, but the attack came from Dostman Khan – Murrum Khan's enemy. There will be divisions of feeling, since some of the *maliks* will have been for Dostman Khan and some for Murrum Khan, and others for their own communities alone.'

'Well?'

Ogilvie smiled. 'Razjah Shah's men, as I said, know the hills and the hillmen. We may be able to take advantage of the rivalries—'

'Find help to put you on Murrum Khan's track, d'you mean?'

'Yes, sir.'

'You may be right,' Norris said. He rode his horse a little way from the group of officers, looking thoughtfully towards the city, and at the bleak surround of hills beneath the snow, and back along the halted column with its greatcoated men and its mountain guns; back towards the camp with its transport animals and followers. To send a small party of men to penetrate the hills and passes in the snow, to offer themselves as targets for the sniper's bullet ... it was to send them to likely death. On the other hand, every patrol that had ever been sent out from Peshawar or Kohat, Bannu or Mardan had faced a similar situation; and a brigade with all its impedimenta was certainly slow on the move by comparison...

Norris rode back. 'Very well, Captain Ogilvie. Your suggestion's a good one. Lord Brora, if you please, make the arrangements within your battalion ... Captain Ogilvie should be given the choice of men.'

'As you say, sir.' Brora stared at Ogilvie. 'Well, what's your wish, Captain Ogilvie?'

'Half my own company, Major, volunteers, with Colour-Sar'nt MacTrease as second-in-command.'

'Subalterns are available,' Brora snapped.

'Yes, Major. But MacTrease is better acquainted with the Frontier. He's been out here as long as I have, ever since the regiment arrived.'

Norris interrupted as Brora's mouth opened again. 'Give him what he asks for, Major. Time's short. Captain Ogilvie, take your volunteer detachment back to camp and see it fully provisioned and mounted. You'll ride out the moment you're ready. Brigade Major?'

'Sir?'

'The column is to move on as soon as Captain Ogilvie has detached his men, with the guns brought forward to the van.'

Ogilvie's whole company had volunteered

and selection was difficult. On arrival in the camp, Ogilvie went at once to the Colonel's tent to report to Lord Dornoch. He found him pale and weak but in fair spirits though full of frustration at being out of action on the Brigadier-General's order. However, he had no intention of remaining long on the Sick List, much to Ogilvie's relief: one spell of Brora as acting commanding officer had been more than enough. Dornoch wished Ogilvie well. 'You'll be out of communication, James,' he said, 'but every man's thoughts will be with you and your half company.'

'Thank you, Colonel.' Saluting smartly, Ogilvie left the tent and crunched through the snow towards his company's lines where the men were making ready under Mac-Trease's orders and with the assistance of the RQMS and his staff. Enough dry provisions and water were being taken for fourteen days and the half company, formed into Mounted Infantry, would take transport mules to carry the stores and the ammunition for the rifles and a stripped-down Maxim gun. Mr Cunningham, who had been retained in camp as senior warrant officer of the brigade to stiffen defence, marched up as the small force made ready. He was delighted to see Ogilvie back. His eagle eye scanned equipment and weapons without seeming to undermine Colour-

Sergeant MacTrease's authority.

'A hard task faces you, Captain Ogilvie, sir.'

'Yes. But we'll survive!'

Cunningham smiled. 'I know you will, sir. And I'll be praying you find the lady – and you'll do that too, with God's help.'

Ogilvie nodded; he was not too sanguine about his chances, though he believed, as he had told the Brigadier-General, that he would have the best hope possible. The Frontier was vast and wild and full of hiding places; but men and animals left spoor that could be read by the experienced. In a little more than an hour after reaching the camp, Ogilvie was ready to ride out. With Mac-Trease on one side of him and Razjah Shah's successor Mohammad Yusuf on the other, he led his troop across the ditch and the rampart and headed on the bandit's advice towards the north-western edge of the plateau. Here the party was unavoidably obvious to any watchers and the word of their coming would be sent ahead; but Murrum Khan would be expecting some sort of pursuit notwithstanding his message, and it could be presumed that little would be lost. Before they reached the shelter of the mountains a horseman was seen behind, riding hell-for-leather from the direction of Mana: Ogilvie's field glasses identified him as the Brigadier-General's orderly officer and he halted his troop for the rider to reach them. The orderly officer reported a peaceful entry into Mana and the palace; the latter, void of any of Murrum Khan's followers, and of Murrum Khan himself, had been found sacked by the mob on the instigation of a one-armed *fakir*. There had been no trace of Angela Ogilvie.

'The pool?'

'No one there. There was blood in the water, and the upper half of a man's body, a native, beside the pool. That's all.'

Ogilvie watched the orderly officer ride back at the gallop. Later when he began the climb into the hills, he heard from far behind the skirl of the pipes and the beat of the drummers sounding clear across the plain as the brigade marched out again from Mana. Then the snow began falling once more and the sounds were muffled behind a screen of white that blotted out sight as well.

In Nowshera, as the days dragged past without news from the south, faces had grown longer. Fettleworth's Divisional Headquarters were like a mortuary, albeit a gilded and busy one. No one liked to think of a woman helpless in the hands of bandits, and there were other considerations too that weighed like lead upon highly-placed military minds: the Civilians were always a damned nuisance but when the military failed to come up to

243

expectations they became incomparably worse and their memoranda, issuing in streams from Calcutta, developed a cutting edge that infuriated Bloody Francis and Sir Iain Ogilvie alike. Fettleworth knew that only the latter's presence in Nowshera kept from his own head the strictures of clerkly pimps in Calcutta and Whitehall who, having never in their miserable lives wielded anything more lethal than a pen-nib, which in all conscience could be lethal enough when dipped in poison, attacked with file and paper-clip any general whom fate had unkindly delivered into their hands. Fettleworth writhed beneath it all: the telegraph lines across the ocean from Whitehall had borne his discomfiture and the next mail from home would bring copies of *The Times* and *The Morning Post* to make him writhe more. The Prime Minister was deeply concerned, so was Her Majesty, and the latter had prodded her Viceroy with a personal cable, clearly against Lord Salisbury's advice, stating baldly that she was shocked and dismayed and expected much better news before Christmas.

'Christmas my backside,' Sir Iain said when word of the Queen's expectations reached him in Fettleworth's headquarters. 'She ought to try the passes herself, with a full pack and rifle!'

Fettleworth was shocked at such a thought.

He coughed and said sharply, 'My dear Ogilvie, Her Majesty—'

'I wish she'd damn well keep her mouth shut. She often does more harm than good. Can't you see the damn newspapers, Fettleworth? The Queen's Christmas spoiled by lack of news from India. Why bring Christmas into it? You know how damn sentimental the public are! Why focus attention on *Christmas*, for God's sake? Don't you see what I mean?'

Fettleworth nodded reluctantly. 'Yes. But we shouldn't make too much of that. Her Majesty has the very best of intentions, she always has.'

'Which doesn't help my son and my niece.'

'Er – no. No, of course not.' Fettleworth hesitated, cleared his throat, coughed; he was debating within himself whether or not to offer his panacea, the one thing that in his view solved everything along the North-West Frontier: a massive show of strength, a review by the General Officer Commanding of the power and might of the Raj, a great assembly of infantry and cavalry and field guns, the combined divisions of the British and Indian Armies of the North marching past the dais behind the pomp of the brass bands and the rolling thunder of the drums. The natives had to be shown the tremendous power of the Raj and of Her Majesty, and then, by Gad, they became willing to talk turkey! Fettleworth's chest swelled behind the scarlet tunic of the General Staff, and, almost without volition, he said, 'Ogilvie, why not put on a show to impress the natives, let 'em see what's what – hey?'

'One of your parades, Fettleworth?'

'Yes! Since you're here, you're available to—'

'You're as bad as the Queen.' Sir Iain turned away angrily and stalked from the room, leaving Fettleworth to simmer and wonder if personal anxieties could have unhinged the GOC's mind. To talk like that ... and everyone knew the efficacy of parades! Apart from anything else, they put heart into the garrison. The men loved the splendour and the smartness and the music of the regimental fifes and drums – loved it! Fettleworth banged at a bell on his desk; a native entered, salaaming.

'*Chota peg.*'

'Yes, sahib.'

'Quickly.'

'Yes, sahib.' The bearer backed away from the Divisional Commander's august presence. When the next person entered, it was not the bearer with his silver salver and the whisky, but Fettleworth's Chief of Staff.

'What is it, Lakenham?'

'Bad news, sir.'

Fettleworth looked bleak. 'Well, out with

it, then.'

'The husband – Hector Ogilvie. He's disappeared. We must inform Sir Iain.' As Fettleworth sat with a sagging jaw, wondering what the Civilians would say now, Lakenham put the facts before him concisely: there had apparently been no disturbance of Hector Ogilvie's quarters and no evidence at all of any penetration by natives. Hector's horse had also been found missing from its stable and his *khansamma* had reported a quantity of basic foodstuffs missing from the kitchen. 'I don't know what all that suggests to you, sir,' Lakenham finished, 'but I know what it suggests to me.'

'Gone looking for his wife?'

'Yes.'

'Poor fellow – poor fellow! He'll not stand a chance – a very foolish thing to do, if natural. And I wish he hadn't done it.' Fettleworth put his head in his hands for a moment and when he looked up his face was haggard. 'Take word to Sir Iain, Lakenham, and then come back here.'

'I'd never have thought it of him,' Sir Iain said. 'My own flesh and blood, I know – but his own father would say the same. Dreadful as a boy – one graze on a knee and he'd run indoors blubbing! Must be some guts somewhere, give him his due, but it's a confounded bloody nuisance. What are you going to do about it, Fettleworth?'

'I'm waiting for your orders, Ogilvie.'

'Are you?' Sir Iain stared. 'Then here they are: have him found, bring him back, tell him to report to me! I'll handle it from there. See to that at once.'

Fettleworth went speedily into action, ordering mounted patrols to scour the open country around Nowshera, and alerting the provost corps to go through the town with a fine-toothed comb. Lakenham saw personally to the close questioning of Hector's domestic staff and of all other persons who might have had some knowledge of the missing man's movements. Fettleworth waited in severe agitation for the reports to come in; by the end of the day it was clear that Hector Ogilvie had vanished somewhere in the snow that lay around Nowshera and Peshawar and had left no traces as the flakes continued to fall and the bitter wind blew out of the north.

Fifteen

For Ogilvie's half company, it became a desperate business as, slowly, they penetrated the little-known passes of the northward-leading Waziri hills. The snow came intermittently ahead of blizzard force winds that drove the bitter flakes into men's eyes and made it painful to face their front as lips and cheeks froze blue. Ever present was the nightmare thought of frostbite. Only Mohammad Yusuf and his tribesmen were able to face the terrible ride philosophically; and in so doing proved an encouraging example to the soldiers. If they could survive, then so could Scots.

Now and again when the snowfall eased and the skies cleared to reveal the sun, wild men were glimpsed along the crests that ran across the border into Afghanistan, figures that quickly vanished, though occasionally there was some exchange of fire. They were close now to Afghanistan and Ogilvie's hopes had begun to fade.

'It's no use, Colour,' he said to MacTrease.

249

'He'll have crossed the Frontier by this time.'

'He had little start on us, sir.'

'Enough, probably!'

'Never say die, sir.' MacTrease hesitated. 'You'll follow into Afghanistan, sir?'

'Follow what?' Ogilvie responded with bitterness. 'What *are* we following, when all's said and done – other than Mohammad Yusuf's nose?' He waved a hand around. 'The snow's blotted out all tracks even if they existed in the first place!'

'Aye, sir,' MacTrease said quietly, 'but yon's nose is a good one. There's a purpose about the man, sir. He's not riding blind.'

Ogilvie nodded: that was true. Razjah Shah's successor was a man of few words but firm action; all along his guidance had been positive and he seemed to know well what he was doing. There was no hesitation; it was as though he had an inbuilt compass the needle of which indicated not north necessarily but the lodestone of Murrum Khan, the killer of a revered leader. As to a penetration of Afghanistan, this was something Ogilvie had pondered much, knowing that it would be on the cards. Once into Afghanistan they would find few friends: they would come firmly into the territory of the wild men whose whole way of life was the antithesis of the Raj, the territory of the border raider and the thief in a much more positive sense than was Waziristan. Murrum Khan would be the one who was at home. There was another consideration as well, an important one: Calcutta might have reservations about the crossing of the North-West Frontier in depth. It was not normally up to an officer of captain's rank to take it upon himself to pre-empt government decisions and the repercussions of action inside Afghanistan could be serious. Nevertheless, Ogilvie's decision had been made already: he would follow Angela to the death.

Many miles to the north and east of Ogilvie's blind advance into the snows, Hector Ogilvie, now riding south by way of a pass leading from the Peshawar-Fort Jamrud track, was facing similar conditions and facing them alone. His equipment for his self-imposed task was entirely inadequate. He had coffee but no means of heating the water for it; he had food but no means of cooking, and the food he had brought in his panic haste was not of a sort that lent itself to eating raw: packets of porridge, of flour ... even a jar of marmalade had found their way into his haversack and saddle-bags. Such might provide some energy but would scarcely prove sustaining. Something else was providing Hector Ogilvie with courage and a crazy determination: a flask of whisky that could be refilled from half-a-dozen bottles of

251

Dewar's that he had found in his allotted quarter, which was normally inhabited by a major of Probyn's Horse temporarily absent on detachment to Quetta. In his anxieties for his wife, Hector had discovered belatedly the anaesthesia to be found in a bottle of spirits...

Desperation had been his driver, whisky had been his final impeller along a chaotic course. He had no plan in mind other than to find Angela – simply that. In a confused way he had thought that he might fall in with natives who could be bribed into his service, men who might form a force to attack Murrum Khan and release Angela. He was not unimportant in the governance of the Raj and his promises would carry weight. He rode on into the whitened hills and behind him the snow covered his horse's tracks. The cold was intense and terrible but was held at bay by Dewar's whisky, and over the horizon was a vision of Angela ... tears flowed down Hector's face until they froze and formed icicles that cracked away as he drank from the flask and filled out his cheeks. He knew a moment of terror as a bank of snow crashed down the hillside and almost submerged him. It worked down his neck in freezing rivers and he cried out aloud to the unfriendly, uncaring immensities of distance.

In camp outside Mana, Brigadier-General

252

Norris, after long and earnest consultation with his Brigade Major and Sir Lawrence Bindle, had reached a decision. The High Commissioner had admitted that he saw little point in remaining immobile in the hopes of being able to convene another *jirgah*; the *maliks* had been kidnapped and that was that. A peaceful solution now seemed unlikely in any case, though it was manifestly no fault of his. Shivering and miserable and far from the comforts of Calcutta, Sir Lawrence had no objection to withdrawing from the Mana plateau and advancing northwards and thus coming gradually into rather more friendly territory; the closer one got to Peshawar and Nowshera and the seats of the military power of the Raj, the less one needed to be in constant fear of the natives. The Brigadier-General, however, having drawn these admissions from the High Commissioner, had then proceeded a step further during his later briefing of his colonels. It seemed that he intended advancing, not safely upon Peshawar, but dangerously upon the entry to the notorious Khyber Pass...

'We're serving no useful purpose here,' Norris said. 'It's still true we'll be slow and ponderous on the move as compared with Ogilvie, but he may have a need of us, and unless we're coming up behind him he'll remain out of communication. In the absence of any orders from Division, I propose to march my brigade towards Fort Jamrud. Not as a tight formation, however. I shall split the brigade into three groups.' Using a pointer, he indicated the positions on a large map hung upon an easel. 'I myself, with the two native battalions or what's left of them, will advance centrally along this line.' He traced it with the pointer. 'Colonel Hinde with the Border Regiment will advance towards Kohat and then close the Khyber after crossing the railway line from Parachinar. Lord Dornoch and the 114th will make their advance on the west flank, keeping as close as possible to the Afghan border. That will give us a reasonably broad and comprehensive sweep, I fancy.' Norris raised his eyebrows. 'Yes, Brora?'

'Lord Dornoch is not yet fully fit. *I* command the 114th Highlanders.'

'Indeed you do – a slip of the tongue. Is there anything else?'

'Yes,' Brora said arrogantly. 'You speak of a comprehensive sweep, sir. I fail to find it such. If Murrum Khan back-tracks, which I would gather is what you have in mind—'

'It is.'

'Well, then he'll find it abominably easy to slip down between the three lines of advance, will he not?'

'Very easy, I regret to say! However, I'm in no position to block him entirely—'

'I think you could split your brigade more, sir. Why not advance in half battalions?'

Norris frowned. 'For many reasons, Brora. For one thing, I haven't enough guns to distribute between six columns. For another, the front would still not be anything like fully covered and to split the brigade too far would leave each sector severely weakened with no useful result brought about.'

'Your plan's nothing but a compromise,' Brora said loudly and contemptuously.

'Compromise is what war is all about,' Norris said, 'as you will find if you reach the Staff. In the meantime, since you've not yet achieved that, you'll kindly see your regiment prepared to move out in accordance with my orders.' He pulled his watch from a pocket. 'Camp is to be struck forthwith, gentlemen, and the three columns will march out with the divided artillery in two hours from now.'

For a while now there had been no fresh snow; Ogilvie's Scots crawled out from their bivouacs after a few hours' respite to find the day clear and bright as the sun came up, thinly enough to be sure, over the eastern peaks to spread soft colourings of gold and pink and green. Ogilvie, up and about before his men and standing with MacTrease scanning the summits of the hills, heard his Colour-Sergeant's sudden warning.

'A horseman, sir, approaching from the north.'

Ogilvie brought up his field glasses. 'Mohammad Yusuf, Colour. He must have scouted ahead on his own.'

'Then the picquets should have reported, sir. I'll be having a word with them.' MacTrease sucked at his teeth, angrily, as the horseman rode in. Mohammad Yusuf seemed pleased with himself, grinning all over his face as he pulled his horse up before the two men.

'Good news, Ogilvie sahib!'

'Well?'

'Over the hills lies a village, a small place which I know and where I have a kinswoman on my mother's father's side, an ancient woman but with all her wits—'

'You said nothing of this?'

'No, Ogilvie sahib. A visit by myself alone was better for many reasons, chiefly for the sake of the village, also because my kinswoman would not have talked to the British—'

'But she has talked to you, Mohammad Yusuf? What did she say?'

The smile was broad; the face showed excitement and the lust for blood. 'Murrum Khan passed through yesterday, Ogilvie sahib. He demanded food, which was provided, and he left in peace. He did not say where he was going, but he was seen to ride

256

westerly from the village.'

'And the mem'sahib, Mohammad Yusuf?'

'There was talk of a woman, Ogilvie sahib, a woman closely veiled who seemed to be captive and whom no one was permitted to approach, nor to see her face or hands.'

'And Murrum Khan's route? It leads into Afghanistan?'

'Assuredly, Ogilvie sahib. It is a route well known to me. Murrum Khan must have been in much need of foodstuffs, and therefore had to ride into the village. Had this not been the case he would assuredly have taken another track, one that branches off before the village—'

'A shorter one, Mohammad Yusuf?'

'Much shorter. Farther to the north-west, it joins the one now taken by Murrum Khan. And that is the track we must now take, Ogilvie sahib, for we may cut across in front of Murrum Khan, and turn him aside from entering Afghanistan.'

'How far ahead is this shorter track, Mohammad Yusuf?'

'Little more than a mile, Ogilvie sahib.'

'And how far from there to the point where it meets the track Murrum Khan has taken?'

'About twenty-five miles more, sahib.'

Ogilvie swore. 'Almost a day's ride in these conditions! At what hour did Murrum Khan enter the village?'

'Towards last sunset, Ogilvie sahib, and he

left within the hour. But by the track he has taken, he will have twice the distance to ride.'

'Touch and go,' Ogilvie said, and turned to MacTrease. 'We'll take breakfast quickly, Colour, then mount and ride at once.'

By now Hector was in a bad way. Weariness and the whisky had forced him to halt for rest, and left him with wit enough to tether his horse to a jag of rock that thrust up from the snow like a stalagmite. There, he had virtually collapsed; but his clothing had been thick and he had enveloped himself from head to foot in a vast cloak of heavy tweed from Harris, and he survived to wake into total darkness and an eerie silence, a silence so complete that it came close to unnerving him to screaming point. But once again Dewar's had come to his aid and had calmed his nerves and brought to his body a comforting if misleading sensation of warmth.

He pulled himself together, got to his feet, stood swaying for a while and half crying, then remounted his horse and once again set out along the pass, quite fortuitously choosing the direction in which he had been headed earlier, deeper into the hills and treacherous rocks of Waziristan, his mind beginning, although he was unaware of this, to slip its moorings. Soon, he began to feel almost warm, and there was a stupid grin on his face as he lurched onward.

The Earl of Elgin, Her Majesty's Viceroy of India, faced the Commander-in-Chief, Sir George White, and Colonel Durand the Military Secretary, across the fireplace where the coals blazed in red and yellow flickers to bring perhaps the one piece of Christmas cheer to Government House. Outside as the guard was changed, a splash of colour was provided by men of the Viceregal Bodyguard in scarlet and gold, shining leather thigh boots, and striped puggarees. Inside, all except for that warming fire seemed dour and bodeful. As His Excellency had already said, the stability of the Raj was threatened by the news, such as there had been, from the North-West Frontier – always like tinder, always the weak spot from which trouble might emerge.

Lord Elgin lifted a hand and ticked off the points in summary. 'Item, where's Mrs Ogilvie? Item, what's become of Norris's brigade and the High Commissioner? Item, has Mr Hector Ogilvie ridden slap into the hands of more bandits, and if so, are we shortly to be faced with another demand with him as yet another hostage? Finally, where's young Ogilvie? Sir George?'

White shook his head. 'He was last reported as being in Murrum Khan's hands. No answer's been given to Murrum Khan's

259

demands, as you know, Your Excellency.'

'Not good for Ogilvie or the girl.'

'Indeed not, but we know the alternative only too well, sir.' White pulled his shoulders back, and met the Viceroy's eye. 'We can't concede, sir. We can't possibly.'

'Yet to leave them will be nearly as bad.'

'No, sir. I must disagree.'

'What will be the view of the tribes? That we left a white officer and a white woman to be slaughtered ... it diminishes the Raj, Sir George. It diminishes our honour.'

'Not as much as concessions made under duress, sir. We must never allow the Pathan to find hostages effective – if we do, it'll become a daily occurrence and we shall never rule again. It would not be the first time sacrifices have been made, and made willingly too.' The Commander-in-Chief shrugged. 'Nevertheless, like you, Your Excellency, I shrink from leaving them to it. That was the whole point of my submission that an expeditionary force should march at once.'

'I don't wish to inflame the situation. In any case, I can't move without Whitehall's approval—'

'For which there is no time, sir!' White's voice rose, urgently. 'The telegraph's fast enough, no doubt, but Whitehall is not! Cabinets ... a fuss in parliament, and a debate ... Lord Salisbury going down by coach to Windsor, and being kept cooling his heels while Her Majesty—'

'Yes, yes. I take your point.' Morning-coated, Lord Elgin paced up and down before the fire, his hands clasped beneath the coat tails. Minutes passed, and then, with clear reluctance, he reached a decision. 'Very well, Sir George, you may assemble troops as you wish so that they're ready, but the GOC in Murree is to be instructed beyond all doubt that they're not to move until they have my personal order as from the Governor-General in Council. Is that clear?'

'Quite clear, sir. It's not, frankly, enough but—'

'I can go no further. Where, pray, are the Ootacamund drafts now?'

'One day by train from Peshawar, Your Excellency.' Sir George reached for his ostrich-plumed cocked hat. 'I shall see personally to the despatches,' he said, bowing formally to Her Majesty's representative and at once taking his leave. Half a loaf was better than no bread. Within the hour the word had gone westward by the telegraph. Nowshera and Peshawar and all other garrisons and outposts along the North-West Frontier were to be brought immediately to a full war footing. The regiments about to arrive from Southern Army as reinforcements would be further stiffened by yet more drafts from Ootacamund; and from

Bombay within the next few days would come two battalions of infantry and a cavalry brigade with field artillery attached, all newly trooped from home. Units of all arms due for relief would have their home drafts stopped until further orders. The Pathan was to be made to realise that the Raj would move in strength to protect its own, and the Raj was now almost committed to the brink.

'And about time,' Sir Iain Ogilvie remarked to Fettleworth in Nowshera when the orders reached Division.

'What's HE's intention, precisely? Has he been specific?'

Sir Iain chuckled. 'I doubt it, but I understand White's pressing him.'

'How far?' Fettleworth asked.

'All the way to Kabul! White wants HE to put pressure on the Amir ... in short, to announce that if the Amir doesn't round up his bandits and deprive Murrum Khan of succour, then the Raj will march through the Khyber. That's what we've to be ready for, Fettleworth.'

Bloody Francis nodded, his chest swelling. 'D'you think it'll happen?'

'At the moment,' Sir Iain answered, 'it's a threat. A counter-threat if you like, such as should have been made much earlier. No more than that. Officially the next step's up to Whitehall, and HE will stick to that.' He paused. 'I'm not sure I shall! Nelson used his blind eye in the hour of his country's need and I call that a very good precedent ... but that's between you and me, remember.'

'Of course...'

'In the meantime you'd better mount that parade of yours.'

The short cut towards the track taken by Murrum Khan had considerably lessened the distance but the conditions had been extreme and the progress slow, and it had been necessary to make many halts. However, Ogilvie felt there was good hope that they might reach the main track before Murrum Khan. As before, occasional ragged figures had been glimpsed against the snow along the crests until the light had gone; two had been shot down, their bodies falling outwards, arcing down into the pass to shatter on the jags of rock. As the next day's dawn came up Mohammad Yusuf announced that the track into Afghanistan was some three miles ahead. Ogilvie kept up the pace until the junction was in view, then he ordered his small force to halt.

He turned and rode down the line. 'Into cover,' he called. 'Dismount and get in the lee of the rocks and bushes. See the mules and horses hidden as best you can. Colour MacTrease?'

'Sir?'

'A lance-corporal and three men to climb the eastern side and act as scouts. They're to watch for Murrum Khan's party and report the moment he's seen.'

'Sir!'

'I'll ride ahead myself to reconnoitre while they're taking post.'

'Aye, sir.' MacTrease, with his rifle at the slope, marched away to detail the scouts. Ogilvie lifted a hand to Mohammad Yusuf, who joined him for the ride down towards the main pass. They dismounted a little way short of the junction, and moved ahead on foot, carefully and watchfully. Ogilvie looked each way along the pass: there was nothing moving. The track was under lying snow and at first sight there were no traces of men or horses. Closer inspection, however, showed some faint indentations almost filled by a fall of snow that had come since the last travellers had gone by.

'What d'you think, Mohammad Yusuf?'

'The direction is towards Afghanistan—'

'Yes. I saw that. How likely is it that Murrum Khan has gone through already?'

The native shrugged. 'The possibilities are equal, Ogilvie sahib.'

'Do many people use this pass?'

'Not very many, but some. The tracks may not be those of Murrum Khan.'

Ogilvie nodded, frowning, in a quandary. The tracks were not very recent or they would not be snow-covered; when the dawn had come up, there was no snowfall either upon his force or ahead. But there was no knowing when, before that, the snow might have fallen again in the main pass; and there was nothing to be gained by entering the pass ahead of Murrum Khan and in effect preceding him and his bandits into his own land. Ogilvie put a hand on Mohammad Yusuf's shoulder and they turned back towards the south. 'It's a guess and no more than a guess,' Ogilvie said, 'but I'm going to assume he's not gone through yet. In the meantime I'll move the men down closer to the junction.' He indicated a big bluff at the westward end of the side pass, a mass of overhanging rock that circled back to form first-class natural cover. 'I'll hold them in there, and we'll have plenty of warning from the scouts.' He had seen for himself that the pass was clear and open, with no twists or turns, for a good distance along to the east. 'All right, Mohammad Yusuf?'

The Mahsud, who had been looking doubtful, shook his head. 'I am sorry, Ogilvie sahib, but I think such a place would appear natural for an ambush, and Murrum Khan will be ready.'

'True. But what's the alternative?'

'A little way to the west there is a better place. It may be known to Murrum Khan or it may not, but what is certain is that this

265

place here will be known to him.'

'And this other one?'

'A false front of rock, detached from the side of the pass. that forms a long and narrow *nullah*, open at both ends. There is much room. Come and I will show you.'

They went back towards the junction, with Mohammad Yusuf in the lead. Although the way from the east was clear and open, the pass turned a little as it left the junction behind it, leading around the rock bluff which had to be negotiated before the route ahead could be seen: which, as it turned out, was just as well. As Ogilvie began to move round the bluff, Mohammad Yusuf stopped very suddenly and waved him urgently back. Ogilvie asked no questions until they were both safely in the side pass. Mohammad Yusuf said, 'There was a man, a Pathan – an Afridi, Ogilvie sahib. His back was to me ... but he was on watch!'

'What does that mean, Mohammad Yusuf?'

'Perhaps that Murrum Khan has reached there – certainly that the place is occupied.'

'Murrum Khan ... in ambush waiting for us?'

The tribesman nodded. 'This is possible, yes. The men on the peaks may well have passed on word of our coming, and the word has reached Murrum Khan, and now he waits. The boot is on the other foot, Ogilvie sahib – but perhaps not for long?'

Ogilvie grinned. 'Perhaps not for long!' With Mohammad Yusuf he went back towards MacTrease and the half company and told the Colour-Sergeant the facts. 'I think we must attack, Colour, though we can't be sure it's Murrum Khan'

'With respect, sir, I'd suggest we wait a wee while to see if he shows up from the east. We can't afford to lose men by engaging other persons who may not be him, sir.'

'We can't afford to be caught on two fronts if Murrum Khan does turn up from the east, Colour, that's for certain. It's not likely the men in the *nullah* are friendly to us, and I—'

He broke off sharply: a shot had come from one of the scouts positioned on the eastern heights, and the man was calling down urgently. His voice was lost in more rifle fire from high up to the west, and then the side of the pass seemed to come alive as wild-looking men poured like a wave over the crests and bounded down behind puffs of smoke.

Sixteen

It was cold to be standing around, but pride was keeping Lieutenant-General Francis Fettleworth warm on the windswept dais. With him was the General Officer Commanding, Northern Army, to take the salute as the reinforced garrison marched past, the infantry with fixed bayonets and lively tunes from the fifes and drums boosted by the brass of the headquarters band; the cavalry behind the kettle-drums on the drum-horses and their somewhat muted wind instruments; the artillery with the thunder of the guns and limbers, the wheels of which sent up the snow in great gouts behind them. Snow was again falling, but thinly before the wind, powdering the uniform greatcoats, the dais itself, and the *maidan* upon which the great parade was being held. It was different from previous parades: for one thing no spectating women were present, partly because of the cold but principally because Sir Iain Ogilvie had expressed the view, irritably, that no damn women should stare and chatter at what was a soldier's occasion.

For another, this was more a review and inspection of men going to their war stations rather than a pure parade: action was in the air and from the *maidan* the soldiers would march into cantonments to be on stand-to, with all arms and equipment ready, to await the orders from Calcutta.

When the review was over and the last files had marched off parade into the falling snow, there were *chota pegs* at Division. Sir Iain was morose, taciturn; the lack of news wrenched at his nerves and for the first time he wondered what he was doing in Nowshera when he might have been better employed in Murree comforting his wife – but it had been partly to avoid the look in his wife's eyes that he had come to Nowshera to sit upon the back of Bloody Francis Fettleworth ... and he wished to God His Excellency the Viceroy would stir himself and act before it was too late! So often, as he remarked now to Fettleworth and Lakenham, no news along the Frontier was bad news. Lakenham agreed, but was about to utter some comforting platitude when Fettleworth's ADC entered the room looking portentous.

'Sir—'

'What is it?' Fettleworth demanded, putting down his glass of whisky.

'Word from Fort Jamrud, sir. They've received a report from some friendly Waziris

of a body of tribesmen, Afridis, having crossed the border into Afghanistan with prisoners.'

Sir Iain crossed the room and stood in
front of the ADC. 'Where was the crossing?'

'A pass south of the Khyber, sir – that's all
that's known, apparently.'

'No distance given?'

'No, sir.'

Sir Iain waved an arm at Fettleworth.
'Maps, and quickly!' He turned back to the
ADC. 'These prisoners. Is anything known
about *them*?'

'Largely men of a Highland regiment, sir.'

'I see.' Sir Iain whitened for a moment,
then his mouth set hard. 'Any officers?'

'That was not reported, sir.' The ADC
added, 'There's believed to have been a
woman, sir. A veiled figure that *could* have
been a woman.'

The GOC swung round on his heel, saw
that Lakenham had unrolled maps and was
hanging them on the wall. He marched
across, a mist before his eyes but otherwise
in full control. For a few moments he
studied the border area south of the Khyber,
then swung round to face Fettleworth. 'I'm
about to make assumptions, General. If
there are Scottish troops taken prisoner,
then I shall assume Norris's brigade has
been under further attack and has again
been cut up. The 114th are the only Scots

currently south of the Khyber, are they not?'

It was Lakenham who answered: 'Yes, sir.'

'I further assume the bandits to be Murrum Khan's Afridis and the veiled woman to be Mrs Hector Ogilvie.'

'A large assumption—'

'No! A reasonable one!' Sir Iain blew through his moustache, angrily. 'If my assumptions are correct, as I believe them to be, there is little time left. From now, gentlemen, we must consider the Raj to be under extreme threat and to be at war—'

'Sir, I am forced to protest. The Viceroy—'

'The Viceroy fiddlesticks. He is in Calcutta, the Queen awaits Christmas in Windsor. I am here. General Fettleworth, as Commander of the First Division, you will at once march out all available men. Barrack guards only will be left in cantonments. You are to march your division upon the Khyber, and I shall accompany you myself. I want a message sent ahead by the field telegraph to Fort Jamrud: they are to pressure the men who brought word of the crossing, and when I reach the Khyber I shall expect to know precisely where the crossing was made.'

Soon after, Nowshera was in a state of controlled turbulence as the regiments made their final preparations for action. The many hundreds of animals – riding horses, pack mules, ponies and camels – that accompanied a division on the march were made ready

and loaded with their burdens by detach-
ments of the Supply and Transport; the final
touches were put by the Ordnance to the
guns and the ammunition trains, and the
field ambulance sections were checked over
for full complements of supplies and spare
horses. In the infantry lines rifles were given
one more pull through with four-by-two
dipped in oil, and the bayonets were given an
extra shine so that they might the more
easily slide into native bodies.

The ride to the west was ignominy, utter
failure. The assault had been well conceived
and Ogilvie knew that he had been guilty of
over-confidence. The attackers had poured
down upon the Scots before the Maxim
could be assembled and at the same time
more men had come in at the rush from the
main pass and the Scots had been open to
enfilading fire. In fact not many casualties
had been suffered: two men dead and eight
wounded, only one seriously. Not one of the
attackers had been accounted for. They had
come too suddenly and they had come in
overwhelming numbers and it had all been
over in less than two minutes. Murrum
Khan, it seemed, still had plenty of willing
support in the Waziri hills! Ogilvie and his
Scots now rode with ropes bound tight
about their arms and bodies, and their mules
led by armed tribesmen, as did Mohammad

272

Yusuf's men; the latter were clearly terrified of the vengeance that would be wrought upon them by Murrum Khan. They had proved brave in action but had been as helpless as the Scots in the sudden fury of the onslaught.

Behind Ogilvie, in the centre of the mounted bandits, was Angela, still veiled from head to foot. Gloatingly, Murrum Khan had confirmed to Ogilvie the identity of the shrouded figure. Ogilvie's thoughts were in tumult: Murrum Khan now had his two hostages back and they would be used against the Raj. And Ogilvie had no doubt that the whole affair had now gone far beyond the original boundary dispute and that Murrum Khan's ambitions would have grown bigger. Unless the British reaction to stepped-up demands was extremely cool and cautious, the Raj might become drawn into war. A rising all along the Frontier was a different kettle of fish from a boundary dispute in the localised area of Mana. There might be many pressures, particularly from Whitehall with world power alignments in mind, to concede enough to avoid the bigger risk. Ogilvie found this unwelcome. Anxious enough to live himself and to see Angela freed, he disliked the notion of being returned to the Raj like a parcel by a triumphant Murrum Khan to become a person to be stared at and even cold-shouldered as the officer who had dropped into enemy hands and become a pawn of natives to be used to discomfit the mighty Raj. An officer's career was always strewn with impediments to honour and promotion and this could certainly be considered one of them.

The ride continued, painfully and in biting cold that was the worse for the fact that he was bound and therefore unable to move to circulate the blood. The nearer they approached the Afghan border the worse the weather became. They advanced through a blizzard; exposed areas of flesh lost all feeling. Murrum Khan, however, was stopping for nothing now. The ride continued. After a long time the track took a downward slant, ziz-zagging through the mountains, and the blizzard eased. Murrum Khan rode ahead to come up alongside Ogilvie.

'Now we are in Afghanistan,' he said. 'We have left the Raj behind.'

'Where are you heading?'

'For a village where I am known and expected.'

'How far?'

'A long way yet. Soon we shall rest. It is quite safe to do so now.' Murrum Khan turned his horse away, and rode back down the line. Shortly afterwards he passed the word to halt, and his men dismounted and led the animals off the track into a deep cleft in the hills where they were protected from the weather. Ogilvie and the other prisoners were lifted down and, under strong guard, their hands and feet were untied so that they could stamp and flail the blood back into circulation, a process slow at first and painful. The horses and mules were fed from nosebags, and a meal of rice was given to the men. They drank from melted snow. After a four-hour halt during which the guards snatched sleep in watches, they were ordered to mount again and they rode deeper into the wild Afghan hills, coming at nightfall into a broad plain, a kind of bowl with more hills rising beyond and extending all around into immense distances, range upon range of utter loneliness and desolation. The wind howled and the cold was bitter but now the snow had stopped falling. A village lay ahead, a place with a remote look as though it had withdrawn from the world. As the bandits rode on, shadowy figures were seen ahead in the dimming light, men riding out in welcome. There was noisy acclaim for Murrum Khan, shouts of anger and derision against the bound natives, the Mahsuds of Mohammad Yusuf, traitors to the Pathan cause: it seemed that the bush telegraph had already brought word ahead that Razjah Shah had taken up arms against Murrum Khan and before dying had rendered assistance to the British Raj.

In the middle of an excited throng, they

moved into the village, riding past rude huts and hovels and a mixture of wild-looking, ragged men and women, children, goats and domestic animals. Hands reached out, plucking with interest at the British uniforms, pulling at the cloak that covered Angela until the villagers were pushed back by the armed riders. There was a wait while Murrum Khan dismounted and went into the headman's hut, a long wait in the freezing cold under the light of flares that smoked and flamed eerily. Then Murrum Khan came into view again and called orders, and the prisoners were removed from the mules and horses. All except Angela were led under guard of the *jezails* and the knives to a hut larger than all the others, a place that looked like a meeting hut. The interior, as Ogilvie ducked down below the lintel of a low doorway, was seen to be completely bare of any furnishing. It had a floor of well-trodden earth, and the walls were of wood and stone and looked strong. Two Pathans remained inside as guards and the door was shut upon them, and a heavy beam was set in place outside. Light was given by a flare set in a metal holder on an upright pole that stood in the hut's centre and helped, presumably, to support the roof. The place was at least warmer than the outside air and gave full protection from the wind. Ogilvie tried to keep a cheerful face for the benefit of his

Scots, but when he offered some words of encouragement he was at once stopped by one of the guards, speaking roughly in Pushtu: 'There will be no speech.' To lend emphasis to his words, the man darted across like a snake, squatted before Ogilvie and laid the tip of a dagger against his throat, remaining for perhaps half a minute staring into his eyes from behind a mass of facial hair and sweeping his nostrils with foul breath.

By now an intense weariness had set in and some of the men had fallen into sleep already, heads lolling and shoulders slumped one against another. It was not long before Ogilvie joined them, totally unable to keep his eyelids from closing. When he woke he felt much refreshed, though hungry and thirsty. Dawn was showing through the crack above the top of the door, and the guard had been changed while he had slept. Soon after he had woken, the door was opened and Murrum Khan came in. With him were four of his tribesmen. These men, ignoring the Scots, went across to Mohammad Yusuf and dragged him to his feet. As he was pushed towards the door, the Mahsud met Ogilvie's eye and smiled.

'*Salaam*, Ogilvie sahib, and farewell. We shall not meet again—' He staggered as the butt of a *jezail* took him a viciously heavy blow in the side. Ogilvie called out to him; as he did so Murrum Khan came over and struck hard with the back of his hand, a blow that left red weals and blotches on Ogilvie's cheek. Mohammad Yusuf was taken outside, dragged along by the Pathans. A rising murmur was heard as he went out, a murmur that grew to an angry baying sound, a sound of blood-lust and savage cruelty, then this sound was stilled as Murrum Khan began haranguing the mob. Ogilvie was unable to catch his words, though he picked up an occasional reference in Pushtu to the Raj. After this there came a hush, and the hush was broken by a faint swishing sound, a sound of displaced air followed closely by a long drawn scream, and then another swish, then silence, then a noisy outbreak of savage pleasure. As the happy shouts continued, the door came open again and, as in the case of Razjah Shah far to the south and east in Mana, the bloody head of Mohammad Yusuf rolled along the floor beneath the flare's flickering light.

Murrum Khan did not come back. Ogilvie sat on with his Scots and the natives of Mohammad Yusuf, all of the latter at least now clearly facing something similar to their leader's execution. Rice was brought, and water-bottles, and all were fed by a veiled woman while the armed guards stood ready. There was no word of Angela. But as the day wore on into evening, tremendous news reached the village. From the hut Ogilvie heard the galloping hooves of horses: two riders, he fancied. The hoofbeats slowed and stopped not far from the hut, and Ogilvie heard the excited voices clearly, speaking in Pushtu and asking for Murrum Khan.

'A great British force has passed Fort Jamrud and is within the Khyber ... many, many thousands of soldiers and beasts and heavy guns ... and with them is the great warrior, the General sahib who commands in Murree...'

Seventeen

Sir Iain Ogilvie was in an angry mood: the men who had brought the word to Fort Jamrud, those friendly Waziris, had been of no further help at all. They did not know the route Murrum Khan had taken; their message was in fact at second hand, and their own informant had not known or would not say. But they had a grudge against Murrum Khan whom they would like to see brought to British justice and Sir Iain, who had spoken to them himself, had seen that they were speaking the truth. Had they known –

having reported in the first place – they would have told all they knew. All they could say was that there were very many avenues into Afghanistan for those that knew them, and Murrum Khan could have taken any one of these.

'What do we do now?' Fettleworth enquired anxiously, but not as anxiously as he would have done had he had the responsibility himself. 'Where do we march?'

Sir Iain pointed ahead. 'Into the Khyber. Where else?'

'The weather's putrid.'

'I've marched in worse.'

'But what are you going to *do*?'

'I'm going to damn well advance into the Khyber!' Sir Iain snapped.

'But really—'

'We may get further word at Ali Masjid or Landi Kotal. If we don't,' Sir Iain said with grim passion, 'it'll be the bloody Amir who'll get word from *me* by the time we reach Fort Dhaka at the western end!'

Fettleworth blew out a long breath that lifted the trailing ends of his moustache. 'What word, sir, pray?'

'That I intend marching on Kabul if he doesn't have Murrum Khan arrested and handed over with his hostages.' Sir Iain passed the order for the long column to get on the move, and somewhat cumbersomely it did so. Regiment upon regiment, squadron upon squadron, battery upon battery with all the paraphernalia of supply and its hundreds of camp followers, the latter ragged and unkempt and dirty, the low caste sweepers who did the housework of any formation on the march, an appallingly spread-out mass of men and animals for a winter advance through the terrible mountains of the Safed Koh. Fettleworth muttered and rumbled unavailingly: Sir Iain was set upon his madness and that was that. Not that Fettleworth ever shrank from a fight; he certainly did not. But in the circumstances the wrath from Calcutta would be terrible and Sir Iain was putting his head firmly on the chopping-block. His career in the army was virtually finished from this moment, in Fettleworth's view. Generals, however highly placed in their commands, did not declare war on their own, and this was war. Some of the opprobrium would rub off upon himself – bound to! Part of the column was formed by his own First Division, indeed all of it since the reinforcements had been incorporated. He was the Divisional Commander ... well, he had already protested, of course! Lakenham had heard him do so, and would have to testify. But he tried again. Sir Iain wouldn't listen, merely set his face ahead and rode on before his massive force, into the gathering gloom beneath the enormous jagged peaks that rose in some cases 3,000 feet above the pass – 14,000 feet above sea level – hostile and cruel even in summer, grim and grey and concealing tribesmen with rifles who would snipe continually from their safe vantage points above.

Pushing north, the three separated columns of Norris's brigade had made fair progress, mostly unimpeded by the Waziris although there had been a handful of attacks, as always expected, upon all three columns. These had been fought off without loss. The Royal Strathspey had followed the route taken by Ogilvie and his half company: having noted the position where Ogilvie had entered the hills, as reported by the Brigadier-General's orderly officer, Lord Brora had made for the same spot and from there had followed willy-nilly, hemmed into the pass by the hills to either side. Later, the battalion had had a stroke of luck: a native had been brought before him by the Regimental Sergeant-Major – a boy searching for strayed goats in the snow.

'What's this, Mr Cunningham?'

Cunningham explained. 'You may wish him questioned, sir.'

'I may, and indeed do, Mr Cunningham! You shall ask the questions. If he's slow to answer, prod him.'

'He's but a child, sir.'

Brora stared down from his horse. 'Don't

argue with me, Mr Cunningham, if you please. Child or not, he's to answer fully. Where's he from, has he seen Murrum Khan, has he seen Captain Ogilvie?'

The boy was cheerful under Cunningham's questions and answered willingly. He came from the village that had been visited by Mohammad Yusuf, and had heard talk of both Murrum Khan and of British soldiers. He was able to tell the Sergeant-Major sahib which track Murrum Khan had taken; but, because the Major sahib on the horse had spoken with an arrogance that came clearly through the foreign tongue, and because the Major sahib looked down at him with disdain and contempt, the boy did not point out the short cut that lay ahead and which could have saved the Major sahib many miles of dreadful progress. Released, he skipped through the snow after his goats and not until he was a long way off did he turn and put fingers to his nose towards the Major sahib.

Lord Brora spoke to Andrew Black. 'That was helpful. Move the battalion out.'

Black, who had been studying a map, said, 'I believe the track that boy indicated leads into Afghanistan, Major.'

'No doubt. And no doubt that was why Murrum Khan's taken it.'

Black looked nettled. 'Quite. My point was, are you going to ride across the border?'

'I don't know till I get there, my dear fellow. We may overtake Murrum Khan on the way, may we not?'

'I think not, Major. As for entering Afghanistan, our orders from the Brigadier-General are for Fort Jamrud, and—'

Brora interrupted rudely. 'You have no damn initiative, I think, Captain Black. I am Lord Brora. I shall act as I think fit when occasion demands.' He rode forward, large, handsome and dark, somewhat obviously making no reference to the Colonel, still under Corton's orders and being borne along in a *doolie* in the centre of the advance.

Murrum Khan himself brought the already overheard news of the Khyber penetration to his prisoners. 'There is no cause to rejoice, Ogilvie sahib, even though your own father marches with the soldiers. None of you shall benefit. If the British happen to come this way, all of you will die before they reach the village.'

'So you're not moving on, Murrum Khan?'

'Not moving, no.' Murrum Khan waved a hand, airily. 'The village is in fact quite safe from the British, and will not be troubled. The British are many miles away.'

'And you?'

'I?' Murrum Khan stared down, eyebrows lifted. 'I do not understand.'

'What can you achieve from here, from

your safe isolation, Murrum Khan? How do you propose to make use of hostages?'

The Afridi smiled and shrugged. 'I have messengers, Ogilvie sahib. Soon the Raj will know that you and the mem'sahib are in Afghanistan and beyond reach of the British Army – and will know also, as indeed they know already, that both will die if my demands are not met ... my demands for the cession of the border lands. More than this I have no need to do. I wait, and all will come to me.'

More, perhaps, than you bargain for, Ogilvie thought; but without real hope. Murrum Khan went away, refusing to answer questions about Angela beyond saying that currently she was safe and well and recovered from the rigours of the journey through the passes. Ogilvie eased his neck in his uniform tunic, trying to shift the headache that had come with the increasing fug in the hut. The many exhaled breaths, the smoke from the ever-guttering flare on its pole, used up the air faster than the chinks in the walls and the occasional opening of the door could replace it. The men, both British and native, sat about listlessly, unable to move hand or foot. Helplessness was becoming hopelessness ... Ogilvie looked across at MacTrease, too far off for any exchange of talk, of views and plans that might have led to some sort of concerted action. Ogilvie bared his teeth in a savage, self-rebuking grin: how could action of any kind come from bound men, with a vigilant armed guard watching every movement? Yet action there had to be if they were to avoid the slaughter that if it didn't come sooner was certain to come when the Raj rejected Murrum Khan's demands.

Something had to be thought of, and quickly. Clearly it could not at this moment be physical. Unless their situation changed dramatically, and this was improbable to say the least, Murrum Khan had to be countered by other means, the means of the mind. Ogilvie sat with closed eyes, trying desperately to get his brain working along constructive lines, but found himself unable to see the wood for the trees, the trees of the actual military and political situation as he saw it. It was known now that the Raj had entered the Khyber in strength; that must mean the First Division under Fettleworth, possible with reinforcements from Murree. As for his father's presence ... it was not the Army Commander's proper duty to leave his headquarters for the field, but James Ogilvie knew his father's often impulsive reaction and his liking for a fight. It was many years now since Sir Iain had been promoted from command of the Royal Strathspey to the Staff, but at heart the old man was a regimental soldier still and chafed at the restrictions of high command. With his son and his nephew's wife in tribal hands, he was likely enough to cut right through the red tape and put himself at the head of the expeditionary force...

Ogilvie's thoughts flew on: what would be the purpose of a penetration in strength, a penetration that seemed likely to go beyond the boundaries of the Raj, though the Khyber itself was British territory? Was the First Division marching upon a needle-in-a-haystack chase, a mere hope that they might fall in with Murrum Khan or be led to him by bandits taken along the way? Again – if indeed Sir Iain was with the column – James knew his father's way. Often bull-at-a-gate, he was inclined to charge past the small fry and attack the pinnacle of power. In Afghanistan the pinnacle was the Amir, and the power lay in the city of Kabul. If you took Kabul, you took Afghanistan. The Amir would not wish that; the Anglo-Afghan border had been satisfactorily settled by the Durand mission as recently as 1893, in which year the Amir's subsidy from the Queen-Empress had been increased from twelve to sixteen lakhs of rupees. The Amir Abdur-Rahman had effectively broken the power of the tribal chiefs – all except Murrum Khan, it seemed now – and had since maintained a standing army of some 80,000 men with many thousands of horses and a respectable number of field guns. There would be a bloody battle if the Amir chose to resist, but he was well disposed towards the British and might be reluctant to jeopardise his position for the sake of a warring tribal leader.

All this, Murrum Khan must be presumed to know; however, there would be nothing lost by reminding him of it. Ogilvie reached a decision and called out in Pushtu, addressing the Pathan on guard.

'I wish words with Murrum Khan. The matter is important.'

The guard came over and stood looking down at Ogilvie, the bayonet of his *jezail* pointed towards him. 'You must wait. Murrum Khan has left the village.'

This was contrary to what Murrum Khan had said. Ogilvie asked, 'To go where?'

'I do not know.'

'When will he return?'

'This also I do not know.'

'I have said the matter is important. Murrum Khan will have left a trusted tribesman in charge?'

'Yes.'

'I must speak to this man.'

There was uncertainty in the Pathan's dark, watchful face, and Ogilvie pressed. 'If my words remain unsaid, Murrum Khan will be angry upon his return.'

There was a pause; the man stared at

Ogilvie, then shrugged and backed away towards the door. He banged with the butt of his rifle on the wood, and the door was opened. The Pathan spoke rapidly, and the door was shut again. All the men in the hut were watchful now, on edge, awaiting the next move. After a long interval the door was opened once more, and a short, thickset man came in wearing a filthy sheepskin coat with a round fur hat on his head. Ogilvie recognised him from their arrival: the village *malik*. Approaching, the man asked, 'What does the British officer wish?'

Ogilvie answered as the *malik* had spoken – in Pushtu. 'I wish to utter a warning. The British force in the Khyber is said to be strong. That means the Raj is marching upon Kabul. There will be war between the Raj and Afghanistan ... between Her Majesty the Queen-Empress with her many divisions and guns, and ships to bring more men, and the army of the Amir. This you know?'

'It is possible.'

'But more possible is this, my friend: the Amir will send his army to rout out Murrum Khan, rather than offend the Raj.'

There was an oily grin. 'Not so. Persons in Kabul who have the ear of Amir Abdur-Rahman promise help of his army for Murrum Khan. It is wished to push back the border into territory held by the Raj.'

'So there will be war?'

'There will be war, yes.' The headman spoke flatly. 'You speak of nothing important, nothing new.'

'Yet I think it is new that so strong a British force is on the march. I believe this will cause the Amir much thought and his mind may well be changed thereby. I believe you should consider this in the absence of Murrum Khan.'

The *malik* shrugged. 'It is not needed for me to consider.'

'What happens if the Amir withdraws his support for Murrum Khan? What happens if the Amir sends men to take Murrum Khan, and then casts him and his tribesmen into jail in Kabul, or perhaps delivers them to the Raj for justice?'

'The Amir will not do this.'

'I wouldn't be so confident were I in your shoes, my friend. Sixteen *lakhs* of rupees is much money, and this can be lost. The minds of princes are frequently changed when they see trouble coming for a way of life to which they've grown accustomed. They begin to think of the advantages of the *status quo*. And Kabul has many reasons to fear the Raj, as you know beyond doubt, remembering General Roberts sahib. You should think well, friend, in the best interest of your leader, Murrum Khan.'

The eyes had narrowed to slits, and the face was watchful and tense. 'And when I have thought – what then?'

'Come back, and I will offer you a solution.'

'No. The solution now.'

'Very well – the solution now, to aid thought.' Ogilvie stared back at the squat, dirty headman, holding his gaze in his own. 'I also have no wish for the Raj to involve the Amir in war. My reasons are personal ... because I am told that my father marches with the British force. My father is a man of much impetuosity, who does not always follow the wishes or the commands of the Queen-Empress. He is liable to exceed his orders and put Kabul to the sword. This, the Raj may not want.'

The headman seemed to understand, and grinned. 'The great Queen-Empress will be angry?'

'Yes. My father may suffer much.'

'It is an affair between him and the Queen-Empress.'

'And Murrum Khan. Because of my father, I am willing to assist Murrum Khan.'

'How?'

The crucial question that had to be answered; and the answer must convince beyond doubt. Ogilvie said steadily, 'I am willing to go as an emissary to the British column and negotiate on Murrum Khan's behalf—'

He was interrupted by jeering laughter.

'You are willing, Ogilvie sahib? Willing to be handed back safely to your Raj? Who would not be found willing for that?'

'You misunderstand,' Ogilvie said quietly. 'I am willing to go under escort, under a flag of truce, to talk at a distance to the commander of the column. I do not ask to be handed back. I shall tell the British that it is best for them to agree to Murrum Khan's demands and march back upon Fort Jamrud. And that when they have done this, and when the new boundaries have been drawn up, then the mem'sahib and I will be released.'

'But already the Raj knows the terms of Murrum Khan! You suggest nothing different.'

'Only that I shall myself be the envoy. I can convince them.'

'And your father ... an illustrious soldier, a warrior, known along the Frontier and throughout the Raj, so it is said ... he will feel no shame for you?'

Ogilvie said, 'I think not. I'll be acting for the mem'sahib ... who will remain meanwhile in your hands.'

The *malik* said no more, but looked thoughtful and grave, and at the same time disdainful of the cowardice that allowed an officer of the Raj to leave a mem'sahib in hostile hands: neither side loved a traitor. As the headman turned and walked out of the hut, Ogilvie felt his contempt like a physical force. He found his forehead dripping with sweat as he caught the looks of his Scots. Many of them had enough Pushtu to have followed the conversation, MacTrease being one. MacTrease's face was scornful, his words cutting. 'Man, I'd never have thought it of an Ogilvie.'

Ogilvie flushed. 'You'll kindly remember your rank, Colour-Sar'nt MacTrease.'

'Aye! And more worthy, I hope, to hold it than you are yours, *Captain* Ogilvie!'

Ogilvie held on to his tongue and endured the bitterness that came across like knives to wound. It was better so; unpromoted, un-rehearsed reactions were always the more convincing if overheard. For the next hour or so he was subject to every kind of insult, some of them muttered, some of them hurled openly. Had the men's hands and feet not been tied, he would, he believed truly, have been lynched. A Scots regiment was like no other, save perhaps an Irish one: the loyalty was intense and personal, but when it was flouted not even the hierarchy could hold the men down. They would have their say and make no bones about it: that was part and parcel of their race. Each man had his dignity as an individual, and in the High-lands there was no touching of the forelock to the squire and never had been. Army discipline they accepted up to ninety-nine

293

parts in a hundred: today the hundredth part had been reached. Ogilvie sat pale-faced while the *malik* pondered and consulted his village lieutenants. The pressures upon him would be heavy: he must act for Murrum Khan and for his own headmanship, his own head too. He was being offered possible peace and a full acceptance of his leader's demands, and it must seem to him that he could scarcely lose by agreeing to Ogilvie's suggestion. Besides, the aspect of concern for a father would ring true: the Pathan understood and respected concern for the elders.

The headman came back and stood looking down at Ogilvie, alone but for the guard as before.

'I have considered, Ogilvie sahib.'

'Good! And the result?'

'You shall go.'

Ogilvie sat tensed, and more jeers came from the Scots. 'I am ready as I promised.'

'There will be an escort of twenty men, and you shall go mounted to the Khyber Pass.'

Ogilvie nodded, licked at dry lips as he approached the next hurdle. 'I am sore from the ropes, and my flesh has lost feeling. In the cold weather that is not good. I must be untied and not ride like a bound sack. If I am not freed, I shall not go.'

The headman puffed out his cheeks, but

after some thought nodded reluctantly. 'You shall be untied.'

'And my colour-sergeant, who is to ride with me.'

There was an oath from MacTrease. The *malik* shook his head in refusal. Ogilvie said, 'I must have corroboration for what I am to say. This is surely obvious. My colour-sergeant is a man of known sound character, and will convince.'

'You ask more than you asked at first, Ogilvie sahib.'

'Yes. But I offer much, and will go only on these conditions.'

Once again, though reluctantly, the head-man conceded the point. He gestured to the armed guard, who came across and held his *jezail* pointed at Ogilvie's chest. The head-man himself bent and cut away Ogilvie's bonds at wrists and feet. The returning blood came painfully, and as MacTrease was freed Ogilvie lay working hands and toes, finding them useless for the time being, stiff as boards. MacTrease was cursing savagely across the hut. Leaving the guard on watch, the headman went to the door and called an order. A few moments later there was a sound of hooves on hard, icy ground – the horses mustering for the ride. When the headman returned both Ogilvie and Mac-Trease were getting to their feet, stumbling painfully. Movement was coming back.

Ogilvie took a turn or two up and down the hut, watched by the Scots and the captured Mahsuds of Razjah Shah, and the terrible feeling of powerlessness vanished gradually.

'You are ready, Ogilvie sahib?' the headman asked.

'I am ready,' Ogilvie answered. He caught MacTrease's eye. *'Craig Elachaidh!'* he called out, using the regiment's Gaelic battle cry. 'Stand fast, Craigellachie!' MacTrease looked much puzzled, but only for a moment; then he gave Ogilvie a fractional wink. Ogilvie said, 'The *jezail*, Colour.' As Mac-Trease moved for the guard with his eyes shining, Ogilvie flung himself bodily against the central pole, sending it clear away from its seating. There was a creaking sound and the roof began to sag downwards; the flare shot off its hook and arced down into a corner of the hut, smoking and sputtering. Ogilvie recovered himself just as Mac-Trease's knee came up hard into the sentry's groin. As the man fell screaming, MacTrease grabbed the *jezail* and swung it on the *malik*, driving it deep into the chest and twisting the blade to withdraw it. Then with Ogilvie he moved back to where the torch was flaring and igniting the wood walls, firing towards a press of men coming in through the open doorway.

Eighteen

The flames and the shooting so close at hand had panicked the horses: bucking hooves beat at the hut's walls, and there were cries from outside as the villagers were caught by flailing legs. While MacTrease covered him with the captured *jezail* Ogilvie used the headman's knife to cut the ropes binding the captives, working fast before the smoke could choke him. As the mob closed in, the Colour-Sergeant reversed the *jezail* and used the butt as a club, smashing heads. As the flames got a grip MacTrease burst backwards through the burning woodwork, clearing a way for the Scots and Mohammad Yusuf's bandits to be dragged out to safety. There were casualties but two of the Scots at least, quickly regaining circulation, were in action now; Ogilvie was aware of a lance-corporal and a private making short work of one of the villagers and getting possession of knives and another rifle. The lance-corporal tore like a maniac into the natives, thrusting with the snaky bayonet so that they pressed back, yelling and in disarray, to be taken in the rear by the flames. More and more of the ex-prisoners came back to vigour and joined in, two of them taking up flaming pieces of wood to bring fire to more of the huts before Ogilvie could stop them. MacTrease with a corporal and four men moved at the double for the compound where the mules had been tethered; within a matter of minutes they had the Maxim assembled. It began stuttering out fire, sweeping the village to leave bloodstained figures on the frozen snow. After that the former prisoners, under Ogilvie, ran for the headman's hut: on their first arrival in the village they had seen their captured arms being taken under the headman's charge. They were there still. As the rifles and bayonets were reissued, MacTrease marched up to Ogilvie and saluted.

'God forgive me, sir,' he said. 'I thought you meant what you said.'

Ogilvie smiled. 'You were meant to, Colour. Part of it was genuine, the part that said I'd ride to join the advance through the Khyber and stop it before it goes too far.'

'The lady, sir—'

'First the lady. She's not been found yet. Right through the village now, Colour, and let's hope she's not in any of the burning huts.'

Saluting again, MacTrease turned about smartly and began shouting for the section sergeants and corporals to muster search parties and provide a perimeter guard. The men moved among the huts, some of which had already burned to the ground. It was Ogilvie himself who found Angela in a strongly-built structure with a stone floor and heavily bolted doors, a grain store in the centre of the village. Tied hand and foot as he himself had been earlier, and gagged, she was lying on a bed of sacks and matting. Quickly he released her. Bending, he kissed her cheek. Tears came. He said, 'It's all right now. You're back ... we've a long ride ahead, but you're back.'

Most of the villagers had fled into the hills in the fading light, but they would return when the British had gone. In the meantime they had left some of the elderly and immobile behind, also some frightened children who had hidden when the fighting started and the huts had begun to burn. MacTrease asked what was to be done with them and with the village.

'They've asked for punishment, sir. They harboured Murrum Khan.'

'Who has yet to be found ... yes, they've asked for it, but I'll leave them in peace, Colour. *Badal's* for the Pathan, not for us.'

'Aye, I dare say you're right, sir. Time moves on, and punitive expeditions don't look as right as once they did, though I don't know if Bloody Francis'll agree, sir ...

begging your pardon.' There was an expression of innocence on the Colour-Sergeant's leathery face. 'Is the lady fit to move out, sir?'

'Yes, she is, though the sooner we find a field ambulance section the better, both for her and the casualties. She and they will have to be carried as best we can manage on the mules and horses – and speed's the watchword now, Colour.' Ogilvie paused, looking about him. 'Talking of which, we'll move faster with a guide, I fancy.'

'Razjah Shah's bandits, sir—'

'No. I've had a word – they intend to leave us at a crossing track once we're clear of the village and I can't say I blame them! Can you rustle up a guide from the people of the village?'

'Leave it to me, sir.' MacTrease marched away. Ogilvie turned for the headman's hut, to which Angela had been taken. Darkness had come down now, thick darkness with no moon or stars to lighten it. Ogilvie feared more snow in the overcast sky. He prayed that it might not come to delay their ride upon the Khyber; once the British force had passed Fort Dhaka at the Khyber's western end, and there was no knowing when that might be, a boundary violation on the part of the Raj would have taken place and the results would be incalculable. A positive advance of a division was a very different thing from the inadvertent border crossing of a patrol ... Ogilvie ducked down into the head-man's hut and smiled at his cousin's wife lying on a more comfortable bed now, in the light of a flare. Rough food, and water, and a liberal amount of whisky from Ogilvie's flask, had brought improvement.

'Better?'

'Much, thank you, James.' In fact she looked a very sick woman, he thought, and would need weeks of good care after they reached Nowshera. Hector was going to need to spoil her for a while. 'Have we far to go, to reach Uncle Iain?'

'I don't know.' He added, 'You'll make it, Angela.'

She answered in a whisper: 'Yes...' Ogilvie looked at her narrowly: for his part he was not too sure, but he had no alternative but to head for the Khyber. Even had he not a positive duty to deflect the main advance, he could not remain in the village. His force was small, and before long the displaced villagers would gather support from neigh-bouring hill villages and a strong attack would come, and Angela would be worse off by far than if the ride to the north had been risked. But she was so frail and weak; her skin was almost transparent, her eyes haunt-ed, dark and shadowed in a haggard white face. Her thinness was now skeletonic; a puff of the wind would blow her from her mule ...

it would be tragic if she died on the march. Hector would never forgive him; he would never forgive himself, but what had to be, had to be and that was that. Ogilvie stiffened himself, gave her a word or two of cheer, and left the hut again to see to the preparations for moving out. The men were falling in, and a mount was being brought up for Angela while the wounded, the casualties from the hut action, were lifted as carefully as possible to the saddles of the fit men who would tend them along the way. Through the darkness came Colour-Sergeant MacTrease, pushing an old man and a young boy ahead of him.

'The guide, sir.'

'Which?'

'The grandfather, sir – and that's what he is. The lad's his grandson.'

'He knows the tracks?'

'He says he does not, sir, but I know well he must do, like all the villagers.'

Ogilvie nodded. 'Very well, Colour. Warn him of the consequences if he refuses to speak or leads us astray.'

'Aye, sir. That I have! Not against himself.'

'The boy?'

'Aye, sir,' MacTrease said again, firmly. 'A false move, said I, and the grandson's spitted like a pig by the bayonets. We need to be bastards, sir, at a time like this.'

Murrum Khan would have done just the

same thing: the knowledge made Mac-Trease's words no easier to stomach. Ogilvie, however, made no comment; the threat, he felt, would be an empty one, but should prove effective. In the light from a flare held by one of the Mahsuds, he saw the boy's eyes. He had never before seen such hate in the face of a child; it was like a blow, a blow struck against the Raj by one who also had his loyalties. That child, for certain, would never point out the way; it was only to be hoped that the grandfather was made of lesser stuff! Ogilvie turned away and went back into the hut behind him, beckoning two privates to follow. Angela was lifted gently and brought out into the cold night's darkness, and set on the waiting horse, her rough cloak pulled up around her knees, awkwardly, as she sat stride. The two privates who had carried her out mounted to Ogilvie's orders and brought their mules alongside her, with a lance-corporal in rear, to act as close escort and to tend her along the rigours of the track.

As soon as the Scots and the Mahsuds were ready, Ogilvie passed the order to move out. They rode from the village, now almost deserted, in as much silence as possible: it was better that the scattered inhabitants should believe for as long as possible that they were still there. Ogilvie in the lead rode almost blind: the night's darkness was intense, still unrelieved by any moon. Beside him rode MacTrease with a hand on the bridle of the boy's mule. On Ogilvie's other side rode the ancient guide, muttering to himself as he indicated the way ahead. They made fair speed, but could have ridden faster had not the animals' hooves been impeded by the depth of the lying snow. After some five miles, appalling miles, they reached a cross track, the one expected by Mohammad Yusuf's bandits. The wild men broke off and rode away to the east, after each had gripped Ogilvie's hand; not for them the Khyber and the army of the Raj! Ogilvie's feelings were mixed: once, Razjah Shah had spoken of forming his own great army in Waziristan against the Raj. Now he was dead, and so was Mohammad Yusuf: had a dream ended with those deaths? And these men had taken part in the killing of his own patrol of Bengal Lancers in the Rahkand Pass, and this could not be forgiven though it had to be as it were pardoned since there was nothing he could do in the circumstances. There were too many to be arrested and escorted to justice, and in any case his word to Razjah Shah still held; and their subsequent help had been invaluable. He was sorry to see them go. The Scots rode on to their guide's instructions, taking the track that stretched towards the west – deeper for a time into Afghanistan, but soon they would turn to the north.

As dawn broke over the Khyber, the long divisional column from Nowshera began to come beneath the high-set fortress of Landi Kotal, pinnacled on the rearing peaks. From the fortress a man stepped into bold view, waving his arms, and was observed by Sir Iain Ogilvie.

'Fettleworth!'

'I've seen him,' Fettleworth said grumpily, and turned to his Chief of Staff. 'Semaphore, Lakenham. Fetch up the signallers.'

Lakenham turned in his saddle and lifted an arm. Soon the acknowledgment was made from the column and the signaller of the Khyber Rifles in Landi Kotal sent the message, which was duly reported to Sir Iain by the Chief of Staff.

'From Calcutta, sir – His Excellency himself. No advance is to be made past Fort Dhaka—'

'Balls,' Sir Iain said. 'But that is not my official reply to His Excellency. I shall make *no* reply.'

Fettleworth blew out his moustache and recalled an earlier conversation with the Army Commander. 'My dear sir, Lord Nelson was in a somewhat different position. The confusion of battle at Copenhagen—'

'I am aware of Lord Nelson's position, thank you, General Fettleworth.'

'As you wish, of course.' Fettleworth shrugged.

A cough came from Lakenham. 'There was more to the message, sir. Information has been passed that Amir Abdur-Rahman has word of our advance. He's already marching from Kabul towards the mouth of the Khyber.'

Fettleworth cleared his throat and addressed Sir Iain with much meaning. 'I suggest we take note of that, General, and use caution.'

'What sort of caution?'

'Heed His Excellency's orders,' Fettleworth answered huffily.

Sir Iain gave a harsh laugh. 'Damn it, the Raj wasn't built on namby-pambyism and running from a fight! I'm certain I shall have the Commander-in-Chief's backing. I'll make my final decision in the light of what we find upon reaching Fort Dhaka, as I indicated much earlier. There is no change in plan, General. The advance continues.'

The column ground on behind the fifes and drums of the battalions. They moved over lying snow, through narrow gorges that extended the column's length but checked it like London traffic moving through the Marble Arch, under sheer hillsides and past long drops to sharp and jagged rock below. They marched on to a seemingly inevitable and unauthorised clash with the massed armies of Afghanistan as, around 150 miles distant, the 20,000-foot peaks of the Hindu Kush came up in clearing weather to the north-west of Kabul.

'A wrong direction somewhere, I fear, Major.'

'Whose fault,' Brora snapped, 'is that, I wonder?'

Black remained silent: he had been reading the map, but the thick blanket of snow had confounded him by virtually obliterating all the landmarks other than the peaks themselves, and even they had seemed to lose their contours when they were visible at all.

'Halt the column!' Brora ordered sharply, swinging his arms and beating his hands upon the opposite shoulders. The liberal supply of blood always noticeable in his heavy face had turned blue, and the rest of him, like all the others, was white. 'Damned incompetence, which shall not go unreported I may say—'

'The maps are seldom to be relied upon in Waziristan, Major.'

'Nor, it seems, are adjutants. The bad workman always blames his tools, Captain Black, have you not heard that said before?'

Black scowled and once again remained silent. The column halted behind him. Cunningham, beaten by the snow as to his marching, clumped to the head of the column, lifting his feet high. Disregarding him, Lord Brora called loudly for all company commanders to attend upon him. When they had mustered the Major made no bones about their plight.

'Gentlemen, we've become lost. I have no idea where we are, Waziristan or Afghanistan. Let the blame for that rest where it sticks. As for myself, I accept to share. If any of you can advise the Adjutant, he will be happy to listen.' He paused. 'Yes, Captain Stuart, what is it?'

'We've been making a fair amount of northing, Major—'

'Until we turned to the west, yes. Well?'

'I think we're not far to the track for Peshawar ... the track from Fort Jamrud—'

'Nonsense!' Brora interrupted tartly. 'Damn it all, man, we've been moving *west* this last day and a night, as the compass bears witness even though the damn sun and moon have been hidden.'

'I agree, Major. I think the basic error occurred farther back—'

'Farther back my arse. Where, pray?'

'After leaving the young goatherd. I believe we missed the right track soon after, and went too far north ... or I should say northeast. You'll remember the track veered a little eastward for some way, Major.'

Brora scowled and blew up the ends of his

moustache in an angry snort. 'Why didn't you damn well say we'd gone wrong at the time, Captain Stuart – if indeed we did?'

'I was not in possession of the maps. I assumed that whoever had the maps would—'

'Would know his job! There I'm in agreement with you! Kindly proceed, Captain Stuart.'

Stuart said, pointing towards an outstanding peak in a great range lofting across the eastward sky, 'There's a leading mark that I believe I know, Major. That peak ... it's visible from the Jamrud–Peshawar track.'

Brora had turned and was staring, his face truculent. 'Peaks can look very different, depending on the angle of sight.'

'That's right, Major—'

'Does anyone else recognise it?' Brora called in a loud voice, pointing to the peak. There was no response, and he glared at Stuart. 'Well?'

'I was about to say I'd seen it from this angle when on patrol. Not so far southward, that's all.'

'How certain are you?'

Stuart said, 'Pretty certain, but not positive.'

'Ha!' Brora ejaculated harshly. 'Well, Captain Know-All, you shall damn well ride out and take a closer look and come back when you *are* positive! Try not to lose yourself. If the peak is what you say, and can be used as a safe landmark, then I shall strike north for the Peshawar track and enter the Khyber where we're not likely to lose our way – are we, Captain Black?' Without waiting for an answer Brora turned upon the Regimental Sergeant-Major. 'Mr Cunningham, I intend to fall out and rest while Captain Stuart makes his probe. See that the men are kept active, however, or they'll freeze.'

'Aye, sir.' Cunningham saluted and started moving down the column, with difficulty. Robin Stuart rode to the rear, passing Lord Dornoch cocooned in thick clothing in his *doolie*. Dornoch called to him, and he dismounted and approached the *doolie*. The Colonel looked far from well; his shoulder was not healing, and there was some fever. If he should grow worse while Brora lost his way, there would be strong feeling throughout the regiment.

Dornoch said, 'I have a suspicion we're lost. Am I right?'

Stuart hesitated. A white lie might be in order for a sick man, but the truth would out soon enough. He said, 'Yes, Colonel, but only temporarily.' He explained his present orders. 'I shall be back as soon as I'm sure, Colonel.'

'That peak...' Dornoch had lifted his body on the *doolie* to take a look. 'I'm not familiar

310

with it, at any rate with this aspect of it.' He paused and fell back with a sigh. 'The Major's not accustomed yet to winter in the hills, Robin. I feel the situation's unfair upon him. I'm not bad enough to be lying here so uselessly.'

'All's well, Colonel, under full control.'

There was a thin and shaky smile. 'I take leave to doubt that, my boy! I'm getting out of this confounded contraption.' He put a leg out, still booted and spurred and trewed. Stuart looked round somewhat wildly and with much gratitude saw the Surgeon Major tramping through the snow towards them. Corton summed up the situation quickly and acted with firmness: on no account was the Colonel to leave the *doolie*. If necessary, Colonel or not, he would be strapped in.

Stuart saluted formally and rode away to the north. Behind him the battalion settled down to rest, but it was rest according to Brora's orders, sensible enough ones, as given to the Regimental Sergeant-Major. Idle bodies were not permitted and the men were set to cleaning their rifles as if for an arms inspection in cantonments, after flapping the snow from heads and uniforms and the Slade Wallace leather equipment that hung from their shoulders in a spider's-web of belts; and meanwhile the field kitchen was set up and a makeshift meal was prepared, and steaming mugs of tea, strong and sweet, were sent down the line. There was a good deal of muttering and sarcastic comment: every man knew they were lost despite the maps and compasses and that the best hope of finding any track at all lay now with the eventual return of Captain Stuart. They were all anxious to be on the move, and their wishes went behind Stuart as he rode out. He rode until, bringing his landmark on to a more familiar bearing, he was able to make a positive identification and be sure that the Fort Jamrud to Peshawar track lay ahead. Before returning he rode a little farther to the north and east, coming up rising ground to look ahead through his field glasses in the hope that he might pick out the track itself so that Brora could be fully convinced. He was still too far off to identify anything beyond that one outstanding peak; the snow was an excellently covering blanket that deceived the eye. But something he did see as he lowered his glasses: not far ahead of him, a large hummock in the snow with a dark protrusion visible to the naked eye.

He rode forward, dismounted when he reached the hummock. The protrusion was a horse's hoof. Stuart scuffed at the snow with his hoot. The horse, a black one, was cold and dead. Something made him scuff around further, some feeling of eeriness that was making his hair rise. Then he found the body. A man, as cold and dead as the horse, lay against the animal's stomach, right between forelegs and hindquarters, as though he had crawled there hoping to find warmth and shelter. The body wore a fur hat and a tweed cloak and in the saddlebags of the horse Stuart found, incredibly, packets of porridge and a jar of marmalade. Beneath the body was an empty bottle of Dewar's whisky. Stuart reached into the pockets beneath the cloak and found identifying papers that caused his lips to frame a whistle.

He stood up: no point in taking the body back to the regiment. The regiment would march this way shortly, and Lord Brora could decide then what was to be done. Stuart mounted and rode back as fast as possible, bringing word that Hector Ogilvie was unaccountably dead in a Waziri pass.

As Ogilvie's half company advanced, they found a strange absence of any opposition; it was as though the men of the Afghan tribes were wary now, that the word of the great force in the Khyber had had its due effect. By the time the next day had darkened into evening, and still no further snow had come, they were not far off the Khyber – the old grandfather guide had confirmed this, and said that the track they were now on would bring them into the pass through the Safed Koh at a spot a little way to the eastward of Fort Dhaka.

'D'you think he's telling the truth, Colour?' Ogilvie asked MacTrease.

'There's no knowing, sir, but he knows what'll happen to the lad if he's found to be lying. On balance, sir, I'd say he's not lying.'

Ogilvie was dubious. 'The boy's probably the key factor, Colour. The old man's fairly senile, I think.'

'Being led by the nose, sir, by the lad?'

'He could be. The boy hates our guts, that's been obvious all along. It's possible he's blackmailing grandfather into resistance to threats ... the boy's full of courage and I've no doubt he feels he holds the honour of every tribesman in Afghanistan in his hands! He's to be watched closely, Colour Mac-Trease.'

'Aye, sir, he'll be that.'

'Full alertness from now, Colour – we're coming into the most dangerous stretch and it'll last till we make contact with Division.'

'Aye, sir. *If* we make contact with Division, sir.' The Colour-Sergeant brushed the back of a hand across his moustache. 'There's no knowing yet how far they've advanced.'

'True.'

'You'll march through the night, sir, I take it?'

'Yes, Colour.' Ogilvie had halted his force a little before the light had gone; the horses and mules, even more than the men, needed a respite from the eternal slog through the snow, but after this there would be no more halts until they had reached the Khyber. With MacTrease Ogilvie walked down the resting line, having words personally with the men and stressing the need for every one to be watchful and ready for instant action. Ogilvie didn't trust the silence of the hills, the absence of tribesmen, the total lack of dark faces along the peaks. There was some falsity, some lulling. Once again he thought about the Afghan youngster. But now they were in the hands of the boy and his ancient grandfather and there was nothing they could do but advance and be on their guard. Ogilvie passed the word to MacTrease to move out the half company and maintain scouts and picquets. The Scots mounted again and rode into the darkness towards the Khyber, behind their officer and the old man and the boy. As they went along the skies started to clear a little, and stars were seen, though as yet no direct moonlight. Palely those stars shone down on the snow and the lonely hills, bringing a touch of silver and, almost, of magic. It was very lovely, and nothing moved except the men and animals who were the only things to break that intense and brooding silence that hung over the whole land to link the Scots as one with the distant ranges of Himalaya.

Nineteen

A man rode back from the advanced scouting party to report to Ogilvie. 'A fork ahead, sir.'

'Thank you, MacKendrick.' Ogilvie turned in his saddle. He spoke in Pushtu to the old man. 'Which should we take, the right or the left fork?'

The old man mumbled something that Ogilvie didn't catch; it was the boy who answered in a loud, clear voice: 'The left fork.'

'That leads into the Khyber?'

'Yes.'

'And the right one, where does that lead?'

The boy said, 'It turns upon itself, leading back to the south by way of the east.'

'If you speak falsely, you know what will happen. My Colour-Sergeant is ready with the bayonet.'

The boy seemed about to spit, but changed his mind. He smiled sweetly. 'I speak true words. You should take the left fork.'

'I shall take the right.'

For a moment hate showed again, then the boy shrugged with apparent indifference. 'I have said. it is for the sahib to decide.' The word sahib came out with a terrible disdain. Ogilvie stuck to his decision to move right, and instructed Private MacKendrick to ride back and rejoin the scouting party with his orders. MacKendrick rode away, his mule kicking up the snow in powder. The moon was up now and the whitened hills stood out clearly. The faces of the guides were clear also; the old man was registering nothing, continuing with a toothless mumble, chewing upon nothing. The boy's expression was calm, almost bored. Was there triumph in it? Worry and uncertainty nagged at Ogilvie. The Afghans were wily, and the boy's face was an intelligent one. Had he fooled his captors after all? Had he set them by contrariness on the path he, the boy, wanted?

It was only too possible; a toss of a coin would be as effective now as a considered judgment! Mentally, Ogilvie tossed one then spoke softly to MacTrease: 'A rider to the scouts, Colour. I shall advance to the left.'

'Sir!' MacTrease handed over guard of the boy to a private, then turned aside and rode down the small column. A man went ahead to overtake the scouts with the changed orders. Soon the main body came up to the fork: Ogilvie watched the face of the young boy as he moved into the lefthand track. There was a flicker, no more; Ogilvie was still unsure. Despite the change, the boy said nothing. The grandfather went on chewing, black eyes glittering from a mass of wrinkles in the moonlight. The advance continued; MacTrease rode again down the column to sharpen the men's watchfulness. No reports came back from the scouts or the picquets as they came between close-set hillsides, higher and steeper than hitherto. Underfoot the going became much rougher, and the mules' hooves slithered over rock, and jags rose up to impede their way. Ogilvie turned to look back at Angela: she was bearing up well enough so far, but Ogilvie knew she couldn't go on taking the ride for much longer. It was urgent that she should have medical attention and soon it might become necessary for her to be carried and a rough *doolie* fashioned for the purpose. That would slow the advance, and time was vital. But an impediment might have to be accepted. Another dilemma of command: was it more important to preserve the life of the woman who had set the Raj upon the march, or more important to preserve the Pax Britannica itself?

They rode on, deeper into the ravine. By now it was so precipitous that the picquets could no longer function, and had descended to join the main body of the advance. Ogilvie ordered them to fall back to form a rearguard five hundred yards behind.

The silence was there still, and was to

Ogilvie still false. Somewhere the tribes must be in pursuit ... Murrum Khan, unaccounted for since he had ridden out from the village, must for a certainty be wishful to stop his hostages riding to the safety of the British column in the Khyber. And for an equal certainty the men of the tribes must, somewhere along the line, have noted the movement of Ogilvie and his men, and would have sent the word through to the right quarter. Icy fingers plucked at Ogilvie: everything, he felt, depended on whether or not his assessment of the boy's veracity had been correct. There had been ways of making more sure, but he had shrunk from the idea of torture upon a mere boy, and he had felt the boy wouldn't have uttered in any case. The face held dedication to the cause of his fathers. MacTrease, he knew, was silently critical of his officer on that score, but in any case it was too late now.

On and on beneath the moon, its light now largely obscured by the high hillsides. Still the silence, deep and foreboding, broken only by the crunch of the hooves, the rattle of arms and equipment and the occasional oath, almost involuntarily stilled before it broke right out, from a man whose mount had slipped on the snow or who had bruised a leg from a hidden outcropping of rock. It was as though all were trying not to break that quietness, as if to do so might bring a concealed enemy down upon them or, alternatively, overlay the sound of his approach.

Ogilvie watched the face of the boy as closely as he could: it might give some sign, the aloof coldness might well hide knowledge of where an attack might come. The boy gave the impression of knowing the wild tracks intimately; young as he was, he had no doubt taken part in tribal affrays, internecine battles or forays against the Raj. He was old beyond his years, but excitement and anticipation might show through in a boyish way. Meanwhile the soldiers were advancing towards a bend where the track ahead bore easterly, and always in the passes bends were dangerous. As they approached it Ogilvie sent back a warning for extra caution. Just here the sides rose higher, and the moon's light was taken away altogether; the boy's face was no longer visible. Flesh tingling, the half company of the Royal Strathspey rode on, into the bend.

Nothing happened: all was peace, and still the brooding silence. The track continued easterly. Savagely, Ogilvie swore. The sides lowered again, enough to admit the moon, and in the silver light Ogilvie saw the track extending ahead into the far distance, due east now by his compass, running more or less parallel with the Khyber and back towards Waziristan. The boy was grinning: he was delighted with himself. He had fooled the officer sahib, the colour-sergeant sahib, all the sahibs. They were idiots! He murmured in Pushtu to his grandfather, and the old man cackled suddenly. Ogilvie halted the advance and rounded on the boy. 'The track,' he said roughly. 'It is this one that leads back upon itself?'

The boy's smile grew wider. 'It leads east. You will not reach the Khyber.'

'Where will I reach?'

'Not the Khyber. I say no more.' There was an indifferent shrug.

Ogilvie turned before he spoke. 'Colour-Sar'nt MacTrease?'

'Sir?'

'We can go back to the fork. And still be lost when we get there! I'll take a gamble the right fork leads into this track – and it wouldn't have mattered which we took.'

'But the boy, sir. *He* knows, the little bugger!'

'Yes. Find out, if you please, Colour. But be careful.'

'Aye, sir.' MacTrease dismounted and went over to the boy's mule. A strong arm wrenched the youngster from the saddle. Grandfartherly mumblings came but were disregarded. 'Now,' MacTrease said grimly, and marched the boy to the rear at bayonet point. Ogilvie sat waiting, keeping an eye on the grandfather. Minutes passed; there were no cries of pain. After almost fifteen minutes

MacTrease marched back; the boy looked baleful but unharmed.

'Well, Colour?'

MacTrease gave a harsh laugh. 'There's more ways than one, sir, of killing the cat. He's unharmed except in his pride, sir. The Pathan respects age, sir, and grandfathers are almost holy ... and are not to have their guts disembowelled by the bayonet and taken into Peshawar to be fed to the pigs. The track, sir, leads back into Waziristan, into the Rahkand Pass. And that's the nearest we'll get to the Khyber, Captain Ogilvie, sir.'

Ogilvie let out a long breath of fury, frustration and self-blame: he had selected, or had allowed MacTrease to select, the wrong person as the lever and had been led astray accordingly. He said, 'Thank you, Colour.'

'Do we go on, sir?'

'We've no alternative, have we? The Rahkand leads north and the mouth's not far from Fort Jamrud. We must be content with sending a message on to Division from Fort Jamrud, and hope it reaches them in time – that's all!' He paused. 'What about an attack?'

'He would not say, sir. It's my belief he has no knowledge of Murrum Khan's intentions, sir.'

Ogilvie nodded. 'All right. Move out,

Colour. Keep up the best speed possible.'
Wearily, they rode on. It was, Ogilvie
thought, coming full circle now in a
geographical sense and was bringing him
back to the wrong end of the Khyber. From
Fort Jamrud he had ridden south along the
Rahkand Pass himself; in the Rahkand he
had been ambushed by the bandits of Razjah
Shah, in the biting winds of the Rahkand he
had lost a patrol of the Bengal Lancers. In
point of fact he was probably even now not
so far off the entrance to the Khyber as the
crow flew, but by the time he reached Fort
Jamrud via the Rahkand his father might
well be past Fort Dhaka and deep into
Afghan territory, and no one could forecast
the reaction of the Amir in Kabul. Time
pressed more urgently now than ever. Ogilvie dropped back towards Angela and spoke
to her of the situation. He asked, 'Can you
go on, Angela?'

'I'll be all right, James.'

'Truly?'

'Yes, truly. I've got to get there ... and I will
get there, James, I promise. Hector will be so
worried.'

Hector! Ogilvie caught his breath: he'd
forgotten about Hector, anxiously pacing the
corridors of Fettleworth's headquarters in
Nowshera. Of course Hector would be
worried sick, and would be making himself a
confounded nuisance all round – naturally

enough, but a worried Hector would be far worse an affliction to endure than would anyone else in a similar situation. However, Hector was having a useful effect now: Ogilvie believed that Angela was keeping herself going by thoughts of her husband's current purgatory; for his sake she must win through, and she would, and then she would give way to reaction. There was more steel in Angela than there was in Hector despite her surface frailty; Hector was a lucky man. After giving another assurance that her ordeal would not last much longer, Ogilvie rode back to the head of the column and they continued easterly through the night.

They made good speed as they came into easier ground, a wider track with less impedimenta. When at last the attack came it came suddenly and swiftly in unexpected surroundings, and it caught them with their defences lowered by sheer weariness and by an over-confidence that attack would come only in the narrow passes. It came before the dawn, when the moon was still bright: from points of cover on the hillsides rising gently to right and left of the track, tribesmen emerged behind a hail of bullets that cut down the picquets before they could give the alarm. Ahead, the scouts went down as though scythed like hay, and then bullets from more than a hundred *jezails* ripped into the riders. As Ogilvie shouted the order to dismount and scatter to the flanks but to have a care for the previously wounded men, he caught sight of the old grandfather's face in the second that it disintegrated into blood and shattered bone. The old man drooped sideways in the saddle and his mule took fright: it galloped ahead towards the ambushing tribesmen, dragging the body with the left foot caught in the stirrup. After it, as the Scots returned the fire from the cover of rocks and bushes, went the boy, head low, body held flat along the neck of his mule. Towards him streamed a horde of tribesmen, ragged garments and wild hair flying out in the cold wind, flashes of fire coming from their rifles as they stormed for the Scots. Ogilvie was firing his revolver point blank, reloading again and again as the attack came down and passed him to the rear. The moon showed the slaughter: Scots and natives together, in huddles along the track. Angela, in the care of her close escort, was in cover beneath a rock ledge like a roof, and behind the carcass of a mule. The lance-corporal and the two privates were firing into the howling mob over the mule's dead flank. Ogilvie ceased his own firing for a moment while he took stock: the men were in good cover now and this looked like becoming a battle of attrition; soon the natives would realise this and would themselves take cover, and both sides would become locked into a stalemate situation that could hold for days until one side or the other was starved out. That must not be allowed to happen: time was still vital.

Ogilvie saw MacTrease a little to his left, and called out to him.

'Sir!' Flat on his paunch, the Colour-Sergeant wormed his way to Ogilvie's side.

'We're going to be stuck here a while, I fancy, Colour. I have to get word through to Fort Jamrud.'

'Aye, sir. Are you thinking of a runner, sir?'

'Yes. Two men, to outflank on right and left and join up farther along.'

'I doubt if they'd have much hope yet, sir.'

'No. But once the natives go into cover, as they must soon. It's the only way I can see, Colour. Detail two good men and have them report to me for orders.'

'Aye, sir.' MacTrease still sounded dubious: two men, riding out from cover, could not be otherwise than seen immediately, and brought down by the *jezails*. He said as much; Ogilvie was about to tell him, abruptly, to carry out his orders when he saw, clearly beneath the moon, a tall man riding fast from out of the native mass, making along the track towards Angela and her escort: a man of imperious bearing, with a cloak of dark, probably maroon, cloth worked with gold thread – Murrum Khan beyond a doubt. Gold fire flashed in the moonlight from the heavy, medallion-hung earrings ... Ogilvie, disregarding MacTrease now, got to his feet, came out of cover and ran along towards where Angela lay, keeping on the high ground leading to the rock ledge. Bullets hummed and sang around him; he rushed on. Murrum Khan seemed equally impervious to bullets. Beside Angela, the lance-corporal of the close escort gave a curious leap into the air, clutched at his throat, and fell back. Angela seemed to be screaming, though she remained unheard in the mêlée and the shouting of the tribesmen. Ogilvie and Murrum Khan reached her position simultaneously; Ogilvie halted on the overhanging ledge just as the tribal leader pulled up his horse by the mule's carcase, and reached down to slice at the two Scots privates with a bloody-bladed scimitar. As the arm lifted, Ogilvie jumped from his point of vantage. He took the native fair and square, coming down astride the man's shoulders. The scimitar blade dipped sharply and plunged into the horse's neck. There was a spurting fountain of blood and a high whinny, and the animal reared up, hooves flailing dangerously over Angela's head. As the privates of the escort opened fire into the body of the horse, Murrum Khan and Ogilvie crashed backwards, with Ogilvie underneath. Murrum Khan was like an eel, wriggling and contorting, his face almost black with fury as Ogilvie tried to hold his arms to his sides. He wrenched them free and got a grip around Ogilvie's throat, and squeezed. Fire from his tribesmen swept the ground all round, pinning the escort down in the lee of the dead mule. Ogilvie's eyes began to dim, then he became aware of MacTrease poised behind Murrum Khan. All at once there was a high shriek of agony, the grip of the hands relaxed, and Murrum Khan fell aside. As MacTrease grabbed hold of Ogilvie and dragged him behind the mule, the firing continued all around. Panting, drawing in air through a bruised throat, Ogilvie found that MacTrease had also brought Murrum Khan in. Murrum Khan looked dead, but MacTrease said he was only knocked out.

'The butt of a rifle, sir, in the kidneys. Mind, he'll not be the same man again, but he'll live long enough to swing in Nowshera.' MacTrease brushed at his moustache. 'I take it you wanted him alive, sir?'

'Yes, Colour. There's still a boundary to be sorted out!' Ogilvie grinned breathlessly. 'That's if we come through this little lot, and...' His voice died away, and he cocked an ear to listen, looking at first puzzled, then incredulous. 'Do you hear what I hear, Colour?'

MacTrease was grinning himself, and pulling his uniform straight. 'I do, sir. The pipes an' drums, sir! And you'll recognise the tune I don't doubt, Captain Ogilvie!'

Ogilvie did. It was 'Farewell to Invermore,' Pipe-Major Ross's own composition, written when first they had sailed for India years before. As Ogilvie and MacTrease listened the tune shifted to 'Cock o' the North,' clear and totally unexpected signal that the 114th Highlanders, The Queen's Own Royal Strathspeys, were coming in to action. From all along the line of cover, a great cheer went up as the sound of the pipes and drums overlaid the diminishing rattle of rifle fire, and grew louder. The tribesmen began to stream away to the flanks, and the pipes and drums stopped abruptly, and from the advancing battalion, now coming on at the double, a great barrage of fire was opened upon the retreating backs. In the last of the moon's light before the fingers of the dawn spread over the waste of hills and the snow, the figure of Major Lord Brora was seen, swaggering into battle on his horse.

Brora was never a tactful man. The news having been broken, he elaborated in forthright manner. 'We have your husband's body with us, ma'am. I'm sorry. I make the assumption he was looking for you. If that's the case, then it was remarkably foolish but he died well and you should be proud.'

'Proud!' Angela covered her face with her

hands and her body trembled. Ogilvie, at her side, held her close.

'Oh, no doubt you'd prefer him safe and alive – that's natural. But pride's no bad mainstay all the same.' Brora began to look irritable: tears were not soldiers' business and failed to impress him. 'Captain Ogilvie, we have much to discuss.' He waved a hand towards Angela, and gave a jerk of his head as much as to say, get her out of my sight. 'I wish no delay now.'

Ogilvie handed Angela over to Robin Stuart, who, he had been told, had found the body. He might be of some comfort, or he might not ... when Ogilvie rejoined the Major, Brora was talking loudly to Andrew Black. 'Women are an odd lot. I doubt if my words registered. Perhaps I should have buried the feller where he fell upon his Dewar's ... ah, Captain Ogilvie. Your cousin was of some importance. All Civilians rate themselves as such, anyhow – that's why I brought the body on. He'll have to have a proper funeral, I don't doubt.'

'I think he's earned that, Major.'

Brora sniffed. 'I don't underestimate what he did, but he didn't do it with efficiency. Whisky and porridge are good Scots materials, and sustaining, but are not enough by themselves. Now, Captain Ogilvie, a full report at once, if you please.'

'Very good, Major. It's a long one.'

'No doubt! Kindly make it fast.'

Ogilvie did so, and made representations as to the need for immediate contact with Division. Brora saw the point. Permission was given for Ogilvie to ride out independently with two mounted privates and head for Fort Jamrud with his urgent despatch to go by the telegraph to Fort Dhaka and the General Officer Commanding. Behind him as he rode away, the dead from the recent action were buried in shallow graves marked with roughly-made wooden crosses bearing names, rank and regiment to become yet another landmark of the Raj and the maintenance of the Pax Britannica. Ogilvie had gathered the facts from Robin Stuart before leaving, and could not but be thankful for Andrew Black's poor map-reading and for Stuart's sighting that in the event had brought the battalion within hearing of the rifle fire. Murrum Khan remained in the custody of the battalion, a man in much agony but a man who, according to the doctor, would reach Peshawar to face charges of murder and of conspiracy against the Raj. Ogilvie reached Fort Jamrud in good time and had his message passed on along the Khyber; and sent another to Peshawar asking for a field ambulance bearer company with attached transport to drive out and collect Lord Dornoch, who was still in poor condition but was expected to mend, and Angela Ogilvie together with the body of her husband, and the many wounded, plus a few men in danger of contracting frostbite. He waited for long enough to learn that the division had been contacted when just past Fort Dhaka, and to receive word back that Sir Iain Ogilvie had agreed in the circumstances to withdraw.

When many days later the huge divisional column had marched back through the Khyber and entered cantonments at Peshawar, Ogilvie was sent for to report at Brigade, where his father greeted him in company with Bloody Francis Fettleworth. 'You don't appear too heartbroken by your cousin's death,' were his first words.

Ogilvie was taken aback. He said, 'He died well, sir.'

'Certainly he did. But it's your uncle I feel for, James. Hector was ... well, I'll not speak ill of him now.' Sir Iain, showing signs of strain, coughed. 'How's Angela?'

'Well, sir. That is, she's improving. The funeral was an ordeal.'

Sir Iain's eyebrows went up. 'She didn't attend?'

'She did, sir. She insisted.'

'Not quite the thing, for a woman to attend,' the GOC said grumpily. 'However, that's her business. Now to the future: you did well, James, and I'm pleased.'

'Thank you, sir.'

'With Murrum Khan in custody, the tribal demands will collapse. I've read your reports ... I'll see to it that the dispute's settled in favour of whatsisname's people—'

'Razjah Shah, sir.'

'Yes. A bloody murderer and thief, but on the right side this time, apart from those poor fellers of the Bengal Lancers. I gather he was helpful.'

'Invaluable, sir.'

'Yes. Good! And the Raj always shows gratitude. So that's that. The High Commissioner will damn well do as I tell him. That village now, the one you were taken to by Murrum Khan. Know its name and location?'

'Not the name, sir. The location, yes.'

'Good.' The GOC rubbed his hands together and went across to hold them out to a coal fire burning beneath the portrait of the Queen-Empress. He glanced up at it. 'It's not quite Christmas ... Her Majesty's got her wish. She'll be delighted with the news. Delighted! Won't she, Fettleworth?'

'Indeed she will.' Bloody Francis met the Queen's eye; he gave a small inclination of his head. 'The village, General. You mentioned—'

'Oh, yes. It'll receive a visit. A punitive expedition ... your report says much of it was burned down, James. They will have started rebuilding. That won't avail them for long.'

'The village was in Afghanistan, sir.'

'I know that.' Sir Iain stared; his blue eyes bulged towards his son. 'Beyond Fort Dhaka, I encountered Amir Abdur-Rahman in person, at the head of his army. Your message came just in time, James – *just* in time! Anyway, we had a parley afterwards, all very friendly. Abdur-Rahman's most obliging ... he's grateful for the subsidy and he doesn't want war. He'll see to the village, I'm certain.' He broke off. 'Care to spend Christmas in Murree? Your mother would like that. I'll speak to Dornoch, or Brora if Dornoch's not yet resumed command.' Once again he coughed, and cleared his throat with a rumbling sound. 'There's another thing your mother would be pleased about, but of course it's early days yet and no doubt indelicate. What?'

Ogilvie felt himself flushing like a schoolboy: he knew very well what his father's reference was and he considered it more than indelicate within a matter of days of the funeral. He said, 'Really, I don't—'

'Don't argue, boy, don't argue. Think about Christmas. Off you go now.' Sir Iain waved a dismissive hand, and James, saluting smartly, turned about with a crash of boots and marched from the room. Outside headquarters, Brigade's standard floated from the flagstaff, emblem of the power of the Raj and the Queen-Empress, symbolic of

334

all the British Empire. At Brigade there was already a *soupçon* of holly and mistletoe, of whisky and plum pudding and crackers amidst the regimental silver, and loyal toasts and eyes misty when they thought of home beyond an immensity of sea. Christmas was a time for home. And Christmas, of course, was in the air. The Queen, who would be so delighted, was safe in Windsor Castle with her Guard outside. A village in Afghanistan was waiting for bullets and flame from its Amir. The dead were in their graves. Ogilvie mounted his horse and rode back to the 114th's cantonment.